FINKS

FINKS

How the CIA Tricked
the World's Best Writers

Joel Whitney

OR Books
New York · London

Published for the book trade by OR Books in partnership with Counterpoint Press.
Distributed to the trade by Publishers Group West

All rights information: rights@orbooks.com

First trade printing 2016

Cataloging-in-Publication data is available from the Library of Congress.
A catalog record for this book is available from the British Library.

ISBN 978-1-944869-13-7

Text design by Under|Over. Typeset by AarkMany Media, Chennai, India.

10 9 8 7 6 5 4 3 2 1

TABLE OF CONTENTS

If you speak for the wolf, speak against
him as well.
                    —Aleksandr Solzhenitsyn

INTRODUCTION

A LIT'R'Y COUP

Where else but in Eden could we find
our freedom only by losing it. . .

—Richard Howard, *Lining Up*

In early 1966, Harold "Doc" Humes, one of the founders of *The Paris Review*, wrote a well-intentioned ultimatum to George Plimpton, another founder. Having left it to Plimpton to run the famous magazine long before, Humes was floundering. Living in London, where his wife Anna Lou had left him over the holidays, he was dogged by bouts of extreme paranoia and convinced that he was under surveillance. According to Anna Lou, he believed that the bedposts in his London home recorded whatever he said, and that the recordings were then played directly for Queen Elizabeth.

Yet in his March 1966 letter to Plimpton, he was clear and reasonable, writing that Peter Matthiessen, another *Paris Review* founder, had just visited London and had told Humes an astonishing story. During his stay, Matthiessen had admitted that *"The Paris Review* was originally set up and used as a cover for [Matthiessen's] activities as an agent for the Central Intelligence Agency." Humes continued,

He further said that you [Plimpton] knew nothing about this until recently, that in fact when he told you your face "turned the color of (my) sweater" which I hasten to inform you is neither red nor blue but a very dirty grey-white, my having worn nothing else since my wife left. It precisely matches my spirits; they get greyer every day.[1]

Humes even sympathized. "I believe Peter when he says he is properly ashamed of involving the [Paris Review] in his youthful folly, and, true, this was all 15 years ago. BUT. . ."[2]

Humes was just one of The Paris Review's larger-than-life personalities. The magazine received early praise from American publications like Time and Newsweek, and also from magazines and newspapers all over Europe. It helped launch the careers of William Styron, Terry Southern, T.C. Boyle, and Philip Roth, among others. It threw legendary parties where, for decades, actors like Warren Beatty and political and cultural figures like Jackie Kennedy would rub shoulders with New York City's writers and book publishing rank and file. Its editor-in-chief Plimpton was already a best-selling author, a friend of the Kennedys, one of Esquire magazine's "most attractive men in America,"[3] and, according to Norman Mailer, the most popular man in New York City.[4] His personal entourage drew attention, too. A 1963 Cornell Capa photograph shows a group assembled for one of the famous cocktail parties in Plimpton's apartment. In the picture are Truman Capote, Ralph Ellison, Humes, Matthiessen, Styron, Southern, and Godfather author Mario Puzo.

In Paris in the 1950s, long before they were famous, Matthiessen, Humes, Plimpton, and a few classmates debated what to call the magazine. They couldn't decide between the name that eventually stuck and other suggestions, such as Baccarat.[5] Having initially collaborated on Humes's Paris News Post, later dubbed "a fourth-rate New Yorker,"[6] Humes and Matthiessen were already involved with the project of launching a new magazine in Paris before Plimpton was called over from Cambridge. Handing off their project, Humes and Matthiessen both left decisions largely to Plimpton in order to attend to their writing careers. On his way to becoming a Zen master and an award-winning novelist and nature writer, Matthiessen published early, including in The Paris Review's first issue, and won fans for his fiction and nonfiction alike. Plimpton became a participatory sports writer, whose best-selling book on quarterbacking for the Detroit Lions was made into a film with Alan Alda. No slouch himself, Humes published a pair of novels in 1958 and 1959 that earned praise in The New York Times and elsewhere.

Humes's diverse lifetime accomplishments would include a scheme to make affordable homes for poor people out of pressed newspapers and cardboard, running Norman Mailer's New York City mayoral campaign, dropping LSD with Timothy Leary, and successfully fighting the New York City police over the racist Cabaret Card laws in effect at the time. But, as with so many young people who were acutely sensitive to the changes of the 1960s, Humes began to veer off the path, casting about for his calling. He thought he was being watched—watched from above. Especially after the Kennedy assassination, Humes was growing increasingly paranoid, railing about being bugged and followed. After his marriage unraveled, he wandered the ruins of Rome, started a new family, witnessed the 1968 student protests in Paris, produced a Beat-poetry-inspired short film titled *Don Peyote*, and gave away thousands of dollars of his inheritance as anti-capitalist performance art around Columbia University in uptown Manhattan (where he squatted in the young Paul Auster's dorm). But in his letter to Plimpton, he was acting in his capacity as a founder of *The Paris Review*, claiming he had the best interests of the magazine in mind.

Arguing that an association with secret institutions like the CIA would inevitably lead to "rot," Humes advised Plimpton that, for the integrity of the magazine, he should make Matthiessen's ties during the magazine's founding public. Citing Edmund Burke's line "that it is enough for evil to triumph that good men do nothing," Humes wrote, "I have deeply believed in the *Review* and all that we hoped it stood for, but until this matter is righted I feel I have no honorable choice but to resolutely resign. Even if I have to split an infinitive to do it." He went on to suggest that Matthiessen might "laugh the matter off in print in a manner calculated to restore our tarnished escutcheon. . ." Under these circumstances, he would stay. Barring that, however, "I should like my name removed from the masthead. I'm sure it will not be missed."[7]

In attempting to inspire his colleagues to come clean, Humes cited an opinion that grew increasingly common as revelations of the CIA's vast propaganda apparatus were published in *Ramparts* magazine and *The New York Times* in 1964, 1966, and 1967. Namely, that any association with the super-secret spy agency—notorious for coups, assassinations, and undermining democracy in the name of fighting Communism—tainted the reputations of those involved. Humes pressed the point forcefully. "Since this was apparently a formal arrangement, involving his being trained in a New York safehouse and being paid through a cover name, then without doubt the fact is recorded in some or several dusty functionarys' [sic] files in Washington or around the world that our hapless magazine was created and used as an engine in the damned cold war. . ." He continued,

> although Peter is not [to] be blamed for a paranoid system that makes victims of its instruments, nevertheless what of Styron? . . . What of half the young writers in America who have been netted in our basket? What color would their faces turn?

In his reply, Plimpton batted away the suggestion that he divulge Matthiessen's secret or that he encourage Matthiessen himself to do so. Moreover, while downplaying the significance of Matthiessen's CIA stint and his using the magazine as a cover in Paris, Plimpton failed to confess his own ties to the CIA, ties that, however subtle, would not emerge definitively until 2012, when several years' worth of correspondence between Plimpton, his staff, and functionaries of the CIA-funded Congress for Cultural Freedom were unearthed in *The Paris Review*'s archives at the Morgan Library in midtown Manhattan.

Indeed, *The Paris Review* was one of the Congress for Cultural Freedom's many active partners that agreed to syndicate "content." These were magazines not necessarily founded or run by the Congress (though *The Paris Review* was indeed founded by one agent) but whose editors were willing to work with the Congress for Cultural Freedom—or CCF—on a slew of collaborations large and small. *The Paris Review* was one of these CCF-friendly literary magazines (call them semi-official), which joined more than two dozen official magazines like *Preuves* in France, *Der Monat* in Germany, and *Encounter* in London—plus the lesser known *Quest* in India, *Mundo Nuevo* in Paris (for Hispanic readers), and *Jiyu* in Japan. These official magazines were conceived, created, named, and even overseen by CIA officers who consulted directly with the likes of CIA Director Allen Dulles and a handful of other agency or foreign intelligence officials about their editorial operations. But unlike these official CIA magazines, *The Paris Review* was left almost entirely to its own devices.

Nevertheless, at key moments beginning with its founding in the early 1950s and continuing beyond the exposure of the CIA's growing propaganda and censorship networks, *The Paris Review*, through Plimpton—not Matthiessen—consciously aligned its mission with this apparatus. It did so likely knowing what that apparatus was doing. Despite himself and backlit by history, Plimpton's 1966 correspondence with Doc Humes makes this clear.

Even if *The Paris Review* played only a small role in the Cold War's marshalling of culture against the Soviets, the magazine's history nevertheless opens a compelling window onto forces that still direct, mesmerize, and affect our understanding of culture in times of political crisis. We understand vaguely that our media are linked to our government still today, and to government's stated foreign policy; and this understanding is enhanced by eavesdropping on *The Paris Review*'s bit part in this massive secret performance that drove a nation for nearly two decades, and whose hangover drives us still.

What follows is by necessity a group biography, reconstructed from splintered histories of the time. These histories have been scattered around the world in books, archives, and occasionally rising up on websites; I have collected several of them together again in a way that might suggest the vastness of the project that involved them. *The Paris Review* will disappear and reappear beside portraits of liberal hawks, nonaligned leftist novelists and Western-yearning Russian dissidents, characters such as Dwight Macdonald, Arthur Schlesinger, Sol Stein, Boris Pasternak, Nelson Aldrich, John Berger, James Baldwin, Stokely Carmichael, Jayaprakash Narayan, Pablo Neruda, Arthur Miller, Ernesto Che Guevara, Keith Botsford, Emir Rodríguez Monegal, and Gabriel García Márquez. The whistleblower-journalists, many of them women, who fought against a long-entrenched habit of secrecy and deception—Immy Humes, Frances Stonor Saunders, Angus Mackenzie, and Michèle Ray-Gavras—will also make their way into these pages, especially when their attempts merely to do their jobs were thwarted, dramatically or instructively, by one of the finks the book is named for.[8]

This account relies on as many primary documents as possible, most of them letters, and leans on a structure that might be closer to *1001 Nights* than a straightforward biography of three friends who founded a magazine. This is because the book that you hold is really the biography of an idea. Compared by one critic to a case of the measles, that idea starts with well-intentioned men who agreed, winking and invoicing, to promote an anti-Communist ideology through secret patronage; it ends with a totalitarian system where secret agents spy on the media and sabotage free speech and press freedom. As Humes cautioned, that evolution was inevitable, and its inevitability was understood in the United States' founding documents.

•   •   •

The partnership between *The Paris Review* and the CIA's Congress for Cultural Freedom began with ad exchanges and the CIA reprinting *The Paris Review*'s famous author interviews in its official magazines.

Some of *The Paris Review*'s early praise came from functionaries within CIA circles. This was beyond *The Paris Review*'s direct control, but it still made them passive beneficiaries of CIA propaganda that posed as spontaneous and free critical praise. On the surface, the publicity came as a result of something that looked like networking and successful marketing. But when you dust off the archival letters, it places the editors in a role that, from the very beginning, blurs the line between criticism, journalism, and the needs of the state; between aesthetics and the political requirements of the Cold War. What many, including the CIA itself, would simply call propaganda.

First á la carte, then en masse, *The Paris Review* granted reprint rights for its interviews to the Congress's official magazines. The understanding was clear: the Congress could take what it liked and pay the magazine what it thought fair later on. It was a little extra cash for the fledgling magazine and a good deal more international publicity beyond those places where it was officially distributed (New York, London, and Paris).

But then the quarterly pursued an arrangement by which it shared the costs of an editor's living expenses with the CIA. This editor would do double duty, working simultaneously for the magazine and in the publishing wing of the Congress for Cultural Freedom's headquarters in Paris. The editor who initially championed this arrangement, Nelson Aldrich, called it a "joint emploi," playfully blending the English and French in letters between the Paris office and Plimpton. Aldrich, Plimpton, and the other editors also arranged for the Congress for Cultural Freedom to vet the candidate in New York before sending him to start work in Paris. To work at the apolitical magazine, then, in its Paris office, you went through a cultural version of a security clearance. And it wasn't just Nelson Aldrich who moved from his work in the magazine's Paris office to join the staff of the Congress for Cultural Freedom; New York poet Frederick Seidel and journalist (and CIA daughter) Frances Fitzgerald followed the same trajectory.

Even while the scheme was incipient, one sees in *The Paris Review*'s archives that the CIA's cultural functionaries took advantage of this arrangement to influence the magazine's coverage, ordering up, as it were, interviews that *The Paris Review* had yet to conduct or commission, and affirming their interest in interviews *The Review* hoped to conduct in the future. Innocent enough? Humes, if he'd known of this other CIA tie, might not have thought so. Humes wrote his colleagues in 1966 of his apprehension toward secret organizations and their inevitable rot: "[H]owever much one might agree with Peter that 'in those days the CIA was just a collection of college kids,'"

> it would appear that the activities of this Kollection of Kollege Kids is inKreasingly Kriminal in nature. I don't believe that the principles of freedom and justice and respect for Law—which after all are the very foundation of western civilization—are best upheld by raping those principles on the pretext of defending their honor; but, as history repeatedly teaches, this is what any unchecked secret organization invariably ends in doing.[9]

Implicit in Plimpton's response, detailed in the pages to come, is the notion that became chronic throughout the American media that working journalists may justifiably do double duty as CIA assets, and that CIA assets may use the media in its many forms as cover, and as a soft power method of dampening blowback against its unpopular operations. Even after Humes begged his colleagues to come clean, Matthiessen's work for the CIA, however short-lived, remained secret until a 1977 article in *The New York Times* by John M. Crewdson outed him among scores of others embedded across media as undercover agents. If Plimpton and Matthiessen had listened to Humes, there would have been no story implicating *The Paris Review*. In the same article identifying Matthiessen's past service in that agency—out just a year before he won the National Book Award for *The Snow Leopard*—a former agent is quoted claiming, "We 'had' at least one newspaper in every foreign capital . . . ." Crewdson added a claim that those which "the CIA did not own outright or subsidize heavily it infiltrated with paid agents or staff officers who could have stories printed that were useful to the agency and not print those it found detrimental."[10] It seems likely, given new archival evidence to come at the end of this book, that yet another *Paris Review* co-founder's intelligence ties in that period bolstered Matthiessen and Plimpton's silence.

The program that *The Paris Review* was part of—Matthiessen through the front door and Plimpton through the back—was astonishingly vast. While Humes argued for transparency, Plimpton, for reasons we can imagine, balked. Many of the liberal interventionists who turned to culture to beat back Soviet influence were of course well-intentioned and were legitimately concerned about the spread of Soviet ideology at home and abroad. But good intentions or not, Plimpton and Matthiessen's silence was collusion with those who would weaken American media. If *The Paris Review* played a relatively small part in the CIA's media war, it also had many friends who joined the young CIA. Even if some could guess, no one, obviously, could know for sure what the young agency, born in the late 1940s, would become. Furthermore, those tied to the CIA through funding designated for cultural programming were often unaware, as has been said many times before, where the money originated. But many others would lean on the contradictory line of being unaware, yet being nevertheless proud. It reeked of doublespeak and of hedging: *if I had known who paid the bill, I'd have been proud to do exactly what I did do. But I didn't know.* The pride argument has held up behind a second argument that the CIA and its editors never censored. But the record shows they censored repeatedly.

Exposing these ties is not for the purpose of moral condemnation. It marks my attempt to look through a keyhole into the vast engine room of the cultural Cold War, to see if this ideology—one favoring paranoid intervention into the media over adherence to democratic principle—remains with us. If so, what do we lose by accepting that our media exist, in part, to encourage support for our interventions? And if we're ok with it during one administration, are we still ok with our tax dollars fostering the nexus of CIA contractors, military propagandists, and journalists even when the opposition runs the government? Most important, what—if anything—can we do about it all?

1

GRADUATES

At first we received a not inconsiderable honorarium for the meetings we attended. . .

—Jorge Luis Borges, "The Congress"

Matthiessen made the decision, which he would downplay for the rest of his life, at Yale.

Like many young Ivy League men in the late 1940s and early 1950s, his CIA career began with a nod from his English professor. By all accounts a brilliant scholar, Norman Holmes Pearson became a professor of English while still a young man himself, then a professor of American Studies. During World War II, Pearson worked in the Office of Strategic Services, the country's fledgling wartime intelligence service. He also joined a team of men who formed a postwar brain trust that helped to lobby for the CIA's creation.

Some of the young agency's earliest recruits were Pearson's students—many of whom first saw publication in the prestigious *Yale Literary Magazine*, the school's student-run magazine and the oldest literary magazine in the country. Like scores of early agency men (they were usually men), Pearson's career is a mashup of literature and spying. A friend of the modernist poet Hilda Doolittle (aka, "H.D."), he hired H.D.'s daughter as his secretary. She later became the secretary of his protégé, the CIA's counter-intelligence chief, James Jesus Angleton—famous for the CIA's great mole-hunt in the 1960s and 1970s, the failure of which would lead to Angleton's resignation. During World War II, Pearson ran the Art Looting Unit, recently fictionalized in the Hollywood film *Monuments Men*.[1]

After an illustrious record in the OSS alongside Allen Dulles, Frank Wisner, and CIA founder William "Wild Bill" Donovan, Pearson returned to academia to launch Yale's American Studies program. A letter from Yale's dean laid out the explicit propaganda aims of the program: "In the international scene it is clear that our government has not been too effective in blazoning to Europe and Asia, as a weapon in the 'cold war' the merits of our way of thinking and living . . . . Until we put more vigor and conviction into our own cause . . . it is not likely that we shall be able to convince the wavering peoples of the world that we have something infinitely better than Communism. . ."[2]

It was into this shifting milieu that Matthiessen was first thrust, in pursuit of those wavering peoples. He wanted to be a writer of important books. In a 1945 photograph from his Hotchkiss School yearbook, young Peter's stare is blank. He has the same extended chin, the same long neck and large ears, the same prominent eyebrows and penetrating look that he would show in later photographs. But the eyelines and crinkling forehead that give the older Matthiessen a gentle, if slightly fierce wisdom, haven't yet appeared.

Where better for this young American blueblood to study the American century than at Yale, as a family legacy, where the brilliant Professor Pearson straddled the English and American Studies departments? Yale's American Studies program would be, as one scholar has written, "not a matter of preaching against Communism, but one of advocacy for the American alternative."[3] Call it "positive propaganda." When the literary CIA got into the game—deploying cultural propaganda or psychological warfare techniques—it would use both positive and negative means, celebrating American cultural achievements on one hand and attacking Soviet ideas and policies on the other.

According to Matthiessen, it was a paper on William Faulkner that caught the attention of Pearson—and the CIA. Although he was a less than diligent student, Matthiessen formed a friendship with Professor Pearson, who had once been a friend of Peter's father's cousin, F.O. Matthiessen.

F.O. Matthiessen, as Peter points out in an unpublished interview, "killed himself at Harvard, rather long story." An expert on the American Transcendentalists, and author of *The American Renaissance* ("the great text about nineteenth century American writers," Peter called it), F.O. had been friends with Pearson—which touched Peter—and Pearson was also a friend of Wallace Stevens, which impressed him.[4]

Peter grew up the son of an architect in a well-to-do environment, and attended the Hotchkiss School in Lakeville, Connecticut. It was while working in a camp for troubled kids one summer during boarding school that he had what he reports to be his first glimpse into politics. Seeing how hard these kids from "troubled backgrounds" had it in life woke him to a vague sense of being sheltered.[5] Likewise, his experience in World War II, where he spent two years during college, deepened his perspective. In the South Pacific one night, Matthiessen saw a glimpse of what he later described as the "primordial longing." If the camp counseling for troubled kids was a political glimpse into a larger narrative, a raging storm during his naval service was a spiritual one. "One night in 1945," he wrote, "on a Navy vessel in a Pacific storm, my relief on bow watch, seasick, failed to appear, and I was alone for eight hours in a maelstrom of wind and water, noise and iron; again and again, waves crashed across the deck, until water, air and iron became one. Overwhelmed, exhausted, all thought and emotion beaten out of me, I lost my sense of self, the heartbeat I heard was the heart of the world, I breathed with the mighty risings and declines of earth, and this evanescence seemed less frightening than exalting."[6]

The year of his graduation from Yale, Peter's cousin's suicide helped solidify his bond with Pearson. He recalled Pearson showing him letters about "Matty," as F.O. Matthiessen was called. "My father was also called Matty," he said, "and they were first cousins. But Pearson and I were pretty close, [and] we would heckle each other. I'd been goofing off, going to Smith [College] and drinking much too much. I never spent a Saturday night at Yale the whole time I was there. And Pearson was kind of ticked off at me because he thought I was an irresponsible youth."[7]

Even if Peter grew serious about one of those Smith girls he was always rushing off to see—named Patsy Southgate, whom he wound up marrying—the stain of irresponsibility colored his relationship with Pearson. Then he wrote a paper on William Faulkner, recalling proudly, "I knew about Faulkner and I had ideas about Faulkner. And I remember it very well; [Pearson] called me in and said, 'Where have you *been* for the last three years?'" With work like this, Pearson told him, "You could have won the

English prize."[8] Was it good enough work for the CIA? So common was recruitment for the Agency from Ivy League schools it was given the code-name "P SOURCE"—P for professor.

William Lippincott, a recruiter at Princeton, used his influential place as dean to staff the agency with new blood. His refrain? "How would you like to serve your country in a different way?" Skip Walz was the Yale crew coach who "would work the boathouse and the field house, Mory's and fraternity row, looking for strong young shoulders and quick minds. When the Korean War called for some beef, he broadened his recruiting ground to the National Football League, producing twenty-five former football players who would be trained, he was told, for parachuting behind enemy lines."[9] So whether he wrote an insightful Faulkner paper or not mattered more to Matthiessen than to Pearson; a taste of his professor's approval, playing on his sense of patriotism, was the beginning, and it would lead him into Yale's secret societies. Pearson, Matthiessen recalled, "was a member of this Yale literary thing called the Jacobean club. And a great friend of Pearson, I'm sorry to say, was Mr. James Jesus Angleton."[10]

The head of counterintelligence from 1954 until the 1970s, Angleton was charged with, among other tasks, eliminating Soviet agents posing as spies for the CIA. The moles. Arguably, this was that most paranoid agency's most paranoid task, revealing itself as a veritable "wilderness of mirrors," the image of T.S. Eliot's.[11]

"And as it turned out, Pearson recruited a great great many Yale seniors for the CIA," said Matthiessen. "Now this was right after the war, when the CIA was starting up, [and was] an offshoot of the OSS, and not into assassinations and all the ugly stuff yet. But I'm afraid that I was one of the ones conscripted, and I was sent to Paris. And I was writing—before I left Yale I was publishing my first short stories in *The Atlantic*, I already had an agent, I was more or less established, and [was] working on my second novel. But Patsy [Southgate] and I wanted to go back to Paris, and I thought, 'Hey, here's a great way to get to Paris free, and adventure.' I didn't know about the CIA from anything, I was just a greenhorn."[12]

Matthiessen repeated many times how the CIA's reputation was not yet destroyed by its subsequent law breaking. "The ugly stuff," he called it. And it's true that this would obviously depend on how informed you were. Given how the press often saw itself then as partners with government in its Cold War efforts on foreign policy, Matthiessen like many others might not have initially known much about the agency. Yet it was indeed into plenty of ugly stuff by 1950.

When he got to Paris after his training, Matthiessen "discovered that we [he and Southgate] were being shadowed, that we were being followed where we were going, and I don't know who that was, but it was one of the intelligence services trying to find out what I was up to."[13] Matthiessen eventually linked up with Harold "Doc" Humes, who had already established a magazine, called the *Paris News Post*. Humes grew up in Princeton, New Jersey, did a stint at MIT and the US Navy, and then made his way to Paris in 1948. As the *News Post*'s fiction editor, Matthiessen exploited its infrastructure, even if he didn't think much of what Humes had built. The idea for *The Paris Review* grew out of these false starts.

"Doc loved James Baldwin, absolutely idolized James Baldwin, and he says they talked about making a magazine—how great it would be if there were an outlet, and a safe space for writers by writers," said Humes's daughter, the filmmaker Immy Humes. "Doc always talked about *The Paris Review* as an anti-anxiety measure . . . [that] was going to be this protected space, and it was going to be criticism free . . . a measure against this 'age of anxiety'. . ."[14] Baldwin was an expat black writer in Paris whose relationship with others at the magazine, like Matthiessen, was fraught, and who would go on to write the best-selling novel *Another Country*. The anxiety these writers sought to escape came from McCarthyism, white supremacy, Jim Crow, domestic espionage by the FBI, and a list of other American maladies. The year Humes got to Paris, Richard Nixon made his name by grandstanding before the House Un-American Activities Committee, and helped tear down popular New Deal figures, like Alger Hiss, by tarring them as Communists. Occasionally, as with Hiss, they scored a hit.

Plimpton was Matthiessen's childhood friend in New York, the two having attended St. Bernard's together. Plimpton could see the school through the window of his childhood home on Fifth Avenue in midtown Manhattan. Their school days together ended after fourth grade. "Somehow I kept up with George enough to know he was in [the UK]. 'How would you like to come to Paris to run a little magazine'?" Matthiessen asked him. Plimpton had worked on the *Harvard Lampoon*, where he had known John Train and Sadruddin Aga Khan, the magazine's respective managing editor and publisher, and where he had been accepted into poet Archibald MacLeish's highly selective creative writing class.[15] MacLeish, like Pearson, had ties to the founding elements of the CIA, and inspired Plimpton's choice of Cambridge for postgraduate work.[16] Plimpton hadn't been known for his academics at St. Bernard's, or Exeter, where he went next. But he got a little more serious about literature after studying with MacLeish and Matthiessen's cousin, F.O.

The son of a prominent New York lawyer who was appointed deputy ambassador to the United Nations under President Kennedy, Plimpton grew up in Manhattan and spent summers in Long Island. In the middle of his undergraduate work at Harvard, he did a stint in the military during World War II, where, as the war was ending, he taught public speaking to soldiers. Or as one comrade called it, "social graces."[17] Many have described how his patrician accent might put a new friend off, until it sank in how immensely friendly and charismatic the tall, slender fellow was, and that the Mid-Atlantic accent was permanent more than affected. The proud descendent of a lionized Union general,[18] Plimpton had the charm of a Kennedy; indeed, his brother said in an interview, "I think George might have even dated" Jacqueline Kennedy.[19] "I really didn't like [George] at first, mistaking the apparent snobbishness and studied front for gratuitous thoughtlessness, rather than recognizing the necessary camouflage of an almost tenderly vulnerable man," wrote Doc Humes years later. "I know a lot about [him] now that I didn't when I first met him, and he is a complex, lonely, rather brave human being."[20]

Given the constant allegations of CIA ties that clung to *The Paris Review* throughout its life, one admires the language, straight out of spy thrillers, that Matthiessen used in an undated letter during the period in which he recruited Plimpton for the magazine. "Michael tells me you are planning to come here and join forces with us, which is very cheering intelligence indeed. I have had a long letter from Humes, presently in Portugal, full of bright ideas, and if we can lure Guinzburg into the trap, which I think we can, all will be well."[21]

It's unclear to which Michael he refers.[22] Thomas Guinzburg was another founder, and a classmate of Matthiessen's at Yale. The first managing editor, he was unable to run the magazine after falling in love with Francine du Plessix (now Gray). He was too heartsick to work.[23] Like Matthiessen, Guinzburg was a Hotchkiss alumnus, the son of a publishing magnate, and a member of Skull & Bones, and worked under William F. Buckley on the *Yale Daily News*. During Matthiessen's final year at Yale, Guinzburg was his roommate.[24]

"Meanwhile," Matthiessen recalled, "in making contacts around Paris for the CIA, my politics by this time had really changed. I was not only going left, I was veering left very hard. And I wrote a book which began actually as part of my cover, my second novel, called *Partisans*. But when I ended up, it was a kind of a statement of belief. And it was so left that the *Chicago Tribune* told me to go back to Moscow, which was ridiculous."[25]

Matthiessen's CIA liaison didn't think the novel was enough of a cover and kept asking, what else can you do in Paris? There was no issue of the new magazine he proposed, but there was letterhead, and an office. Compared to some expat magazines there, *The Review*'s first Paris office stood out. "The rue Garancière, where *The Paris Review* had its office, contained within the larger office of [French publisher] La Table Ronde, was just around the corner from the Tournon [café], and the magazine's editorial team settled into the café and made it their local." Plimpton mused that the publishing house "worked with the kind of silence one associates with clerking in nineteenth-century banking institutions," but "the *Paris* team preferred instead to read galleys and new submissions snugly enveloped in the congenial smoke of the Tournon."[26] The office was posh enough to stimulate casual rumors of CIA ties. "*The Paris Review* . . . seems at first sight an unlikely recipient of ideologically determined disbursements; but the other side of the bill says that publications generally reflective of 'American values' and broadly in line with the American government's hatred of Communism might be looked on favorably if a request for funding were to be made."[27]

Plimpton denied ties to the CIA, recalling, "Many people felt that *The Paris Review* was somehow involved with the CIA as a recipient of its funds through the agency of the Congress for Cultural Freedom. That was not true." But from nearly day one, the rumors stuck, and some speculated that there would soon be quid pro quo for such funding. "There would have had to be a return somehow," thought Otto Friedrich, the journalist and author. "It might have just been a matter of the CIA asking these people to keep an eye on things around their café tables and in their hotels. There was lots of it going on at the time. There wasn't anything even particularly sinister about it."[28] The Congress for Cultural Freedom was the CIA's new propaganda front, its attempt to offset the use of culture by the Soviets to lure intellectuals to the fringe benefits of Communism—which included government funding for the arts.

Plimpton acknowledged the rumors occasionally in interviews, but was "adamant that there were no government favors done for favors returned." "*The Paris Review* was started with private money," he told James Campbell. "The families of Peter Matthiessen, myself, and John Train each gave $500. That got the magazine off the ground." Plimpton did admit "that one prominent member of *The Paris Review*'s editorial team was actually working for the CIA at the time, as he confessed to colleagues in later life.

He resigned his security position . . . after being asked to spy on the expatriate community."[29]

The New York Times revealed Matthiessen's CIA ties in 1977,[30] somewhat against his will. Matthiessen claimed that he spoke on the understanding that the journalist would not use his name. But the journalist reneged. "I knew and he admitted that a lot of people he was talking to weren't using their names," said Matthiessen, who attempted to make the same arrangement to speak anonymously. But then, "he had this long gray piece and needed a little spice in it. So he threw my name in it."[31] It was precisely because the CIA had already launched magazines that such suspicions were attached to the group's office, which was luxe compared to the Left Bank dives where rival magazines like *Merlin* were located. *Preuves*, launched in October 1951—the year *The Paris Review* crowd was planning its first issue and debating the new magazine's name—was already under suspicion, as it "was unmistakably the house organ of the Congress [for Cultural Freedom], giving it a voice as well as advertising its activities. As such it immediately faced . . . [hostility], but stood firm in the face of virulent attacks from both the left and the right."[32]

If Matthiessen had been asked to spy on his expat friends, he was not alone. Richard Wright, author of the acclaimed novel *Native Son*, began to suspect he was being watched. Wright had founded a group called the Franco-American Fellowship. Its mission involved elucidating "the problem of human freedom. . .[in order] to combat the . . . extension of racist ideas and practices . . ." He and his group were relentlessly spied on. Though he was an anti-Communist, Wright was an activist writer with a political bent, who lobbied for more employment of "'Americans of African ancestry' in US government jobs in Paris," and observations by informants found their way into his FBI file. One of the informants who spied on Wright was known to be mentally imbalanced, described in Wright's file as having a "mental quirk."[33]

Aware he was being spied on, Wright resigned as president, and this group that might have gotten more jobs for black expat Americans, such as the perpetually broke James Baldwin, folded for want of his leadership. It turned out that Wright's extensive FBI file was constructed mostly from spies from military intelligence, though the US Information Agency and the Foreign Liaison Service also helped keep a covert eye on Wright. In fact, in a photograph in Nelson Aldrich's oral history of Plimpton, *George, Being George*, a handsome young Peter Matthiessen, flanked by writer Max Steele on one side, laughs with Wright in front of a Paris cathedral. Wright, too, laughs, and the scene looks like a jolly one between friends. But during the period that the photograph was taken, Matthiessen was a covert counter-intelligence agent of the CIA, and Wright was being spied on by multiple acquaintances in multiple agencies. The fact of having to resign from a group due to infiltration by intelligence agents naturally embittered Wright. Years later, he told a group on the Quai D'Orsay that "most revolutionary movements in the West are government-sponsored. They are launched by *agents provocateurs* to organize the discontented so that the government can keep an eye on them."[34] As we shall see, the CIA's cloak of secrecy would tempt it to suppress lawful political activists, and this à la carte suppression would then lead to Operations Chaos and Mockingbird, involving exactly the sort of mass infiltration Wright described.

"I remember I was trained in New York that winter," Matthiessen said of the time before his trip to Paris. "I went to Paris in the spring." Training consisted of "how to photograph documents, surveillance, the usual. I thought it was kind of fun. I really did. They had a safe house and every day [Matthiessen and his trainer] would work together."[35] After training as an intelligence officer for around three months, the senior agent challenged Matthiessen: "'I could find out your real name and this is how I would go about it,' [he said]. So I came back a few days later, and said, 'I can find out your real name, too, and this is what I would do, bing bing bing,' and he said, 'Right, stop right there,' and 'more or less your training is [done].'" Though Matthiessen impressed his CIA trainer, he admitted, "I never learned who he really was. . ."[36]

.   .   .

Instead of telling people he was training for the CIA, Matthiessen said he was beginning work on his novel. "Which I was. We only worked a few hours a day." But the first uncomfortable request came up. "They wanted me to come to Washington. [But] I said, 'Look, if I do that, my cover is blown right away. Either you train me in New York or there's no go.' That was the first sticking point right there. Because there were so many guys signing up for the CIA."[37] Apparently, it was such a high number from his social circle that a trip to Washington, Matthiessen felt, would blow his cover with the others that he would see there. "I have a lot of friends who did it [joined the CIA]. So does George. We still do."[38]

But the pressure—and guilt—were mounting. His boss in the agency "kept hitting that patriotic note. And when he sent me to Washington, guess who he sent me to? James Jesus Angleton. The headquarters at that time, temporary housing in the woods, [had] buildings thrown up, like they do for migrant workers, by no means a big operation." Initially his wife Patsy was in favor of Peter's new vocation. "But she wasn't all for it later on, after we lost our first kid. I started getting followed every time I left the place," in Paris. She would say, "'We don't need this.' But also for political reasons, this was not my gang. I realized that all these Ivy League rich people, [from] wealthy families . . . this isn't where reality is at all." Matthiessen said he "was reading the Communist papers for research purposes to keep up to date about France. But I really found that—[the French Communist Party] weren't a very humorous bunch, I'll tell you—but they were the only honest party in France at that time; everybody had their hand in the till. So, I respected the people I was supposed to be spying on, more than the ones that" he was spying for.[39]

Irwin Shaw, a novelist from the older generation who had befriended *The Paris Review* group in Paris, described the privileged milieu that was wearying Matthiessen: "The literary hopefuls of the Paris contingent spoke in the casual tones of the good schools and could be found surrounded by flocks of pretty and nobly acquiescent girls, in chic places like Lipp's on the Boulevard St-Germain or on the roads to Deauville or Biarritz for month-long holidays." He continued, "They were mild-mannered, beautifully polite, recoiled from the appearance of seeming ambitious and were ready at all times to drop whatever they were almost secretly composing to play tennis (usually very well), drive down to Spain for a bullfight, fly to Rome for a wedding . . . they gave the impression they were going through a period of Gallic slumming for the fun of it. One guessed that there were wealthy and benevolent parents on the other side of the Atlantic."[40]

Attractive qualities emanated from these figures, and these qualities didn't go unnoticed. For one young writer in Paris and New York during that time, Matthiessen especially stood out. "Peter Matthiessen was not just a long-legged prep-school-looking man," wrote Anne Roiphe, "he also had appeared to be a man who hunted and climbed mountains and spoke in native languages and lay down in the tall grass and let bugs crawl over his chest." She was referring to the reputation increasingly arising from his nature writing, in books like *The Cloud Forest* and, later, *The Snow Leopard*. "He had a quiet fierce intelligence that came from his eyes, the cut of his jaw." She thought "a wise goodness was moving within him. . ."[41]

Working on his first novel while in the Agency's employ, Matthiessen joined a long tradition of writer-spies. This relationship wasn't incidental.

This aspect of the "P Source," especially as exemplified at Yale, emerged from a kind of close reading popularized by the movement known as the "New Criticism." The New Critics' method for studying a literary text owed much to an understanding of language put forth by Sir William Empson in his *Seven Types of Ambiguity*: "Empson's peculiar achievement," wrote one scholar, "was to find a way of talking about poetry which was at once exemplary of the commitment to literature that he found essential in a critic . . . exact, teachable, and seemingly quite detached from the political quarrels of the day."[42] Other scholarly methods of criticism emphasized the historical context of a literary text. Upending this, New Criticism sought to examine texts ahistorically, as closed, self-contained systems.

Angleton, Matthiessen's ultimate boss at the CIA, came of age intellectually within this tradition. His official CIA photo shows a man with deeply subdued, quietly distracted eyes, borne by a slightly gaunt face, with pronounced cheekbones resembling the young Sinatra, but with the large ears of Mickey Mouse, which make him seem both boyish and underline the degree to which he was a human antenna searching for signals.

Angleton's father was from Idaho. He started in sales and eventually owned a successful cash register business, and his mother was from Nogales, Mexico. He met her on an expedition to capture Pancho Villa. His father's business took him to Italy, so that young Angleton grew up speaking Italian in addition to Spanish. His English schooling gave him an appreciation for expensive English-cut suits, and a sense of his Americanness as *containing*, owning, the European culture to which he was now heir.[43] Even if his literary publishing at Yale wasn't exactly his cover, in the way it was for Matthiessen, it at least led him *into* the CIA. First, Angleton launched a Francophone student literary magazine called *Vif*, then another, *Furioso*.[44] *Furioso* spurred Angleton's correspondence with T.S. Eliot and William Carlos Williams, who said of Angleton's own poetry, "I like the rich color and intensity (a bit nostalgic) of the feeling—but I'd rather see more before judging." *Furioso* also fostered his friendship with poets Ezra Pound, E.E. Cummings, and Reed Whittemore. After graduation, Angleton hoped to go to Harvard Law School, but he was rejected. He then enlisted Professor Pearson, who wrote a letter praising how serious *Furioso* was. It got him in.[45] Though Angleton would call himself a lawyer when testifying before lawmakers later in his career, he actually enlisted to fight in World War II before graduating from Harvard Law, never finishing. Pearson eventually yanked Angleton into the OSS, and, before long, he was serving as an intelligence official in Italy, the country he knew so well. Among the "ugly stuff" from those early years (of which Matthiessen denied knowledge) was the huge infusion of CIA bribe money for the 1948 Italian elections, which initiated more than two decades' worth of subsequent Italian election bribes. "'All in all, between 1948 and 1975, over $75 million was spent by the CIA on Italian elections,' part of a worldwide program of secret and illicit support for . . . Christian Democrat parties and their analogues, like the particularly corrupt Japanese Liberal Party. . ."[46] Other early efforts would see the useless march of Albanians and other Eastern Europeans to death and capture behind the Iron Curtain in guerrilla operations meant to spark regime change, operations that had already been compromised.[47] These missions were betrayed by early double agents, "moles," and would become Angleton's key obsession beginning in the years he had Matthiessen in his employment at the Agency. This was likely why Matthiessen read the Communist newspapers in Paris.

But as *The Paris Review* editors sifted through copy for their first issue, the CIA was shifting focus. In the wake of President Eisenhower's January 1953 inauguration, Allen Dulles took over as director, having served under Walter Bedell Smith as deputy director. The following year James Jesus Angleton was named chief of counterintelligence. "At this point, long before I left Paris, they came to me, the government did, and wanted me to go very much deeper," said Matthiessen.[48] Counterintelligence Chief Angleton had an army of journalists who were under what was called "deep snow" cover. "I spoke good French by that time. I had good contacts; apparently mine were good." Matthiessen had taken his junior year at Yale abroad at the Sorbonne. "I said nope, and not only am I not going to do that, I'm going to resign from the CIA right now. And I did. And I've [been] going leftward ever since."[49]

As vague as Matthiessen's post-training responsibilities were—did he spy on his friends, sabotage the French left?—the above is more than anyone has gotten him to say on the record. These details about his recruitment, training, and chain of command were given in an on-camera interview to Doc Humes's daughter, the filmmaker Immy Humes, who sought to untangle her father's paranoia in a documentary about his life. Once Matthiessen agreed to the interview, and signed a release, it was all Humes could do to keep any of the details about his CIA service in her film. After Matthiessen saw a cut of the film, he began a campaign to browbeat her to take his own confession out of her film. Much of the above wound up on the cutting room floor.

2

THE RESPONSIBILITY OF EDITORS

A very good editor is almost a collaborator. —Ken Follett

But literature was not just a cover; it was a weapon in its own right. The need for amped-up Cold War cultural propaganda—a sort of international American Studies—grew out of the reaction to Soviet cultural programming in post–World War II Western Europe. George F. Kennan, the founding father of American "containment," worried in his "Long Telegram" from Moscow that the Soviets were infiltrating organizations throughout the world.[1] Many policymakers felt that Western Europeans were being softened to the horror of Communism thanks to towering Soviet and Russian cultural achievements. Americans, in a word, needed to become boosters of their high culture. But the same men who agitated for an agency to champion culture also believed the Americans needed to fight fire with fire, employing sabotage, covert warfare, and all sorts of nefarious activities that Kennan and others insisted the Soviets were engaged in.

This thinking eventually spurred the creation of the Office of Policy Coordination and the International Organizations Division, out of which would emerge the CIA's Congress for Cultural Freedom. The Congress itself dwelt within a slew of propaganda agents who worked in radio, books, film, art, music, labor, student groups, and so on. In 1952, the OPC, having started under the State Department, was merged into the CIA. Out of this grew the new umbrella for propaganda, covert ops and psychological warfare,[2] the Directorate of Plans. Under this behemoth sat the new magazines, usually under the Congress's sovereignty. A use for culture had finally been found; it was a weapon. The CIA sent the Boston Symphony Orchestra on its first European tour and covertly sponsored abstract expressionism's first European exhibition. Like the New Critics' ahistorical approach to a text, the paint splashes of Jackson Pollock did not lend themselves to a Marxist or anti-imperialist narrative the way Diego Rivera's sweeping murals did. This American expressionism pointed instead to individual freedom in a tacit campaign against social realism, a style that Franklin D. Roosevelt had funded openly during the Depression. Now, twenty years later, this art that was sensitive to history was anathema: a tool of the enemy. Those conservative figures leading the reaction against the New Deal's popular programs were themselves curmudgeons about funding art. Whether it could be used for soft power purposes or not was beside the point. These modern, decadent paint splashers, let alone writers who depicted the realities of the poor and marginalized, should be banned, not funded. Rather than educate through public discussion, instead these would-be builders of the non-Communist consensus "did it black," to use their later phrasing. This meant funding their scheme for cultural propaganda secretly through the unaccountable new agency, rather than rally for consensus before lawmakers and the public. The expressionist painters would be championed. The canonical writers would be too. But in order not to raise the reactionaries' hackles, the social realists would be marginalized. This sloppy compromise was papered over by CIA secrecy.

The Wall Street lawyer Frank Wisner was head of both propaganda schemes and covert operations. The diminutive manic-depressive had been a World War II adventurer who would head up the Directorate of Plans, and thus, ultimately, the Congress for Cultural Freedom, as well as its sibling offices in coups and assassinations. The Congress had offices in dozens of countries, employed hundreds of personnel, published dozens of intellectual and anti-Communist magazines, and "held art exhibitions, owned a news and feature service, organized high-profile international conferences, and rewarded musicians and artists with prizes and public performances. Its mission was to nudge the intelligentsia of Western Europe away from its lingering Marxism and Communism towards a view more accommodating of 'the American way.'"[3]

And it wasn't just government propaganda outfits that Wisner and his CIA boss Allen Dulles directed, but cover businesses—airlines and paper factories and film production fronts. Sometimes a legitimate company housed within it a CIA shell company to lend it a veneer of legitimacy. The CIA's "empire," as Evan Thomas called it, expanded into Asia, Africa, and Latin America, and—according to one of its boosters—the flagship Congress for Cultural Freedom was "the only outfit . . . making an anti-Communist anti-neutralist dent with intellectuals in Europe and Asia."[4]

The neutralists and avowed leftists of Europe, men like existentialist writer Jean-Paul Sartre, were one test of sorts for the CIA's efforts. Some results can certainly be claimed in Europe, as when Sartre denounced the Soviets for their repression in Hungary in 1956. But the neutralist intellectuals of Asia and the developing world, a key area of focus when Dulles became Eisenhower's Director of Central Intelligence, were left cold by often clumsy, ham-fisted efforts to win them over with a schizophrenic cocktail of perfidy, coups, and culture.

The CCF would not just do positive propaganda, like reminding our European and global friends about our Nobel Prize winners. The CCF and its CIA partner agencies would also engage in negative propaganda, exposing the "lies" of "coexistence," "neutrality," "non-alignment," "peace," "anti-racism," and other buzzwords alleged to originate with the Communist front groups. Like its parent agency, the CCF was enlisted not just to spread criticism, but outright disinformation to foreigners and Americans alike.

The Congress for Cultural Freedom's CIA funding was kept secret. Yet those working within its vast apparatus knew the rumors, according to several well established accounts.[5]

. . .

As *The Paris Review* founders trickled back to New York in the middle and late 1950s, a group dubbed the New York Intellectuals had laid down arguments that would affect the fledgling magazine's long-term prospects. The New York Intellectuals were a clutch of leftists associated with the magazine *Partisan Review*. They had renounced their former Communist sympathies during the worst of Stalin's purges in the 1930s, and after the Hitler–Stalin non-aggression pact of 1939.[6] Well-informed in the nature of Soviet tactics, these intellectuals, under the banner of the American Committee for Cultural Freedom, a nonprofit foundation sometimes called the American Committee for short, began to crusade for anti-Communist causes. They disrupted conferences and critiqued supposed Communist front activities and groups, writing letters to editors and government officials, holding public forums, discussions, and debates. When the international Congress for Cultural Freedom formed in Paris in 1950, the American Committee became the US affiliate.

Sidney Hook, a pragmatist philosopher at NYU and the chair of its philosophy department, was the most hard-line of these ex-leftists, and Dwight Macdonald, a contrarian critic, author, and professor, was the most ambivalent. Respectively, these two formed the right and left wings of the group. Sol Stein—the novelist, playwright, and propagandist, and the only member alive today—claimed the center. Dan Bell, the sociologist editor, and Arthur Schlesinger, the historian, helped round out Macdonald's liberal-left camp of the American Committee.

Macdonald was another Yalie who became known for his outspokenness. After a stint with *Partisan Review*, he worked at *The New Yorker*. The contrarian magazine he had founded, *Politics*, was an outlet for the vestiges of his pacifism. But in the late 1940s, he was so depressed about politics that he flirted with giving it up for cultural criticism. His marriage was stagnant; as an anarchist he attacked all the presidential candidates of the liberal-left in the 1948 election. According to Macdonald, Henry Wallace, the socialist running for the Democratic nomination against Truman, was an apologist for the monstrous dictator in the Soviet Union, Josef Stalin. Macdonald saw Wallace's naïveté toward Stalin as unforgivable and relentlessly attacked him. While Harry Truman ultimately upset Republican Governor Thomas Dewey of New York, neither candidate was good enough for Macdonald: they were more of the same. Even if one them had to win (it was Truman), Macdonald was consoled that the election was marked by the fact that almost half of the eligible electorate had opted not to vote—a victory for Macdonald's anarchist views.

By March 1949, Macdonald and the American Committee were united in a great plan of subversion that embodied their consensus. They gathered like covert action spies at New York's Waldorf-Astoria Hotel to disrupt the "Cultural and Scientific Conference for World Peace," which they thought was a Communist Trojan horse. Attending in the name of cultural exchange were dramatist Lillian Hellman, playwright Clifford Odets, composer

Leonard Bernstein, playwright Arthur Miller, NAACP co-founder W.E.B. Du Bois, and author Dashiell Hammett. Young Peter Matthiessen's cousin, F.O. Matthiessen, also attended. The Soviets who came were the composer Dmitri Shostakovich and Alexander Fadeyev, head of the Soviet Writers' Union. Priests, nuns, and political conservatives organized by the American Legion picketed outside the hotel in very cold New York weather, jeering and booing.[7]

Contrasting this "unintelligent anticommunism," Macdonald's and the American Committee's style was designed to play better to educated anti-Communists, thanks to the group's trademarked brand of urbane gravitas, the beloved intellectuals who lined its letterhead and the sober, meticulous tone of their public takedowns. The NYU philosopher Hook had written several books on Marx, but his hero was pragmatist philosopher John Dewey.[8] Hook's second book on Dewey was nearly out, and as a frequent commentator on politics to the media, Hook represented an outsized fear of Soviet penetration of American institutions.

In addition to Macdonald and Hook, the novelist Mary McCarthy, poet Robert Lowell, novelist Elizabeth Hardwick, composer Nicolas Nabokov (first cousin to Vladimir), and future Kennedy administration historian Arthur Schlesinger all crammed into one of the Waldorf suites, their makeshift command center. At stake was more than peace. "The Cultural and Scientific Conference for World Peace . . . was widely suspected of being underwritten by the Soviet Union (a claim, which, to this day, is impossible to verify). Anticommunists feared that the Soviets were co-opting intellectuals with words like 'peace' and 'freedom,' and thus winning the Cold War by controlling the terms of the debate."[9] Whether it could be proven or not, the American Committee thought the Waldorf conference was a dangerous foothold in the heart of New York City, and planned a bit of theatrical counter-debate bordering on counter-insurgency.

During those days in late March, hard-liners like Hook seemed almost disappointed that rather than being tossed ignominiously into the chilled air amidst those picketing crowds outside, they simply had to wait their turn. Since Hook had insisted they'd be shouted down or removed, they had written their comments down on tear sheets to be handed to the media. But they were treated well, asked pointedly not to shout interruptions; in a few minutes they would have the floor. The warfare Hook had prepared them for was not necessary. The more moderate among them saw that there were distortions within this "paranoid style."[10]

When their turn came, it was a lesson in public shaming. Mary McCarthy asked *American Renaissance* author and Transcendentalist scholar F.O. Matthiessen if he thought that Emerson would be free to write and live as he liked in the Soviet Union. Matthiessen acknowledged he would not but added that Lenin would not be allowed to live in the United States either.[11] (F.O. Matthiessen was not long for this world. Soon he would be hounded into suicide like many leftists after him, the abuse at the Waldorf exacerbating a long depression that he went into after the death of his domestic partner.) Macdonald asked the Russian writer Fadeyev why he had allowed the Politburo to make such drastic edits to his novel *The Young Guard*.[12] Robert Lowell asked the composer Shostakovich whether the state's criticism of his work had been helpful.[13]

But the Committee's militancy was only embarrassing them. After banging her umbrella to be heard and receiving a polite response in return, Mary McCarthy "blushed" at her rudeness and later resented Hook's distortions about the monstrous treatment they should expect. According to his biographer, Macdonald, too, came prepared for warfare but was won over by an aura of shopworn humanity in some of the men demonized by their group. He rightly sensed clumsiness in the soft-spoken Matthiessen, this "fellow traveler," the term for those sympathetic to Communist ideology who were therefore nearly as dangerous as the Communists themselves. Looking back and forth between the composer Shostakovich and the writer Fadeyev, Macdonald divided Russian cultural warriors, respectively, into victims and bureaucrats. The victims were the artists like Shostakovich, sensitive, always pale and thin like the embattled composer, who until that year had been severely criticized by the Soviet Union's official organs. Fadeyev on the other hand, was large, cold, and wooden, more like a "plainclothes detective."[14] Whatever differences officialdom had lavished on these men, the members of the Committee were impaling both.

When Mary McCarthy's argument turned into a discussion, she and the others were cordially invited by members of the National Council of the Arts, Sciences, and Professions to a reception at the run-down Hotel Seymour. On the way inside, Macdonald had handed out copies of his magazine *Politics*. But coming out of the Waldorf, his own dissenters' camp was booed alongside the so-called Stalinists and fellow travelers. Rather than glimpsing a window into a plot to penetrate America, Macdonald found himself a little bored, and somewhat charmed. "But despite his boredom he did get a much different impression of the Stalinists than he had previously gleaned," his biographer, Michael Wreszin, recalled.

He found it possible to communicate with them, since . . . they shared a common culture and political background. They read many of the same books, went to the same art shows, foreign films, held the "same conviction in favor of the (American) underdog— the Negroes, the Jews, the economically underprivileged"—and against the Catholic hierarchy and the US State Department.[15]

In the next issue of *Politics*, Macdonald ran a piece that he'd written before the conference taking the State Department line that you couldn't talk to "Stalinists" and fellow travelers. But when he recapped the reception after the Waldorf panel, he made it clear that you could. After readers pointed to the contradiction, he tried to clarify that so long as you stayed clear of the "main point" you were fine.[16] But the whole episode seems to have reminded him that the Stalinists and Communists may have begun their decline. They were shabbily arrayed; they apparently had little funding and this made their influence seem questionable. They weren't so fearsome after all. And the consensus items he shared with them—fighting for the underprivileged, for black Americans, for Jews—was being overshadowed by the fight against Communism.

Other events might have made Macdonald suspicious of the paranoia in the air. Weeks before the Waldorf battle, Macdonald was embroiled in a battle over Yaddo, the writers' and artists' colony in Saratoga Springs, New York. As it is today, Yaddo was a beloved retreat space to write and create and Macdonald had been accepted to take up residency there to work on a book. But underneath Yaddo's idyllic landscape, J. Edgar Hoover was rattling the retreat space's bedrock. Hoover's FBI was investigating an alleged sympathizer with Chinese Communism, Agnes Smedley, who had written books about China. Smedley was friends with Yaddo's leadership and was busily working on her next project there. Robert Lowell, an acclaimed poet from New England and a manic depressive member of the Waldorf action, was provoked by news of the FBI investigation.[17]

Lowell and his cohort accused Yaddo's beloved director, Elizabeth Ames, of being a Communist spy, however indirectly. The incident led to a board meeting meant to oust her from her position. Although Ames asked Smedley to clarify her sympathies or leave Yaddo, and Smedley left, Lowell had already called up applicants to get them to boycott, including Macdonald. "Although there was little offered in the way of supporting evidence," wrote Macdonald's biographer, "Dwight immediately wrote Ames a rude and blistering letter declining his appointment and condemning [Smedley] for turning the retreat into a 'center for pro-Soviet propaganda.'"[18]

As part of the liberal-left wing of the American Committee, Macdonald's ambivalence and even tenderness later in March 1949 toward those at the Waldorf whom he considered Stalinists-in-decline, alongside his militancy when it came to Smedley and Ames, offer a glimpse into the confusing nature of the times. But it got even stranger when Ames was cleared.

Novelist Malcolm Cowley, a Yaddo board member, recapped for his friend Ernest Hemingway the strange turn events took next. Cowley noted the "happy end" after Ames was cleared. But he went on to describe how Lowell nevertheless had "gone out of his head" in the days afterward and "had to be put in handcuffs by four sweating policemen and carried off for treatment. Paranoid psychosis was the doctor's verdict." Cowley saw in the incident a collective, not a singular psychosis. "What we had really been living through was paranoia that had passed from mind to mind like measles running through a school. Not so long afterwards," Cowley concluded, Washington gossip columnist "Drew Pearson gave his famous broadcast about [Secretary of Defense James] Forrestal and how he had been carried off to the loony bin shouting, 'The Russians are after me.' This great nation has been adopting its policies on the advice of a paranoiac Secretary of Defense. Maybe this is the age of paranoia, of international delusions of persecution and grandeur. Maybe persons like Forrestal and Robert Lowell are the chosen representatives and suffering Christs of an era."[19]

Having been born in this paranoid age, the American Committee for Cultural Freedom was an attempt to create an eloquent, outspoken coalition of liberal and conservative anti-Communists. Their reasonableness came and went, along with their bipartisan anti-Communist consensus. But these episodes show how a militant anticommunism was being used by upstarts in the FBI and Congress with little to no real experience who could make a name for themselves by denouncing the FDR and then the Truman administrations—and American institutions—as hotbeds for Communists and fellow travelers. And the American Committee was the cultural supplement to this work, done—if in public at all—often without due process.

As the decade wore on, the American Committee injected an adrenalized activist-interventionist impulse into the media, particularly with respect to opinion pages, criticism, and literary journals, or "little magazines," as they were sometimes called, over which the Committee presided like literary agents.

. . .

In the early 1950s, the House Un-American Activities Committe and its Senate counterpart, driven by Joseph McCarthy, had put the nation on edge. And while some saw it as evidence of an American strain of reactionary repression that echoed Puritanism—and thus had to be challenged in order to protect civil freedoms—the American Committee was divided over how much to push back in defense of civil liberties at home. All were concerned about Communism; they just weren't unanimous that the threat was as significant inside the United States as it had once been.

Apart from its work coordinating magazines, a large percentage of the American Committee's day-to-day focus was spent writing proposals to would-be funders like the Ford Foundation, the Fund for the Republic, and the Asia Foundation. (The last turned out to be a CIA front.) The Committee published books and white papers and helped ensure that its friends in the United States Information Service bought them up for dispersal in its international offices.

As its archives show, members of the American Committee presumed to know which arguments for civil liberties were sincere and which ill-intentioned, and which to brand as those of a Communist front. In some cases, the implication of Soviet influence turned out to be true. Certainly the occasional spy for the Soviet Union turned up. But in other cases, this denunciatory behavior was blind, wrong, destructive, and tantamount to blacklisting. It killed careers, forced people into poverty, and even triggered the occasional suicide.[20]

At times, the Committee seemed wary of alarmism and sensitive to the importance of due process. When the city council of San Antonio, Texas, was considering labeling its local library books with a warning if an author had once been accused of an "affiliation with subversive organizations," the Committee's chairman Dan Bell called the proposal "reprehensible" and compared it to Communist attempts to "'control' thoughts."[21] But on other issues it was clear that the appearance of this more liberal line was used to rationalize hard-line anticommunism. Writing to the New York State Education Commissioner in 1952, the American Committee's executive director, Irving Kristol, discouraged the compilation of a list of subversive organizations, but he did so on logistical grounds. Kristol, later the father of neoconservatism, suggested that the lists could be drawn up instead from public debates. He also commended Sidney Hook's expertise on such matters.[22] For his part, Sidney Hook had smeared the liberal professors at UC Berkeley as dangerous "fellow travelers" for refusing to sign a loyalty oath, which they thought violated their academic freedom.[23]

Requests for funding to the Ford Foundation and other grantmakers during the early 1950s show that the group strained to make anticommunism palatable, drawing up these lists of subversives, branding the likes of Agnes Smedley and Berkeley's psychology professor Edward Tolman as fellow travelers or Communist sympathizers, while masking the work under what one member called a tone of "tolerable urbanity."[24]

Among the most ambitious projects the American Commitee proposed was a master list of subversives, extremists, and front groups. The proposal sought funding for a nascent think tank of experts doing round-the-clock analysis on Communist front organizations and extremist groups in the United States. The proposal made the rounds at the Ford Foundation, getting as high up as Henry Ford himself. In one draft of the proposal they asked for nearly $130,000 to carry out all the associated tasks involved in researching the list. This would be about a million dollars in today's currency. They hoped to create a permanent research staff led by an executive staff of eight public experts and promised to release their findings in regular reports.[25]

The suspect groups who were listed in the proposal were divided into Communist fronts—the Civil Rights Congress, the National Council of the Arts, the Committee to Save the Rosenbergs, the American Women for Peace—and "extremist groups of the Right"—the Christian Nationalist Crusade, the Minute Women of the USA, Inc., the American Protestant Defense League, the Patriotic Research Bureau, and the Protestant War Veterans of the US, Inc.[26]

One of the project's chief aims was to "convince those who collaborate, often unwittingly, with extremist groups that they are aiding forces antagonistic to the best American traditions and the ideals of the Constitution of the United States." The words "unwittingly" and "extremist" jump out from the text as especially ironic, given that the majority of the American Committee's budget was paid by the CIA through a front organization headed by Julius Fleischmann, the bon vivant, sailor, and the son of a Cincinnati yeast magnate.

When it began to pay the Committee its monthly $2,500 stipend, Fleischmann's CIA front organization was called the Heritage Foundation, Inc. Within weeks of the first monthly stipend, the name was changed to the Farfield Foundation. When the CIA ties to these groups were outed, collaborators like Kristol would claim not to have known of CIA sponsorship. But whether that's true or not, these fronts paid the American Committee a minimum of about $30,000 per year in the early 1950s, the equivalent of nearly

$280,000 today. But this amount shields the real money that was available for project proposals and other anti-Communist tasks. In one letter to a potential collaborator at Columbia University in 1954, for example, the American Committee's Arnold Beichman, an author and scholar associated later with Stanford's Hoover Institution, sent a "partial list of some of the major contributors of the American Committee over the past year or two." The first section lists donations from foundations amounting to $167,500. These contributions came from such CIA front groups as the Fleischmann Foundation ($40,000), Hayfields Foundation ($20,000), National Committee for a Free Europe ($35,000), Free Europe University in Exile ($4,500), Heritage Foundation ($41,000), Farfield Foundation ($10,000), and so on. Many of these pointed to Julius Fleischmann, whose foundation for laundering CIA money had changed its name from Heritage to Fleischmann to Farfield, and so on. The total listed, $167,500 (which doesn't count the amounts given by private and individual donors), would amount to $1,475,220.45 in today's dollars. If you divide that in half to account for the phrase above—"the past year or two"—you have a minimum of $737,610.22 per year from CIA and likely CIA front groups alone for the years 1953 and 1954.[27]

What's more, to get funded, they played into an already widespread blacklisting tendency aimed at legitimate American groups. In the mid-1950s, when the Civil Rights Congress was being maligned in the mainstream media as a Communist front, for example, African Americans were being punished and sometimes killed for the Supreme Court's decision to desegregate schools in the American South. The pushback by entrenched racists was part of a wider effort to preserve white supremacy and Jim Crow in American institutions, both north and south. Among the many victims of this pushback was young Emmett Till, a fourteen-year-old from Chicago who was murdered while visiting relatives in Mississippi in 1955. His crime was talking to, perhaps flirting with, a white woman in the Jim Crow South. Hundreds of thousands of readers saw an image of the murdered boy on the cover of *Jet*, "the Weekly Negro News Magazine." Side-by-side photos showed the innocent, bright, and handsome face of Emmett when he was still alive and preparing to start eighth grade. Beside this cheerful image was another of water-damaged lesions and swelling that beset the boy's skin, eyes, and mouth as a result of his killers dumping him in the muddy river after they tormented and shot him. "Closeup of lynch victim bares mute evidence of horrible slaying," read the caption.[28]

Accused repeatedly of being a Communist front, the Civil Rights Congress had launched a campaign in years prior to Till's murder that lobbied to prevent such murders. It culminated in a program called "We Charge Genocide," which brought an inquiry into America's racial hatred and crimes against black Americans before the United Nations. In the race to win over hearts and minds against Communism, this was obviously an act of war. This, and the CRC's attempts to bail out alleged "Communists" who were arrested at protests, sealed its fate. New Cold War laws like the Smith and McCarran Acts effectively banned the Communist Party and labor, and split organizations that had former or current Communist members by making these groups register with the government.

While the American Committee believed the Communist threat serious enough to warrant such study, how should we see these episodes today? Given our widespread understanding of the horror of the Soviet gulag system, did the CRC's ties amount to support for Soviet or Stalinist Communism? Among the CRC's broad patchwork of constituencies dominated by labor and antiracism activists—and lawyers advocating Constitutional protections—some Communists indeed took part. But the CRC's civil rights work was effective. Gerald Horne, in his book on the Civil Rights Congress, has written that the Congress's vaunted ties to the Kremlin were exaggerated. "In state and federal courts [the CRC] argued landmark cases in areas as disparate as extradition, standing, excessive bail, the right to be silent before a grand jury, and many more."[29] In this portrayal, "Communist front" was too clumsy a description.

The Communist Party USA itself was hardly the demonic cabal it was made out to be, as Paul Robeson told a group of US senators. The internationally beloved actor and singer, who was black, defended the Communist Party USA as a legal entity that stood for "complete equality of the Negro people" and denied that the party was "an offshoot of Russian Communism." In the event, he must have incensed the American Committee, as it sought its funding to bolster efforts to ban civil rights groups for their association with the party. The senators must have spoken for the American Committee consensus when one argued, "surely the American people were better protected in their rights than the Russian people, who faced 'liquidation' if they dissented from official policy." "I have been threatened with death two or three times," Robeson replied. He added that his "sharecropping relatives" in North Carolina were threatened with lynching on a daily basis "if they dared assert even their minimal rights." Deaf to the irony of answering these depictions of threats of violence with yet another, Republican Senator Edward Hall Moore from Oklahoma told reporters that "Robeson seem[ed] to want to be made a martyr. Maybe we ought to make him one."[30]

The American Committee may have been correct that former or current Communist Party members were associated with the Civil Rights Congress. Still, for the American Committee to seek funding to study the group played into the reaction against the group's work. This reaction saw the FBI breaking into its office, bugging the CRC's phones, McCarthy's henchmen dragging its activists before Congressional witch hunts, their meetings being disrupted by thugs, *agents provocateurs* and informants, and their leader, Ida Rothstein, dying in mysterious circumstances.[31] To do more on racism would not have amounted to less for the American Committee on anticommunism. On the contrary, it would have entailed a style of prosecuting the cultural Cold War that would have empowered, rather than marginalized, American minority groups, thereby offering leadership by example, not by bayonet.

· · ·

Another American Committee proposal from April 1954 lobbied for funding to create a conference of magazine editors. The conference would establish a political line that was not to be crossed, and that would essentially amount to an explicit ban on robust criticism of the United States. It would implicitly pull *The Paris Review* back into the CIA's publishing fold after its ties had supposedly ended with Matthiessen's resignation. The proposal begins with a dire warning that European pessimism will have a direct effect on the outcome of the Cold War: "Pessimism pervades every report about the ideological climate in present-day Europe. . ." From all quarters, the proposal warned, "the message is: 'In Europe, America is an unknown continent. . .'"[32] The proposal cites American stereotypes of Europe as problematic, too, and goes on to call the "lack of a genuine cultural and political transatlantic discourse" nothing less than "shocking," as well as "dangerous and frightening." Even worse, it was Europe's very intellectuals "who show the latest lack of understanding for the other partner in the transatlantic community. . ."[33]

At the end of all this fulmination on anti-Americanism came a plan involving little magazines. The Committee sought to leverage these so-called "little"—or intellectual—magazines and bring them together with established American magazines of opinion as part of a transatlantic alliance. And it called for action "to stimulate a more effective transatlantic discourse among opinion leaders. We cannot afford to let dissension prevail among the members of the free world . . . . A sense of cultural cohesion is an indispensable condition for any effective political or cultural cooperation.

We must strive to strengthen the cultural unity of the Atlantic nations that has been damaged by ignorance and misinformation."[34]

In its calls for unity and its fear of criticism or disharmony between Western allies, the proposal echoed one from seven or so years before, by Melvin Lasky. Writing from Berlin, Lasky, a former City College Trotskyite who served in World War II, also pointed to anti-Americanism in Europe as a geostrategic problem. "The same old anti-democratic anti-American formulas on which many European generations have been fed," Lasky wrote, "are now being reworked. Viz., the alleged economic selfishness of the USA (Uncle Sam as Shylock); its alleged deep political reaction (a 'mercenary capitalist press,' etc.); its alleged cultural waywardness (the 'jazz and swing mania'; radio advertisements, Hollywood 'inanities,' 'cheese-cake and leg-art'); its alleged moral hypocrisy (the Negro question, sharecroppers, Okies).... We have not succeeded in combating the variety of factors—political, psychological, cultural—which work against US foreign policy [and]... the success of the Marshall Plan in Europe..."[35] Lasky's plan—the Lasky Proposal, as it was known—also sought to correct America's failure with intellectuals, and "to win the educated and cultured classes—which in the long run provide moral and political leadership in the community." What you had above, then, were the first articulations of official taboos about the United States, whether true or not, that were now declared beyond the pale for associated editors to print or even debate. Here was the proposed establishment of political correctness before the kind commonly associated with the term today.

The first such magazine launched to tackle this challenge, fittingly, was Lasky's own, *Der Monat*, which translates to *The Month*. Launched on October 1, 1948 and printed in Munich, it was a concrete embodiment of this fight against the anti-Americanism described by Lasky, and was conceived as a means to help achieve America's foreign policy goals by winning sympathy for its statesmen and cultural creators alike, as well as by ridiculing the common lines of criticism against American policies and assumptions. "Across the years, *Der Monat* was financed through 'confidential funds' from the Marshall Plan, then from the coffers of the Central Intelligence Agency, then with Ford Foundation money, and then again with CIA dollars," wrote Frances Stonor Saunders. "For its financing alone, the magazine was absolutely a product—and an exemplar of—American Cold War strategies in the cultural field."[36]

Der Monat may have been the first, but dozens more would arise in its wake—so many, in fact, we're still discovering them. Each new magazine targeted intellectuals. In England and France, these magazines were *Encounter* and *Preuves*. Between Yale's American Studies proposal, and "the Melvin Lasky Proposal," sometimes called a proposal for "The American Review," these proposals were drafted secretly in bureaucrats' offices and reeked of stale cigarette smoke, weak corner-office coffee, and sour bourbon–induced glee in throwing CIA money at the wall.

In pursuit of that money, the American Committee—back in midtown Manhattan—went on to scheme its way into a position of central control over these magazines. It cited "over forty magazines that are serious in tone, nontechnical in nature, and that consistently publish material that is of intellectual interest. . ." The Committee wanted to bring together the editors of these magazines to improve the "transatlantic discourse." But it was predominantly what people in the magazine industry would call a business-side scheme, rather than an editorial one.[37]

The Committee cited the *Partisan Review*'s anthology, the *Partisan Review Reader*, whose high sales indicated "that the circulation problem of the 'little' magazines are [sic] not entirely due to the content of these magazines." The improvement in sales came not by changing the "esoteric" content but through "a new format and entirely new distribution mechanics. The editors of the opinion magazines in the United States will want to examine the implications of this development in publishing technique."[38]

Nevertheless, CIA control over the magazines' editorial line would be the proposal's most important legacy.

．　．　．

As multipliers of the right kind of media, the American Committee also had an internal newsletter. If an article of interest came along they would select it for reproduction. Members' articles basked in this extra publicity through the Committee's elite circuits. For instance, after it was accepted to run in French in a condensed form in *Preuves*, scholar Gleb Struve's article on Chekhov—and Soviet attempts to use the fiftieth anniversary of his death for cultural propaganda—was sent by his "agents" at the Committee to *The New York Times Book Review*, *The New Leader*, *Book Review*, and other outlets. This was an attempt to double and triple his fees and multiply the outlets where the work ran.[39]

There were other perks—though to get them you might have to agitate. The conservative Peter Viereck was one of many Cold War writers lucky enough to be sent to Europe by the CCF. He coordinated his trip through the

American Committee, traveling on the US taxpayer's dime. Viereck was the son of a poet described by *Slate* as a "German propagandist" whose meddling in the United States helped spur the Espionage Act, under which Julian Assange and many other journalists have been persecuted under the Obama administration.[40] Though Viereck disagreed with many of his father's ideas, and had denounced McCarthyism, propaganda was apparently in his genes. As his trip approached, Viereck wrote to the American Committee to get his European junket upgraded. "If a certain affluent Yeast man likes us going in Grand Style (with better speech-typing conditions, not to mention better dissipation conditions) it wd be good to check with the boat companies if they can switch the cabin class reservations to 1st-class. . ."[41]

This was another reference to Julius Fleischmann. But beyond Fleischmann-funded junkets, there were other ways that Viereck's affiliation with the American Committee helped his career. When the *Hudson Review* attacked Viereck's book *Shame and Glory of the Intellectuals*, the American Committee's Sol Stein petitioned *Hudson Review* to run a rebuttal.[42]

So the idea for a conference of magazine editors to discuss how to monetize and mass-distribute writers' work was part of a coordinated effort to unite intellectuals in a common cause. Already experienced at tapping its network of friends, colleagues, and fellow board members to maximize the benefits of participation and membership, the American Committee sought in 1954 to formalize those benefits for magazines and their stakeholders. And all these ideas for sharing developments in publishing techniques came with certain responsibilities. The proposal promised to "make clear the responsibilities assumed by the editors of the American journals and would try to prevail upon their European counterparts to assume similar responsibilities."[43]

What sorts of responsibilities?

Combatting anti-Americanism comes up most often on the list of goals, among other worthwhile objectives, like intercultural exchange, and challenging American cultural insularity with international trends and ideas. Most importantly, the proposal notes that the American Committee wants to play the role of an editorial command center—a patriotic literary agency—for such CCF magazines as *Preuves, Encounter, Cuadernos, Der Monat*, and *Forum* (the CCF magazine in Austria). It also lists non-CCF magazines in the United States and overseas for whom it has performed this "clearinghouse" service, including *The Twentieth Century* in England, and *The New Leader*[44], *Partisan Review*, and *Commentary* in the United States. The American Committee was essentially offering literary agency services at large, telling members that if you write pieces that fit with our broader aims of fending off critiques of the United States, and if you are a member or friend of the American Committee, we can help you get published in multiple markets. With this, the quid pro quo was revealed. For if the American Committee helped these magazines on the business side, the Committee assumed that the magazines' editorial lines would reflect this help.

The specific editors whom the American Committee wanted to tap to co-present the conference were Elliot Cohen of *Commentary*, Norman Cousins of the *Saturday Review*, Gilbert Harrison of *The New Republic*, Sol Levitas of *The New Leader*, Russell Lynes of *Harper's*, Frederick Morgan of *Hudson Review*, William Phillips of *Partisan Review*, Paul Pickerel of the *Yale Review*, and Edward Skillin of *Commonweal*. *The Yale Review* agreed to host the conference in New Haven, and the Committee planned to invite the following additional magazines to be represented: *Accent, American Quarterly, American Scholar, Antioch Review, Arizona Quarterly, Art News, Atlantic, Bulletin of the Atomic Scientists, California Quarterly, Christian Century, Colorado Quarterly, Discovery, Dissent, Epoch, Foreign Affairs, Freedom and Union, Freeman, Georgia Review, Kenyon Review, New Mexico Quarterly, New Yorker, New World Writing, Northern Review, Pacific Spectator, Perspectives USA, Poetry, Queen's Quarterly, Quarterly Review of Literature, Review of Politics, Sewanee Review, South Atlantic Quarterly, Southwest Review, The Reporter, Theatre Arts, University of Kansas City Review, Virginia Quarterly Review*, and *Western Review*.[45]

As a new and unknown magazine, *The Paris Review* wasn't yet on the American Committee's list. But as more CCF magazines launched, it would find itself welcome among them.

. . .

The Paris Review launched the same year as the flagship magazine of the Congress for Cultural Freedom. *Encounter* was the CCF's London magazine. But of all the Congress's literary gems, *Encounter*'s reach was most global. It was born in planning meetings between Michael Josselson, who would covertly lead the CCF as executive secretary on behalf of the CIA for most of its life, and Christopher Montague Woodhouse, a British intelligence officer.[46] The composer Nicolas Nabokov, who had attended the American Committee's Waldorf protest, also consulted over the new magazine in the spring of 1953.[47]

Somewhat resembling the living American actor Paul Giamatti, Josselson was Estonian-Russian and described himself as apolitical at the end of World War II. At the war's end he worked in the US Office of Military Government—or OMGUS—helping oversee the de-Nazification of artists and functionaries. After spending the war interrogating German prisoners to separate out true Nazis from those pressured into supporting the party, he made a name for himself as a brilliant procurer and a talented fixer.[48]

Nicolas Nabokov was Josselson's old friend from Berlin in the 1920s. During the war, Nabokov worked with W.H. Auden and John Kenneth Galbraith in the US Strategic Bombing Survey Unit's Morale Division. He then worked with Josselson in the Information Control Division. After the war, given his musical talents, he was tasked with separating actual Nazi believers from the musicians who had just kept their heads down to avoid danger, while monitoring the "programmes of German concerts and see[ing] to it that they would not turn into nationalist manifestations."[49]

Christopher Montague Woodhouse, the Fifth Baron Terrington, had spent the war in Greece. He worked as a saboteur who blew up bridges and finally became head of the British Military Mission. After the war, he was the British Secret Intelligence Services' Tehran station chief. In November 1952, he traveled to Washington to float the idea of ousting Iran's elected prime minister (*Time* magazine's Man of the Year), Mohammad Mosaddegh. After enlisting opposition politicians, religious leaders, and journalists in his various propaganda campaigns, Woodhouse and his staff were tossed out of Iran. While developing the scheme to launch *Encounter*, he simultaneously convinced CIA men Allen Dulles and Frank Wisner that he wasn't merely trying to use Americans "to rescue British oil interests" in Iran (he was) but rather emphasized "the anti-Communist element in our plans."[50]

Though its first issue would launch in October 1953, *Encounter* was already operational in the summer of that year. The magazine's expenses were covered by an initial grant of $40,000. Money was channeled via its publishers at Secker & Warburg on the British side, and via Julius Fleischmann on the American side. Fleischmann, the yeast and gin heir, served as the most important "quiet channel" for the CCF. His reputation must have been growing; *The Paris Review* also sought Fleischmann's patronage from its inception.

．　．　．

"Dear Mr. Fleischmann," wrote Peter Matthiessen on *Paris Review* letter-head sometime before the first issue (in Spring 1953). "Here at last is a pro-spectus of the fine new literary review I mentioned to you in June. I sincerely believe . . . it will be the best literary quarterly since the TRANSITION of the Hemingway-Pound-Gertrude Stein era." He goes on to request funding[51] and, according to Nelson Aldrich, he got at least $1,000 from Fleischmann. Matthiessen always claimed that the CIA ties to the magazine consisted solely of his own short service in the early 1950s, and that there were no ties through the Congress. The fact of Fleischmann's donation contradicted this. It "muddies" the picture, Matthiessen later admitted.[52]

Matthiessen was still in Paris when *The Paris Review*'s first issue came out in the spring of 1953. It included fiction by Matthiessen, Terry Southern, Eugene Walter, and Antoine Blondin, and poetry by Robert Bly, George Steiner, and Donald Hall. The issue was crowned by what became the magazine's most enduring legacy, an interview: in this case one with E.M. Forster, whom Plimpton met at Cambridge. Of course, the hip young editors of magazines like *Merlin* and *Point* noted ruefully that Forster hadn't written a novel in decades.[53]

Co-founders John Train and William Styron wrote "features" for this first issue. Styron's feature was a self-conscious anti-manifesto, promising readers no punditry, noting that they wanted to favor creative work, and leave out the political, to "welcome" "into its pages—the good writers and good poets, the non-drumbeaters and non-axe-grinders."

> Let's by all means leave out the lordly tone and merely say: dear reader, THE PARIS REVIEW hopes to emphasize creative work—fiction and poetry . . . with the aim in mind of merely removing criticism from the dominating place it holds in most literary mag-azines and putting it pretty much where it belongs, i.e., somewhere near the back of the book.[54]

Reading Styron's editorial, it was clear that the magazine would forego poli-tics, too. "This would have been evident in the list of contents, which included the name of Henri de Montherlant," wrote one scholar. De Montherlant "had recently been shunned in France for having been a supporter of the collab-orationist Vichy government during the war."[55]

Or were they disguising their politics? Writing to Plimpton about a Jean-Paul Sartre interview, Matthiessen called for them to "offset" its poli-tics. Sartre was very much out of favor with the Cold War interventionists of the CCF. He was seen as a Communist sympathizer. Matthiessen wrote that the Sartre "material is good but . . . it must be supplemented by further material of a literary and non-political nature. . ." He added that the interview is "interesting and politically the sort of stuff to offset the Catholic-Fascist-Reactionary [word missing] that Sindbad and co. attach to us."[56]

The Sindbad to which he referred, Sindbad Vail, was part of this expat literary scene who worked on the magazine *Point*, of which Plimpton had claimed once to be jealous. Vail was Peggy Guggenheim's son and would become heir to her fortune, so *Point* was hardly a broke Left Bank magazine like *Merlin*. However, in order to compete, Matthiessen here in fact articulated a core strategy of the CCF—to appear culturally liberal, left-wing even.

Another letter from this time suggests that the editors were also cautious about appearing *too* liberal. This was, after all, the McCarthy era in the United States. After listing a number of font and design problems among ads in the most recent issue, co-founder Tom Guinzburg wrote to Plimpton, whose father was increasingly engaged in legal work with the Democratic Party. He raised a red flag about an ad for in-house organ of the Party called the *Democratic Digest*: "I should have paid more attention when you intimated that you were contemplating some sort of decent relationship with the [*Democratic*] *Digest*." He continued,

> You will recall that we have gone to very special lengths to disassociate ourselves from any political fence. No one is quite so naïve as to think that this ad found its way into our pages through any normal space selling or advertising appropriation. It stinks of duplicity, it fairly screams "deal". . . . I envision it losing us a host of friends and I can't think of any excuse for its presence. Truly Grand Maigre, I cannot tell you how upset I am . . .[57]

A reminder of the patriotic politics of the time, Guinzburg, who worked at Viking Books, wrote in the same letter of a visit to the Department of Defense's in-house newspaper: "I went and saw the representatives of *Stars and Stripes*, who control the newsstand distribution in Germany, etc., and they were courteous and showed signs of interest. I gave them a cock and bull harangue on the fact that a large percentage of our contributers [sic] were G.I.s and that G.I.s were writing in in droves for subscriptions, etc. I don't expect anything to come of it really, but there is just the chance and it would be a magnificent break."[58]

Matthiessen ran Mac Hyman's short story "The Hundredth Centennial." Sending the piece along to Plimpton, he wrote that Plimpton wouldn't be able to change anything without asking the author, who struck Matthiessen as "a latter-day Ku Kluxer. . ." Matthiessen thought "this kid Hyman was one of the boys who dropped the big boomer on Nagasaki . . . and probably volunteered for the duty into the bargain."[59]

Despite rumors of CIA ties to *Encounter*, however, no such warning letter appeared to come from Guinzburg when *The Paris Review* began running ads for the CCF's London-based magazine in 1954. How was it that running ads for a publication openly affiliated with a legitimate political party was forbidden when ties to a CIA front group were fine? Even the actual naming of the magazine was an attempt to position it with respect to its politics. *The Paris Review* is said to have gotten its name from John Train, who also nudged the quarterly away from a focus on criticism.[60] The brilliant young men who founded and launched the magazine met in Matthiessen's flat on 14, rue Perceval, which he described as his "wonderful flat." The CIA had paid for it. Present at this planning meeting were Matthiessen, Humes, Plimpton, Styron, William Pene du Bois (an illustrator), and John Train, who said later, "Matthiessen favored a magazine to be called *Baccarat*—hyper literary. I claim to have come up with the name *The Paris Review* and lobbied for that because it seemed very logical."[61] Plimpton was against the one-word names of the high-minded, self-flattering (and broke) literary quarterly scene. Additionally, he didn't think *The Paris Review* could last without a traditional editor-in-chief, a Grand Maigre, the Great Slender, as Guinzburg liked to call Plimpton.

Justifying his position about both the magazine's name and its editorial structure, Plimpton wrote in his diary that "there must be an absolute boss if one agrees that the magazine is more important than feelings."

Example is [the recent] argument about cover. I *know The Paris Review* is a sensible and safe title. It may not sell a million copies but . . . . It has snob appeal . . . . But . . . *Merde, Phusct, Venture, MS, Manuscript, Counterpoint, Baccarat*, all these evocative names which symbolize countless magazines . . . which have failed . . .— *zero, Blast, Transition* (although that a fine one), *Wake*, etc. I said I'd never read a literary magazine of any sort with a one name supposedly striking title which hadn't folded within a year or so. "*Time, Life, Fortune?*" asked du Bois. Well, he may be right . . . The title can certainly ruin it. . . . I hope if there's a better one and a safer one than *The Paris Review* I can open my mind to it.[62]

. . .

The idea for "an English language *Preuves*" was simultaneously envisioned by the American Committee and the British Society for Cultural Freedom. The CIA had money and a variety of groups were vying for it. Rumors that Plimpton was constantly putting down—that there were early CCF ties to *The Paris Review*—deserve some considering. *Encounter* and *The Paris Review* may have represented competing visions for the role of the so-called English-language *Preuves*. A magazine created as CIA cover for an asset would have appealed to CCF officials—a magazine created by an agent who may have been resigning, but who had friends at CIA, and who was recruited, trained, and "patriotic." Matthiessen had already written to the "quiet channel," Julius Fleischmann, who may have passed this idea along.

Then in the winter of 1953–54, after he said he left the CIA, Matthiessen wrote to Plimpton—who had since become the magazine's public face and, in Matthiessen's words, its "nominal" head—and offered funding largesse in the amount of $20,000 by unnamed backers. But these backers would need to be convinced the money could be used to put *The Review*, beset by funding and communication problems, on "an efficient working basis." Alluding to its most recent issue (No. 4) having arrived late, annoying its advertisers, Matthiessen asked Plimpton to consider the offer carefully; it would require putting Matthiessen back in charge since he would be accountable for the money.[63] The sum of $20,000 in 1953 is the equivalent of around $180,000 today.

Other evidence for an early tie to the CCF lies in the American Committee's archives. *Encounter*'s British editor, the poet Stephen Spender, suggested this in a letter to his American counterpart, Irving Kristol.[64] Kristol was recruited from the American Committee to co-edit *Encounter* in early 1953 before it was named. Spender was part of a poetry "brat pack" of sorts, and had turned against Communism and recorded it in an essay in the anthology *The God That Failed*. In their correspondence over the so-called English-language *Preuves*, Kristol wrote, "I wish I could resolve the questions you raise about the projected English language magazine (or magazines), but at the moment I am not in a position to."

During the quick trip to Paris I made a couple of weeks back I spent a good deal of time discussing this problem . . . Josselson and myself went to London for a day to talk the matter over with [members of the British Society for Cultural Freedom]. There seemed to be two magazine ideas floating around, and whether they are compatible, and what the relation between the two is, are matters on which I myself am far from clear.[65]

One of the magazines to which he refers was certainly *Encounter*. Was the other *The Paris Review*? Another rumor held that the CCF was looking to do an international *Partisan Review*.[66] Sol Levitas's *The New Leader* was also jockeying for funding amidst this CIA publishing exuberance, and saw itself as poised to launch a French version. Levitas had taken the newsprint magazine into the "little magazine," digest-bound format that the CIA preferred. He did so after the CIA prodded him to, in return for funding. The funding was very slow to materialize. He wrote to agents Carmel Offie and Jay Lovestone in the late 1940s, pleading that they pay him back; the expense of the transition had destroyed *The New Leader*'s finances. He referred to the project as akin to an English *Preuves*.[67] The English-language *Preuves* probably meant many things to many aspiring editors. Do these unnamed backers whom Matthiessen dug up, and his bid to retake control, suggest that *The Paris Review* was one such candidate for official CCF sponsorship?

Maybe the funders themselves were entertaining multiple visions. And the different editorial voices could complement each other in support of the CIA's efforts toward intellectuals.

. . .

Encounter would not take the same apolitical posture as *The Paris Review*, nor would it relegate criticism merely "toward the back of the book." But the magazines dovetailed in other ways. *Encounter* and *The Paris Review* both wanted to pursue William Faulkner, Hemingway, and Forster, obvious choices for their first issues, and both had distribution primarily in New York, London, and Paris. But given that *Encounter* didn't want to do interviews and *The Paris Review* all but disavowed criticism, they were perfect complements, a one-two punch where one could make the case that Americans were rich with not just CIA slush money but also with great authors—through its now-famous author interviews—while the other could make a sustained assault on global neutrality and buttress any burgeoning special transatlantic friendships.

Whatever the deepest concerns of *The Paris Review*, rolling back the stereotypes against Americans in Western Europe was foremost in the minds of *Encounter*'s founders. Among the names for the fledgling magazine bandied about in letters between New York, where Kristol was, and the Midwest, where Spender was, were *Congress* and *Culture and Politics*.[68]

In response, Spender suggested *Witness*, *Vista*, *Testimony*, and *Writing & Freedom*. "Culture" puts people off, Spender argued. He likewise wanted to avoid "politics." Kristol had suggested they avoid "liberty" and "freedom." These were already Cold War clichés.[69] Kristol suggested *Messenger*, *Across Seas*, and *Compass*. To further emphasize the geographical range envisioned, and the eastward gaze, he added *East West Review* or *East West*. The world's most populous democracy, India would increasingly be seen as crucial to win over, and that was certainly embedded in these choices.

The final name for the CCF's London magazine, like many of its subsequent decisions, was dictated from high up the chain of command, over the heads of its nominal founding editors. *Encounter* represented these NATO as well as East-West alliances and conversations. But when it did finally launch, there was much to recommend it: "It was here Nancy Mitford published her famous article 'The English Aristocracy,' . . . Isaiah Berlin's 'A Marvellous Decade,' four memorable essays on Russian literature, Vladimir Nabokov on Pushkin, Irving Howe on Edith Wharton, David Marquand on 'The Liberal Revival,' stories by Jorge Luis Borges, critical essays by Richard Ellmann, Jayaprakash Narayan, W.H. Auden, Arnold Toynbee, Bertrand Russell, Herbert Read, Hugh Trevor-Roper . . ."[70] Thanks to its sponsors, its reach was truly global.

. . .

While *Encounter*'s purpose and origins are now relatively clear, *The Paris Review*'s CIA birth remains complex. Even the question of who founded the quarterly was still being argued as recently as 2008. Note these two somewhat contrasting assertions by Peter Matthiessen. Statement one: "I was very proud of the magazine and . . . petty enough to bristle occasionally when . . . George permitted people to describe him in interviews as 'The founder and editor of *The Paris Review*.'" He explained, "This was technically untrue."

The magazine was under way when George was invited to Paris: but that founding was nebulous and mostly talk. The real founding did not take place until George and Billy Pene du Bois had joined us. Patsy Southgate made many contributions, including a fine translation for the first issue, and Styron, Guinzburg and Train were also important participants in that spring and summer of 1952.[71]

Matthiessen exudes certainty that he was there from day one, a primary founder, unlike Plimpton. But notice how this statement is more cagy (emphasis added): "For many years I have stated flatly that the rumors that *The Paris Review* was founded or influenced by the CIA are simply untrue. *Though I still believe that, it now appears* that some of our startup funding may have come from an acquaintance of George's and mine, a rich, cultured Chicagoan living in Paris at the time, who, many years later, around 1966, turned out to have been associated with a CIA-sponsored outfit called the Congress for Cultural Freedom." Matthiessen was of course talking about Julius Fleischmann, the CIA's most famous conduit, or quiet channel used to launder its money to its operatives and secret collaborators. Matthiessen describes Fleischmann as "one of several friends of our parents who donated money to help print and publish the first issue of the *Review*. George and I had no idea—not then, certainly—and by the time we learned of it we'd forgotten about his donation. Now, of course, I've seen the letter George wrote his parents about our fund raising efforts, and, difficult though it is to believe that an utterly unknown apolitical magazine of laughable potential circulation was a likely recruit for ideological warfare, the name Fleischmann in that letter muddies the picture a bit."

Was this the opening salvo of a confession? No, Matthiessen decided to swerve: "What muddies it even more, though, is that the Fleischmann George refers to—Raoul, the publisher of *The New Yorker*, who was Junkie's cousin, *I believe*—was a man who *as far as I know* had no connection with either the Congress or *The Paris Review*. Perhaps George confused his Fleischmanns; perhaps we both did."[72]

Though a reporter well versed in *The New Yorker* fact check regimen, Matthiessen couldn't get his story straight. Internal documents include Julius "Junkie" Fleischmann's full name and Cincinnati address on a list of *The Paris Review*'s backers in its Morgan Library Archives.[73] One critic writing in *The Nation* was eloquent on Matthiessen's ambiguities. "In assessing the history of the journal," he wrote, "how consequential was its early liaison with the CIA? In light of the paucity of scholarly material, the person most qualified to make that assessment is Peter Matthiessen. If he believes the waters have been 'muddied' by recent revelations, then he should endeavor to cleanse them. But over the years, and to this day, Matthiessen, who says he quit the CIA in disgust in 1953, has been tight-lipped."[74] As we shall see, Matthiessen did make one attempt to confess during an interview with filmmaker Immy Humes. But then he fought to suppress the interview, even after signing a legal release.

But as much as outside journalists or the *Review*'s readers, the figure who deserved answers most of all was Matthiessen's co-founder, Harold "Doc" Humes. Humes was present at Matthiessen's apartment when they named the magazine, he made regular contributions and suggestions, and took trips to drum up pieces for the first issue; he founded the original magazine that lent its infrastructure and resources to *The Paris Review*. Instead of rewarding him by making his role as a co-founder public, Humes was left off the first issue's masthead. John P.C. Train served as *The Paris Review*'s de facto managing editor for the first issue. After it was printed in Europe, he got the issue transported on the ship *The United States* in exchange for an ad from the ship company. But they put the shipment in such a large container that no one could move it on the docks in New York: "[S]everal thousand copies of *The Paris Review* were plopped down by crane into the New York docks in an immense, immovable carton," Train recalled. "The dockworkers refused to touch it, so we had to assemble a kind of ant army of volunteers to break up the crate on a dock and carry the copies into a warehouse. That was when Doc Humes turned up. He got hold of a rubber stamp and stamped them all 'Harold Humes, New York Representative.' He was miffed that his role . . . had not been acknowledged on the masthead."[75] Gay Talese depicts Humes, in his beret and with his silver-tipped cane, shouting defiantly, "Le Paris Review c'est moi!"

> "But . . . but . . . how *could* you have *done* such a thing?" George Plimpton asked when he next saw Humes. Humes was sad, almost tearful. With a final flash of righteous anger he said, "I am damned well not going to get shoved around!"[76]

3

PASTERNAK, THE CIA, AND FELTRINELLI

I do not want to turn the history into a novel, but rather to anchor the novel in history.

—Paolo Mancosu

In 1958, the Soviet Union stifled a major novel by a man many called "the greatest living Russian writer." Boris Pasternak's highly anticipated *Doctor Zhivago* had been suppressed by the Soviet Writers' Union, the official Soviet literary magazines, and the official Soviet publishing house. This created an opportunity for covert assistance from the CIA, who schemed to secretly publish the book in Russian with a short publishing turnaround so it could be handed out to Russians at the 1958 World's Fair in Belgium that fall. To the degree that it could, *The Paris Review* hoped to leverage the controversy by seeking funding from the Congress for Cultural Freedom—which resulted in *The Paris Review*'s supporting role in the ongoing US/Soviet propaganda wars, and strengthening the magazine's erstwhile ties to the CIA. When Pasternak died in the wake of the controversy, he may have sensed that he'd been used as a symbol, an instrument even, by both sides. Arguably, as a string of typos in his masterpiece suggested, he had been.

From the time of its inception, the CIA was operating covertly in Eastern and Southern Europe, especially aiming its early paramilitary operations at incitement and liberation of those populations locked behind the Iron Curtain. Frank Wisner was in charge of operations; his division of the CIA, the Office of Policy Coordination (OPC), was initially its own independent body. When it was moved into the newly formed CIA from its former State Department home, the OPC encompassed both covert operations—by decade's end, this would increasingly mean assassinations—as well as psychological warfare, which contained radio stations like Radio Free Europe, book publishers like Free Europe Press (both overseen by the Free Europe Committee, or FEC), and the literary magazines. These covert efforts were distinguished from the intelligence-gathering side.

Wisner was a University of Virginia man, both for undergraduate studies and law school. Short, wiry, compelling, energetic, a track star in college, he came from such a genteel Southern background that as a child he never dressed himself; instead, he merely stuck out his arms and legs while lying on his bed for his maids to dress him. One colleague wondered whether Wisner's constant muscle flexing was a self-conscious projection of strength to offset his small physical stature, or an unconscious trick of the nerves. Wisner was known to scoff at the dutiful intelligence gathering of the former OSO, or Office of Strategic Operations, as the boring work of "Prudent Professionals," his nickname for people like Richard Helms, future CIA director.[1]

After buying off the Italian elections to break a Communist/socialist majority, Wisner's CIA next targeted Albania for what it called rollback. Rollback meant reversing the spread of Communism by forcibly changing a nation's political leadership—a more proactive endeavor than mere containment, bribery, or election tampering. Later this was renamed "regime change." In this particular area, Albanian refugees were trained and sent across the border from Italy or by boat, most never to return. Like the overthrow of Prime Minister Mossadegh in Iran (known as Operation AJAX), the Albanian operation, codenamed BGFIEND, was conceived initially by the British. Unlike the Americans, the British had centuries of experience in what experts liked to call international "spycraft." But the Brits were too broke to run BGFIEND alone, so a mutually beneficial partnership bloomed.[2]

"Wisner was happy to help," recalled one official. "He had enormous respect, as well as some envy, for the British, who had vastly more experience with spying than the Americans. The British would provide the know how, and in the beginning at least, the manpower; the Americans would provide the cash. Wisner was taken with the idea of using the British to inherit their role as global power."[3] During joint operations, the Brits could show off the perks of their shrinking empire. "Whenever we want to subvert any place, we find the British own an island nearby," Wisner told Kim Philby, the famed British intelligence officer.[4] Indeed, the amount of land the British and its associated Western powers once held was staggering to those who did the math.[5]

Edward Said, the scholar and critic of imperialism, believed that after World War II, the Americans effectively inherited those holdings not as sites of physical control, but as select bases to control remotely through surveillance technology, proxy governments, mass communications, and propaganda. "A vast web of interests now links all parts of the former colonial world to the United States," he wrote, "just as a proliferation of academic subspecies divides (and yet connects) all the former disciplines like Orientalism." This could be seen in James Jesus Angleton's and Frank Wisner's European-informed sense of their American entitlement to take on, possess, and protect allies' former holdings while at the same time envisioning themselves as heirs to all of European culture, and it could be seen in the propaganda imperative that swallowed media, the arts, and academia in one large covert gulp.

When the first attempt to rollback Albania's Communism resulted in twenty percent of the exile invasion force being killed and most of the rest captured—the operation having been anticipated and thwarted—Wisner insisted this was normal; they should press on. Disgusted at the losses, the British pulled out. Yet Wisner continued to discuss the operation with the congenial, if unkempt, Philby. In 1951 and 1952, Wisner sent sixty Albanian exiles back across the border. Almost all of them were captured or killed, including a whole group that was burned alive. "The Albanian security service always seemed to be waiting for them."[6] When it became clear that Philby had most likely been part of a team of moles who had compromised many of these covert infiltrations, American exuberance stalled out, if only for a moment. "I began to have real doubts about rolling back the Iron Curtain," said one of Wisner's operatives. "It was peacetime, not wartime. The stuff that had worked against the Germans did not work against the Russians, who seemed impervious. It was time to go back and think this business through."[7]

The eminence grise behind many of these activities, George Kennan, had his own doubts. Kennan had written the "Long Memo," citing Soviet perfidy, and much of the fight-fire-with-fire thinking of the period harkened back to his warnings from Moscow. It was his unshakable conviction that the huge propaganda and penetration apparatuses of the Soviet Union would seize American institutions if Americans didn't take action. "It did not work out at all the way I conceived it," Kennan later said of his plans for covert operations. "We had thought this would be a facility which could be used when and if any occasion arose where it might be needed."[8] Instead, Wisner was dipping into Marshall Funds to keep these operations going virtually full-time. Covert actions drew the CIA to Italy and Albania—executed, despite his public disavowals, during Peter Matthiessen's stint under Angleton—continued through the early 1950s with the Korean War, made a detour for the US coups in Iran and Guatemala in 1953 and 1954, respectively, and finally settled onto Hungary and Poland in late 1956.

. . .

One clear success of the early CIA was its leak of Khrushchev's Secret Speech. On February 25, 1956, the new Soviet leader gave a critical and galling account of the reign of terror to which Josef Stalin had subjected the Russian people. In a fifty-eight-page report, Khrushchev denounced Stalin's atrocities before the Twentieth Party Congress of the Communist Party of the Soviet Union. After hearing reports of the speech's existence, Wisner had challenged his men to "bring home the bacon" and Angleton delivered a copy of the speech that he obtained through his new Israeli spy contacts.[9] Wisner and Angleton wanted to leak out parts of the speech piecemeal through Wisner's propaganda empire, which included radio stations and the many literary and opinion journals, and which could draw on the satellite journals of the "clearinghouse," book publishing assets, friendly opinion columnists across the country, not to mention a motion picture studio called Touchstone, Inc., as well as undercover agents inside mainstream studios like Paramount. The machine grew so large that Wisner called it his Mighty Wurlitzer, where he could play the media like it was his own personal silent film soundtrack.[10] One of the reasons Angleton wanted to wait was to build up saboteurs through the secret Operation Red Sox/Red Cap, where "Eastern Europeans from Hungary, Poland, Rumania and Czechoslovakia were trained to become the CIA's entry in anti-Soviet struggles."[11]

But the Dulles brothers and Eisenhower wanted to release the speech all at once.[12] Excerpts ran in *The New York Times* on June 5, 1956. The CIA even planned a film on it, but this never came to be. The leak worked, in its way, leading to unrest in both Poland and Hungary. But having failed at rollback in Albania, Wisner's OPC was caught between philosophies. If they had continued to recruit from the emigre community, to build an army of agent provocateurs and store weapons, then it might make sense for Radio Free Europe to egg the protesters on, implying that NATO troops and Western-trained exiles would help defend them. However, Wisner had only a single agent inside Hungary.[13]

Despite its evolving mission to do objective news, and despite explicit orders not to escalate or instigate dissidents, Radio Free Europe provoked uprisings so that when the Soviet forces entered Budapest, thousands of civilian protesters were reportedly killed. One Hungarian protester cabled the Western democrats he expected would help them, reporting: "RUSSIAN GANGSTERS HAVE BETRAYED US; THEY ARE OPENING FIRE ON ALL OF BUDAPEST. PLEASE INFORM EUROPE AND THE AUSTRIAN GOVERNMENT. . ." The protester continued,

> WE ARE UNDER HEAVY MACHINE GUN FIRE . . . HAVE YOU INFORMATION YOU CAN PASS ON? TELL ME, URGENT, URGENT. (And minutes later, after no answer came.) ANY NEWS ABOUT HELP? QUICKLY, QUICKLY. WE HAVE NO TIME TO LOSE. . . . (And after that connection ended, came more. . .) S.O.S. S.O.S. S.O.S. . . .I DON'T KNOW HOW LONG WE CAN RESIST . . . HEAVY SHELLS ARE EXPLODING NEARBY . . . WHAT IS THE UNITED NATIONS DOING? GIVE US A LITTLE ENCOURAGEMENT. THEY'VE JUST BROUGHT A RUMOR AMERICAN TROOPS WILL BE HERE WITHIN ONE OR TWO HOURS. . . . (And finally, when those troops never appeared, the dissident continued) GOODBYE FRIENDS. GOODBYE FRIENDS. GOD SAVE OUR SOULS. THE RUSSIAN SOLDIERS ARE TOO NEAR. . .[14]

On the Cold War scoreboard, however, Western powers ultimately gained from this bloody episode of repression. Jean-Paul Sartre finally denounced the Soviets. On the front page of the Indian CCF's newsletter, alongside Sartre's denunciation of Khrushchev, appeared activist and prominent CCF member Jayaprakash Narayan's denunciation of Indian leader Jawaharlal Nehru, whose stubborn neutrality prevented him from immediately condemning the atrocities, though he would later.[15] Despite the soft public relations win, it was a pyrrhic victory, one that came with considerable recrimination. For one, the Soviet geopolitical position had changed little, nothing had rolled back, and the United States' instigation of the dissidents was a severe breach of trust for dissidents around the world in similar circumstances.

As the news cycle morphed, the US betrayal of the Hungarian protesters traveled alongside news of Soviet atrocities. Radio Free Europe, or RFE, had escalated the unfolding events, even suggesting that Western troops would come and liberate them. "Sure, we never said rise up and revolt," the CIA's Thomas Polgar conceded, "but there was a lot of propaganda that led the Hungarians to believe that we would help." Wisner was aware of these views, cabling his boss Allen Dulles that "discussion with refugees shows some criticism of RFE broadcasts into Hungary."[16] As CIA officer Richard Bissell recalled, "No one had thought it through. I think Frank [Wisner] thought it was better to have a little bloodletting, and give the Russians a header."[17] So began a pattern where Soviets and Americans were partners in violence that one instigated covertly, the other committed overtly.

In one iconic scene in the annals of CIA lore, Wisner, touring his international agency holdings, went from Vienna to the border with Hungary to watch refugees flee across wooded hills, scrambling over the frontier, many bloodied from their encounters. Face to face with the victims of the Soviet atrocities, he was forced to decline repeated requests for various forms of assistance.[18] A manic depressive, Wisner was never the same after watching those refugees crossing in droves while having to deny them help.[19] He knew the Soviets were to blame, but he must have felt the full futility of his work. As one agent put it, "By reestablishing control over Hungary and by exposing—more dramatically than in 1953—the emptiness of the 'roll back' and 'liberation' rhetoric in the West, the Soviet invasion in November of 1956 stemmed any further loss of Soviet power in Eastern Europe.... Any lingering US hopes of directly challenging Moscow's sphere of influence in Eastern Europe thus effectively ended."[20]

The CIA's earliest years had already been so frustratingly fruitless that one operative, Miles Copeland, who participated in the Iran coup, had said of the years leading to Philby's exposure that, "when you look at that whole period ... the entire Western intelligence effort, which was pretty big, was what you might call minus advantage. We'd have been better off doing nothing."[21] And now in the middle 1950s, the years after Philby's virtual banishment to the Middle East (where he took to—what else?—journalism) were stained for Wisner by this terrible setback. Rollback was dead, liberation was nothing more than a propaganda campaign, and American leadership could not be believed. And then there were all those dead Hungarians and Albanians. After a manic spell, Wisner had a nervous collapse that gave way to crippling depression and, years later, suicide. Many closest to him blamed his ongoing despair on his heartbreak over Hungary. When recounting the episode to a friend, he wept.[22] He was never the same: hubris had stripped him of his confidence, the way his childhood maids had stripped him of his clothes.

．　．　．

That same year, the battlefield moved from *The New York Times* leaks and the streets of Hungary to the pages of a literary magazine, when the Soviet cultural apparatus issued a new challenge to the West.

The challenge came via novelist Mikhail Sholokhov's open letter in the Soviet magazine *Foreign Literature*. In a letter to the editor, Sholokhov wrote, "Our nation has made a great contribution to the treasure house of world culture."[23] He criticized the Cold War—that is, the United States—for frustrating the desires of the Soviet people to have true cultural exchanges. In a breathless letter reacting to the Sholokhov challenge, the United States Information Agency's John Pauker laid out for the American Committee's Sol Stein a possible US response. The response amounted to a frenzied attempt to fact-check Sholokhov's disingenuous invitation. If cultural exchange was so important to the Soviet elite, why did *Foreign Literature* publish a story that was chosen clearly to beat up on American capitalism? The story was Erskine Caldwell's "Masses of Men," and—according to Pauker—it "is vicious: it . . . deals with corporate knavery, negro poverty, and the rape of a 10-year-old-girl for 25 cents."[24] The Soviets would eagerly champion a writer who rankled their enemies.

Pauker then suggested that a response go out as a press release and reported on Voice of America radio. Stein was proud of the response his press releases got from mainstream outlets, writing that the American Committee had so much clout it simply picked up the phone and called its press releases in to a service, "which then transmits it by teletype to the city desks of New York newspapers and wire services."[25] This was what the American Committee called its "publicity machine." Pauker also suggested that *The New York Times Book Review*'s Harvey Breit call Caldwell in Arizona to confirm that he didn't authorize this story printed to bash US culture in

Foreign Literature, that the Soviets therefore didn't have permission to run it, and that they hadn't paid him.[26] Ironic, as we shall see, that the Americans were concerned for his copyright.

Throughout the mid-1950s, the American Committee struggled to define its role. After boasting of his work in propaganda ("a script prepared by me for broadcast to Czechoslovakia was sent by Radio Free Europe . . . as a model for scriptwriters preparing propaganda broadcasts to Eastern Europe . . . .") Stein bragged further, "Public statements made by the American Committee for Cultural Freedom are sometimes particularly valuable to stations which broadcast behind the Iron Curtain . . . several times each month we issue statements reporting the views of the American cultural-intellectual community . . . . A recent one applauded the capture of the Rumanian embassy in Berne, Switzerland, by a group of Rumanian exiles who protested the imprisonment of a number of anti-Communist democratic leaders in Rumania . . ."[27] The Berne incident, which took place February 14–16, 1955, was an act of anti-Communist terrorism not unlike the Benghazi embassy attack of September 11, 2012. Only one embassy staffer was killed, as opposed to four in Benghazi. A cheerleader for such terrorist acts, Stein was likewise nostalgic for the drama of the Korean War, writing to Sidney Hook that "Things were easier" for anti-Communists "when the conflict was more dramatic . . ."[28] These past public incitements, losses of territory, and fatalaties explain Stein and the American Committee's glee for militant action and drama. And his peers in CIA propaganda saw an opportunity for such drama with respect to Pasternak.

In the fall of 1958 *The New York Times* reported that Boris Pasternak had been coerced to turn down his Nobel Prize. "Pasternak cabled to the Swedish Academy today his voluntary refusal of the 1958 Nobel Prize for literature," ran a *Times* article of October 29.[29] The assumption was that the Soviet authorities had in fact forced Pasternak to renounce the prize for having published his novel abroad before doing so in the Soviet Union. Acting in secret, the CIA had shaped these events and the news cycle both, and *The Paris Review* would follow suit. "The Pasternak affair has caused such a stir here," Plimpton wrote from the journal's New York office just after the *Times* report that fall, "and is in itself an event of such importance in lit'r'y history that we feel the *Review* somehow should chronicle what has happened . . ." Writing to Nelson Aldrich, his Paris editor, Plimpton suggested a special issue be built around the incident, with short statements by a "variety of authors asked to comment. What does Sartre have to say on this matter . . .[Louis] Aragon, [Pablo] Neruda, [Evelyn] Waugh? Here [in New

York] we have Niccolo Tucci . . . digging up statements, mostly from writers who (as he is himself) are refugees from tyranny . . ."[30]

If the Soviets championed disapproved American writers like Erskine Caldwell, then shouldn't the Americans champion those who irked the Soviets, like Pasternak? Plimpton went on to suggest that the CCF be approached to fund brochures to publicize the issue. Conveniently, the Paris editor to whom he was writing, Nelson Aldrich, would himself soon be on staff with the CCF in its Paris headquarters.

· · ·

Pasternak finished a draft of *Doctor Zhivago* in 1956. An Italian Communist living in Moscow, Sergio D'Angelo, visited him in late May in the Soviet writers' resort sixteen miles southwest of Moscow, called Peredelkino. Peredelkino "was created in 1934 to reward the Soviet Union's most prominent authors with a retreat that provided escape from their apartments in the city."[31] Stalin had a plan for these writers. "The production of souls is more important than the production of tanks," he said in 1932, toasting to a new social mission for writers in the USSR. ". . . [S]omeone correctly said that a writer must not sit still, that a writer must know the life of a country . . . . Man is remade by life itself. But you, too, will assist in remaking his soul . . . . And that is why I raise my glass to you, writers, the engineers of the human soul."[32]

Upon his Peredelkino visit, Sergio D'Angelo hadn't yet read the great Pasternak.[33] Pasternak occupied a unique space in the Soviet establishment. The wide recognition of his talent was marred by a sense of danger surrounding his perceived lack of revolutionary fervor, his love of the foreign, and his recurring identification with the West. After all, England, where two of his sisters lived, was the original dark heart of retrograde imperialism. Who was more colonialist than the British? Foreigners like D'Angelo were a new treat in the Soviet Union, which had loosened the ban on outside visitors after Stalin's 1953 death. Pasternak, D'Angelo, and D'Angelo's travel companion (and occasional interpreter) Vladen Vladimirsky sat among the larches and May breezes while the poet talked fondly of his studies in Germany, and of his trip to Italy in the summer of 1912.[34]

No doubt charmed by the magnetic writer, D'Angelo finally explained why he was there. He was a part-time agent for the leftist Italian publisher and scion Giangiacomo Feltrinelli. Rumor had it that

Pasternak had written a novel. After it came out in the Soviet Union, Feltrinelli hoped to bring it out in other languages. "Pasternak interrupted the Italian's pitch with a wave of his hand. 'In the USSR,' he said, 'the novel will not come out. It doesn't conform to official cultural guidelines.'"[35] To publish *Doctor Zhivago* overseas first would be disastrous. Boris Pilnyak, "Pasternak's former next-door neighbor in Peredelkino (the side gate between their gardens was never closed)," was shot in the head in April 1938.[36] Among his crimes? Foreign publication. Pasternak was present the day the secret police came for Pilnyak. On October 28 of the year before his death, "it was the birthday of Pilnyak's three-year-old son, also named Boris. . . . [A] car pulled up and several men in uniform got out. It was all very polite. Pilnyak was needed on urgent business . . ."[37] But despite this red flag for Pasternak, D'Angelo must have been charming and Pasternak had big dreams. Pasternak "emerged from the dacha a short time later with a large package wrapped in a covering of newspaper."

> The manuscript was 433 closely typed pages divided into five parts. Each part, bound in soft paper or cardboard, was held together by twine that was threaded through rough holes in the pages and then knotted. The first section was dated 1948, and the work was still littered with Pasternak's handwritten corrections. "This is *Doctor Zhivago*," Pasternak said. "May it make its way around the world."[38]

D'Angelo must have been gratified, if confused. For Pasternak concluded, "You are hereby invited to watch me face the firing squad."[39] The next day, Pasternak's literary partner and mistress, Olga Ivinskaya, tried to recover the manuscript[40] but D'Angelo told her she was too late. He had handed the manuscript to Feltrinelli in Berlin[41] the same day.

. . .

Pasternak's relationship to Soviet power was complex. During the early years of the Revolution, Pasternak was as enthusiastic as any young idealist. As Yuri Zhivago says in the pages of his novel: "I watched a meeting last night. An astounding spectacle. . . . Mother Russia has begun to move, she won't stay put, she walks and never tires of walking, she talks and can't talk enough." The novel continues,

And it's not as if only people are talking. Stars and trees come together and converse, night flowers philosophize, and stone buildings hold meetings. Something gospel-like, isn't it? As in the time of the apostles. Remember, in Paul? "Speak in tongue and prophecy. Pray for the gift of interpretation."[42]

The eponymous protagonist describes those early events breathlessly, intimating within the sweeping changes how "the roof over the whole of Russia had been torn off."[43] "What magnificent surgery!" Pasternak writes. "To take and at one stroke artistically cut out the old, stinking sores!"[44] But at the same time there was disillusionment. Pasternak channeled it defiantly, as when Zhivago tells the revolutionaries: "I grant you're all bright lights and liberators of Russia . . . and nevertheless I can't be bothered with you, and I spit on you, and I don't like you, and you can all go to the devil."[45]

Isaiah Berlin, philosopher and CCF advisor, thought that Pasternak bore "a passionate, almost obsessive desire to be thought a Russian writer with roots deep in Russian soil." This trait was "particularly evident in his negative feelings towards his Jewish origins . . . he wished the Jews to assimilate, to disappear as a people."[46] Berlin exaggerated when he pointed to Pasternak's oddly twinned response to power, a response of both attraction and defiance. This response was partially a survival mechanism. The poet's father, Leonid, was a painter and his memoir records him painting distractedly one afternoon just after the turn of the century in an aristocrat's living room, when he felt, with a chill, someone behind him. "It was the Grand Duke Sergei, the tsar's uncle who became governor of Moscow in 1891, the same year that twenty thousand Jews were expelled from the city. Leonid Pasternak may well have been the first and last Jew the grand duke ever encountered in a drawing room."[47] Beyond the filial chill it gave him, did such stories instill in Pasternak a writerly obsession with the power of the solitary voice speaking against corrupted powers?

When Stalin's wife committed suicide in 1932 in response to the dictator's many affairs, writers were expected to sign a collective letter of condolence. Pasternak instead wrote his own note: "I share in the feelings of my comrades. On the evening before I had for the first time thought about Stalin deeply and intensively as an artist. In the morning I read the news. I was shaken as if I had actually been there, living by his side, and seen everything."[48] His separate piece, beyond what was required, seems to have moved Stalin.

In April 1934, Pasternak saw his friend the poet Osip Mandelstam on the street. Mandelstam recited a poem mocking Stalin:

We live, deaf to the land beneath us,
ten steps away no one hears our speeches.

All we hear is the Kremlin mountaineer,
The murderer and peasant-slayer. [49]

Olga Ivinskaya captured her lover's response to the poetic heresy. "I didn't hear this," he said. "You didn't recite it to me, because, you know, very strange and terrible things are happening now: they've begun to pick people up. I'm afraid the walls have ears and perhaps even these benches on the boulevard here may be able to listen and tell tales. So let's make out that I heard nothing."[50]

When Mandelstam was picked up, Pasternak did his best to help him, and Stalin's chilling order, "Isolate but preserve"[51] led to Mandelstam's institutionalization rather than his immediate murder. The episode prompted an unusual, though much discussed, event. Stalin phoned up Pasternak. According to Ivinskaya, Pasternak was speechless. "He was totally unprepared for such a conversation. But then he heard his voice, the voice of Stalin, coming over the line. The Leader addressed him in a rather bluff uncouth fashion, using the familiar thou form: 'Tell me, what are they saying in your literary circles about the arrest of Mandelstam?'"[52] Pasternak rambled evasively.

Stalin: Why didn't you come to me instead of Bukharin? If I were a poet and a poet friend of mine were in trouble, I would do anything to help him.
Pasternak: If I hadn't tried to do something you probably never would have heard about it.
Stalin: But after all he is your friend.

Playing it safe, Pasternak muttered vaguely, how "poets, like women, are always jealous of one another."

Stalin: But he's a master, isn't he?
Pasternak: But that's not the point.
Stalin: What is then?

Pasternak sensed that Stalin—notoriously fearful of genius—was thinking of the attack poem, and changed the subject.

> Pasternak: Why do you keep on about Mandelstam? I have long wanted to meet you for a serious discussion.
> Stalin: About what?
> Pasternak: About life and death.
> Stalin hangs up.[53]

Word of the conversation traveled rapidly, many believing that Pasternak had failed to muster the courage to defend his friend with conviction.[54] But according to other accounts Mandelstam was pleased, noting, "He was quite right to say that whether I'm a master or not is beside the point."[55] Nadezhda Mandelstam, Osip's wife, thought Pasternak saw the dictator as the embodiment of the age and was disappointed not to meet him after that mysterious call. Pasternak even wrote an ode to Stalin, which he published in the New Year's Day 1936 edition of *Izvestiya*. Though he described the dictator as "not so much a man as action/ incarnate" and "a genius of action,"[56] he had been terrified the first time he met the figure, who emerged from the darkness in a way that made him resemble "a crab."[57] Pasternak later spoke of the more flattering notes as "a sincere and one of the most intense of my endeavors . . . to think the thoughts of the era, and to live in tune with it."[58]

Vladimir Nabokov had a conspiracy theory about the so-called Zhivago Affair. After Pasternak's participation in the first Congress of Soviet Writers in 1934 and the pro-Soviet International Writers' Conference in Paris, and after his odes to Stalin in 1936, Nabokov believed that the incident "was planned by the Soviets for a single goal: to guarantee the commercial success of the novel so that the hard currency earnings could be used to finance Communist propaganda abroad."[59] Events have not borne out Nabokov's conspiracy theory. Yet Nabokov remained a skeptic toward Pasternak's novel, describing *Doctor Zhivago* as "sorry . . . clumsy, trite . . . melodramatic. . ."[60] What's interesting about Nabokov's theory, however, is the sense of a hidden hand influencing events from the shadows.

.   .   .

Pasternak was already an international notable.[61] Even if this protected him to some degree, Ivinskaya, Pasternak's mistress, was not immune. Punishing her was a clever way for the Party to punish Pasternak's unorthodoxies. In

October 1949, she was seized, roughly interrogated, and even psychologically tortured with the threat of her lover's death.[62] She also miscarried her child with Pasternak and debated government spooks about aesthetics of Russian poetry.[63]

During her interrogation, Ivinskaya was asked about *Doctor Zhivago*: "You are aware of the anti-Soviet nature of the novel?"[64] After being forced to write down a synopsis of the novel, she was told to prepare to meet her lover and driven to a secret police facility just outside Moscow. "The smell was odd. . . .'There was the unmistakable sweetish smell of a morgue. Could it be that one of these corpses was the man I loved?'"[65] Recognizing that they intended to terrorize her was strangely calming. "For some reason, as though God had put it in my mind, it dawned on me that the whole thing was a monstrous hoax, and that Boria (Boris) could not possibly be here."[66] What did they want? Probably she was meant to send a message to unruly writers like Pasternak: defy us and see what happens. In July 1950, Ivinskaya was sentenced to five years of hard labor for "close contact with persons suspected of espionage."[67] Pasternak had a heart attack two years later, which led to a protracted health scare, making him sensitive to the least of stresses. On March 5, 1953, Stalin died. Stalin's death was followed by an amnesty for many prisoners that freed Ivinskaya;[68] hopes bloomed for what the world called a thaw. After Stalin, the embargo on Pasternak's work, and that of other proscribed writers, was briefly lifted. He published his first poems in almost a decade in 1954, a packet of "Poems from the novel *Doctor Zhivago*." It was also his own first public announcement of the novel.[69] Pasternak's translation of *Hamlet* was performed in Leningrad in this period, too, and it was rewritten to revel in the Thaw, the production ending not with Fortinbras but with Shakespeare's Sonnet 74, a meditation on arrest.[70] It begins,

> But be contented when that fell arrest
> Without all bail shall carry me away;[71]

But conservative figures began to bite back. The publication *Pravda* attacked the Zhivago poems. At the end of 1955, Pasternak reported that his novel was complete, though he didn't think he would be able to publish it. When Pasternak told his wife, Zinaida, that he had given Feltrinelli the novel, she asked, "What kind of nonsense is this?" It was Ivinskaya's reaction, however, that carried the weight of hard prison time and real suffering. Aware that no post-Stalinist thaw would shield Pasternak from news of his consorting with foreign publishers, she was apoplectic: "I've been in prison once, remember, and already then, in the Lubyanka, they questioned me endlessly about what the novel would say. . . . I'm really amazed you could do this."[72]

. . .

In June 1956, Feltrinelli sent a courier with Pasternak's contract and a letter. Pasternak let Feltrinelli off the hook. "If its publication here, promised by several of our magazines, were to be delayed and your version were to come before it, I would find myself in a tragically difficult situation. But this is not your concern. In the name of God, feel free to go with the translation and the printing of the book, and good luck! Ideas are not born to be hidden or smothered at birth, but to be communicated to others."[73]

Hearing of these arrangements for foreign publication, the Kremlin wondered if the book could be spot-censored and rewritten for publication in Russian. To the Americans, it must have seemed as if karma were answering Sholokhov's provocation of 1955. But to the Soviets, the novel simply wouldn't do; it was too anti-Soviet. The Soviets tried to suppress the book from coming out anywhere, and to coerce Pasternak to get his manuscript back from Italy. In anticipation of this, Pasternak sent word to Feltrinelli with a code: "If ever you receive a letter in any language other than French, you absolutely must not do what is requested of you—the only valid letters shall be those written in French."[74]

In mid-September of 1956, *Novy Mir* (*New World*), a Soviet literary magazine, formally rejected the prospect of excerpting *Doctor Zhivago*. It cited "non-acceptance" of socialism and "viciousness." Pasternak's most radical insinuation went unstated: that Stalinism was a natural outgrowth of Bolshevism, and that the book made this all too clear.[75] In its ploy to recall the novel from Feltrinelli, the state book publisher, Goslitizdat, offered Pasternak a phony contract for *Doctor Zhivago* in January 1957. By now the Soviets had crushed rebellions in Hungary and Poland. There would be no thaw.[76] Playing along warily, Pasternak signed. He then wrote Feltrinelli asking him to delay publication until the Soviet-Russian version could be published. In a followup letter, he admitted that it wouldn't come out in Russia. It was a stalling technique. "A mutual bluffing game," he called it.[77]

In late 1957, excerpts of the novel appeared in the new Polish journal *Opinie*. This infuriated the Soviets, who, after a call to the Polish leadership, had the magazine discontinued.[78] But Pasternak still thought there was a small chance that the threat of Western publication might prompt the Soviet apparatus to publish the novel. A final August 1957 meeting with Goslitizdat's editor, Anatoli Starostin, ended this possibility for good. Feltrinelli responded sharply to "Pasternak," (that is, to his handlers) insisting that the book was great and warning that any further attempts to retrieve it, whether for edits or any other reason, would only lend power to the publicity storm that was brewing. Their actions, he wrote, "would lend the entire affair a tone of political scandal that we have never sought nor wish to create."[79]

The Soviet writer Alexei Surkov, Secretary General of the Writers' Union, visited Feltrinelli in Milan, browbeating him shrilly for three hours to get him to return the manuscript. Surkov cited Pasternak's coerced letters. Feltrinelli shouted back, "I know how such letters are written." And he added for good measure that he was "a free publisher in a free country."[80] Surkov left with nothing, retaliating in an Italian Communist Party newspaper: "The Cold War is beginning to involve literature. If this is freedom seen through Western eyes, well, I must say we have a different view of it. Thus it is . . . for the second time in our literary history, after *Mahogany* by Boris Pilnyak, a book by a Russian will be first published abroad."[81] Several Pasternak biographers rightly point to the threat of violence implicit in this comment, given Pilnyak's fate.[82]

Another fake telegram was forced out of Pasternak that autumn. But he followed it with a real one, stating, "The future will reward us, you and me, for the vile humiliations we have suffered." He continued,

Oh, how happy I am that neither you, nor Gallimard, nor Collins [his French and British publishers, respectively] have been fooled by those idiotic and brutal appeals accompanied by my signature (!) . . . extorted from me by a blend of fraud and violence. The unheard-of arrogance to wax indignant over the "violence" employed by you against my "literary freedom," when exactly the same violence was being used against me, covertly. And that this vandalism should be disguised as concern for me, for the sacred rights of the artist! But we shall soon have an Italian Zhivago, French, English, and German Zhivagos—and one day perhaps a geographically distant but Russian Zhivago! And this is a great deal, a very great deal, so let's do our best and what will be will be.[83]

That phrase "geographically distant" matters. It writes into the record one of many markers suggesting that for all Pasternak's literary brinksmanship, he drew lines where his safety was concerned. To publish the novel cautiously in Russian outside the territory, on terms he set out carefully with his Italian publisher, was one thing. To smuggle it back in was another.

First published in Italy in November 1957, 6,000 copies of *Doctor Zhivago*—the whole run—sold out on the first day.[84] A second run was published five days later. It was, thanks partly no doubt to overbearing Soviet attempts to quash it, an immediate best-seller. The author of *Lolita* had rightly been skeptical; it was astounding that Soviet censors could be so stupid as to try to suppress a book, not recognizing how their efforts would work against them. "The very passages that had embarrassed and frightened the Soviet censors most of all, and that Pasternak was ready to remove, were now widely quoted in the world press." And then the foreign editions began rolling off the presses to boot. What the poet Marina Tsvetaeva had long called Pasternak's "subterranean fame" in the winter and spring of 1958 came out fully from underground,[85] though this fame had been rising all year.[86] One biographer noted that Pasternak was a reluctant cold warrior. "The poet, who had always refused to take part in Soviet propaganda activities, did not want to be drawn into anti-Soviet political propaganda [either]."[87] But the CIA had other plans.

. . .

In early January 1958, the Russian version of the manuscript landed at CIA headquarters in its temporary offices in Washington, DC. It arrived on two rolls of film[88] via British intelligence, whose London source was kept secret. The CIA's Western Europe chief wrote that the British were "in favor of exploiting" the book and offered their help. The Soviet Russia Division chief, John Maury, wrote to Wisner, describing the novel as "the most heretical literary work by a Soviet author since Stalin's death."

> Pasternak's humanistic message—that every person is entitled to a private life and deserves respect as a human being, irrespective of his political loyalty or contribution to state—poses a fundamental challenge to the Soviet ethic of sacrifice of the individual to the Communist system. There is no call to revolt against the regime in the novel, but the heresy which [Doctor] Zhivago preaches—political passivity—is fundamental. Pasternak suggests that the small

unimportant people who remain passive to the regime's demands for active participation and emotional involvement in official campaigns are superior to the political "activists" favored by the system. Further, he dares hint that society might function better without these fanatics.[89]

According to internal CIA memos released to journalist Peter Finn, the English translation that the CIA was keeping its eyes on had been delayed by translator Max Hayward. In particular, the difficulty of translating the poems embedded in the novel into "fluent English" had slowed the work. *Encounter*'s "Stephen Spender may work on this problem," explained a CIA agent. The agent added, "It is requested that Headquarters keep us informed of its plans concerning the book so that we may continue to discuss its exploitation with the [British] as closely as possible."[90]

The CIA was "deeply concerned that [*Zhivago*'s] exploitation in the West be handled with care." This particular agent, name deleted by CIA censors, recommended that "*Dr. Zhivago* should be published in a maximum number of foreign editions, for maximum free world discussion and acclaim and consideration for such honor as the Nobel prize." If the CIA couldn't get the Russian edition published through Feltrinelli, recapped one agent, "We'll do it black."[91]

. . .

By the second week of January, 1958, the CIA was also coordinating to have the work done for a Pasternak issue of a certain magazine whose name was whited out in the CIA's declassified files.[92]

Given the degree to which Eastern bloc and other emigre publications like *Opinie* in Poland or *Facets* in Munich had inflamed Soviet tempers, Pasternak was prudent to ask that no Russian-language edition be published either by emigre groups or in the United States—or by any American-affiliated group. While he wanted a Russian edition printed, he knew that an American fingerprint would prove his critics right; the work was being used as Cold War propaganda. Not involving US agencies in its printing would of course preclude the CIA from taking a role. But the Eisenhower administration trusted that the Agency would be able to keep its fingerprints off the job; any of its other agencies would be more easily caught.

During the days of rollback, emigre groups funded by the CIA had learned the hard way that the very paper they used for falsified documents had been analyzed and found to be of American origin, which told hostile analysts that the documents were forgeries. The CIA subcontracted the job of publishing the Russian-language version of *Zhivago* to the American Felix Morrow, who had several ties to the American Committee for Cultural Freedom. Morrow had a profile similar to many New York Intellectuals; he had made the journey from City College leftist to ardent Red hater and had even studied with Hook at NYU. The CIA liked him; Morrow was a man "who occasionally lunched with CIA agents [who] . . . visited Morrow at his house in Great Neck, Long Island . . . always arriving with a bottle of whiskey and a box of chocolates."[93]

. . .

In June 1958, Morrow signed a contract with a lawyer representing the CIA to publish *Doctor Zhivago* on a secret basis, in Russian, in time for the World's Fair in Brussels that fall. Morrow's violations of this secrecy agreement began immediately. He told his friend Fred Wieck at the University of Michigan Press about the project and even gave Wieck a copy of the microfilm with the manuscript; Wieck moved to publish his own Michigan Press version of *Zhivago* in Russian, in defiance of Pasternak's safety, Feltrinelli's copyright, and the CIA's propaganda plans. Morrow also consulted a press in New York with strong ties to the Russian emigre community, in effect fueling rumors of a Russian edition of *Zhivago* within this contentious community and potentially endangering Pasternak.

In its attempts to rein in Morrow, the CIA offered to sell him rights to the Russian edition of the book to be exploited after the World's Fair version was done; this was, of course, again in violation of Feltrinelli's agreement with Pasternak. Sensing weakness in his CIA handlers, Morrow threatened to walk, to "commandeer" the proofs and print on his own without CIA involvement.[94] When the University of Michigan Press petitioned the CIA to buy Russian copies of the novel from them, the CIA wrote back objecting to Michigan's right to publish due to concerns surrounding Feltrinelli's copyright. Yet the same argument made by Michigan's lawyers—that the copyright didn't apply as the Soviet Union was not a signatory to the Berne Convention, which regulated international copyright—was used by the CIA in-house, in memos justifying further exploiting Pasternak's work, for instance, in Radio Free Europe and Radio Liberation broadcasts.[95]

Finally, the Russian edition was published by the Dutch publishing house Mouton in time for the World's Fair, and the Vatican's exhibition staff helped distribute the pocket-size edition among Russian visitors and others who might be heading to the Soviet Union. In late October, Pasternak was forced to turn down the Nobel. Less than a week later, the CIA, Air Force, and US Information Services convened a meeting whose aim was encapsulated in a memo: "We should exploit the Soviet position on the award of the Nobel Prize to Boris Pasternak."[96] But the CIA wanted to shepherd publications around the world to publish on the topic. This was revealed in a coy letter by Dulles. On January 5, 1959, Victor Bator wrote Dulles to request that *Zhivago* be translated into various Eastern European and other languages. Dulles responded, downplaying CIA involvement. "According to our information *Doctor Zhivago* in fact has been or is being translated into more than 20 languages, among them Polish, Serbian, Finnish, Chinese and several Indian tongues."[97]

In February 1959, the CIA's chief of Commercial Staff wrote its General Counsel to seek legal advice on the feasibility of an anthology of Pasternak's poetry from the 1920s and 1930s. "Reportedly, this material is in the public domain because of Russia's nonparticipation in certain international copyright conventions. . ." This was Michigan's argument that the CIA disputed when it didn't favor their wishes. The CIA wanted to include an autobiographical essay in the anthology but Feltrinelli held the copyright on this, as well. The CIA also wanted to get around Feltrinelli's rights and Pasternak's wishes in granting him those rights.[98] Within this flurry of memos, CIA lawyers gave the American Committee for Liberation the green light to broadcast selections from *Doctor Zhivago* on the "radio in Russia." Given the rules of the Berne convention, it was unlikely "any competent authority would award substantial damages to Mr. Pasternak," the CIA argued.[99] For the Convention to apply, these lawyers argued that Pasternak would have to be ejected from the USSR. The consequences of this bullish argument left Pasternak unprotected from cultural brinksmanship with a whiff of 1956 Hungary to it. And it wasn't the most sound legal reasoning, as one dissenting CIA contract lawyer believed.[100]

The CIA's justifications rested on the fact that the Russian-language edition of the book published in Holland was not authorized (because the CIA ensured it would not be authorized). It also rested on the alleged fact that the first (Italian) translation was published by Feltrinelli "despite the protests of Mr. Pasternak." But the CIA knew that Pasternak's protests were faked for his safety. Such selective legal reasoning not only favored the more precipitous CIA hard-liners, it also further disenfranchised Pasternak, making him into that which he detested—a propaganda tool and an instrument. The

CIA knew Feltrinelli was likely to sue,[101] which he did, calling the Mouton Russian edition illegal, and one in-house CIA lawyer saw this phase of the operation, its Pasternak Phase 2, as so legally untenable that he asked to be recused.[102]

After Mouton published its unauthorized Russian version from CIA proofs, the only way for Feltrinelli to maintain his copyright was to sue. The compromise that resulted forced Feltrinelli to take over publication of the error-ridden Mouton text, which had spelt Feltrinelli's own name wrong in Russian.[103]

. . .

After Pasternak won the Nobel, the CIA gave itself even more leeway to exploit him, by looking to Radio Free Europe and Radio Liberation in Munich. The Soviets saw these stations as "center[s] of subversion," as roughly a third of the people in the Soviet Union's cities listened to their programs, write Peter Finn and Petra Couvée.[104] Writer Aleksandr Solzhenitsyn called Western broadcasting "the mighty non-military force which resides in the airwaves and whose kindling power in the midst of Communist darkness cannot even be grasped by the Western imagination."[105]

It's clear the agency chose to measure the Pasternak operation's success from the standpoint of embarrassing the Soviets. With a running tally of translations it approved and oversaw, the agency was exuberant. An expanded "clearinghouse" of sorts as recorded in one CIA memo listed book editions and serialization in magazines and newspapers as far-flung as Vietnam, where *Zhivago* was published by the Front for Defense of Cultural Freedom. Further, the CIA tallied—and may have arranged—reviews and coverage in friendly media by CIA assets and other writers.[106] In its March 23, 1959 memorandum, the Agency recorded fifty editions worldwide. Of these, however, less than half were known to be legal editions with rights granted—the rest presumably pirated.[107]

Having embarrassed the Soviets, the CIA arranged a renewal of the Pasternak operation, code-named AEDINOSAUR, turning it into an ongoing propaganda campaign to send up to a dozen banned books per year into the Soviet Union.[108] By one of its own measures, though—keeping US government fingerprints off the operation in the name of Pasternak's safety—the CIA failed, and it knew this. By broadcasting *Doctor Zhivago* to captive audiences and overseeing its publication in dozens of languages, the CIA gambled not just with Pasternak's safety when he was frail, but with that of his family. One memo showed that after Pasternak renounced the Nobel, European and American media tied the *Zhivago* publications to American intelligence, specifically to the CIA's Free Europe Committee, or FEC. The memo cited France's "*People* magazine," *Paris Match*, and just a week after the announcement of the Nobel kerfuffle, Germany's *Der Spiegel*. *Der Spiegel* correctly tied the affair to the FEC, adding mysterious ties to writer Count Leo Tolstoy's relatives through a foundation named for him. The right-wing *National Review* (and its *National Review Bulletin*) alleged CIA/FEC ties too. *The New York Times* book columnist asked what was the source of the Russian version being handed out in Brussels—answer: "classified."[109] So that, whether in New York or Europe, it would have been hard to miss the news of CIA involvement. It was baked into the Pasternak Affair's global media coverage.[110]

Pasternak read the *Spiegel* story, saw a copy of the error-riddled Russian and was livid, but initially didn't know whom to blame.

4

THE PARIS REVIEW GOES TO MOSCOW

Aldrich became Paris editor of *The Paris Review*.
I followed him and Blair Fuller in the job. Youth! Paris des reves!
Fifty years later, Barack Obama rules.
Lady Gaga reigns.
Lorin Stein seizes the *Paris Review* reins.
The joy or whatever
Of being the new editor begins, as it happens, April Fools' Day.
You know what I'm going to say. . .

—Frederick Seidel[1]

In the last months of his life, Boris Pasternak raced to finish his play *Blind Beauty* while receiving a slew of international visitors. They were a distraction, to be sure. But to the Soviet leadership, the visitors from abroad were unwelcome or even illicit. Among them was a young painter sent by George Plimpton and Doc Humes. Olga Carlisle traveled to Peredelkino in January

1960 to secure an Art of Fiction interview for *The Paris Review*. Her interview marked the quarterly's attempt to salvage its great Pasternak symposium, which Plimpton envisioned the Congress for Cultural Freedom sponsoring days after the Nobel Prize announcement, when Pasternak's reputation and safety were most under attack. Plimpton wrote to Aldrich in Paris, suggesting that "the *Review* somehow should chronicle what has happened"[2] with a symposium.

Wary of a tally of jargon-filled denunciations, Plimpton suggested that "What would give such a collection impact and importance would be the variety of authors asked to comment." He listed both well-known leftists such as Pablo Neruda as well as "refugees from tyranny" who were now anti-Communists, like Niccolo Tucci. "Naturally, the main difficulty will be that one Ringing Assertion ('a blot on the escutcheon, etc.') sounds much the same as another."[3]

With issue 19 still on newsstands, Plimpton expected this issue to come together at an unprecedented speed, envisioning it as part of the next issue, 20. "In that publication of such a collection in the *Review* (for issue 20) would be picked up by the press, that a pamphlet would undoubtedly be the result (financed by such a group as the Congress for Cultural Freedom) with credit for the compilation going to the *Review*, don't you think the idea has enough merit for you yourself, or perhaps for someone else of your choice, to haunt European writers, their journals, for views on this extraordinary case. Please advise."[4] Plimpton had deferred to the wisdom of the first managing editor John Train on the timing, writing that "Train is right, I hope, in supposing that we can hold off distribution of issue #20 until #19 has had a chance. But in theory #20 must get here before the first of the year."[5]

The letter illuminates how friends of the Congress at magazines like *The Paris Review* might conceive of their work backlit by Congress for Cultural Freedom sponsorship. The details are interesting. By emphasizing his distaste for the Ringing Assertion, Plimpton was merely hewing to the magazine's aesthetic–editorial line, which was belletristic, seeing itself as above politics. But by seeking funding from what Aldrich called "a well known CIA front," wasn't he also disguising a political act as an aesthetic one? The most significant hints of where the magazine was going in its willingness to work with the Congress are in the two-word sentence to Aldrich ("Please advise.") and in the wise counsel that had already been received by John Train. Aldrich and Train are two figures who take *The Paris Review* deeper into the world of covert propaganda, as the archival record shows. Aldrich linked *The Paris Review* to the CCF by occupying positions at both organizations. Train's ties to state propaganda are more nebulous. If they start here in Paris during the late 1950s, they climax in Afghanistan during the 1980s.

Meanwhile, magazines like *Tempo Presente*, the Congress's monthly publication in Italy, worked at a speed Plimpton hoped *The Paris Review* might match. In its November issue, just weeks after the Pasternak Affair had blown up, the Italian magazine printed a piece called "The Pasternak Case."[6] And in December,[7] it translated a discussion published in *Dissent* between Lionel Abel and Nicola Chiaromonte on the literary merits of *Doctor Zhivago*.[8] *Encounter* had already run pieces on the coming Pasternak affair even before he won the Nobel. Gerd Ruge's "A Visit to Pasternak" was a literary portrait of his life in Peredelkino in the March 1958 issue.[9] Two months later, translator Max Hayward recounted the whispers of ideological ire that the book was already anticipating inside the Soviet Union.[10]

But as a quarterly that frequently missed an issue and bundled two together to compensate (e.g., Fall–Winter 1958–1959), *The Paris Review* was unaccustomed to speedy deadline publishing. Though she hadn't written before, the painter Olga Carlisle's maiden name, Andreyev, echoed with her forbears' literary roots. Carlisle was born and raised in France. Her parents had fled the Soviet Union but had retained their Soviet citizenship. Carlisle's interview with Pasternak was timed with new interest in Russian writers in the West. AEDINOSAUR, the CIA's covert operation to smuggle a Russian edition of *Doctor Zhivago* back into Soviet territory, had been expanded by the end of 1958. With this operation, a cottage industry cropped up within American book publishing to launch translations of Russian writers previously unknown in the West while (more secretly) working to smuggle dissident writers back into the territory and distribute them as *samizdat*, or forbidden texts. This was the invisibly guided ebb and flow of relevance in the literary Cold War. Immigrant fiction or nonfiction or dissident poetry smuggled back in—alongside constant reminders of their presence through new translations of them abroad—cleverly blurred the distinction between negative and positive propaganda. Each Russian cultural achievement, what could be positive propaganda for the Soviet Union, could instead remind readers of the lack of freedoms typifying the Soviet system as it then operated. The FEC—with its book publishing wing and its radio transmissions— was just one of the CIA's channels for these publishing and broadcast coups. The CCF was another.

·   ·   ·

Olga Ivinskaya met Pasternak in 1946 when he was one of Russia's most beloved poets and when whispers about and progress on the novel were incipient.[11] They became lovers, worked on literary translations together, happily accepted work from the Soviet state cultural apparatus and grew exceedingly close. Pasternak split time between her "little house" in the writers' retreat town outside Moscow, Peredelkino, and the "big house" he lived in with his wife, Zinaida, and their sons. When the regime sought to punish Pasternak for his political independence, it was forced to do so—due to his fame around the world—through Ivinskaya. A few years before Stalin's death, as we have seen, she was arrested and served time in a labor camp.

During the propaganda battle over *Doctor Zhivago*, Pasternak had been thoroughly denounced at Writers' Union meetings by his literary comrades. They argued for the removal of his citizenship and he was harangued and threatened. But much of this was felt directly by Ivinskaya, sent to represent him. It was she who, in person, bore those infamous and demoralizing denunciations and reported them back to Pasternak. Defending him from these insults, she explained that he only gave the novel to D'Angelo merely to read.[12] Before the members of the Writers' Union, Alexei Surkov, who opposed the Thaw, denounced Pasternak hysterically while Ivinskaya watched. A chorus of voices followed, denouncing Pasternak's "political and mercenary motives."[13] Olga, finding the group shouting over her, yelled into the noise: "If you won't let me speak, then there's no point in my being here." She was defending a traitor, they told her.[14]

She had come with Anatoli Starostin,[15] State Publishing House editor and one of three allies during the *Zhivago* shitstorm whom she singled out for praise.[16] Starostin, too, spoke in defense of the novel, arguing that it could bring glory upon Russia. He insisted that it was not considered to be in its final draft even by Pasternak. These pleas did little to counter hostilities the poet faced for selling out to the worldwide capitalist conspiracy.[17]

Though she and Pasternak sought to find humor where they could, Ivinskaya thought Pasternak "was unable to take an ironical view of things that seemed almost idiotic to others. . ."[18] In private, his loneliness came through. It was fated, he told Ivinskaya, that he "drink his cup of suffering to the end."[19]

When asked yet again to face the Writers' Union, though, Pasternak admitted that he couldn't face the "monstrous display" he expected there. Though he offered a few concessions, he did so again through Ivinskaya. "I continue to believe it was possible to write *Doctor Zhivago* without ceasing to be Soviet," he stated in a letter of self-defense.[20] While he had "expected that the translation would be censored," and "was willing to cut out [unacceptable] passages" from *Doctor Zhivago*, he had "expected friendly criticism," not the vitriol he was undergoing on a nonstop basis. As a last concession, he said that he was "ready to hand over the [Nobel Prize] money to the Peace Committee." "I do not expect justice from you," he concluded. "You may have me shot, or expelled from the country, or do anything you like. All I ask of you is: do not be in too much of a hurry over it. It will bring you no increase of either happiness or of glory."[21]

These were hardly the conciliatory grovelings they must have hoped for. On the catchall list of violations that Pasternak was guilty of, one item, a passive crime, stands out as actually being true: Pasternak "has become a tool of bourgeois propaganda. . ."[22] Eventually it came out that the CIA had played a role in the Pasternak affair even after Pasternak had requested the Americans not get involved. *Paris Match*, *Der Spiegel*, *The New York Times*, even the CIA-friendly *National Review* had reported this, as we have seen.

Like Matthiessen and Patsy Southgate in Paris, Olga and Boris were soon being followed wherever they went.[23] They were surveilled by male agents badly disguised as young women; agents in bad drag usually lurked outside Olga's little house. Olga feared, further, that a bug had been installed in one of her walls. "Good day to you, microphone!" Pasternak used to say. He didn't believe it was there. But he "would say [this], bowing low to the wall, and hanging his cap on a nail next to the place where . . . the microphone really had been hidden." And "the mere thought that there might be [a bug] helped to create a feeling of being harassed on all sides," Ivinskaya recalled.[24]

Between this chilling surveillance and his fears of being shot, Pasternak grew desperate. In October, he told Olga in front of her son that he could not "stand this business anymore. I think it's time to leave this life . . . If you think we must stay together then . . . we'll just sit here this evening . . . and that's how they'll find us. You once said that eleven tablets of Nembutal is a fatal dose—well, I have twenty two here. Let's do it. . . .it will cost [Soviet authorities] very dearly. . . . It will be a slap in the face."[25] Trudging the muddy way to Pasternak's neighbor Fedin's house during a downpour, Ivinskaya "told him [Boris] was on the verge of suicide, and had just proposed this to me as a way out." "You have told me a terrible thing," the neighbor said, finally getting choked up. Fedin had previously shown no courage in defending his neighbor and friend. He finally seemed to be acting honorably toward that friendship. "Can you repeat it in another place?" At the Writers' Union the next day, the high-ranking Dimitri Polikarpov scolded Ivinskaya. "If you allow Pasternak to commit suicide, you will be aiding and abetting a second stab in the back for Russia."[26] A settlement was offered. "He must say something. . ."[27] Though she was wary of what Pasternak might have to say, Ivinskaya thought the matter was settled. But Pasternak was threatened with exile on television that night. India's Prime Minister Jawaharlal Nehru was among those who offered asylum.[28] Ernest Hemingway also offered refuge in the Republic of Letters. "I shall give him a house to make his life in the West easier. I want to create for him the conditions he needs to carry on with his writing." But Hemingway understood what it meant to be estranged from the land you love. "I can understand how divided Boris must be . . . I know how deeply . . . he is attached to Russia. . . . But if he comes to us, we shall not disappoint him. I shall do everything in my modest powers to save this genius for the world."[29] Indeed, Pasternak couldn't leave his homeland.[30] Later, in order to stay, Ivinskaya brought him something to sign. And to both their regret, he signed it.[31]

One day, Ivinskaya heard "the wind . . . sighing in the pine trees and we could hear electric trains hooting in the distance. It was the sort of moment at which we felt terribly afraid for ourselves—but particularly for this one man, who seemed the most lonely and defenseless of all . . . . As we stood there with our gloomy thoughts, we suddenly heard loud, unrestrainable sobs. Rushing in we saw [Boris] crying on the phone." He had just telephoned a friend who spoke as if she had been waiting for his call and cried out: "Boria, my dear, what is all this? What are they doing to you?"[32]

These events took a toll on Pasternak's health. "The violence done to him was overwhelming," Ivinskaya wrote. "It broke and then killed him. Slowly but surely his strength was undermined, and his heart and nervous system began to fail."[33] The constant flow of visitors brought him joy but those visitors were troubling. Their appearance intensified authorities' fears of foreign ties and of a well-funded capitalist wind stoking the flames of controversy like a bellows. One at a time, Olga and Boris were hauled to Moscow in official black cars and told to avoid foreigners. But how could they make any promises if visitors came of their own will? They acknowledged the request but made no commitment.[34]

To protect Boris, however, they put up a sign at his house: "Pasternak does not receive, he is forbidden to receive foreigners." They wrote it in French, German, and English.[35] It was usually ignored. In January 1959, with the promise of the New Year and Pasternak's work life (and some peace) relatively restored, he tried to show his gratitude to Ivinskaya by breaking with the "big house"—his wife. In the end, he couldn't follow through. This upset Olga, who left town and said it was over. A bereft Pasternak wrote a poem in which he expressed his long-repressed cries over the storm surrounding the novel and lamenting the loss of Ivinskaya. "I am caught like a beast at bay," he wrote. "Somewhere are people, freedom, light, / But all I hear is the baying of the pack, / . . . As the noose tightens around my neck, / At the hour when death is so near, / I should like my right hand near me / To wipe away my tears."[36] He handed the poem to a foreign reporter hounding him for an interview. The reporter had the poem printed. Soviet bureaucrats called in Olga—the poet's right hand—and took an unusual tack. They begged her to take him back at once for fear of international denunciations resurfacing. It was an initial climax to the affair that must have signaled not so subtly that the Soviets had lost the most in this battle over Pasternak's novel. Having heard of these events and read the poem, Olga did return, chiding her lover: "Surely, you don't imagine I would leave you. . .? My poor dunderhead."[37]

Much later she saw that there had been strategy in her lover's hysteria. "With this poem he canceled out all the efforts of his persecutors to deceive posterity into believing that his renunciation of the prize had been 'completely voluntary. . .'"[38] In one spontaneous deed, Pasternak was able to proclaim his love for his right hand, lament the persecution he had faced, and retract the letters he had been coerced into signing. Into this maelstrom came *The Paris Review*'s roving interviewer.

. . .

Olga Carlisle arrived at Pasternak's dacha in Peredelkino on a Sunday in January 1960. Harold Humes knew Carlisle's parents. In her memoir, *Under a New Sky*, Carlisle writes, "It had been our friend Harold Humes's idea. An eccentric, adventuresome novelist, the author of *The Underground City*, Humes was acquainted with my father. . . . Not averse to the notion of international intrigue, Humes became convinced that, though I was a painter and not a writer, I could nonetheless obtain an interview that would be a journalistic scoop for the *Review*."[39]

During the previous fall, Plimpton had already made his enthusiasm for the topic clear. What could Carlisle have meant when she wrote that "George Plimpton did not quite share Humes's enthusiasm for the undertaking, but he allowed himself to be persuaded"? Did her lack of experience as a writer give Plimpton pause? Or was it the potential for an international incident that made him hesitate? Once he warmed to the idea, Plimpton was keen to tap the editorial treasures behind the Iron Curtain. "He stressed the fact that interviews with other, unspecified important Soviet writers might also be welcomed by *The Paris Review*," Carlisle recalled. "But the most desirable would indeed be" the Pasternak interview,[40] which would do its work as propaganda. This was assured by the apparatus growing up within American publishing, and beneath *The Paris Review*.

At *The Review*'s office at 16 rue Vernet—mere blocks from the Arc de Triomphe—Nelson Aldrich's enthusiasm for the original symposium matched Plimpton's in the aftermath of the announcement of the Nobel. "[W]hat a marvelous coup that will be!" Aldrich wrote Plimpton of the Congress-funded brochures. "I think of huge international mailing drives, droves of publicity," he continued. "To come out just before Christmas?"[41] Aldrich has been described by *People* magazine as "the son, grandson and great-grandson of millionaires." His pedigree included the posh private schools of New England followed by Harvard's Porcellian club. Both as the magazine's Paris editor and afterward, he was often lackadaisical—sensitive to "the airy inconsequentiality of working," he told one interviewer.[42] So his enthusiasim for the publishing coup was met by long periods of inaction and broken correspondence with Plimpton.

After her first visit that January Sunday, Carlisle visited Pasternak twice more, ignoring the sign reminding visitors of the ban. The writer was anxious to get on with his work and the visits that were so frowned upon by the Soviet censors, and which he clearly enjoyed, took too much time from his writing. "To speak the truth," he wrote a friend in New York that winter, "I should disappear and hide . . . and write in secret whatever I can still do— but in Russian conditions this is impossible."[43] Given this anxiety, Carlisle couldn't keep him still enough to record him—so she pieced together a blend of interview and profile. It wasn't to be a typical Art of Fiction interview; she admits in her memoir, *Voices in the Snow*, that he never technically granted a formal interview.[44] Her descriptions of what she brought back on Pasternak failed to inspire confidence.

"I am very anxious to know what this great Pasternak interview looks like," Aldrich wrote Plimpton. "I had a talk with Robie McAuley of *Kenyon* [*Review*] who said he had a very banal little piece from the young lady [Carlisle]—a bad auspice from a good bird. If it is good, I will sell it to all 16 of the Freedom magazines from here to Manila."[45] *The Kenyon Review*'s Robie McAuley had been recruited to the CIA by Cord Meyer in the summer of 1953. Meyer ran the International Organizations Division, which housed all propaganda fronts, from the Free Europe Committee to the Congress for Cultural Freedom, and sat under what today is called the National Clandestine Services.[46]

Plimpton confirmed Aldrich's concerns. "The Pasternak, frankly, is unknown quality," he wrote. "Our splendid Olga darted over there full of energy and determination, to be sure, and saw Pasternak on three separate occasions; but one has the feeling talking to her that Pasternak was so starved for information about the Western world . . . that she spent most of her time filling him in. What she got in return is sketchy, at best," Plimpton continued,

> and since she can't write, it's going to be a monstrous and sensitive job of editing to produce something of value. She does have excellent recall, however, so I feel we'll have enough to create a stir. After all, she was the last westerner to see him, and she's intelligent and well-informed on his work. She's a pretty girl, and Pasternak adored her. I wish she hadn't talked so much, and had dutifully listened.[47]

Carlisle depicts Pasternak as hard at work on *The Blind Beauty*. "What I want to show," Pasternak said of the trilogy of plays, "is . . . the birth of an enlightened and affluent middle class [in Russia], open to occidental influences, progressive, intelligent, artistic. . . ." He also told Carlisle that time to write was now "something I have to fight for. All those demands by scholars, editors, readers cannot be ignored, but together with the translations they devour my time. . . . You must tell people abroad who are interested in me that this is my only serious problem—this terrible lack of time."[48] In the weeks after Carlisle returned to the United States, Pasternak told Ivinskaya that he needed about two months of solid writing to finish the play.[49] As it turned out, he wouldn't make it.

Recounting her encounters with Pasternak, Carlisle claimed much later that in the study of his dacha, "Pasternak entrusted me with a mission consistent with my family's legacy: to join in the Russian intelligentsia's cause against a repressive government." The writers and intellectuals in her family had been persecuted and forced into exile. She claimed that Pasternak told her that anyone with her "background must tell the truth about us. Remember that one of the goals of the Terror was to make us forget what the truth is—truth is especially elusive in a dictatorial world. Of course, you'll also have to be careful about how you speak of us, since we live in a police state."[50] She admits that this was her paraphrase and that she "should have been more subtle."[51]

As per instructions, Carlisle returned with interviews with other Russian writers, some better known outside the Soviet Union than others. Aldrich, doing double duty for the CCF, broached the idea of the CCF publishing those interviews that *The Paris Review* didn't want. In early 1960, Aldrich wrote Plimpton that "Blair [Fuller, the next Paris editor] tells me that Mrs. Carlisle has also done an interview with Sukolov (?) *Quiet Flows the Don*." By this Aldrich seems to have conflated Sholokhov, the writer who challenged Americans in the magazine *Foreign Literature* to a true cultural exchange, and Alexei Surkov, the conservative aristocratic opponent of the Thaw, who shouted at Feltrinelli in Milan and denounced Pasternak before the Writers' Union. "Have you read it?" Aldrich continued. "Is it publishable, if not by the *Review*, then by one of the Congress magazines? Has she disposed of it elsewhere? May I try to sell (not for very much) one or both of these pieces to such embattled outposts of freedom as Brazil and Japan?"[52] The CCF magazine in Brazil was called *Cadernos Brasileiros* and in Japan, *Jiyu*. This was the Japanese word for "freedom."

But beyond the failed Pasternak issue and the choppy interview, Aldrich proposed a number of anti-Communist writers, who increasingly found their way into the quarterly's pages, mostly as interviews. The makeup of *The Paris Review* was changing then. Aldrich was well established in the quarterly's Paris office in early 1958 and left the *Review* to join the CIA's Congress for Cultural Freedom. "I stayed at the *Review* for only a year and then went on to a better-paid job at the Congress for Cultural Freedom, which by 1959 was already a well-known CIA front, but no less admired for that."[53] By the time he stopped receiving editorial instructions and requests from Plimpton in New York, it was already 1961. This was because his new job was, in part, to help magazines like *The Paris Review* into the Congress for Cultural Freedom's press division. So from early 1958 until summer of 1961, he effectively worked at both organizations.

.   .   .

The Review's ties to the Congress went back to the early days of the magazine. Aldrich's predecessor, Robert Silvers, wrote Plimpton in 1956 that he "greedily" sought out the CCF magazines to reprint *The Paris Review*'s interview with Faulkner.[54] Something of a prodigy, Silvers had written speeches for the one-term Connecticut governor Chester Bowles and had then worked at Supreme Headquarters Allied Command Europe (SHAPE), a NATO base, before he met Plimpton. They hit it off and he took the position as Paris editor. Later, in 1963, he founded *The New York Review of Books*. Previous mentions of the CCF in the magazine's archives are business-side matters, such as ad exchanges, or those early letters to Julius Fleischmann requesting funding. This Faulkner interview that Silvers cites appears to be the earliest direct mention of editorial cooperation. Silvers said later that he sought out the CCF just that once for the widened readership for *The Paris Review*. He stipulated that he would have had no knowledge of whether the money the magazine got from the CCF for the reprint rights would in the end go to the interviewer, Jean Stein, or the magazine.[55] "I should also make it clear that during these Paris years, I had no idea of CIA or US government funding of the Congress," he added.[56] But the editorial cooperation grew during Silvers's tenure and he was included in multiple editorial planning letters arranging for other interviews to serve the CCF's insatiable content needs. *The Paris Review* syndicated its interviews to CCF-affiliated magazines for reprint, often before those interviews were completed, as was the case with Hemingway, Pasternak, and Faulkner. Eventually, Plimpton told another Paris editor he could negotiate the fee for the interview reprints but he shouldn't price the Congress out of buying them.[57]

. . .

One day toward the end of his life Pasternak said to Ivinskaya, "How late everything has come for me. . . . But we did get through all our troubles together, Oliusha. And everything is alright now! If only we could live forever like this." He thought for a moment about this feeling of abundance and added a disclaimer: "Only I'm ashamed of those Polikarpov letters. What a pity you got me to sign them," he scolded her. These were the letters they signed, in which Pasternak admitted, browbeaten and under duress, that he had given up the Nobel Prize of his own volition, and more. "I protested indignantly," Ivinskaya writes, "how soon he had forgotten the state of desperate anxiety we had been in!" To these protests, Pasternak countered: "We only took fright out of politeness, you must admit!"[58]

What else did Pasternak regret? A year before he got sick, Pasternak saw the CIA's Russian-language version of *Doctor Zhivago*. A decade's worth of work—bringing together the lyricism he'd spent a lifetime honing as a poet along with his spiritual views, views on creativity, freedom of expression, the Bolshevik revolution, his love for Olga/Lara, and his native Russia—had come to him riddled with errors. Pasternak read in Germany's *Der Spiegel* of the CIA's role in crash-printing his novel. An error-filled edition printed by Mouton (and the CIA) had been smuggled back to Moscow. CIA spying had revealed that Feltrinelli had sold the Dutch rights to Hague-based publishers, Mouton, though negotiations were not complete. The CIA briefed Mouton on their scheme to print and distribute the book at the World's Fair, and Mouton tried to call Feltrinelli, who was on vacation in Scandinavia, and couldn't be reached. Mouton had to decide whether to join the scheme, and they did so; as the World's Fair batch was being finished, the company added Feltrinelli's name to the copyright to try to salvage their original agreement, hoping the advance printing would escape his notice. But given the errors, which originated in the CIA's pre-production text prepared in New York by Felix Morrow, including the typo in his surname, Feltrinelli sued.[59]

For his part, Pasternak was livid; everything he'd worked for had been compromised. "It abounds with errata," Pasternak wrote Feltrinelli.[60] With these mistakes, Morrow—the contract agent hired by the spooks who was a lesser member of the New York Intellectuals, a fervent anti-Communist, a clumsy and rogue freelance propagandist hired to do a rush job— had written himself (and the CIA) into Pasternak's legacy—clumsily if not violently so. "This is almost another text, not the one I wrote," Pasternak griped to French translator Jacqueline de Proyart,[61] to whom he immediately signed over all remaining rights to his novel. Make a "faithful edition," he asked.[62] Ivinskaya calmed him, persuading him that abruptly transferring rights to the French publishers would lead to lawsuits; he must work it out with Feltrinelli.[63] It's not clear if Pasternak ever understood how the CIA had undermined Feltrinelli's arrangements with Mouton. But this coda to the Pasternak affair of March 1959 was clearly one of his last serious regrets.

As a Peredelkino winter became spring—and before finishing his play— Pasternak's health took a drastic turn. After suffering angina, from then until the end, he and Ivinskaya barely saw each other. His death came in late May. Hearing from one of the servants, she ran to the big house so long forbidden to her and rushed inside to find his body warm. At the funeral, a professor lamented how "Everything that brings us glory we banish."[64] Someone read out the line from Pasternak's poem, "Hamlet": "To live your life is not as simple as to cross a field." Ivinskaya was unable to hold back her tears. "Glory to Pasternak," some chanted, as church bells rang across the field. A frightened bureaucrat in gray trousers insisted that the coffin be closed, the ceremony disbanded. But the young, the poets, and Ivinskaya stayed a little longer. When she left, she heard them reciting Pasternak's poems while clumps of dirt landed on his coffin and a heavy downpour began.[65] Two days after the funeral, on her "Name Day," the KGB stormed into her house and demanded she hand over the play. She gave them an uncorrected copy and kept the true one hidden in Moscow.[66]

In August, on the Day of Flowers, she was arrested.[67] Her role as liaison between Pasternak and the endless stream of Western visitors, many of whom the Soviet authorities considered spies, was the pretext for the arrest.[68] They made her out to be a spy herself, claiming she had ghost-written *Doctor Zhivago* so they could could blame its political unorthodoxies on her. But what appeared to hold the most legal traction was her reception of foreign visitors, which was tied to the claim that she helped smuggle in money (Pasternak's royalties).

. . .

The January after the interview ran, Plimpton was keen to syndicate it. But the Ivinskaya arrest was a red flag. Hearing through Aldrich of the interest of multiple CCF magazines, Plimpton hoped to be cautious politically while exploiting the Pasternak material. "Will you let me know exactly which Congress magazines wish to publish the Pasternak, if any," he wrote Aldrich. "Olga Carlisle is worried that publication in them may jeopardize her chances of returning to the USSR, and wants to be sure that political overtones are slight indeed."[69]

In the face of this interest, Plimpton demonstrated his awareness of the politics of partnering with the CCF magazines. For instance, while receiving the "good news about the lively and universal interest shown by the Congress magazines" Plimpton nonetheless warned Aldrich to "be sure you don't make any commitments until publication plans have been cleared through Olga."

> She is delighted to think that her work will be read by as many as will through Congress publications, but in this present turmoil of the Olga Ivinskaya imprisonment she's been spooked: the point is that her parents are Soviet citizens, and she worries that things might not go well with them if her piece on an author the Soviets are obviously extremely sensitive about appears in such politically engaged magazines as the Congress publications. Both RBS [Robert Silvers] and I have tried to allay her fears—on the Congress' degree of engagement, this and other factors—but

while Olga herself does want that large audience she does feel strongly that she owes it to her parents at least to ask their advice.[70]

Later Nelson Aldrich told me he thought that Plimpton knew that the Congress for Cultural Freedom was a CIA front.[71] Many of the CCF's friends in Paris knew, he told me. Well, if not "knew," then "believed," he said.[72] While Plimpton's caution on behalf of Carlisle's parents was admirable, Plimpton nevertheless downplayed the CCF's engagement in order to enable mass syndication of the interview, and within two months Plimpton and Carlisle resolved their fears for her parents. On March 5, 1961, Plimpton wrote Aldrich and Fuller, "We've decided with Olga to split the proceeds of her interview . . . fifty-fifty. Interest in that issue continues to mount. Random House wanted 300 more copies today. We had only 100 to give them. In view of a 1-hour television show that Robert Lowell has arranged with CBS (on which Olga, Mary McCarthy, Edmund Wilson, and T.S. Eliot are scheduled to appear—Olga to talk about her interview) it was certainly a wise decision of yours to keep the [printing] plates."[73] Carlisle confirmed that the show was filmed in Los Angeles and thought it was overseen by Lowell's prep school friend Blair Clarke, an executive at CBS.[74]

Here the covert industry rising up within New York publishing to disseminate the work of persecuted Russians is seen doing two things: contributing to the coffers of *The Paris Review* while rippling out from a small-audience literary quarterly to mainstream broadcast outlets. Ivinskaya's arrest revealed not just another cruel Soviet blunder (that hounded its best living poet to his early death, at age 70, and reeked of collective punishment) but it also made a mediocre Art of Fiction interview, by Plimpton's standards, newsworthy once again almost a year after Pasternak's death—newsworthy enough for TV.

Like other CCF-friendly magazines, *The Paris Review* learned to tap the patronage. Increasingly, the magazine was subsidized through government subscription and issue purchases. The CCF's national offices around the world subscribed to *The Paris Review* while the USIS, the agency tapped for overseas propaganda, also boosted the magazine's circulation. These CCF national offices were mailed lists that ushered the magazine into the Congress's clearinghouse fold and assured that *The Paris Review* was self-consciously publishing with this audience in mind. In one letter, Aldrich wrote the New York office asking about print runs. "What is the run to be on this issue? Here we can use perhaps a thousand, though that may be overly optimistic. The USIS may repeat their largesse and buy another few hundred copies, but I doubt it. (Did I tell you that they have now bought 460 copies of No. 18 and taken out 10 subscriptions?) As far as possible, this information should remain secret; I tremble to think of Congress discovering such a thing."[75] The print runs at this time could be as high as ten or twenty thousand, the majority shipped to New York. Issue number 18, cited here, was the Hemingway issue.

Founded by President Eisenhower in 1953, the US Information Service kept a list of anti-Communist and pro-American books to disseminate at American embassies around the world. The American Committee had mastered the art of using these lists to help sell books, as we see in Chapter 6. It did so by adding favored authors to USIS lists. It kept tabs on pro-American and anti-Communist writers and sent the USIS updates. This was part of the setup that helped make the American Committee's books into the occasional best-seller, exemplifying the greater "clearinghouse" spirit throughout small magazines and book publishing.

The note from Aldrich above shows that entities like USIS were recognized by *The Paris Review* as government propaganda fronts. Indeed, this was no secret. As with the American Committee's activities in the United States, the line was blurred between funding for propaganda aimed abroad and at home. The Committee, itself funded through the Farfield Foundation, a CIA conduit, served as the US distribution and fulfillment agent for *Preuves*, whose vast audience was in Paris, and sometimes *Encounter*, and for several years the American Committee served to publish *Partisan Review*. With no mission to fund news or culture except in the service of its mission to do propaganda abroad, and banned from operating in the United States, all the CIA's funding efforts in these fields legally had to be aimed outside the country. But they weren't, and Aldrich seemed to understand this; he also said the place he worked was a well-known CIA front, suggesting he knew this by 1959 when he joined.

Beyond the USIS publicity, rewards from *The Paris Review*'s dalliances with the CCF included direct financial ones for disseminating American greats like Hemingway and persecuted Russian dissidents like Pasternak, but also free publicity in international media. Thanks "to the kindness of Francois Bondy of *Preuves*," Aldrich wrote in 1959, "the *Review* has been raved about at great length in *Der Tagesspiegel* and a Swiss newspaper . . . . both . . . as widely read (almost) as the *New York Times*. Also we had a shorter but just as flattering notice in *Preuves*. Not surprising since Bondy wrote all three."[76] Bondy was the editor of *Preuves*, funded secretly by the CIA. Here he was planting stories favoring a CIA-founded magazine, with an emerging "clearinghouse" deal with the CCF through Aldrich. This was exactly what the American Committee had anticipated by serving as de facto literary agents for anti-Communist writers. An editorial payola was arising to reward anti-Communist writers with higher fees.

But this partnership went further. In his recollection of joining the CCF, Aldrich suggested his joining meant leaving *The Paris Review*. In fact, letters show that the work overlapped and Aldrich hoped to design it that way for his replacement, too. When mentioning his New York return, he wrote to Plimpton, "I recently got another job (in the press division) at the HQ of the intellectual Cold War, the Congress of Cultural Freedom. I am happy there, but I don't know for how long."[77] Aldrich hoped he could continue to do both jobs. Plimpton entertained the same idea. In July 1960, Plimpton wrote, "I see no reason why it shouldn't be as possible to collaborate with Blair [Fuller] as it has been for as many as four or five of us to struggle to agreement here in New York.... The financial consideration is trickier. Blair needs and will get that niggardly monthly sum. But if you're staying on, and you let me know quickly, perhaps I can arrange an additional monthly payment. If you need it, or the remuneration from the Congress isn't sufficient . .. then tell me frankly and I'll see what can be done."[78]

But the CCF apparently had plenty of work for Aldrich. He responded, "it is true that I will be working . . . very busily at the Freedom Fighters Guild [his nickname for the Congress]." But whether he could manage to do both jobs or not, his work for the CCF would be good "for the *Review* because there is no Congress sponsored magazine in the States, and since I am supposed to see that the various articles and stories published in *Encounter*, *Preuves*, *Der Monat*, etc. to 16, there is no reason why any really exceptional fiction should not find its way to us."

．．．

By 1961, checks were coming in from the CCF on a regular basis. With Aldrich's exit approaching and a high staff turnaround, a new Paris editor was badly needed. This editor would be conscripted to do double-duty for the two organizations. As letters indicate, the CCF would augment the meager literary quarterly pay—and the many ways to work together had already been discussed. The *Review* was to coordinate the hiring through "friends of the Congress."

Now that Fuller had moved on, *The Paris Review*'s replacement candidates were Frederick Seidel, the New York poet honored in 2014 at the *Paris*

Review Revel, and Roger Klein, a young editor and critic with a passionate expertise in Latin American literature. In February, Plimpton wrote to Blair Fuller and Aldrich with the latest update on Seidel's changing plans: "Fred Seidel has scribbled in a postcard to say that now he's very interested in the *Review* job—a somewhat predictable turnabout I might say. The trouble is that while he sat in his tent another candidate has been suggested—one Roger Klein . . . a brilliant young editor at *Harper's*. He's a linguist, would be an excellent choice . . . for the Congress job which he would need to supplement his [*Paris Review*] salary. Very important, he seems genuinely anxious to do the job for both organizations."[79]

Such were the topsy-turvy maneuverings of the Cold War. The CIA was infusing money into fraternal orders who were then acting as literary agents for their anti-Communist writer friends in New York and around the country. Meanwhile, the nation's "most apolitical literary magazine," half-based in Paris, was vetting candidates for the CIA's propaganda outfit, after its editor had been scolded just a few years before for running an ad for the Democratic Party.

From the CCF's offices on Boulevard Haussmann, Aldrich wrote Plimpton in March: "If . . . you propose [Roger Klein] for the PR and the CCF, I must have a curriculum vitae to show the people here. The language abilities sound auspicious but we've got to have more dope on this fellow." After looking over his CV, Aldrich wanted Klein to "meet Dan Bell or some other 'friend of the Congress' in New York. Having passed that test I don't believe there will be any objection on this side either to hiring him or to sharing him with the PR."[80] But the odds were stacked against poor Klein. In a note inquiring about a Russian poetry issue in the spring, Plimpton asked about the vetting process. "Is the Seidel team a fait accompli?" he wrote. "Somewhat to our dismay the Congress people never sent poor Klein any word on his application." On the bright side for Klein, a colleague in New York was willing to pay him "to act as a Harper [Brothers] watch dog in Paris—not as much as the Congress would have paid but enough . . ."[81]

. . .

Aldrich finally left, and *The Paris Review* wrote the Congress to reestablish its ties. In late June, Fuller wrote on behalf of the magazine that after "Nelson Aldrich, having departed for America, we no longer have a direct link to the Congress."[82] The CCF replied a week later. "Before leaving, Nelson was trying to find out how many interviews have been reprinted in the Japanese magazine *Jiyu*."[83] The letter indicated nine: Faulkner, Francoise Sagan, Francois Mauriac, Alberto Moravia, Hemingway, Eliot, Pasternak, Georges Simenon, and Aldous Huxley. The Congress also stipulated that it would pay three times as much for the Pasternak—which is to say interviews with a higher element of "negative" propaganda, pieces that made the Soviets look bad to the rest of the world. But the Faulkner paid the most: about $1,650 in today's dollars.[84] The money was on its way, wrote the Congress staffer, adding, "*Jiyu* requests Graham Greene, Somerset Maugham, Kingsley Amis, Henry Green, and Arthur Miller."

Seidel's tenure began with him articulating a problem with this request in the summer of 1961. He wrote *Jiyu*'s editor, Hoki Ishihara: "Mr. Ivan Kats of the Congress for Cultural Freedom here in Paris has listed for us a number of interviews that you would be interested in publishing. The list mentions several writers we have not yet interviewed. . ."[85] Arthur Miller, for instance, did not appear in *The Paris Review*'s interviews until 1966, timed with a monumental CCF partnership with PEN, the international advocacy organization for freedom of expression. Kingsley Amis would not appear in the magazine for more than a decade. Maugham, another spy writer like Matthiessen, would never appear in *The Paris Review* interviews, though the British spy-turned-writer John Le Carré would, as would the undercover CIA agent and conservative pundit William F. Buckley. How the anti-civil rights, pro-Vietnam War figure fit into the apolitical *Paris Review* is anyone's guess. (His book editor interviewed him.) But the question before Seidel was, Why was the CCF requesting interviews that didn't exist?

In back of many of its early issues, *The Paris Review* ran lists of authors it thought it might interview in future numbers, including interviews still being edited. The practice allowed the CCF to exert influence over the choice of interviewees on *The Paris Review*'s horizon. Even before they were finished, there were orders for the good ones, usually white males, Europeans and Americans. There was three times the money for Russians who could be turned into anti-Communist dissident symbols to score points against the enemy. Even when diversity dared to creep into the magazine's interview series, it coincided with Cold War cultural wrangling. Ralph Ellison, author of the acclaimed novel *Invisible Man*, was the first black writer to appear in the Art of Fiction Series, in 1955, before Aldrich's emplacement as bridge between the two organizations. Ellison had famously been included in the anthology *The God That Failed* for his turn against Communism, so he covered aesthetics while also being politically correct in the anti-Communist calculus. Not until thirty years later, with its 1984 interview with James

Baldwin, did *The Paris Review* interview another black writer.[86] Throughout the entire 1980s, the only other black writer interviewed was Derek Walcott. For its first roughly forty years, that's just three black writers.

Russians, of course, were more in demand (with seven writers interviewed in the period); even Latin Americans (seven) and Eastern bloc writers did better than black Americans. If the interviews section of *The Paris Review* was any indication, race was at best a distant third after the transatlantic cultural bond and the cultural détente pursued in the 1960s. (Forget entirely about gender balance. "In those years the *Review* was decidedly male-oriented," wrote Carlisle. "Its editors drew inspiration from Ernest Hemingway. . . . It seldom gave assignments to women—at the *Review*, women were employed as typists or volunteer readers of manuscripts."[87])

By 1962, direct links and joint employment were back on the table. The CCF's Irving Jaffe invited Seidel to talk about an editorial assistantship with him and the CCF's number two man in Paris, John Hunt. Over the next two years, more requests came for *Paris Review* interviews to be translated into *Hiwar*, the Congress's "Arab Review," which was preparing its first issue. Requests came from *Jiyu* in Japan, and reprints and subscriptions were paid by the CCF for *Sameekha* in Madras, India. When Seidel left, requests went back and forth between the Congress's Anne Schlumberger, Irving Jaffe, and Ivan Kats, and *The Paris Review*'s Patrick Bowles, who took over Paris duties.[88] In *The Paris Review* of the late 1950s and early 1960s, then, one finds a potent recipe. While culture was being subtly weaponized for reasons practical and ideological, the politics remained camouflaged within a belletristic literary review.

5

DID THE CIA CENSOR ITS MAGAZINES?

Encounter, Preuves, and other magazines supported by the Congress were superb publications—with no strings attached in terms of what was published that I could ever see.

—George Plimpton

When news broke in the late 1960s that the CIA had secretly funded the Congress for Cultural Freedom, defenders of the program were forced to contend with Dwight Macdonald's 1958 essay "America! America!" Seen as anti-American, the essay had been censored by the CIA's flagship magazine, *Encounter*, and the episode had remained on people's minds because when the piece was finally published elsewhere, Macdonald wrote a famous preamble, discussing the fate of his piece. In addressing the incident, then, those who cited "America! America!" were using a case of censorship, bizarrely but unavoidably, to insist that the CIA rarely—or never—censored. This, after all, is what Macdonald recorded in his preamble.

But a different story was sitting in the Congress for Cultural Freedom's archives in Chicago. 1958 was of course the same year the Soviets suppressed Pasternak's first novel. The authorities in the Soviet Union had called the book "anti-Soviet." And because he had examined the seedy side of American life, the American Cold Warriors were censoring a friend, however unreliably a friend, in Dwight Macdonald. Macdonald was one of the New York Intellectuals often viewed as a maverick. Earlier in his career, he had created the magazine *Politics*, which was an inspiration to Noam Chomsky, among others. After the rumpus they caused at the Waldorf Astoria, he and his fellow American Committee members duked it out over the atrocities of Soviet Communism and the sublimity of the literary avant-garde in *Partisan Review*. But in the mid-1950s, he had also been a roving reporter for *Encounter*, the magazine that wound up censoring him apparently for anti-American reporting and observations.

One of Macdonald's most famous later essays would articulate the phenomena of "Mass Cult" and "Mid Cult," two different forms of mass-produced art. At the heart of this argument was a quasi-Marxist idea that mass-produced art, like religion, was an opiate for the people, something tantamount to propaganda used automatically and routinely to pacify them. But there was also a kind of double-bind in Macdonald as he grew more conservative and argued that the masses were not capable of appreciating high art, which is why they could never be anything but "the masses." The essay and its circular argument were rightly called out for snobbishness, or unsound reasoning.

Elements of these ideas appear in "America! America!," itself a full-frontal assault on American culture. Early in 1958, *Encounter*'s editor Stephen Spender accepted "America! America!" for the magazine. But ultimately Spender reneged, claiming he'd read it too quickly, killing the piece for its depiction of American life as violent, crude, and without style, and—in particular—for its depiction of American prisoners of war in Korea as, more or less, craven cowards with no sense of solidarity for their fellow POWs. Macdonald began the essay by assuming that "No nation in history has been richer or has had so equal a distribution of wealth,"[1] and then he asserted that Americans are nevertheless unhappy. Further, he cited a problem that still hounds the United States, mass shootings and mass violence. Whether it was the American roadside or the American city, we live in ugliness and squalor. Our famous equality would be grand, if not for the fact that, having erased hierarchies, we find that nobody respects one another. We are individualists to our detriment, with no sense of community. We disrespect our elders and worship youth. Finally, he wrote, "When we come into contact with other peoples, as our post-1945 imperial role has forced us to do, we don't impress them."[2]

When Vice President Nixon went on a goodwill tour of Latin America in 1958, he so unimpressed the Venezuelans that his caravan was attacked in an infamous incident of anti-American protest: his car window was pelted with stones and smashed; Nixon was even spat upon. The response? The leadership wanted more Latin American blood. On one hand, Macdonald argued, America is dominated by a naïve "let's-talk-it-over-boys" boosterism, which sent Nixon to Latin America in the first place. And on the other, by a reflex to send in troops at the least provocation. Though digressive and, by design, episodic and subjective, the essay is a hostile and compelling pan d'horizon of American culture at its worst, nowhere more so than when Macdonald cited a military study that found that roughly a third of US prisoners in Korea collaborated with the enemy. It wasn't that the collaborators were mistreated by their Chinese captors: but they were merely told that they had been freed from capitalist hierarchies. Now that they didn't have to listen to orders, they stopped doing so.[3]

The article certainly touched a nerve in the halls of both the CCF on Boulevard Haussmann in Paris, and at CIA headquarters in Washington. It was a dispiriting portrayal of American ugliness, and something so critical of the morality of American soldiers could not be tolerated. We know from the clearinghouse that the main responsibility of the little magazines was to push back against anti-Americanism; here was a celebration of the worst aspects of American culture. The CCF and the CIA both ordered the editors to kill the piece.

Kristol believed that because Spender had initially accepted it they would be forced to run it. He told an interviewer that he "was easily moved not to run it, since I hadn't liked it in the first place."[4] He and Spender were told that the key funding channel, Julius Fleischmann, had said it would hurt the magazine's funding prospects. "Stephen was a little more recalcitrant. But in the end we said . . . if it's really going to make life that much more difficult for you, we can do without the article. And then Dwight published it elsewhere, complaining about censorship. Rejecting an article is not censorship. I've been an editor of magazines all my life, and I've rejected plenty of articles and I've never regarded that as a form of censorship."[5]

Yet when Spender, tasked with killing the essay, informed Macdonald that he had read it too quickly—and that he now felt it was one-sided and harsh—Spender added a damning fact. Nicolas Nabokov of the CCF had read it and it had made him "very upset." This in turn upset Macdonald, who was made aware that officers of the CCF were pressuring editors on strictly editorial matters. Typically in journalism, there is a wall of separation—akin to checks and balances in government—that protects editors' judgments from the interests of investors, advertisers, funders, donors, and in the case of public media, government bureaucrats. If buying an ad in a magazine could get the magazine to stop covering the abuses of a prospective advertiser, then it would amount to a form of buying off magazines (or newspapers, or TV, or radio) and defanging the Fourth Estate. Publishers would be like lobbyists telling their editors which advertisers were to be effectively immune from editorial scrutiny. The same would go for elected and appointed officials who could pull the plug on funding. At *Encounter*, the editorial protection wall was down.

Aware that his piece was read "upstairs," Macdonald suggested sarcastically that maybe *every* piece ought to go right to them *first*, in order to avoid a lag in response time. Little did he know that this was already happening. Spender later insisted that this was the only piece the CCF/CIA ever vetoed. He would also remark that he wished he'd published it anyway, so that his record at *Encounter* could be *completely* without blemishes, rather than mostly.[6] Spender of course was mistaken. The record shows that Josselson at the CCF would never have allowed it. Josselson himself wrote to Macdonald to explain. "You must understand that Irving and Stephen must eat, that you must be paid for your articles, that *Encounter* must be able to say the things it is best qualified to say without jeopardizing its future."[7] This special pleading couldn't be more clear. If they published pieces that government funders did not approve of, the editors might be fired, or the enterprise might be terminated. Diana Josselson, Michael's wife, said later that it "was the one example of editorial intervention by the CIA, and Michael fought it very hard, but he didn't win."[8] Though admitting to one case of what can only be called censorship, her statement was misleading.

Josselson often sent orders to editors. Citing friends of the Congress, he wrote to insist that *Encounter* cover the Asian conference of 1955. "It is essential that this conference be written up in *Encounter*. Many of our friends . . . have the same wish." Josselson was known to tell his editors, "I think it is quite important that this book[9] be reviewed in *Encounter* by one of 'our' people."[10] Francois Bondy, *Preuves*'s editor, bristled at the frequency with which Josselson made editorial suggestions, and he threatened to resign over meetings called to discuss *Preuves*'s editorial direction that Bondy himself was not invited to.[11]

. . .

Christopher Montague Woodhouse, who helped set up *Encounter* (and helped install the Shah in Iran), told a journalist that he knew—in general terms—that "the Congress for Cultural Freedom was axing pieces. But I never knew of any formal guidelines for this which were precisely laid down somewhere."[12] Removed from Iran for destabilizing propaganda, Woodhouse was one of several spies who wrote for *Encounter*. As such, he would have been doubly versed in the "responsibility" of journalists. In the case of "America! America!," it was the section about Korea that appeared to have offended Josselson the most. Later that year, after *Dissent* published it, Josselson wrote to Kristol: "Now, as to [Macdonald's] exhibitionist piece about America which you and Stephen were wrong in accepting in the first place, you may also recall that you asked him to re-write it and to leave out the whole section about Korea which had already appeared in the *New Yorker*. He did not do this."[13]

Guidelines on who had the power to accept pieces or "veto" them were made clear from the beginning. Macdonald's sarcastic suggestion (that they send every piece up the chain to the government funders first, to save time) was the actual policy—if the piece was controversial. These guidelines were repeated upon *Encounter*'s one-year anniversary, when a piece on China was accepted.[14] CIA officer Thomas Braden later recalled, "We had some trouble with *Encounter* from time to time, and I used to say, 'Let them publish whatever they want.' But there was one time . . . *Encounter* was to publish a piece that was critical of US policy, and we had a helluva fight back at the office. I remember going up and talking to Allen Dulles, and he refused to get involved. He just said, 'You handle it.' So we finally axed it, and I am sorry we axed it."[15]

This second known *Encounter* piece to have been axed by the CIA in its oversight role toward the CCF was by Emily Hahn, a China expert and contributor to *The New Yorker*. Again it was Spender who may have been the article's early advocate but who sent it along dutifully to Josselson. Josselson wrote back that he "found it utterly shocking. It will certainly not make any new friends in England. I am passing it on to Nicolas [Nabokov] and Francois [Bondy] and shall call you or Irving [Kristol] about it before this letter reaches you."[16] This prompted Nabokov, two days later, to review the editorial approval process. He wrote Kristol and Spender to remind them. "Before going into the matter of Miss Emily Hahn's piece, let me restate some of the principles upon which we had all agreed in the course of the talks we had at the time of launching *Encounter*, as well as in our various subsequent meetings. *We agreed that all articles on controversial topics should be seen by us before they are shown to anybody outside*. We agreed that one of the fundamental policies of *Encounter* should be to work toward a better understanding between England and America and consequently, that all political issues should be discussed on the highest possible plane so that whenever controversy takes place, it should be stated in a manner so as not to be offensive to national feelings on either side of the ocean. We have all read Miss Hahn's piece ... all of us had the same negative reaction to this article. We feel that Miss Hahn gives an erroneous, superficial and slipshod statement of the American point of view on China. We feel that Miss Hahn's article is offensive in matters of style, temper and contents."[17]

The phrase that others—like *Preuves*'s Bondy—leveled at the article, "hysterical abuse," was not only casually misogynist, but conflated criticism with tone.[18] Yet the bigger question was how there could be a singular, pre-designated "American point of view," unless Nabokov meant "American policy"? Nabokov saw a teachable moment in these events. "Now, where do we go from here? We would suggest that you attempt to secure from Miss Hahn a re-write of her article, which would result in a *complete* change of tone eliminating its most abusive passages. In addition to Miss Hahn, you secure another article stating the American point of view on the Chinese problem but on a high and dignified level and in a more concise form. If this cannot be done, we think that Miss Hahn's article should be dropped and this crucial issue raised again at a later date with more responsible persons than Miss Hahn representing the American point of view."[19]

Note the euphemism that persists today for dissent that strikes vigorously at the root of bad policy: irresponsible. The responsibility of editors was to defend the American point of view on any given "problem," and eliminate "abusive" passages toward the United States or its policy. Does this responsibility mean quid pro quo? Where some might call these editorial interventions censorship, the psychological warfare operatives of the CIA, British intelligence, and the CCF called them simply being "axed," "dropped," or, most democratically of all, "vetoed."

The association between these magazines and the CCF, for its part, was not hidden; *Encounter, Preuves*, and *Cuadernos*—the Congress magazine in

Spanish—were even listed on the CCF letterhead in the early to mid-1950s. But whatever the vague role CCF officers played here in editorial oversight, was the CIA directly involved? Braden admitted that he reported to Dulles over one editorial matter. Another agent, Warren Manshel, offered these instructions to Encounter's editors: "We are all in agreement here that it would be unwise to publish the [Hahn] piece. If your commitments are irreversible, however, and the article has to appear, then the following sections will have to be changed as a minimum condition of its publication." In case anyone missed the element of threat, he added "the Hahn may well cook our goose."[20] The CIA's Manshel helped pay the American Committee's bills from Paris when it was approved for monthly subsidies.[21] Later he founded the neoconservative mouthpiece *The Public Interest*, as well as *Foreign Policy* magazine. But in 1958 he was a Deputy Secretary overseeing the Congress for the CIA.[22]

As it turned out, there was no apparent pushback. The "veto" from the CCF and its in-house CIA operatives was not challenged. For its "hysterical" style of abuse and its "irresponsible" attack on US policy, another *Encounter* piece was killed.

· · ·

Defending his role in the episode, one agent sought to draw a clear line between what "they" do directly and what "we" do indirectly. "This was all about efforts to create vehicles which by definition were articulators of Western values, of free and open debate. We didn't tell them what to do, that would've been inconsistent with the American tradition." He continued in euphemism, "This doesn't mean there weren't themes we wanted to see discussed, but we didn't tell them what to do. . . . We did not feed the line to anyone."[23]

Future CIA director William Colby agreed, recalling, "There was not [an] imposition of control from the CIA. We were supporting but not bossing, not telling what to do. You might sit down and as good friends you could argue about whether this particular line would make sense of that, but there was no sense of, This is it, bang! It comes from Washington. . . . That goes for Moscow but it didn't go for Washington."[24]

But the evidence contradicts Colby and Williams, along with several other examples of more subtle censorship. Apparently, Josselson was sensitive to Macdonald's rebelliousness from the time Macdonald was being considered as an in-house and then a roving editor at *Encounter* from 1956 to 1957. When Spender sought to commission a piece by Macdonald on the European coal and steel community, Josselson advised Spender to think the matter over, warning of the "danger of [Macdonald] coming up with a completely destructive piece"[25]—ending the idea. When Macdonald wrote up a recap of the CCF's Milan conference of 1955, his truthful emphasis on the luxury digs and the failed communication between Westerners and their Asian counterparts likewise got swift pushback in the form of more "responsible" rewrites from the CCF brass.[26] But these are only those interventions that are on record. "The pertinent question about *Encounter*'s independence," Peter Steinfels has written, "was not whether there were instructions cabled to the editors from Washington, but who chose the editors in the first place, and who established the clear bounds of 'responsible' opinion within which differences were uninhibitedly explored."[27] One former roving correspondent in Latin America recalled constant pressure, tantamount to censorship and control, coming from Josselson.[28]

· · ·

Eventually, Macdonald was able to publish "America! America!" in England's magazine *Twentieth Century*, yet another member magazine of the CCF "clearinghouse." Its editor stipulated that he would not have published Macdonald's "spirited and witty comment on American life were not Mr. Macdonald himself a good American." Macdonald defended himself against this charge, writing a letter to the editor replacing "good" American with "critical American." Meanwhile, when finally published in the United States in September, his preamble in *Dissent* recalled that the infamous piece had been accepted, rejected, re-accepted, and definitively rejected at *Encounter*. This was not unlike the roller coaster of rejection that Pasternak had faced. He cited the magazine's "front-office Metternichs" of "the Congress for Cultural Freedom in Paris, which publishes the magazine with funds supplied by several American foundations."[29]

He continued, "The people in Paris felt the [essay] was exaggerated, one-sided, unfounded, and in bad taste, and they feared it might cause American foundations to cut off supplies." Macdonald believed that "readers have a right to know when a magazine makes an editorial decision for extraneous reasons. . ." Macdonald then hedged. "But I must also state that (a) the Paris office is not ordinarily consulted about manuscripts (mine apparently was shown to one of the Paris boys merely as a matter of interest—the editor thought he'd enjoy it!) and also that such intervention is extremely rare. I can recall no such pressure from Paris while I was there."[30] Even if the famous gadfly was gentle with his front-office Metternich friends, the incident rankled him in a way that would come back to bite those colleagues defending secret subsidies later on.

But perhaps the Western case most like the Pasternak was John Berger's. This little-known incident targeted a writer of historical fiction. Unlike Pasternak, though, Berger would not change a word, would make no apologies, and would therefore see his book dropped for more than seven years. If this was cultural freedom, it wasn't much to stand on.

. . .

Berger is today one of the most important living art critics, whose book on Picasso has been described in revelatory terms. His reputation as a major novelist was secured when he won the 1972 Man Booker Prize for his fourth novel, *G.* (He famously criticized the prize money's colonialist origins, and donated half the money to the Black Panthers.) But earlier in the culture wars, Berger's first novel caused such distress among the cultural freedom fighters that they promptly suppressed it.

The 1958 novel *A Painter of Our Time* features a narrator named "John," who discovers that his close friend, the painter-in-exile in London, János Lavin, has fled to his native Hungary. János returns there as the Hungarian uprising is gaining momentum in the fall of 1956. While searching the painter's studio for a book János had borrowed, John comes across a diary detailing the painter's intimations about art and politics. As noted earlier, Hungary's uprising was a pivotal moment for Cold Warriors of all stripes. While János's journal entries make up the book's heart, "John's" interpretations clarify them between entries. János not only speaks in beautiful passages, voicing Berger's insights on painting and creativity, but cogently describes events surrounding Hungary's position in the Eastern bloc in the middle 1950s, and the place of the artist amidst turmoil. Many of János's meditations betray regrets over a friend in Budapest who was disappeared by the state. As John comes to the end of János's diary, he imagines his friend heading into the political maelstrom, and massacre, that was about to take place. He muses fatefully: "I myself would like to believe that János, if he is still alive, supports Kádár."[31] János Kádár, to the Americans, was persona non grata for siding with the Soviets in crushing the Hungarian Revolution, and this sentence placed the book beyond the pale.

Encounter editor Stephen Spender, writing in *The Observer*, called Berger an "advocate of judicial murder," and compared the book to something the Nazi propagandist (and novelist) Joseph Goebbels could have written. This was accompanied by several attacks in *Encounter*. The most prominent was Hungarian Paul Ignotus, a frequent contributor who renamed the book *A Fiddler of Our Time*,[32] a reference to Berger's assertion that emergency humanitarian work must take precedence over art.[33] *A Painter of Our Time* had been published in England by Secker & Warburg, the publishing house that collaborated with British intelligence and the CIA to print *Encounter*. The two publishers whose names crowned the brand were publishing giants known for books by Orwell.

Given the public criticism of the book, Secker & Warburg "withdrew the book," according to Berger. "The book was already a little distributed, but very little. And they refused to distribute it anymore. So then it was not published or available until it was published as a paperback."[34] A Penguin edition appeared in 1965, seven years after the book's 1958 debut. This represented a lapse long enough to mark a new era in Cold War debate tactics, nearly arriving at the official beginning of cultural and geostrategic détente. The suppression, which featured *Encounter* and Spender once again playing central roles, didn't bode well for cultural freedom. But it made Berger tough. "I was a writer in opposition," he said by phone from France, "and in those days if you were consciously a writer in opposition you didn't expect to be well treated."[35]

After the line about Kádár, Berger added a better summary of the spirit of the book, a spirit that was being lost on these hard-line and crass culture warriors, "Judge people as you have known them. Do not jump to conclusions."[36]

· · ·

Of course it wasn't just magazines, books, and print media that were controlled by the front-office Metternichs. In the mid-1950s, the Pentagon, the Navy, the National Security Council, and the Operations Coordinating Board coined a slogan to encapsulate the perfect Hollywood film: "militant liberty." Author Hugh Wilford defined it as "a multi-agency propaganda campaign devised in 1954 with the aim of American-style democratic values in foreign cultures, especially in such new theaters of the Cold War as Central America, the Middle East, and Southeast Asia." When it came specifically to films, the goal was "to insert in their scripts and in their action the right ideas with the proper subtlety."[37] Though seldom discussed from this period is how the crucial question of anticommunism would vastly overshadow the so-called "Negro question," a perennial source of American shame and embarrassment.

The slogan "militant liberty" was envisioned to "explain the true conditions existing under Communism in simple terms and to explain the principles upon which the Free World way of life [sic] is based." It should also use cinema "to awaken free people to an understanding of the magnitude of the danger confronting the Free World; and to generate a motivation to combat this threat." In late 1955, the Joint Chiefs of Staff hosted a secret gathering to discuss how it could slip the concept of militant liberty into movies, also calling meetings at director John Ford's office at MGM Studios. Here they test-ran the concept of militant liberty on a focus group comprised of several Hollywood elites.[38]

The initial presentation roused actor John Wayne so much that he signed on immediately. He invited a group of militant liberty shills to his Encino home for dinner and a screening of *They Were Expendable* and *The Quiet Man*. The films were "studied," wrote one attendee, ". . . for the manner in which favorable slants for the Navy and free-world cultural patterns had been introduced in the two films."[39] Director John Ford was gung ho. He asked for copies of the propaganda booklet describing the term for use in explaining it to his staff and writers. He even asked for a consultant from the Joint Chiefs to help insert the concept into his movie *The Wings of Eagles*, then under production in Pensacola.[40]

Another who signed up was Cornelius Vanderbilt Whitney, heir to the Whitney fortune. Whitney had produced *Gone with the Wind* in the late 1930s and was linked to the CIA through his cousin, Tracy Barnes. He allowed his family trust to be used, like Fleischmann's Farfield Foundation, as a CIA conduit for funneling funds to secret recipients in and outside Hollywood. And he vowed to do an American Series,[41] to act as a cinematic, dramatic version of Yale's American Studies program, that sought to woo the world's wavering peoples.

Despite their early efforts to lead the way in cinematic propaganda, the Americans got to the Cannes Film Festival only after the Soviets. In response, the Motion Picture Service came to regulate American participation in international film festivals, and "it worked hard to exclude 'American motion picture producers and films which do not support American foreign policy.'"[42] Propaganda and censorship were increasingly married.

. . .

The CIA also got into producing films, and its first feature was an animated version of Orwell's *Animal Farm*. "The creatures outside looked from pig to man, and from man to pig, and from pig to man again; but already it was impossible to say which was which."[43] That's how Orwell's classic fable ends in the original, capitalists and Communists blurring and merging into one image. Not surprisingly, the CIA version would change this key outcome of the fable. CIA agent and Watergate crook E. Howard Hunt was an operative in the CIA's covert body, the Office of Policy Coordination, or OPC. He recalled in his 2007 memoir, *An American Spy*, how his OPC group championed the CIA's first animated film.[44] The CIA even rewarded Orwell's widow Sonia for the rights by promising her an introduction to her idol, Clark Gable.[45]

But why change the ending? Hunt wrote that his team's plan was to make a film that had been carefully "tweaked to heighten the anti-Communist message, and distribute it throughout the world in the hope that it would be seen by parents and children alike."[46] Anti-Communist though the book was, it upended the typical Cold War rationale that saw US and Western anticommunism as a reaction to Soviet atrocities. Here, in telling the story of Communism, Orwell had started with human (that is, Western) misbehavior that motivated the pigs in the first place. Hunt wasn't interested in that part of the story. In the CIA's film, instead of the pigs morphing into the humans, the other animals overthrow the pigs, whose rank and file and fellow travelers are all too drunk on power, and ale, to defend themselves.

Hunt conceals under bureaucratic jargon his rationale for the changed ending. "[T]he difficult production, made slower by the albatross weight of accountants, budgeters and administrators from within and outside OPC," he wrote, "would eventually take four years to complete. Additionally, *to compete with Disney fare*, jokes and a happy ending were introduced, somewhat dulling the message."[47] So according to the CIA's propagandists, the scrubbing was conflated with reach. A film uncomplicated by the truths of history would simply go further in the market, and compete with Disney. The book's evenhanded critique of both fascistic capitalism and totalitarian Communism would be abridged in the interest of commercial reach. Cultural freedom, in its broadest sense, now meant commercial success, and was aimed not at the intellectuals alone but at a mass audience. An anonymous CIA staffer assigned to the script justified the new ending. "It is reasonable to assume that if Orwell were to write the book today, it would be considerably different, and that the changes would tend to make it even more positively anti-Communist and possibly somewhat more favorable to the Western powers."[48] Orwell's message about dehumanizing and instrumentalizing people was itself instrumentalized and distorted.

One of the major studios even had a spy installed as a covert censor. Scholars have debated whether it was Carlton Alsop, who worked with Hunt, or Luigi G. Luraschi. The more likely mole was Luraschi, "a longtime Paramount executive and, in 1953, head of foreign and domestic censorship of the studio, whose job it was (as he put it himself) 'to iron out any political, religious or moral problems and get rid of the taboos that might keep the picture out of, say, France or India.'"[49] The use of a censor who was merely doing his job to localize movies for international audiences would further disguise the security state's drive to eliminate ideas it saw as unhelpful or irresponsible. The arrangement was properly "subtle," as the CIA argued it must be. In open daylight, Luraschi did his job on behalf of his movie house bosses for profits, taking out elements that might offend India's Hindus or France's Catholics and hinder commercial uptake. But in the shadows, he used this as a cover for his covert mission as booster for the American way, rolling back anti-Americanism, pointed critiques of US foreign policy, and honest depictions of entrenched domestic racism. Here was the perfect blurring of propaganda and art, subtly done.

The above would also establish, logically, that film professionals—who, as such, could vote at the Oscars—were inducted as stewards of America's image as defined by national security hawks, men who hoped to support rather than criticize US foreign policy objectives in the 1950s. (This tradition continued with *Zero Dark Thirty* and *Argo*, two CIA films that would vie for the Best Picture Oscar in 2013, to give just two recent examples.) Uncritical cinematic support for interventionist policies was privileged, while criticism of domestic inequalities, as we shall see, was censored. We were playing the game on the Soviets' terms. Power meant control of the intellectuals and their products—the veritable production of, if not souls, then careers and livelihoods.

Basic codes to censor films that depicted sexuality (even couples kissing for more than three seconds) or taboo views of race (e.g., depictions of intermarriage) had been established in the 1930s and were followed until the late 1950s. Hitchcock got around the kissing ban in *Notorious* by having Cary

Grant and Ingrid Bergman stop kissing every three seconds then resume.[50] Though "militant liberty" was obviously political, Sam Goldwyn was so fond of Moss Hart's anti-polemics line ("If you have a message, call Western Union!") that it was eventually attributed to Goldwyn. It was essentially a ban on progressive messaging in Hollywood, on behalf of a conservative code. This, too, merged with CIA censorship.

And alongside kissing, the Paramount movie mole's reports were equally hard on drunkenness, and this policing of lewdness was illustrative of anxieties over the American image as it went out into the world. In one summary, the agent wrote: "Have succeeded in removing American drunks, generally in prominent, if not principal, roles, from the following pictures. *Houdini*. Drunken American reporter. Cut entirely. This may need a retake to correct. *Legend of the Incas*. Removed all the heavy drinking from American lead from script. *Elephant Walk*. Keeping drunkenness to strict plot purposes only. *Leininger and the Ants*. All heavy drinking by American lead is being cut out of script."[51] Note the punitive retake prescribed in *Houdini*; if you violated accepted social norms over depictions of America, you might be forced to spend more time and money on retakes.

Films that attacked religion were also censored, as were, most unforgivably, scripts aiming to show the realities of American racism and American segregation. Negative portrayals of Southern life were also newly forbidden. In her book, *The Cultural Cold War*, Frances Stonor Saunders captures the noted Republican Eric Johnston, who was president of the Motion Picture Academy of America, quipping, "We'll have no more *Grapes of Wrath*, we'll have no more *Tobacco Roads*. We'll have no more films that show the seamy side of American life."[52]

. . .

The Paramount movie mole wrote his superiors about one film where "he had secured the agreement of several casting directors to plant well dressed negroes as a part of the American scene."[53] Despite this ban on depicting black poverty, the mole understood that a film set in the antebellum south would have to, alas, show "plantation negroes." But this, he wrote, was "being off-set, to a certain degree, by planting a dignified negro butler in one of the principal's homes." Of Jerry Lewis's *Caddy*, he wrote, "some negroes will be planted in the crowd scenes."[54] Depictions of Mexicans being exploited was also sensitive. The script adapted from Edna Ferber's novel *Giant* was "one to watch," since it "touches upon the following three problems: 1. Unflattering portrayal of the rich, uncouth, ruthless Americans (Texans). 2. Racial denigrations of Mexicans in Texas. 3. Implication wealth of Anglo-Texans built by exploiting Mexican labor."

Giant wound up as James Dean's last film. The movie script censor wrote about the film, "I'll see to it that it is killed each time someone tries to reactivate it at Paramount."[55] Killed at Paramount, the film was done instead at Warner Brothers. The way the thinking worked, anything that might serve the Soviets in cinematic depictions of the United States might have to be axed. Truth was not the measure. For instance, a film by Billy Wilder "about the illegitimate Japanese baby of a G.I. 'would prove a wonderful piece of propaganda . . . for the Commies.'" American G.I. rape was evidently not to be depicted. Films we take as American classics were even targeted, such as *High Noon*, starring Gary Cooper. The film had two disadvantages both "in its unsympathetic portrayal of American townsfolk and its featuring a Mexican prostitute character. 'I could write the French, Italian, [and] Belgian commie reviews for this picture right now,' the agent reflected gloomily, before going on to recount his efforts to sabotage the film's chances in the 1953 Academy of Motion Picture Arts and Sciences Awards."[56] Thus, as early as 1953, the CIA was preventing films from winning major Hollywood awards.

. . .

Actors who were liberal or progressive were black- and gray-listed. At the height of this age of anxiety, as Harold Humes had characterized the early Cold War, the atmosphere was so jittery and tense that even the prominent red-baiter and actor Ronald Reagan could be passed over for his youthful pursuit of countercultural ideas. Though Reagan appeared to give no names of suspected Communists before the House Un-American Activities Committee, behind closed doors in conversations with the FBI he famously named names and denounced former comrades. He further forced members of the Screen Actors Guild, of which Reagan was president, to give up names publicly or face expulsion from the Guild. Despite being labeled "friendly" by the forces of McCarthyism, Reagan was nevertheless denied a role in the FBI's production of its 1959 in-house propaganda film, *The FBI Story*. This was for having attended benefits where figures such as actor Paul Robeson had performed, which Reagan had been open about and wrote off to the benefit having been mischaracterized (he concealed that he'd been a chair). But his contrition was not enough for J. Edgar Hoover. Hoover's control over the least detail of *The FBI Story* ensured that Jimmy Stewart scored the lead and Larry Pennell landed the role Reagan wanted, so badly he was willing to halve his usual fee.[57]

The American Committee lent its support to conservative efforts to flush out and expose leftists so enthusiastically that it incensed its left flank. In-house historian Arthur Schlesinger thought the support off-base. In 1954, Schlesinger wrote his colleagues witheringly, "I suspect that AWARE [a magazine whose work the Committee had supported] would be delighted, for example, to drive Charlie Chaplin out of the United States and out of the movie business, but I hardly regard our Chaplin policy as a great American triumph. Nor, I hope, does this Committee . . . . Does any one [sic] seriously think that such Communists and fellow travelers as remain in the entertainment world are a menace to national security?"[58] The answer, evidently, was yes. Many of his colleagues seemed to think so. Quietly or loudly, they collaborated with a system that, in light of evidence of American backwardness and hypocrisy on questions of race and poverty, reflexively changed the subject to freedoms betrayed by our Communist enemies abroad.

• • •

Even if the CCF billed itself as a civil rights organization, its own members saw through this charade—not just on questions of race but on those of due process. Their archives at NYU subtly confess as much. In one letter to the American Committee, the ACLU's Roger Baldwin wrote the American Committee's Sol Stein, insisting "that anticommunism in itself is an inadequate and negative policy, which only partially contributes to cultural freedom."[59] Others complained about a singleminded obsession that inspired American Committee members to the detriment of a more rounded program of civil rights. In 1952, Columbia University's R.M. MacIver briefly joined, then resigned from, the American Committee, as it sought to partner with his American Academic Freedom Project. In his resignation letter, MacIver wrote, "The great problem of dealing with Communism in schools and colleges is one of method, not of goal. I do not feel that we should be committed to what seems to be the approach of the committee leadership to this problem."[60]

On the issue of racism, one sees in many American Committee officials' correspondence an approach that treats racism as little more than a publicity problem. When it came specifically to desegregation, and the long, slow push against American racism—a huge legitimate source of anti-American sentiment—the American Committee, like its Hollywood partners, could only offer to change the subject, or distort the truth. When Jean-Paul Sartre's independent leftist magazine, *Les Temps modernes*, published an article linking the FBI and the Ku Klux Klan, the American Committee responded by rushing a request to one of its members to write a series of rebuttals in *Preuves*. One was titled "Egalitarisme aux USA,"[61] by Ernest van den Haag. Van den Haag was a de facto segregationist who quibbled over the science used in the desegregation decision of *Brown v. Board of Education*. He quibbled further over the questions of *whether* segregation harmed black children and whether it might also harm them to increase contact with the majority white population who feared them. "One need not be a psychologist," he wrote, "to see that many, even of the previously indifferent or well-disposed, are likely to turn against the Negroes: Southern resentment of the imposition is likely to be shifted to those supposed to benefit from it. Is it less damaging for the Negro children to go to school together with resentful whites than separately?"[62] Van den Haag became a regular at *The National Review*, the pro-segregationist magazine also founded with taints of the CIA's DNA.

In 1956, author and American Committee official James T. Farrell wrote to the Fund for the Republic to get American theater producer Kermit Bloomgarden booted as a jury member for a freedom and civil liberties prize. Bloomgarden had produced Arthur Miller's *Death of a Salesman* and later *The Diary of Anne Frank*—stories arguably "about" freedom and civil liberties. But in seeking to create a political test as a qualification, Farrell wanted to reduce his career to one event, Bloomgarden's having attended the Waldorf conference in 1949. To do so, Farrell made a telling analogy. Stating his doubts over Bloomgarden's qualifications to judge such a contest, Farrell wrote to the prize administrators, "I presume that a necessary qualification is . . . disbelief in totalitarianism . . . . I must confess that it seems just as obvious to me as the assumption, say, that only a person who believes in the desirability of better race relations could qualify as a judge in a contest to determine what television show best furthers satisfactory race relations."[63]

Farrell's use of race relations as a yardstick for freedom fighting was ironic, pointing to this organizational blindspot. In the mid to late 1950s the American Committee was already on the verge of splitting up because its members couldn't agree on priorities. American Committee member Norman Jacobs, writing to the board during a debate about the group's direction, noted coldly: "Today the internal Communist threat is admittedly negligible. If it is felt that the negligible proportions of the danger deprive the Committee of its original raison d'etre, then it would seem the time has come for the Committee to dissolve. I myself do not accept the implications of this approach."[64] Jacobs called for the Committee's priorities to shift: "I should cite for example one important problem in which we have a vital role to play: desegregation. It strikes me as a startling fact of omission that the Committee has done virtually nothing in this field."[65]

Scour the letters of the American Committee's archives and you will find scant mention of the likes of Emmett Till or Rosa Parks. The above, in fact, is one of the few mentions of white American racism or black American race martyrs you will find. What does appear are those instances where a man of the vital center, like Ernest van den Haag, was tasked with refuting the notion of American racism as a legitimate concern for our European allies. For a group named after freedom, cultural or other, to ignore what had been done to terrorize, marginalize, keep down, exclude, rape, and murder black Americans—or collude in sophisticated language with such terror— was tantamount to criminal neglect at best, and worse in the case of van den Haag. Others, to be fair, no doubt did desegregation work in their other affiliations, but was it enough for the American Committee to do so little apart from where it affected the transatlantic alliance? Anticommunism had sucked the life from their moral imaginations. And groups like the American Committee helped change the subject from American racism to the latest atrocities committed by the Soviets. It could have championed both but instead it tended to cast every sustained protest, every campaign for racial inequality, at least in the the 1950s and much of the 1960s, as a Communist plot.

. . .

In 1957, the American Committee disbanded. Its members were bickering, its subversives lists were being funded but with little enthusiasm by the CIA's secret patronage conduits. It broke apart at a time when it could have helped speed up the slow, grinding, brutal march toward more inclusive freedom in the United States. They certainly were proud of the credibility they had amassed among conservatives; Irving Kristol bragged in 1953 how the Committee "can command a degree of credence among the conservative-minded that few other organizations can."[66]

The nonprofit that held the American Committee was soon resurrected for the sole purpose of continuing *Partisan Review* magazine. By now, it was hardly the energetic body it had been in the late 1940s and early 1950s, and its members were largely plugged into other channels for their pursuits of culture, politics, and cultural freedom. The Congress for Cultural Freedom, its American members, and the agents of the CIA with a stake in the American image, proved themselves more adept at blacklisting and censorship than at championing those at home who had lost their freedom (or their lives). Cultural freedom may have been in some formulations a defense of American democracy over Soviet tyranny. But in practice it was often an abstraction, a means of changing the subject, and one writer, James Baldwin, was getting sick of it.

6

JAMES BALDWIN'S PROTEST

[T]he only time that nonviolence has been admired is when Negroes practice it.

—James Baldwin[1]

Brand America's sales team thought little of fostering cultural freedom through routine acts of censorship. As in many of the films censored in Hollywood, the list of victims included writers who depicted American anti-religious sentiment, lewdness (sexual, debaucherous or other), Southern or inner city poverty, or the reality of America's virulent white racism. And for stitching together so many of these threads, Dwight Macdonald's "America! America!" was suppressed. Censorship aimed more pointedly at criticism of American foreign policy forced Emily Hahn's piece on China to be stifled by *Encounter* and John Berger's first novel to be "withdrawn" by *Encounter*'s publisher, Secker & Warburg. James Dean's final film was suppressed, at least at the first house that attempted to make it. *High Noon* was sabotaged, though obviously not fatally. Ronald Reagan was blocked from a role in a well-paying FBI propaganda film for his past politics, despite his repentance-through-snitching. These examples are only known because a handful of diligent researcher/writers, like Frances Stonor Saunders, pored through archives to find those rare letters where the CCF's operatives and overlords confessed. But recall, too, how easy it was for agents overseeing the CCF to walk to Allen Dulles's office and check in with the vaunted director—and it brings a new appreciation for how hard its collaborators had to shout, once the scandal of CIA sponsorship broke, to preserve the myth of the uncensoring, so-called "good CIA." Even if claims were true that the literary CIA only censored rarely, it was doing so in an environment that was anything but neutral—in which, for instance, the FBI was already spying on US citizens, such as civil rights activists. And it was doing so structurally, telling its editors that anything controversial should be sent to the CIA overseers; this meant that an untold number of pieces were preemptively chilled, censored by insinuation.

Beyond these few examples where agents did confess, American and allied censorship, therefore, was rife. This was because it was written into the mission statements, into the editorial process, into the founding procedures—into the whiteness—of the American institution. Author James Baldwin understood this. To judge by a pronounced self-conscious tic, Baldwin felt it most when writing for the CIA's official journals of opinion. One meandering report he wrote for *Encounter* prompted refreshers from his editor on what was acceptable to write in the harsh light of the Cold War. Against such admonishments, the pained pleas of his fellow African Americans would radicalize Baldwin and sharpen his critique. It would turn him entirely away from those Soviet and Eastern bloc crimes that the Americans obsessed over, and direct his writerly powers at something he couldn't say enough about, thanks to editorial protectionism: the ongoing barbarism against his fellow Americans, some of them children. "I have never been afraid of Russia, China or Cuba but I am terrified of this country," Baldwin would write.[2]

Baldwin began his rise as one of the Civil Rights era's most important literary spokesmen from obscurity—in late 1940s Paris, among expat American literary figures like author Richard Wright, whose hangout, coincidentally, was *The Paris Review*'s "local," the Tournon Café. In discussions with Humes, Baldwin had been an intellectual forbear to the magazine that became *The Paris Review*, unsung though he is. After writing straightforward book reviews for magazines that were increasingly but secretly entangled in the propaganda battle, Baldwin wrote his first polemical essay on Harriet Beecher Stowe. The essay included a jab aimed at his former mentor, the novelist Richard Wright, embedded as a coda. Baldwin saw

Wright's work as revelatory, and especially his novel *Native Son*, which taught Baldwin how to write in the social realist mode by incorporating the sweat and blood of real places and milieus. Having befriended Wright first in Brooklyn and then in Paris, Baldwin felt beholden to Wright, who agreed to read his work, but nevertheless saw while rereading Stowe that there was something sentimental in her novel. And it mirrored something he now saw in *Native Son*'s beleaguered protagonist, Bigger Thomas. *Uncle Tom's Cabin* is the story of the long-suffering slave, Uncle Tom, who serves as a spine around whom other characters' lives unfurl. *Native Son* is the story of Bigger Thomas, driven to kill a white Communist woman named Mary, the daughter of Bigger's wealthy white employer, so he won't get caught in her room after he has carried her home drunk.

If the white liberal fallacy about black Americans was featured in *Uncle Tom's Cabin*, namely that blacks were helpless without white "grace," Baldwin wrote, then Bigger Thomas, the murderer, was the inverse of this, depicted as violent in a world without that grace. In Stowe, black Americans relied on white goodness and in Wright their self-determination was available only through violence. In either the liberal self-loving or the conservative black-fearing modes, black characters were objects for good liberal whites to prove their goodness or they were repositories for white fears of barbarism, disorder, or terror. Bigger Thomas, Baldwin wrote, was Uncle Tom's offspring, "flesh of his flesh, so exactly opposite a portrait that, when the books are placed together, it seems that the contemporary Negro novelist and the dead New England woman are locked together in a deadly, timeless battle; the one uttering merciless exhortations, the other shouting curses."[3]

The article was published in Paris in *Zero*, before *The Paris Review* launched. *Zero* was one of what Plimpton dismissed as "countless magazines" "with a one name supposedly striking title" that usually "folded within a year or so." Plimpton was right about *Zero*'s short life, but this brevity came with a glorious legacy.[4] Likely, Baldwin's axe-grinding essay, titled "Everybody's Protest Novel," left *The Paris Review* set cold anyway. But what was effective in the famously repressive McCarthy era was how the essay masked its more subversive ideas under a mainstream anti-social realist (read, anti-Communist) title. The title brandishes an eyerolling disdain for "protest novels." But this camouflages its attack on badly done protest novels, ones using sentiment, in a way that transforms it into a protest essay. The only question that Stowe ought to have but failed to ask, Baldwin insists, was "what it was after all that moved her people to such deeds."[5]

That was the key question for anyone living after the period of slavery and for any novel dealing with slavery, Baldwin suggested.

Wright had been a Communist during a long period when many liberals and leftists, including Ronald Reagan himself, were flirting with left wing and socialist ideas. Even if Wright had moved into the anti-Communist camp during World War II, he remained a leftist and his novel remained an instigation to young black and protest writers to strive to depict the social conditions of black Americans, which was how Baldwin had read it initially. Now Baldwin lumped the book together with white sentiment that failed to ask key questions about the denial of black humanity and complexity.

After *Zero* ran Baldwin's essay in Paris, *Partisan Review* reprinted it in the United States.[6] The essay's question would drive Baldwin's writerly output for at least two decades, doing so against mounting opposition from the United States security state. In fact, he was getting so good at the essay—a form drawing on memoir, analysis, anecdotal observations, and voice—that opportunities to write for many magazines, including official CCF magazines like *Encounter*, were opening to him.

"Everybody's Protest Novel" was included in Baldwin's first non-fiction collection, *Notes of a Native Son*—a book so beloved that Maya Angelou once stood at a public reception to applaud its editor for his work on it.[7] But that editor, Sol Stein, was a master of subtly weaponizing books he edited against America's critics. He had launched a full-size, intellectual, polemical paperback line at Beacon Press. Paperbacks were more affordable for general readers but until then they were pocket-sized. In the company of cultural Cold War figures such as George Orwell, Sidney Hook, Arthur Koestler, and Bertram Wolfe, all avowedly anti-Communist writers, Stein's inclusion of Baldwin was curious. (Beacon Press even had Felix Morrow, future publisher of *Doctor Zhivago*, in its sales and publicity department.)[8] But Baldwin's early anti-Communist—or anti-anti-American—stance is often forgotten due to his later radicalism. How he fit into the series comes into sharp focus after you read his essays in order and pair them with marketing and display copy drafts. In Stein's memoir about his work with Baldwin, he includes jacket copy he composed for Baldwin's approval. One of the critiques Europeans leveled against Americans, straining the transatlantic alliance, was over American racism. But *Notes of a Native Son* ends with an example of extreme racial ignorance that Baldwin faced in a Swiss village. Thus, the jacket copy: "Baldwin can make mistakes, but he cannot lie," Stein begins.

His book will therefore earn the hatred of many Negroes and of those white people who are professional champions of Negroes. However, his experience of America will be a wet rag flung across the face of Europe's intellectuals; his experience of Europe will trouble Americans who think that for the dispossessed black man Paris or Switzerland can be a possible home.[9]

Does Stein call these whites allies in the civil rights struggle? Anti-racists? No—"professional champions of Negroes" tips Stein's hand. And the "wet rag" is a flourish around that Swiss village, reminding Europeans that they, too, bear a responsibility for racism. But Stein was only warming up.

When Baldwin covered the Paris Congress of Black Writers and Artists for *Encounter* and *Preuves* in the fall of 1956,[10] the CIA and State Department were already nervous about the conference, as they themselves did not organize it. It was organized by the quarterly *Présence Africaine*, founded by Alioune Diop, a Senegalese philosopher, and associated with African and European leftists like Jean-Paul Sartre. Around the world nationalists in the former European colonies were still recovering from colonialism, throwing off their occupying governments and these movements were joining in solidarity with African Americans engaged in the civil rights struggle. While movements in Africa particularly converged around Black Nationalism and black empowerment, the broader Negritude movement linked adherents not just to political but also artistic empowerment. Even worse, African American leftists like Paul Robeson and W.E.B. Du Bois had been invited by organizers and were widely viewed as Communists by American officialdom. Their presence suggested the conference might not privilege "the responsibility of editors"—or other pro-Western, pro-American organizing principles—as much as the CIA would have liked.

With such organizers and speakers on the roster as Negritude founder Aimé Césaire, Senegal's Léopold Senghor and Alioune Diop, "anti-Americanism"—by way of anti-racism, anti-colonialism, and anti-interventionism—would surely top the conference's agenda. To offset this, the Americans would have to act decisively. In addition to the conference being stacked with a "pro-American" black delegation, which conferred with the now reliably anti-Communist Wright, Du Bois was banned from attending. This was courtesy of the State Department, who denied issuing his passport. This mistake (tantamount to censorship) forced Baldwin's hand. He wrote of the Congress's opening moments, during which Du Bois's letter was read to delegates.

"Of the messages from well-wishers . . . the one which caused the greatest stir came from America's W. E. B. Du Bois," Baldwin wrote. Then he quoted Du Bois, "I am not present at your meeting . . . because the US government will not give me a passport." Baldwin then gave *Encounter*'s readers the upshot.

> The reading was interrupted at this point by great waves of laughter, by no means good-natured, and by a roar of applause, which, as it clearly could not have been intended for the State Department, was intended to express admiration for Du Bois' plain speaking. "Any American Negro travelling abroad today must either not care about Negroes or say what the State Department wishes him to say." This, of course, drew more applause. It also very neatly destroyed whatever effectiveness the five-man American delegation then sitting in the hall might have hoped to have. It was less Du Bois' communication which did this than the incontestable fact that he had not been allowed to leave his country.[11]

In case Baldwin seemed to be laughing at the United States, his caution led him, perhaps unconvincingly, to mock Diop's speech. It was an indictment of Western chauvinism and, by way of an attack on imperialism, an attack of sorts on the United States. But Baldwin deftly distanced himself from the sentiments by suggesting that his fellow attendees wanted the speech even more bitter or demagogical. Changing tacks yet again, though, Baldwin described a palpable sense of the crowd being caught on the battleground between the United States and the Soviet Union during a contest for world domination.[12] Was Baldwin using these meanderings—from mocking American hypocrisy to mocking Third World indignation to flat-out nonalignment—to mask his hostility toward American assumptions? Or was he simply trying to make up his mind? One can almost hear Baldwin toying with his reader, dutifully attacking America's attackers, then miming their more cogent critiques, then denouncing both. It reads as a debriefing for the State Department by a hostile collaborator. When Stein read the piece, he was livid. As agitprop for the American way, this wouldn't do. But even as acceptable discourse, it failed.

Stein had helped recruit his old friend onto the American Committee, briefly. Their connection went all the way back to high school, where they worked on the school's literary magazine, *The Magpie*, together with photographer Richard Avedon. Stein came to know that the CIA was paying his salary, as he admitted in an unpublished piece for *The New York Times*, during the period that he worked with Baldwin.[13] And reading his writer in *Encounter*, Stein helpfully reduced Baldwin's miscues, as a favor between old chums, to a lesson on "accuracy."

"'Princes and Powers' [is] . . . not par," Stein wrote, "especially the long beginning."

> It reads too much like a working paper for a piece rather than the piece itself . . . . The writing is not as uniformly good as I've come to expect of you. Neither is the thinking. Russia and America are not battling for the domination of the world. That's an inaccuracy and all I am quarreling with here is inaccuracy.[14]

This was a common sticking point for Cold Warriors in the United States. One name for this objection was "moral equivalency." It was to be understood at all times that the United States was reacting *against* the USSR, which was evil. To put them on the same plane was a category mistake. They were *not* equivalent. Another name for this mistake was nonalignment, the mistake of seeing both sides' sins or seeing both sides in reaction to the other. As in the Hahn and Macdonald episodes, aesthetics and ideology blur together in Stein's dissection of Baldwin's report on the Congress of Black Writers and Artists. Meandering, thinking aloud on the page, as Baldwin had done, was aesthetically as well as ideologically verboten. But what Stein wrote next was less subtle than his lesson on moral equivalency.

"As for Du Bois," Stein continued, "when you have a teenager with an eight year old mentality who likes to go down to a certain neighborhood every Saturday night and almost always comes back either cut up or with a case of VD,"

> if you're the parent you sometimes reach the point where you don't let him out anymore. It's nice to be able to say, "To hell with it. If he wants to go, let him." How can you say it though when everyone identifies him as a member of your family rather than as a crazy kid. That's America's problem with Du Bois. You look at it much too much in terms of black and white, and I thought you didn't particularly care for those colors.[15]

"America's problem with Du Bois"? If you were looking for a definition of paternalism, with a racist tint, reread the above. Can you imagine Stein talking about Jean-Paul Sartre's left wing politics by referring to him as someone liable to catch VD if you let him out of the house? And in the metaphor, what does catching VD refer to, Du Bois stating his opinion? Freedom of speech? Freedom to disagree with the administration granting the passport? Stein doubled down on his campaigns to publish Baldwin, presumably casting him as a "Negro of the Vital Center," as the last line above suggests this was how he imagined Baldwin. But he had to throw some sharp elbows such as these metaphor-filled notes to keep him in line.

During this exchange about Du Bois and the Paris Congress, Stein was also discussing a second project with Baldwin, an essay titled "Letter to My Younger Brother." The new collaboration elicited from Stein another comment that demonstrated that his efforts to keep Baldwin in line and to publish him had propagandistic and censorship-like components to it. The essay was intended for a new series for the *Mid-Century Club* (a magazine built around a book discussion group). But Baldwin was blocked on the essay, as a result of his confused feelings toward Africans he met at these conferences. Writing from Corsica, Baldwin explained: "'Letter to My Younger Brother' has been suffering from my ignorance concerning Africans . . . [and] from a certain condescension . . . toward Africans." Baldwin continued,

> [This condescension] can't be defended, and I'll probably never entirely overcome it. It was a shock. . . . It mirrors my confusion, certainly, but it also mirrors theirs. . . . I hope to have [the new essay] finally written when I come home—I'm more convinced of its importance. . .[16]

This was Baldwin's declaration of ambivalence, and Stein may have read it as another delay on the book. But Stein was keen for more work from Baldwin. Between letters scolding Baldwin for delays in "Letter to my Younger Brother," Stein promised "that the government is very interested in quantity purchases of the volume."[17] Much is clarified regarding the nature of their collaboration, and the ideological forces channeling the winds blowing at Baldwin's back with this reference (probably to the USIS). Whether for the American Committee, Beacon Press, or the *Mid-Century Club*, the books Stein edited and packaged were doing double duty as American propaganda. Two years earlier, while Stein was considering contracting the paperback for Bertram Wolfe's book *Three Who Made a Revolution*, he first wrote to the USIS to ask if they might agree to buy it for the government in "quantity . . . for distribution abroad."[18] He wanted to secure this agreement before he committed himself to publishing it. Already in 1954, then, Stein knew what he was doing: he was using authors to fight the Cold War, and using a government propaganda agency to subsidize his authors.

Baldwin himself was aware that an official taint came with some of his writerly projects, such as the ample grant money he received during this period from Ford and other foundations. About such grants he wrote later, "I'd have to be a fool to think they were subsidizing me—they were not doing *that*; they were proving to themselves how liberal they were."[19] His many elite patrons would prompt Harlem Renaissance poet Langston Hughes to write Baldwin to settle an old score by alluding to these tricky ties. "I fear you are becoming a NEGRO writer, and a propaganda one, at that!"[20]

But by 1960, in addition to official sources as his patrons, unofficial magazines were also censoring Baldwin along the lines of the nitpicky morality rampant in Hollywood and other national media. When *Partisan Review* excerpted Baldwin's second novel, the best-selling *Another Country*, the magazine's powerful lawyer, William Fitelson, refused to print Baldwin's cusswords. The magazine could be prosecuted, Fitelson had warned Baldwin, adding that *Partisan Review*'s printer refused to print "fuck," "motherfucker," "cocksucker," and "blow job." Baldwin shot back witheringly that he was gratified to have coined this new pair of dirty words: blow and job. He never wrote for *Partisan Review* again.[21]

. . .

One day in the spring a few years later, Harold "Doc" Humes, co-founder of *The Paris Review*, found himself sitting on a magazine with Baldwin's face on the cover. After Baldwin's second novel, *Another Country*, was the second-best-selling book of 1962 (after *Lord of the Flies*), Baldwin's star had risen so high that he was now on the cover of *Time*. As part of the same series on race and civil rights, Abraham Lincoln had graced the cover the week prior, linking the two in the editors' presentation of civil rights. Early 1963 was a pivotal time. Kennedy had yet to be shot, a tragedy that would especially trouble Humes and the world come November. But racial strife was already destroying the country, and a particular incident of violence against an African American boy was circling in Humes's head. Between the initial incident as reported in *The New York Times*, Baldwin's magazine cover, and their old friendship, Humes turned to his old friend Baldwin for counsel.

"It's hard to write you. Indeed, it's hard even to know why I feel so compelled to write you, except to tell you that I've been crippled with depression for the last four days—yesterday morning was the worst, after I saw that photograph in the *Times* of that kid being kicked in the face," Humes began. He called the white-on-black violence prevalent in the news that week "unalloyed insanity," and threatened violence against the white perpetrator, adding,

> It drove me to the wall just thinking about it, and I may as well record the fact that in the full impotence of brokenhearted rage I finally cracked completely and wept for a damned hour. You must know that kind of killing depression. They say depression is the failure of self-esteem and I must confess that my self-esteem failed me completely when I realized that I was too cowardly to take a goddamned gun and go down and shoot that motherfucker. . . . I finally simply sat on the windowsill and looked into the streets and wept . . . tears of impotence and lost innocence and rage. And when I got up I realized that I'd been sitting on your head to boot— *Time Magazine*, that is—and even that gave me a rap of guilt.[22]

Indeed, Baldwin was all too familiar with the sort of crippling depression his old friend Humes was writing about. With racial tension finally starting to be noticed by the white mainstream media—which would culminate in August with the March on Washington and Martin Luther King's powerful "Dream" speech—Baldwin had appeared on the cover of *Time* on May 17, 1963.[23] A week later, he appeared in a nine-page photo spread in *Life*. Though it came against his friend Stein's warnings, Baldwin increasingly accepted his role in deciphering, deconstructing—and denouncing—America's race convulsions. Baldwin refused to be color-blind. Color, irrational bias against one and for another, had created a brutal system of real victims: victims and perpetrators; privilege and violence and marginalization.

During a Hamlet-like period of doubt about this role, Baldwin had indeed had a depressive breakdown. News about violence against Americans of color had typically been minimized in the period leading to this explosion as the "Negro problem" rather than being framed as what it was: irrational white hatred, a *white* problem. As Baldwin's biographer James Campbell has captured, Baldwin saw it epitomized in images of tragic black victims, often young, usually in the South, like Elizabeth Eckford in Little Rock.

When nine children showed up for their first day of classes at Central High, a formerly segregated high school in Little Rock, the National Guard, called by the governor, turned them away, supposedly for their protection. This happened again the next day, except a crowd had come and "thousands

of white protesters swarmed around the building, carrying anti-black plac-
ards and chanting slogans.

> When one of the black girls, Elizabeth Eckford, became sepa-
> rated from her group and tried to approach the military barricade
> for safety, she found a bayonet raised in front of her face and a
> mob at her back yelling, "Lynch her! Drag her over to the tree! No
> nigger bitch is going to get into our school!" Elizabeth Eckford later
> recalled that when she met the eyes of an elderly white woman,
> searching for a look or a word of assistance, "she spat on me."[24]

Clashes like these lured Baldwin back to America after nine years in Paris.
But these incidents were not restricted to the South. When he first returned
in 1952 to sign the contract for his first novel, *Go Tell It on the Mountain*,
with Knopf, he tried to stay for as short a time as possible. He sailed west
for America after a period of writing in a small Swiss village, where—as
depicted in the last essay of *Notes of a Native Son*—the villagers had never
seen a black man; they touched his hair and tried to see if his pigment would
rub off on them.[25]

The Americans he knew in Paris had taken him to a poker game at Peter
Matthiessen's house, where Baldwin, who was gay, had endured an hour's
worth of bigoted statements about "gays" taking over jobs in the arts. Finally
he pushed back, whereupon Matthiessen accused him of "coming on" like
he was straight.[26] Baldwin was unequal in Paris, so long as Americans like
these were there. Who among the expats could help him decipher America's
promise to persecuted Russians while all but ignoring injustices faced by
Emmett Till, the Chicago boy killed and dumped in the river while visiting
family in Mississippi? He couldn't get away from it. Racism was everywhere.
On a return visit to New York two years before, even there he had seen casual
racism, though the country focused usually on the Southern kind. It resulted
when he had planned to meet his mother and some writer friends for dinner
in a Greenwich Village restaurant. When his mother, Berdis, arrived first,
she was turned away for her skin color.

"That's alright, I don't mind," she said. "I understand."[27]

In the summer of 1954, Baldwin came home again; by accident, merely
by wandering the streets, he and a friend found themselves amidst a gang
who had stolen lamps from a New York bar and they were swept up in a
police raid. "They put him in a cell next to me," the friend recalled. "And
he just *screamed*. All night long. I said, Cool it, Jimmy, in the morning

someone'll come for us and get us . . . But Jimmy—'I'm a nigger, they picked me up because I'm black. . . .' And in the morning he was very indignant."[28]

He saw racism on both sides of the Atlantic but he kept going back to Paris to escape the American kind and to write fiction. But the newly integrated high school student in Little Rock, Elizabeth Eckford, had made it harder to maintain his balance between fiction and polemical essays. He kept seeing faces like Elizabeth's in the media, even in Paris, and "could not bear to sit in Paris, 'polishing my fingernails,' trying to explain Little Rock to the French . . . ." He ". . . realized what tremendous things were happening, and that I did have a role to play."[29]

The American South had become a battlefield, and he arrived for his first visit to this ancestral homeland to fight and report. While he left the reporting of "broken noses" to the mass media, his biographer recalls, he was interested in recording the "broken hearts." For example, when an old Southern man in Atlanta brought Baldwin to experience his first segregated bus, the old man "seemed to know . . . that what I was feeling, he had been feeling, at much higher pressure, all his life. But my eyes had never seen the hell his eyes had seen."[30]

Bearing witness was just part of this new role, which would include these reporting trips as well as self-imposed assignments to call out the racism of one of the country's greatest living novelists. When William Faulkner's liberal views on race faltered, Baldwin read the comments with dismay. He had always loved Faulkner's work and appreciated his nuanced, intimate, and lively depictions of black characters. Faulkner had given an interview in the anti-Communist outlet, *The Reporter*, and was asked about civil rights unrest. While the South erupted, Faulkner cautioned black activists to "go slow," suggesting that going fast would lead to riots. He warned further that he might not take the side Baldwin would, saying that "if it came to fighting I'd fight for Mississippi against the United States even if it meant going out onto the street and shooting Negroes. After all, I'm not going to shoot Mississippians." When challenged by the interviewer, who asked whether blacks weren't Mississippians too, Faulkner shot back, "No, I said Mississippians—in Mississippi the problem isn't racial."[31]

Here was the post-racial liberal proclaiming the 1950s version of "All Lives Matter" while only black lives were being snuffed out across the South by the forces of power. In his "Letter from a Birmingham Jail," Martin Luther King explained the urgency of civil rights in spite of the violent retributions and race riots that some cited as reasons to wait. King told these critics that even if protesters drew violence to themselves through passive resistance, to blame them for this violence would be no different than blaming Christ for the actions of Pontius Pilate and the Roman Empire. "Go Slow" was a defense of the status quo. In considering these questions, Baldwin was not just impatient with black Americans' unfreedom. After the Birmingham bombing, he also questioned the "weapon of love," as MLK had called passive resistance. Baldwin said on television that "the only time that nonviolence has been admired is when Negroes practice it."[32] This certainly implicated Faulkner, who doubled down on his earlier comments about Mississippi's problems not being racial, now speaking to an interviewer in *The Paris Review*.

"The people around my home who have caused all the interracial tension," he told *The Paris Review*'s Jean Stein, were "the Milams and the Bryants (in the Emmett Till murder) and the gangs of Negroes who grab a white woman and rape her in revenge, the Hitlers, Napoleons, Lenins . . ." This alleged prevalence of black retaliatory rape was a popular straw man. Faulkner added the warning that "if we in America have reached that point in our desperate culture when we must murder children, no matter for what reason or what color, we don't deserve to survive, and probably won't."[33]

Faulkner's equivocating was too much for Baldwin, who fired back in *Partisan Review*. "Where is the evidence of the struggle [Faulkner] has been carrying on there on behalf of the Negro?" Baldwin asked. "Why, if he and his enlightened confreres in the South have been boring from within to destroy segregation, do they react with such panic when the walls show signs of falling? Why—and how—does one move from the middle of the road where one was aiding Negroes in the street—to shoot them?"[34]

Though Faulkner later disavowed the "shooting Negroes" comments (and he had allegedly been drunk during the *Reporter* interview), Baldwin had shown he could chasten the country's most prominent Southern writer when he veered into racial apologetics typical of so many whites. And so Baldwin became what Peter Matthiessen dismissively called a "polemic" writer[35]—and a politically unreliable one at that. No wonder Humes sought to unburden his "white depression" on Baldwin. Even if many covert official sources had turned against Baldwin, with the FBI bugging his friends and surveilling him, for much of the country he had become the Civil Rights era's literary spokesman. For his part, Humes had written a pair of well received novels, one also dealing with race, and had engaged in a series of what Gay Talese called "tall deeds," such as sponsoring a prototype of a house for the poor made out of pressed newspapers and, in his own way, defending musicians—especially black musicians—against New York City's racist Cabaret Card Laws, for which he was thrown in jail. But he wanted to reach out to his old friend in solidarity.

"Jimmy, I know that I don't feel guilty because I'm white," Humes continued the confessional letter he'd started after sitting on Baldwin's head. "I feel guilty for the same reason I feel enraged—because I'm human."

> You'll laugh if I told you that more than once I thought of committing some outrageous symbolic act—I even thought of trying to get into the Muslims. After all, Malcolm X is on record as saying that one drop of black blood is enough to make a man black and save him from perdition. And for one lousy drop I'm sure I could count on you for the loan. . .[36]

Like Baldwin, Doc Humes had also fled his homeland more than a decade before. He described the "madness, or suicide" that he avoided by fleeing McCarthyite America and going into exile in Paris in the late 1940s, though now the impulse to commit "outrageous" acts was returning. The culture and its wars had followed them both. Indeed, the racial injustice he saw on all sides jarred his self-awareness: "You may think that I've stopped being serious," he wrote. "Well, yes and no."

> Writing you, the simple act itself, has lifted me out of my white depression, and I do feel like frolicking a little, like diving out a window maybe. Well, anyway, please don't lose courage, man. You seem to be put here to say a few things just right, and if it weren't for the fact of your existence the history of the world might be different. I don't mean to throw the weight on you, but . . . remember. . . . The idea of that kid kicking a white man in the foot with his head—it takes guts Jimmy. Don't you let us forget it.
>
> I really don't mean to be flip. I'm just hysterical. If there's anything insane you want done, just pick up the phone and call—I'm in the book . . .[37]

Humes's letter does show the high regard in which he held Baldwin, along-side the birth of the New Left. What Harold Bloom would later dub a "school of resentment," the New Left was the veritable school of American and world dissent that had come into its own, having fermented under its repression by the FBI, CIA, and others in covert ops, intelligence, and propaganda, who did everything they could to keep it marginalized.

Beyond the strictly cultural Cold War, Humes's concerns mirror those of officials during the Kennedy years who were finally starting to pay attention to race. It was a sentiment shared by Richard Wright before he died. Having helped the CIA create AMSAC, the American Société Africaine de Culture, a CCF for black American anti-Communists, Wright had come to realize—as Baldwin was to soon do as well—that officials were spying on him. They penetrated groups he was part of, using both the FBI and the CIA to keep tabs, manage, rein in, bribe, and publicize. The dual role that the CIA played by (likely) spying on and (definitely) funneling money to figures like Wright and Baldwin was positively schizophrenic, Wright himself calling it "the CIA's vacillating between secretly sponsoring and spying." It was enough to finish Wright on anticommunism as a movement: "My attitude to Communism has not altered but my position toward those who are fighting Communism has. I lift my hand to fight Communism and I find that the hand of the Western world is sticking knives into my back. The Western world must make up its mind as to whether it hates colored people more than it hates Communists or . . . Communists more than . . . colored people."[38] Apparently his protégé thought so, too.

Baldwin's response to the surveillance was, consciously or not, to forego his own privacy by making the private public in countless interviews. This, of course, was possible in tandem with his rising prominence. In October, 1963, the year his "voice broke," his biographer James Campbell offers up a typical day in the surveillance life of James Baldwin. He flew with his brother to Birmingham, Alabama, to take part in the protests there; his ride didn't show up at the airport, so he made a call, then went to the Gaston Hotel, where he called Robert Kennedy. When he went to Selma a few days later, the FBI followed him there, on some of these flights taking notes over the least detail of his travel routine secretly from a seat down the aisle.[39] To justify the illegal surveillance, the FBI called Baldwin a Communist (what else?) in internal memos—a laughable charge.

Was it in this light that Baldwin began to renounce his responsibility to the Cold War and instead denounce Americans as "the most unattractive people on earth"?[40]

· · ·

In 1963, Stokely Carmichael, a student at Howard University and a civil rights activist with the Nonviolent Action Group, was ready to testify before the government's Commission on Civil Rights. The problem was that Howard, a traditionally black college, was caught using segregated workers in its new construction projects. The fact was astonishing, and like his friend Baldwin, Carmichael seemed destined to raise the problem to the national level. Carmichael was a confident, inspiring speaker who had befriended veteran activist and March on Washington organizer Bayard Rustin during his high school years: he volunteered under Rustin as a labor organizer. Not yet twenty-two, his talents were already prodigious and his influence rising. With the segregated workers problem at Howard and his pending government testimony, it was a chance for Baldwin's young friend to get national attention and rock the foundations of segregation and white racism nestled cozily in the nation's capital.

President John F. Kennedy understood the stakes the same year when, roughly two months before the March on Washington, he made a speech prompted by heightening violence in places like Cambridge, Maryland. To motivate his power base and the country at large, Kennedy cited America's image overseas. Thanks to the work of activists like Baldwin and Carmichael, the administration had been lured that spring into a reluctant position as an ally to civil rights organizers who had protested Howard's use of segregated labor to build its new men's gymnasium.

"The combination of Carmichael's testimony," his biographer Peniel Joseph noted, plus the school newspaper's "outrage and threats of campus demonstrations and White House pickets caught the Kennedy administration's attention. Attorney General Robert Kennedy obliquely addressed this issue during a March speech on 'international understanding' at Howard. Kennedy identified civil rights as 'the greatest internal problem facing' the nation and lament[ed] the damaging global consequences of domestic racial unrest on America's worldwide reputation."[41]

Was civil rights finally getting its due, now that the internal threat of Communist infiltration—at least by Soviets—was coming to be recognized as overblown? Men and women had been fighting for centuries against structural racism that had crystallized most recently as the reaction to civil rights activism and the Supreme Court's decision to end segregation, and before that as Jim Crow, and peonage (or debt) slavery, and before that outright slavery. Civil rights activists during the Cold War could damage America's reputation with the people who actually mattered to the political elite: the hearts and minds of those to be won over in the very same Cold War, outside the United States. Perhaps calling the activists "Communists" or censoring their literary comrades wasn't the only way to address the matter. The result of Kennedy's visit was that the Labor Department was pressured into enforcing its ban on segregated labor, despite Kennedy's fears that he would lose support in the South. Baldwin was one of many influences on Carmichael's deepening recognition of the power of grassroots organizing to transform government when its heart and soul were elsewhere and when the loudest voices still said to "go slow."

When the nation's eyes turned from Howard to the segregated town of Cambridge, Maryland, the Kennedy administration followed. The town of 15,000, just two hours southeast of the capital—just twenty-five minutes to the Mason Dixon line—was one-third black. Yet it was a bastion of segregation well situated near the heart of the Mid-Atlantic American North. Overseeing the anti-segregation movement's next great push in this critical town, the local SNCC (or Student Nonviolent Coordinating Committee) affiliate was led by fellow Howard graduate Gloria Richardson who pushed for Robert Kennedy's Justice Department to broker a desegregation deal. Discussing the deal, Kennedy asked Richardson, "Do you know how to smile?"[42] Smarm aside, Kennedy's time among the activists moved him to tell SNCC chairman John Lewis that he had been transformed. After reading the SNCC affiliate's "in-depth reports explaining how racial discrimination and poverty impacted the city's African-American community in a way as powerful as Jim Crow," Kennedy confided in Lewis: "John," he said, pulling Lewis in closer to confer, "the people, the young people of SNCC, have educated me. You have changed me. Now I understand."[43]

.   .   .

On June 11, the president delivered his first nationally televised speech on civil rights. Kennedy drew the nation's attention to black Americans. Among the nations' twenty million African Americans were soldiers who had fought and risked their necks beside white fellow soldiers, he said. But they did so for a country where racism in all regions, not just in the South, had left them disadvantaged in education, life expectancy, employment, incarceration, and income. "Difficulties over segregation and discrimination exist, in every city, in every state of the union, producing in many cities a rising tide of discontent that threatens the public safety," the president said.[44] This urgency was a relief to King and the NAACP's Roy Wilkins, who had written to plead with the president to make civil rights a priority.

The next morning one of those black veterans of World War II whom Kennedy alluded to, Medgar Evers, was murdered in Faulkner's Mississippi. Evers was a field secretary with the NAACP. His activities included Biloxi "wade-ins" on segregated beaches, assisting activist James Meredith in enrolling black students at the segregated University of Mississippi, and investigating the murder of young Emmett Till. Evers was also James Baldwin's friend. Evers's killer was white supremacist Byron De La Beckwith, a member of the White Citizens' Council. Baldwin had tried to warn the president, through a testy meeting with his brother Robert, that the problem was more serious than the administration understood. But the attorney general had been too rigid toward Baldwin and his group's angry exhortations, deaf to the content of their warning thanks to the pitch of their voices.[45]

When Baldwin flew home from Paris for the August March on Washington, he thought he would speak on the Washington Mall. Though he was disappointed to be excluded, Baldwin nevertheless joined a TV panel on the day of the March. It was sponsored by the USIA,[46] the outfit Stein once promised would purchase Baldwin's next book in quantity. On the panel, Baldwin appeared alongside Harry Belafonte, Marlon Brando, Charlton Heston, and Sidney Poitier. (If the inclusion of white actors seems anachronistic, these were the white allies who helped draw attention to the problem, but whom Sol Stein wrote off as "professional champions of Negroes.") As far as television programming in the early 1960s goes, it was a revelatory discussion and it owed this to Kennedy's appointment of Edward R. Murrow to head the USIA.[47] But it was hardly a completely free forum, as Baldwin learned; alas, not even Murrow could keep Baldwin's comments in the show that finally aired. In the end, only the more moderate of Baldwin's comments made it onto the half-hour segment (and Murrow was fired, replaced with Carl Rowan, for even allowing the segment to air at all).[48] In a reminder of the strictures of cultural freedom, his most pointed statements—that the FBI was working against black activists and against civil rights—were scrubbed even from the transcript. Here was a writer whose insistence on style and human complexity over polemic had made him seem moderate and color-blind, but whose voice increasingly drew in the great injustices of American life behind it, especially as it pertained to black Americans. The CIA may not have dogged, surveilled, or threatened him as had the FBI— who had it on good authority that Baldwin might write a book exposing them. Yet neither was the CIA a champion of his vaunted cultural freedom, let alone his political freedom—though, to be fair, it *had* published him when he had written what was required.

Indeed, of just sixteen *Encounter* articles from the 1950s that even mention the word "segregation," many referred to class or another kind of segregation. Dwight Macdonald wrote one essay with the word and he uses the word to refer to the civil rights struggles in the South, to be sure. But he discusses this topic for merely two sentences then moves on to anticommunism. (This is not to take away from Macdonald's work elsewhere to honor and prop up the marginalized, including African Americans; it just shows the nature of the diversity that the *Encounter* apologist was defending.)

The most sustained examination of segregation, a book review by Scottish author and historian D.W. Brogan titled "America South," unpacks the challenges for American civil rights activism against stubborn intransigence by Southerners. But Brogan's imperial chauvinism slips through, as when discussing Northern whites demurring as black Southerners moved north to share their children's public schools:

> A "liberal" lawyer who knows that, if he sends his children (as he should) to his neighbourhood public school, they will be swamped by Negro children three or four years behind-hand in academic rating, barely housebroken, and with, as adolescents, a habit of violence that arouses natural alarm, may decide that he doesn't believe in desegregation as much as all that and send his children to a private school or simply move out to an all-white suburb.[49]

The white imperial writer demonstrates in one paragraph in *Encounter* all his race contortions (Brogan was even knighted for such pro-imperial insights). "As he should," of course, preemptively covers him for what will come next; lest you think otherwise, *Encounter* and its writers are sufficiently liberal and entirely urbane. Public schools are a good on both sides of the transatlantic alliance, no matter what we call them. "As he should" indeed. But then there are the two big slips. The phrase "barely housebroken" tips the journalist's hand. Here was all the well-intentioned paternalism in a phrase and in a paragraph of the anti-Communists' flagship intellectual magazine. "A habit of violence that arouses natural alarm" confirms that the racism is not the white northern Americans' alone, onto whom Brogan has been projecting it, but Brogan's—and *Encounter*'s.

Two cheers for anticommunism!

7

INTO INDIA

Such is the spirit that breathes . . . to make loud the . . . insistence that the poor have been placed among us for the primary purpose of affording the comfortable a chance to discover how virtuous they are.

—Murray Kempton[1]

Propaganda is not literature.

—George Saunders[2]

In 1958, Jayaprakash Narayan, a socialist turned Gandhian, took Wendy and Allan Scarfe across India by train. The two Australian tourists watched as Narayan and his wife were greeted by crowds, who hurled garlands and shouted, "Long live Jayaprakash!" Amazed at Narayan and his wife's reception, the Australian couple joined a celebration for a raja who had just given hundreds of acres of property to the area's landless poor. In the 1950s, there were two especially high-ranking taboos for anti-Communists, and either could trigger a CIA intervention. Private corporations had often served Western powers as proxies for the plunder of cheap resources and labor in the developing world. By World War I, these corporate and government holdings had climaxed with Western powers holding or controlling as much as 85 percent of the world's land-mass.[3] People's uprisings in these poorer nations in nationalist and anti-imperialist movements forced Europeans and Americans to relin-quish control over non-European spaces and populations. But while nationalist uprisings in India and around the world could hardly be stopped after World War II, history would prove that if these people dared take control of their resources, this purported act of war could trigger an invasion, one that might be spearheaded by the new agency, the CIA. When Iran nationalized the British oil conglomerate that became BP, the British enlisted the Americans in the summer of 1953 to overthrow Iran's elected president, replacing him with monarchy. The following year, Guatemala sought to distribute the United Fruit Company's unused lands to Guatemala's poor but the United States intervened, replacing democrats with dictatorship.

So what the Scarfes saw in India was an unusual way around the ban on land redistribution. Narayan was part of a movement called Bhoodan, by which rich landholding elite were petitioned to donate land voluntarily to landless Indians. In the world's most populous democracy, this redistri-bution could address the nation's legacy of inequality which, most recently, British occupation had foisted upon the Indians and ruthlessly maintained. What was unusual about the Bhoodan movement was that it was not only approved by anti-Communists but it was also co-led by a figure revered by the Congress for Cultural Freedom; the CCF had even put him on its stationery beside John Dewey, Bertrand Russell, and Reinhold Niebuhr. At the height of the movement, in fact, *Encounter* gave more space to Bhoodan, with its Gandhian and religious tint, and to its founder, Vinoba Bhave, than it gave to American desegregation or a long list of other important topics. In the middle and late 1950s, then, Narayan was a unique figure. Revered by the Congress for Cultural Freedom's anti-Communists, he was at the same time engaged in a form of land redistribution which was largely approved of. His early life also exposed the lie of what would later be called moderni-zation theory: namely, that contact with the West helped bolster democratic institutions in the non-Western world.

Jayaprakash Narayan was born on October 11, 1902, in a village near Patna in Bihar State. Throughout his primary and secondary schooling he paid fees; in this part of India there were no public schools under the

British. His childhood was marked by idyllic nights where his father might invite travelling musicians to play sitar and tabla in the upper courtyard on their riverside house. Yet his father's engineering work kept both parents away from home. And the house itself was prone to flooding. At age 9, Narayan was sent to Patna school, where he devoted himself to his studies and earned a scholarship to Patna College.

As a teenager and idealist, Narayan was inspired by the Bengali freedom fighters who sought India's independence, though at the time doing so through less-than-peaceful techniques. Under these activists' influence, Narayan sought to become Swadeshi, or self-sufficient, and boycotted British institutions when he could, as well as products and textiles—which were made from raw materials stolen from India and sold back to its people.

But his wife Prabhavati Devi—when he married in October 1920—went to work for Gandhi allowing Narayan to finish his studies. Prabhavati Devi's work with Gandhi and his wife Kasturba would keep Narayan close to the Gandhian ban on violence and even coercion. But times of war make for terrible cauldrons for democratic freedoms and India after World War I fell victim to the repressive Rowlatt Act. This was an attempt to preserve the official wartime censorship, along with preemptive and indefinite imprisonment of alleged conspirators against the British. Gandhi called the act, named for Sir Sidney Rowlatt and rubber stamped in March 1919, a form of collective punishment for the political crimes of the few, and responded with a general strike, or hartal, which crippled the Indian economy. After violence erupted, Gandhi called a halt to this campaign, as he frequently did when noncooperation turned violent; he asked those guilty of crimes to confess and announced a fast. But with fears of Hindus and Muslims joining together in the strikes, the government of Punjab seized Congress participants from both religious communities to send a message. When protests resumed, the British sent in Brigadier General Reginald Dyer. Between ten thousand and twenty thousand people descended on Amritsar's public garden for a religious festival that violated the ban on protests, and Dyer ordered his troops to fire on civilians without warning. "With 1,650 bullets he scored 379 dead and 1,137 wounded," recounted Narayan's biographers. With only 134 bullets missing a civilian on average, the British were economical with their hardware. To make it worse, Dyer "made no provision whatsoever for caring for the wounded."[4] Though a commission of inquiry condemned it, Britain's acting-governor applauded the British savagery.

These events filled the Congress Party's rolls and spurred new passions for independence. "In an inspired fervor thousands of students pulled out of schools, giving up their education and future career for achieving the greater, unselfish goal of national liberty."[5] Narayan too was swept away, and the once-enthused scholar walked out of classes. Initially he matriculated in a school set up for walkouts like him. But soon thereafter the Congress was outlawed, and Gandhi was arrested for his retaliatory non-cooperative response, which erupted into violence in which twenty-two policemen were killed. Not only was the most exciting event of Narayan's life apparently quashed, but the institution of higher learning set up for Indians, by Indians, was only able to offer two years of higher education on the donors' funds. Narayan the scholar and activist had come to a frustrating dead end. So he left for America.

But when Narayan returned to India nearly eight years later, in late November 1929, he was a man transformed. He had washed grapes and worked on a vineyard to pay for his studies at the University of California at Berkeley. When a friend had invited him to the University of Wisconsin, where he had earned a Bachelor's degree in sociology, he had absorbed left wing and radical ideas. At Ohio State University, Narayan's Master's thesis "was declared the best paper of the year."[6] His professors said that Narayan had been one of the university's best students ever to attend. One Professor Dumley had written that he bore "the germs of leadership" and "was aggressive in thought but not action" and had noted his high "ideals of human welfare."[7]

During that infamously roaring decade, he had seen American fits of manic spending and self-conscious escapism but alongside it all, he had witnessed how capitalism left its streets lined with castaways and rejects. This had moved him terribly. During a botched tonsil operation, which had left him convalescing for three months, he had gotten to experience this American poverty and inequality firsthand; his bill of $900 would amount to about $12,000 today. Against this backdrop his experience was an under-sung one. The Easterner, emissary from the developing world, had recoiled at US poverty rather than the other way around. He had returned, then, to his native India convinced that inequality "of wealth, property, rank, culture, and opportunity"[8] was the real enemy of the people and—armed with newfound Marxist-Leninist ideas—he had grown determined to end this inequality, which led him right back to the struggle with the British.

Narayan dreamed of opening a sociology department and working in academia. But Gandhi and Nehru pulled him into the Congress apparatus and soon he made himself indispensable, working on labor. Narayan

had been radicalized by the bloody events that had preceded his departure. But as a boy, he had been inspired by tales of Gandhi's great sat-
yagraha in South Africa, where the young lawyer had fought for the rights
of ethnic Indians. These stories "left imprints on [Narayan's] inner being."[9]
But Narayan had also read the socialist M.N. Roy, who had persuaded
Narayan that Gandhi "was against the social revolution and would at a
moment of crisis hasten to hold up the [British] system of exploitation
and inequality."[10] This ambivalence about the Mahatma would bond him
to Nehru.

Nehru, too, harbored left wing and socialist views. When they met
that December Nehru caught Narayan up on political events that had taken
place in his absence, including the resurrection of the Congress Party.
Though Nehru was a socialist of the Fabian variety, preferring a gradual
approach to revolution, they "were both highly educated, highly original
thinkers, saw Indian affairs from an international perspective, and had a
passion for the life of politics and for national independence. Each of them
was critical of Gandhi's economic theories and his technique of civil dis-
obedience and noncooperation, feeling that socialism was more likely to
lead to a better world."[11] A month after Narayan's return, Congress leaders
met at Lahore and declared themselves independent of Great Britain.
Though this was a largely ceremonial act, the emotion of the celebrations
inspired Narayan.

"It is the inalienable right of the Indian people to have freedom.
We hold it a crime against man and God to submit any longer,"[12] read
the declaration. When Lord Irwin, the Viceroy, refused the demands,
Gandhi announced a program of noncooperation that would start with
a march to the sea to make salt. Salt was one of the monopolies the
British had imposed on the Indians, and Gandhi would march two hundred and forty miles, which resulted in a trail of followers that stretched
two miles, in order to break the monopoly. Some feared the sixty-one-
year-old Mahatma would not survive the march. When he did, however,
and he and his fellow protesters heated the water ceremonially for salt,
it marked the beginning of another mass strike. Meanwhile, in the chaos
that ensued around the nation, mass arrests led to more mass protests
and so on, in a rapid spiral, until finally Lord Irwin sent in a battalion
to fire on protesters, but the soldiers refused. But with a media blackout
ordered, including a moratorium on any reporting about his government,
Lord Irwin ordered the military to retake by force the city of Peshawar,
which had been occupied by the so-called Frontier Gandhi, Khan Abdul

Gaffar Khan. Meanwhile, working out of Nehru's old house, Narayan appealed to Indian laborers to stick with the party. He appealed for the return of those who had left. He made international labor contacts. And his group, the Congress Labor Research Department, also managed to bring Indian labor in line with the International Labor Organization's conventions for the first time. When protests brought them scores of injured, Jayaprakash and Prabhavati tended to their bullet wounds. This was another moment that for the rest of his life would nurture Narayan's hatred for British rule, his biographers recall.

Emergency Powers legislation formalized Great Britain's absolute rule and again the Congress Party was banned. "Jayaprakash became an individual atom of a giant movement in which millions of people felt a bond of unity against an oppressor,"[13] wrote Allan and Wendy Scarfe. Negotiations between Gandhi and Lord Irwin incensed British leadership and prompted Lord Irwin's replacement as viceroy with an "anti-negotiator," Lord Willington, who "promulgated new ordinances reintroducing imprisonment without trial, confiscation of property and an Emergency Press Act silencing news of his rule."[14] He also worked to wedge apart the Hindus and Muslims by scheming with the figures who would form the Muslim League and agitate for a separate Muslim state in Pakistan. This group was financed by the Aga Khan. (The Aga Khan's money, incidentally—filtered through his son Sadruddin—helped to finance *The Paris Review*. It was at least in part wedge money to split the same factions the British feared in India: Muslims and Hindus.)

When a British delegation from Parliament came to study Lord Willington's repression, Gandhi and much of the Congress Party were in jail. Narayan had been engaged in printing the Congress's tracts and pamphlets illegally, the Indo-British counterpart to samizdat. But as he had managed to stay out of jail, he now evaded police to meet the Parliamentary delegation. He accompanied the delegates to sites of British atrocities and introduced them to activists around the country. The moment that the Parliamentary delegation left, Narayan was apprehended and sent to prison. There he encountered Minoo Masani and the milieu out of which he would put together the socialist wing of the Congress Party, which he named the Congress Socialist Party. He originally hoped to keep the new party within the Congress fold. But in 1935 the Government of India Act enfranchised thirty-four million Indian voters, a huge new constituency but only one tenth of India's population. Nehru and Gandhi wanted to participate, but Narayan was disgusted with this partial gift and split off. Narayan spent the 1930s and early 1940s in and out of jail, calling for socialist rebellion. His British jailers tortured him.[15] In 1948, after the joys of independence and the horrors of partition, he launched what became one of the most popular unions in India, putting him effectively in charge of a force of a million workers. His relationship with Nehru became increasingly fraught. When the Congress Party won the 1952 elections, Nehru invited Narayan to explore the prospect of socialists rejoining the Congress Party, but these negotiations petered out.

In the early and mid-1950s, Narayan went through a major shift in his thinking. Again disenchanted with the political process, he was moved to do a *jivandan*, which meant "to offer his own life to the service of [a] social movement."[16] His movement would be a middle way between Gandhian care for the poor and socialist land redistribution. In founder Vinoba Bhave's vision, the excess land, or Bhoodan, of rich landholders was donated—voluntarily—to the poor. This excess land gave the movement its name. Instead of asking for money for a nonprofit, in other words, these activists were asking alms in land, sometimes whole villages, redistributed from top to bottom. "Vinoba Bhave started going from village to village on foot and asking those who have land, to give part of it for the benefit of those who do not," Narayan once explained. The scheme's simplicity even to him sounded "nonsensical, foolish, but it seems to be working . . . . We are all human beings," Narayan continued,

> the landlord is a human being, the capitalist is a human being; there is something in all of us to which this man is appealing and there is good response—hundreds and thousands of acres of land have already been given to him. You know that I have dedicated my life to this new movement.[17]

Therefore Bhoodan Narayan explained,

> is an application on a general scale of Mahatma Gandhi's nonviolent technique of revolution. No heart or mind has been changed by law; no individual made virtuous by coercion. Gandhiji's technique of conversion was based on faith in the possibility of improving man.[18]

Narayan soon became second in command of this movement after Bhave himself. As such, Narayan occupied a unique space as the intellectual heir of both Gandhi and of Karl Marx. But in India, the CCF magazines would boost this version of land reform, with nearly a dozen articles in *Encounter* alone during the 1950s and early 1960s. Some of the articles in CCF magazines criticized the scheme. But many approved, though these same magazines would denounce land reform elsewhere, even where done without violence and with vast approval by the public and their elected officials. Never mind that the poor were getting land. What was it that allowed Bhoodan, a unique sort of land redistribution, to be at least debatable in India but inexcusable elsewhere? Was it that a friend of the Congress for Cultural Freedom earned it a pass?

. . .

Narayan shifted his focus around the same time as *Encounter's* launch in England, and the launch of *The Paris Review* in New York and Paris. Independent India's founders were among the leading practitioners of neutrality. This was because of Nehru's socialism and the British occupation confirming much of the socialist critique. But these views were balanced by strong cultural ties to the English-speaking world. As such, India's leaders refused to align solely with either the United States or USSR. Because of this, the CIA sought to penetrate India. It would do so by using the local affiliate of the Congress for Cultural Freedom as a foothold, and that affiliate would include Narayan and Masani among its members. India nevertheless vacillated from side to side, like a sail in changing winds. While US secretary of state John Foster Dulles saw neutrality as "immoral and shortsighted," Nehru sought "to avoid entanglement in power politics and not to join any group of powers as against any other group."[19]

No single event better prescinded the rise of the neutral Third World, later called the Non-Aligned Movement, than the Bandung conference in Indonesia, which began on April 18, 1955. It opened with a speech by the Indonesian president Sukarno, who implored the world's powers to forgo their addiction to intervention and replace it with a principle summed up by the phrase "live and let live!" In the United States, this attitude was traditionally called isolationism. The CIA later came to hate Sukarno so much that they planted fake news pieces about an alleged affair with a Russian stewardess and then shot a porn film, which they called *Happy Days*. Unable to find a decent lookalike, the Agency hired an actor to wear a latex Sukarno mask designed by the CIA's Technical Services Division and distributed the film throughout Southeast Asia.[20]

Such dirty tricks were part of what repelled the nonaligned movement from the United States and may have helped rally those non-aligned nations around China's Zhou En-lai, whose presence at the Bandung conference was significant (not least of all because the US tried to murder him en route). Nevertheless, when Nehru boomed out his neutralist creed, "I do not believe in the Communist or the anti-Communist approach!" Bandung delegates roared with approval. When Egypt's Nasser, also in attendance, declared that "the game of power politics in which small nations can be used as tools must be stopped!"[21] they cheered even more. But some Indians saw that neutralism could cut both ways. When Nehru was initially silent in the face of Soviet bloodletting during the Hungarian uprising of 1956, Narayan and the Indian branch of the CCF were shocked. Though Narayan had dedicated his life—lately—to quieter grassroots campaigns seemingly outside the political fray, he had not withdrawn completely from the ugly world of realpolitik, and this incident elicited a brief return from his focus on the Bhoodan movement. Narayan saw the Soviet move as comparable to the French–English occupation of Egypt, which Nehru had denounced resoundingly in support of Egypt and Nasser. As the Indian CCF's honorary president, Narayan issued a statement: "Russia has no right to be in Hungary. No one can question the right of the Hungarian or any other people, including the Indian people, to choose a Communist form of government, if they so desire." Narayan continued,

> That would be a domestic affair. But when a big power by armed intervention tries to impose in another country its own puppets in power, it no longer remains a domestic question but becomes an international issue of the highest importance.[22]

These statements ran with giant headlines in one of the many national Congress for Cultural Freedom newsletters, and American members delighting over the denunciation of Nehru and recapping the quotations in press releases may have missed that Narayan was privileging national sovereignty above all else, to denounce the Indian leader. Yet the phrase "when a big power by armed intervention" showed that he was speaking to the United States too. As the CCF's honorary president, Narayan still carried water for US anticommunism against Nehru's staunch neutrality. But this anticommunism was defended through a reapplication of the principles of sovereignty, a basic right of nations that the United States was more than a little guilty of breaching. Narayan became known as "Nehru's foremost critic."[23] But he vacillated between his commitments to the poor and his role as public gadfly, keeping in touch with political players and friends, including Nehru himself, whom he continued to write to throughout the 1950s and '60s.

These events, and the Cold War mission in India, were never far from the minds of *Encounter's* editors. "Irving Kristol, the first American coeditor of *Encounter*, suggests in his *Reflections of a Neoconservative* the less than spontaneous nature of that magazine's Indian coverage when he recalls 'gentle interventions' from Congress headquarters (in Paris) to attend to Asia, and particularly to India, the last hope in Asia for 'the free world,'" recalls scholar Margery Sabin.[24] The editors of *Encounter* knew that India was mission-critical and were told by headquarters. *The Paris Review*, on the other hand, almost entirely ignored India and the developing world in favor of the transatlantic cultural alliance. Even so, founding managing editor John Train lamented this absence of India in his editorial critiques to Plimpton and the rest. Train, in the late 1950s, had returned from a short leave and went back and forth between the New York and Paris offices, helping to make the two offices communicate more efficiently. He also supported the magazine financially with a series of ads during the period when *The Review* was working most closely with the Congress for Cultural Freedom. On the subject of India, Train was informed by a Western mastery of the sweeping generalization that informed the mission-critical understanding of India then. "This suddenly occurred to me in meditating on whether to send (issue #) 18 to some Indian writers and booksellers who were promised copies," wrote Train. "There is nothing quite like the PR flavor in Indian writing, and I do not know whether they would be interested or alarmed." He continued to Plimpton in late 1958,

> Indian writing has a lot of suffering but in a stable framework; indeed a framework that has changed little in the memory of the race. (The British were an episode, birds of passage compared to the Moguls, who themselves were simply absorbed.) For the 80 percent of the population who live on the land things have always been much the same; and Indian writers try to be very conscious of the life of the peasant. Almost all write rather awful social realist novels on this theme. While they are . . . generally looking to the west for guidance in many material fields what would they make of [some of the latest fiction in *The Paris Review*]?[25]

In particular, Train cited the most recent Philip Roth story, which would "upset them no end," he wrote. Train's sense of what India and its Asian neighbors needed would culminate in the early to mid-1980s with a plan to fund anti-Soviet propaganda through a refugee advocacy organization that Train founded after the Soviet invasion there.

By some measures, *Encounter* also did a ham-fisted job of covering India. While many magazines of the CCF were intended as the local CCF vehicle for that country alone, *Encounter* on the other hand was special. Remember that the "encounter" of the magazine's title was originally rendered as "East-West Review" and was therefore an "East-West encounter." But by focusing on the US special friendship with England, it gave short shrift to the subcontinent. For instance, there were zero articles devoted to world-renowned Indian film director Satyajit Ray during *Encounter's* run.[26]

To make up for these lapses, the CCF launched a new Indian magazine called *Quest* in August 1955. When the US Ambassador to India, John Kenneth Galbraith, saw the magazine after his appointment in 1961, he was unimpressed, suggesting that the magazine "broke new ground in ponderous, unfocused illiteracy."[27] Indian Communists called it "insidious" American propaganda.[28] But it nevertheless formed yet another invisible tie between Ambassador Galbraith, the intellectual HQ for the Cold War (as Nelson Aldrich called the Congress's Paris office) and magazines like *The Paris Review*, under the great umbrella that Aldrich dubbed the "Congressiste" magazines. *Quest* even ran ads for its sister publication, *Encounter*, promising Indians and Asians that "Time and again you will find that your own problems, the problems of the Far East, are illuminated by articles in *Encounter*."[29] It also ran ads in its first several issues for giant US oil conglomerates like Mobil and Standard Oil. The American Committee advertised *Quest's* birth and sought its funding by other CIA fronts, like Asia Foundation; James Farrell recorded its mission statement for the Foundation: "Considering moral neutrality in the face of totalitarian threat to be a betrayal of mankind, the Congress opposed 'thought control' wherever it appears, whether concealed or active."[30] And one of Quest's columnists, Dilip Chitre, corresponded with *The Paris Review* over editorial matters. The network was growing.[31]

. . .

Despite the United States' best efforts, Nehru clung to his neutrality like a bachelor to his freedom. In 1951, he refused to let the second international CCF convene in India's capital. He purportedly knew that the organization was an "American front."[32] However, given the growing strategic importance of the world's most populous democracy, the CCF planners would not, as it went, "quit India." They merely moved the conference from Delhi to Bombay (now Mumbai).

Alongside Narayan, Minoo Masani rounded out the Indian annex of the Congress for Cultural Freedom's executive committee, which built itself up around a roster of prominent socialists who would operate all over India and fight India's neutrality. A former mayor of Bombay, Masani was a three-time member of parliament, a democratic socialist who opposed monopolies and who went on to co-found the right-leaning Swatantra Party partly in opposition to the nationalization of banks. We've already seen how Masani had in the early 1950s been offered a special welcome at the American Committee's center for foreign visitors, and the American Committee pitched his trip to the United States for press coverage to the *New York Post*.[33] (The Welcome Center itself strengthened the American Committee's tie to the Asia Foundation.) Before Masani swung right, he, too, fought India's neutrality.

Masani and Narayan were joined in the Congress for Cultural Freedom's efforts in India by Nissim Ezekiel, a young Indo-Jewish writer who later achieved renown as a poet. Nirad Chaudhuri, another India CCF-linked writer, published the controversial book, *Autobiography of an Unknown Indian*, and was described by one scholar as "a gadfly" working in opposition to the "culture-wallahs" in the service of Nehru in New Delhi.[34]

As *Quest's* editor, Ezekiel would attempt to navigate India's contentious waters, emphasizing the common ground between the US agenda and the Indian; where that common ground faltered, he wasn't shy about saying so. In his first editorial for *Quest*, for example, he wrote that phrases "like 'cultural freedom,' along with 'peace' and 'social justice,' all belong to the rhetoric of a global conflict not designed to promote India's independent interests."[35] Ezekiel's magazine was taking money from the American side, suggesting a kind of Westward alignment. But at the same time it was all but disavowing this stance by renouncing the buzzwords of both the American and Soviet sides in his first editorial.

This and the conferences' on-the-spot encounters suggested that wounds between Eastern and Western partners were more fresh than either side might have liked. According to one analyst of the period: "In . . . accepting Western sponsorship, *Quest* was choosing the alliance that most supported a version of cultural freedom crucial to and within India, namely the freedom to criticize established authority within the state. Ezekiel . . . wanted to use *Quest* for a specifically Indian project of internal 'opposition to authority,' in accord with the position argued more recently by African critics . . . that after the struggle for anticolonial freedom, there needs to come a 'second phase' of internal debate within postcolonial nations themselves."[36]

Ezekiel instituted principles that would define *Quest* throughout its life: "Everything about it must have some relevance to India. It was to be written by Indians for Indians—for in those days, we still glamourised everything foreign, including writers."[37] Ezekiel's personality charmed many who worked with him long after *Quest*'s demise. A relentless mentor to younger poets and writers, he spent time in Chicago and recited to Saul Bellow the names of his own family members that he found in Bellow's novel *Herzog*.[38]

. . .

One of the first ways the Western funders controlled the content of *Quest*, however, was through editorial orders. *Quest*'s would-be independent intellectuals basking in cultural freedom on the page often took their marching orders directly or indirectly from CCF headquarters in Paris—for instance, when the CCF instructed editors of both *Encounter* and *Quest* to write up CCF conferences.

But this often meant a play-by-play recounting of Eastern resentment against the West or Western bias against the East—the very fraught East-West encounter. in other words. In 1959, it was David McCutchion, a British-born writer interested in India, who was tasked with capturing the Congress's conference in Calcutta. Writing in *Quest*, he grew embroiled less in the text of the many speeches and lectures in favor of the cross-cultural battles. Arthur Koestler, author of *Darkness at Noon*, opened the conference. Koestler had been tortured in one of Franco's prisons during the Spanish Civil War, and had witnessed Soviet repression from an intimate vantage. His illusions had been shattered time and again and yet he kept searching for a place that didn't exist, which after all was the very meaning of utopia. He was accustomed to setting the tone for Congress for Cultural Freedom conferences, even if his compelling rants were anathema to some in both the CIA brass in Washington DC as well as the Congress leadership in Paris. The latter had wanted him sidelined and a letter from the American Committee's James Burnham to the CIA had indeed secured his marginalized status.[39] Yet his sense of entitlement as a rock star of anticommunism was offended when his successor at the podium ignored everything Koestler had said in his opening statements. Koestler would not be setting the agenda and for this he was indignant. The Westerners were often scandalized that their gift horses could be looked in the mouth, or for what they saw as the air of abstraction among the Asians.[40] "The only break came when Koestler interrupted [his successors at the podium] with a 'petulant' demand for more concreteness from the Indian speakers. Briskly enumerating a list of arguable 'greats'—Baudelaire, de Sade, Nietzsche, Céline, Evelyn Waugh, Ezra Pound, Francoise Sagan, and a 'Japanese epic—he did not recall the name—based on a blood-feud code of honour,' Koestler demanded that the Indians be 'democratic' and cast votes on the morality of each. Yea or nay."

Only the Jesuit delegate, Father Fallon, played along, issuing a single yea vote for Baudelaire.[41] Koestler continued ranting. "There is no bringing these people down to earth!" The next day, "a Polish delegate by the name of Szimansky opposed virtually everything Koestler had said … [agreeing] only with Koestler's point about the deplorable haze of abstraction in Calcutta."[42] "Haze of abstraction" joins a long list of Western euphemisms by which to sideline the intellectual efforts of Asians by restricting them to vague, esoteric, or spiritual areas of expertise and little else. Edward Said has traced how Europeans have done this across centuries of studying the East.[43]

The Indians retaliated generously. Announcing a visit to India by the American writer James Farrell, chairman of the American Committee for Cultural Freedom, Ezekiel took to the pages of Quest to praise Farrell's commitment to liberty. But he snuck in a contrast between Farrell's "deliberately fiat and pedestrian style" and the rich "emotional and intellectual texture" of James Joyce in A Portrait of the Artist as a Young Man.[44] This unflattering comparison led Farrell to lambaste the Indian Committee members for their "aristocratic disdain of material things" and to slam them "for reckless anti-Americanism."[45] Nor was he too humble to remind them who was paying. "The American worker, rising at five and six A.M. daily to earn his bread and giving a few weeks of his labour in taxes is not going to react well and in good temper when he learns that some of his foreign friends refer to America as Uncle Shylock and Uncle Sucker.'"[46] But the statement was disingenuous; the arrangement shied away from daring to tell the American worker that his tax dollars funded such counter-productive debates.

One Indian intellectual—who happened to be the head of Fergusson College, alma mater of India's tenth and twelfth prime ministers—took issue with Farrell's veiled threat, pointing to what he saw as the causes of anti-Americanism: "the phenomenon of the US standing on the side of Totalitarian, Imperialistic, and Racist powers." Quick to note the "friendly ways and unassuming manners" of typical Americans, the academic questioned the US government's priorities. "For the Asians and Africans, at least, racial equality is a long way ahead of anticommunism."[47] James Baldwin had tried to say as much for some of his fellow Americans to Robert Kennedy and his FBI.

"Farrell kept the dispute going from New York the following winter," as the scholar Sabin recapped, writing that he wasn't the sort to "go about trying by checkbook and slogan to win quick liking for myself and my country."[48] Farrell met the charge of racism directly and with indignation. But didn't he protest too much? "I happen to be one of the many Americans who has fought in many ways for complete equality in America." He added that he "distinguish[es] between equality and a reversal of roles. A cult of superiority appears at least threatening to break out among the opponents of colonialism."[49] In the face of legitimate criticism, even from allies and recipients of funding, the Americans tried refuting these concerns with the by-now familiar line "not all Americans," or not all whites. Farrell didn't have a leg to stand on.

. . .

In a September 1955 piece for *Encounter* called "No Miracle in Milan," Dwight Macdonald offered a blunt critique of the Congress for Cultural Freedom's "Future of Freedom" conference in Milan. He was particularly attuned to what the Asian delegates had to say about the Americans. Masani "caused a sensation with a speech sharply critical of Western policies in Asia, in which he depicted Indian public opinion as predominantly pro-Soviet and wound up: 'Communism gives us a sense of belonging to something. But we can't belong to America.'"[50] It was a plea for help if the Americans could only hear it properly.

Macdonald also quoted Thailand's Prince Kukrit Pramoj, another US ally who nevertheless quipped, "As a common bond with you Westerners, let me admit that we Asiatics feel as racially superior to you as you do to us. . . . Since my country has never been under the rule of a colonial power, we are in the unhappy position of having to blame ourselves for our short-comings."[51] Macdonald further recorded the gulf between East and West, reversing for Koestler and his Polish counterpart the calculus of who was abstract and who was concrete, noting that "the Western delegates came to Milan to discuss freedom as an abstract philosophical principle, or as a problem in sociology, political theory, other academic disciplines, or as an aspect of European and Anglo-American history and culture; while the

Asian delegates came to find out what 'freedom' really means to people with white skins—and to present to these cultural representatives of their present or former masters a list of complaints and grievances."[52] Could this ill will that the Americans were finding everywhere they traveled really *all* be written off to Communist propaganda? Surely, some of it was the result of Western interventions and institutional racism.

And if the American bosses could order up coverage of their conferences, what other signs of American editorial influence riddled *Quest's* pages? Between Ezekiel's editorial and a piece critical of Bhoodan, a full-page ad for Standard Oil appeared. In the next issue, its comrade, Mobil Oil, ran an ad.[53] Another early piece offered a free speech–based defense of *Encounter's* (and Orwell's) publisher Secker & Warburg, who ran into trouble for publishing D.H. Lawrence's *Lady Chatterley's Lover*. With such signals in its debut and follow-up issues, Ezekiel's second editorial had to refute charges that *Quest* represented "The birth of a new baby in the American lobby." The issue went on to cite Narayan's notion that "the departure of the British was followed by the creation of new elite groups." Issue 2 also ran a review of Nicolas Nabokov's *Old Friends and New Music;*[54] Issue 3 ran CCF official Edward Shils's recap of the "encounter at Milan," which Macdonald also covered above. Later pieces criticized—in between dissections of Indian dance, poetry, and music—India's failure to take more military material and funding from the West, to spend more on military defense, and one article praised the mind of warmonger (and alleged war criminal) Henry Kissinger. Whatever its charms, which were many, its funders' and stakeholders' interests were never very far off-camera in its pages.

And it was one among several of the new babies in the American lobby's growing family.

· · ·

When Australian journalist Phillip Knightley arrived in Bombay in 1960, he didn't expect to spend two years on the subcontinent, marry an Indian woman, and thereby "inheriting two hundred and ten Indian relatives,"[55] as he recounts in his memoir, *A Hack's Progress*. It turns out that after two years in India, he had been unwittingly recruited for literary propaganda work by the CIA and the KGB. He was better at resisting the latter, which was far less subtle.

Knightley's detour began when he found himself unable to leave the country. He discovered that his return passage to Australia was postponed for months. And so he began to adapt. "A new English-language literary magazine called *Imprint* was about to start," he wrote, "and I was offered the post of managing editor—Rupees 1,200 a month (L95), four weeks' annual holiday and a return airline ticket to Australia."[56] He also began working on documentary film scripts for the Government of India Films Division. These ranged from public service projects—"how to understand metric weights; why farmers should use fertiliser"—to life-or-death public education projects, such as films demonstrating how to "give your blood for Indian soldiers on the Indo-Chinese frontier" during the war with China in November 1962.[57] But the films also represented a third government that Knightley worked for during those two years in India.

Knightley's bosses at *Imprint* were an American couple, Glorya Hale, the editor, and her husband, Arthur, the publisher. Knightley found them to be "amusing, cosmopolitan Americans who were fun to work for." They lived and worked out of a luxury high-rise called the Bhaktavar, "that looked out over the approaches to Bombay Harbor."[58]

"Sitting on the balcony one evening" alone . . . "enjoying a quiet beer and watching the lights of small fishing boats," Knightley recalled, "I became aware that someone in the next block was doing the same thing. We nodded to each other and raised glasses. Then he called across the gap, 'What are you drinking?' When I told him it was beer, he said, 'Come over and try vodka.' I went down in the lift, across the courtyard, and up the lift in the next block to the sixth floor where I noticed that a sign on the bell that I was about to ring said SOVEXPORT FILM. Inside I met Igor—I never got to know his other name. . . . Ostensibly Igor represented the Soviet Film industry in India. . ."[59]

Igor and Knightley spent many evenings getting sloshed, going to parties, and eventually Igor confessed to Knightley. He wanted to be a journalist. They decided to write a piece together about the parts of India that Nikita Khrushchev and Nikolai Bulganin wouldn't see on their upcoming state visit: "the poverty-stricken shacks, the notorious caged prostitutes of Bombay, the illicit liquor stills, the villages given over entirely to gold smuggling."[60]

Igor and Knightley placed the article quickly in a Soviet magazine, which Knightley had never heard of. A large check came for Knightley, and when he was asked to sign a receipt he understood how he was being manipulated. Igor, he discovered, was KGB. "I learned that Igor's pitch was typical not only of the KGB but of most intelligence services. If I had accepted the money I would have crossed a barrier. . . . Our joint articles would have delved deeper into areas of Indian affairs that should not have concerned us and if I had complained that the sort of information Igor's Soviet 'editors' wanted was not readily available, he would then have suggested that we try to find an Indian who did have access to such information and pay him for it."[61]

. . .

At the CCF, that binding signature was your byline. Knightley's arm's-length poverty reporting mirrors that of the American Congress President Denis de Rougemont's. De Rougemont was the author of *Love in the Western World*, and was himself the lover of Consuelo de Saint Exupéry, the wife of *Little Prince* author Antoine de Saint Exupéry. De Rougemont is said to have co-authored her vengeful memoir, *The Rose Memoir*.[62] His piece in *Encounter*'s first issue, "Looking for India," features all the clichés of the Western poverty seeker, the occult, diamonds in the rough, hidden wisdom, and visual clichés like half-naked, simple-but-happy locals, always "squatting," their eyes either "burning" or "vacant."

"All this takes place in view of the street," de Rougemont wrote, "a few feet away from the men sprawled in the shops, from the barefooted passers-by who go up and down without casting at us a glance of their fixed and burning eyes." Often all that is captured in the Western gaze are the inscrutable, mystical, and unknowable figures of the developing world:

> A half-naked creature passes us, very old, its skull cropped and two breasts hanging down to its stomach. Women with unbelievably thin and graceful limbs. Little noise, and not a single smile. A temple bell rings, unmusically. One hears the shuffling of bare feet, the swish of pink, violet, and pale-green saris. Eyes gleam in the dark doorways. Here and there a man prays, squatting against a wall. An air of enigmatic and insidious solemnity hangs over the whole quarter, which has about it something dreamlike and animal. Everything is delicate, feline, miserable, and precious, all at once. I feel too heavy and too big in my European clothing.[63]

What has de Rougement learned of these people beyond his inability or unwillingness to talk with them, which he must distract his reader from noticing through his urge to decorate that lack of understanding with colors and sounds? God forbid he should speak to these city and village dwellers. If you compare "Looking for India" with Baldwin's reporting from the United States South, the former is exposed as little more than a restatement of the developing world's poverty with the adornment of a postcard collector and an air of the inscrutable. In the thrill-seeker in the East one thinks of novelist Chinua Achebe's great distrust of writing that seeks to hypnotize the reader. "When a writer while pretending to record scenes, incidents, and their impact is in reality engaged in inducing hypnotic stupor in his readers through a bombardment of emotive words and other forms of trickery, much more has to be at stake than stylistic felicity."[64] Baldwin on the other hand saw emotion in the eyes of the old man in Atlanta as the old man helped Baldwin seek out the segregated buses. And more than an ahistorical dream-like vagueness, Baldwin was able to imbue those emotions and those eyes with the actual events of history and of white persecution. The difference is a step at least. But it wasn't just the capitalists who fetishized such writing.

This kind of poverty reportage was much sought-after on both sides of the ideological divide. The Soviets wanted readers to see the poverty and absorb it as proof of what havoc Western colonialism wrought. Americans and Europeans wanted to find something spiritual and authentic in it, something ultimately condescending, to make themselves feel rich and generous—needed. Both sides were of course too engrossed in their mutual death struggle to do much about such squalor. Removing military spending from the equation, Americans spend little per capita on helping the world's poor. As we will see in Afghanistan in the early 1980s, the only thing either side really wanted at their worst was to turn such scenes into a battlefield upon which to rout the other.

. . .

Such poverty was also an excuse for cultural incursions. At *Imprint*, Knightley's job was to condense classic novels in order to fit several together in one digest. "Western books in India were prohibitively expensive, so *Imprint* would condense four or five bestsellers and publish them in a magazine which because of its advertising would cost only one rupee a copy. It would overcome nationwide distribution problems by soliciting subscriptions by direct mail."[65]

But there were hints that the work was not so benign. "I knew that Hale had been in the American army in Burma during World War II in psychological warfare operations. . . . When I look back now over the early copies of *Imprint* I see that many of the books we chose to condense lauded the American way of life and painted a grim picture of the lack of freedom in the Soviet Union. . . ."[66]

And condensing books was only part of his job. It was paired with what he called "the subsidiary publishing operation." He explains, "At the Hales' request I was writing short histories of American folk heroes—Johnny Appleseed, Casey Jones, Davy Crockett—which *Imprint* was publishing as lavishly illustrated children's books and putting on the Indian market at a ridiculously low price."[67] Knightley was employed at using poverty as an excuse to push obedience to America. "If I had been naïve about Igor's intentions," Knightley recalls, "I was simply *stupid* about *Imprint*."[68]

While out sailing with Arthur Hale one day, he got a brief glimpse into who his employers really were. As much as Knightley favored his adopted India in the recent border dispute with China, he mentioned that he had heard of an academic who had found an old British map of the border in the National Archives in Delhi. "The map clearly showed the disputed territory as being within China's borders. Hale appeared to absorb this without much interest. But back at the landing at the Gateway of India, Hale said, a little too off-handedly I thought, 'That Professor Ghose . . . what were his initials again?'"[69] Knightley thought of this attempt to identify a professor with a dissenting view when he learned much later who his real bosses had been.

Decades later, Knightley had become a journalist and documentarian with an expertise on spying. But he still knew nothing of the official backing behind *Imprint*. While he was working on a documentary on the British double-agent Kim Philby, he found himself at a lunch in Washington with Harry Rositzke, the first Soviet-Russia Division chief of the CIA. After running the CIA's training schools for Eastern European exiles in West Germany in the early 1950s, Rositzke had moved to New Delhi where he was India station chief.[70]

When Knightley told his lunch companions he'd been in India in 1960–62, Rositzke asked what he'd been doing. Knightley said he'd been working on *Imprint*. "I knew it well," Rositzke said. "It was one of my little operations. Shake hands with your ex-boss."[71] "It was a shock to me," Knightley recalled, "that, however unwittingly, I had been an employee of the CIA. Now Igor's attempts to recruit me made sense . . . he was after the employee of a CIA front . . ."[72]

To appreciate how psychological warfare and cultural propaganda ran hand in hand with covert ops and military interventionism, consider Rositzke's journey through the CIA. Rositzke worked not just in India but in Germany during the very first years of Wisner's tenure, presiding over a period marked by "air drops" of emigres behind the Iron Curtain, a brutal practice with such high losses that the Americans' British partners demurred. "No claim can be made for a significant return on the heavy investment in these cross-border operations," recalled Rositzke, discussing the emigre drops decades later.[73] Many of the most disastrous early operations began in an atmosphere of fierce optimism that gave way to stark realism, finally grasping for any practical success at all. As Rositzke noted, "the first generation of CIA operations officers was learning its trade by doing, by developing know-how, both in what to do and what not to do."[74] Arguably, rather than face this legacy, time and again the CIA merely censored it.

Rositzke presided, too, over the active recruitment of Nazi war criminals to the CIA. The CIA's use of Nazis had its origins in Allen Dulles's implausible gospel of the "moderate Nazi." One such program, "Operation Paperclip," brought over 1,600 Nazi scientists, engineers, and doctors to the United States. "In fact, these were people who were directly involved in, for instance, running slave labor factories where thousands and thousands of people died in making Hitler's rockets," *New York Times* reporter Eric Lichtblau told *Democracy Now!* in 2014. "These were doctors who were involved in medical atrocities. They then found homes in the United States. . . . Many of them became US citizens. Many of them [were] honored for their work in the United States."[75]

The reason Rositzke could go from participant in recruiting Nazis for the CIA to then running a magazine in India (even becoming a writer) is because both were on the non-intelligence gathering side of the CIA, under the former OPC and International Organizations Divisions, the same side where covert actions—coups, assassinations, and recruitment of Nazis— were housed.

Let's remember that, implicit in Peter Matthiessen's lifelong self-defense was that he was in the "good CIA," the pre-"ugly-stuff" Agency. Others lionized this early agency for "the atmosphere of an order of Knights Templar, to save Western freedom from Communist darkness," as future director William Colby described it. But the recruitment of Nazis lasted the entirety of Matthiessen's purported service. Rositzke, with less of a literary reputation at stake, explained it simply. "We knew what we were doing. It was a visceral business of using any bastard as long as he was anti-Communist."[76]

As India demonstrates, with *Imprint* run as one of the Soviet-Russia chief's "little operations," and *Quest* out of the Congress for Cultural Freedom's India outpost, the developing world's modernization ran with secrecy, Western patronage, a conflation of spying with literature, and no shortage of editorial meddling across multiple CIA agencies.

8

THE US COUP IN GUATEMALA

Spitting is a despicable custom.

—José Figueres Ferrer

In 1958, Vice President Richard Nixon was attacked by a mob while on a goodwill tour of Latin America. He was in Caracas when his car windows were pelted with stones, and protesters spat at the vice president and his wife Pat Nixon as their cavalcade rolled through the city center. The American media erupted in patriotic support, playing and replaying newsreel footage of the "savage mob" that Nixon himself called "a very small, violent, vocal minority."[1] Later, trying to understand the incident, lawmakers got an earful from Costa Rica's former president José Figueres Ferrer, affectionately known in his homeland as "Don Pepe."

Costa Rica was a US ally. Its diminutive ex-president, José Figueres Ferrer (he stood at 5 feet 3 inches)[2] was something of a national hero who had left office only months before. A decade earlier he had amazed Costa Ricans with his own revolution, which had reversed what he considered to be a fraudulent election. He demilitarized the country and banned Communism. Figueres had spent several years of his youth in the United States. He recalled the time fondly, quoting American officials such as Franklin Delano Roosevelt. He partnered with the United States without hesitation, even arguing for better understanding among other Latin Americans of the culture and concerns of its neighbor to the north, and vice versa.

His first wife was an American, a Southern belle named Henrietta Boggs, who wrote a fond memoir of her time as the American First Lady of Costa Rica. But despite all of his affection for the States, when asked by the Senate Foreign Relations Committee on June 9, 1958 why an official of the United States was spat upon in Latin America, Figueres told the truth as many Latin Americans saw it. "With all due respect to Vice-President Nixon . . . I have no choice but to say that the act of spitting, however vulgar . . . lacks a substitute in our language to express certain emotions . . ."

After praising Nixon's behavior during the incident, and at his press conference after, Figueres offered a more pointed critique. "If you're going to speak of human dignity in Russia, why is it so hard to speak of human dignity in the Dominican Republic? Where is intervention and where is non-intervention? Is it that a simple threat, a potential one, to your liberties, is, essentially, more serious than the kidnapping of our liberties?" He gave other examples of American policies that explained Latin American hostility:

> Of course you have made certain investments in the (Latin) American dictatorships. . . . When your government invited Pedro Estrada, the Himmler of the Western Hemisphere, to be honored in Washington, didn't you spit upon the face of all democrats in (Latin) America?

Estrada was the head of Venezuela's secret police.[3] Secretary of State John Foster Dulles had invited Estrada to Washington in November 1954 to honor the relationship between the United States and this figure who had been behind a long list of atrocities: arbitrary arrest, imprisonment without trial, torture, and extrajudicial assassination.[4]

But while Figueres was lambasting American lawmakers publicly, privately he was planning a magazine, one that would be funded by the CIA. Before the magazine could launch, an internecine battle would play out over how robustly the magazine would be allowed to cover dissent toward US foreign policy. In other words, whether the magazine would be able to retain its editorial freedom. It was one of more than half a dozen CIA-sponsored magazines aimed to influence the region's intellectuals. That these maga-zines tended to launch just before a US-sponsored coup in the region may have been a coincidence, given the number of coups and magazines created there. But the two things these magazines had in common was that they tended to defend US foreign policy at its most egregious, facing censorship when they didn't, and that they learned to disguise this defense.

. . .

Even for pro-US moderates like Figueres, it was far too easy to point to a long list of cases where the United States was guilty of supporting, con-doning, or directly committing atrocities, not to mention breaking the law, thwarting democracy, hurting and killing good people in Latin America and around the world. When planning began for Operation SUCCESS, the US overthrow of Jacobo Árbenz in Guatemala, for instance, Figueres was seen as a regional ally and consulted on the matter. He advised against the invasion, suggesting it might make the United States more unpopular in the region. He was ignored.[5]

The troubles in the region reverberated out from Guatemala, the domain of United Fruit, an American fruit company. Across the nation, the US-backed dictator Jorge Ubico had given the company free rein, allowing it to pay just a pittance to workers and in taxes. But as nation-alist movements swept across Asia, Latin America, and Africa in the 1930s and 1940s, citizens of these countries argued that their own governments or companies ought to own and control their national resources, something wealthy countries took for granted. Elected in 1950, Jacobo Árbenz rode this nationalist wave into office. He was Guatemala's second president[6] after the ouster of the dictator Ubico in protests led by schoolteachers. His succession marked the country's first-ever peaceful transfer of power from one elected official to the next. These two presidencies represented Guatemala's initial—all too brief—"democratic spring." But however it felt about democracy, the CIA was more interested in banana profits.

With fair hair and Germanic features, Jacobo Árbenz was born to a Swiss German father in Guatemala's second largest city, Quetzaltenango. Under his leadership, Guatemala continued a land reform program that was popular across its twenty-two provinces (or departments) and approved by its legislature. Passed in June 1952, the land reform program compelled United Fruit to sell its *excess*, unused lands. The government reimbursed the company for the amount United Fruit had listed as the lands' worth in its tax returns. When United Fruit grumbled in protest that it had undervalued its holdings to pay lower taxes, Árbenz insisted he would pay only what they had listed. So United Fruit turned to the US government.[7]

Secretary of State John Foster Dulles was one of United Fruit's lawyers. His brother, CIA director Allen Dulles, had also done legal work for the company and owned stock. Another State Department official was a large shareholder. That official's brother, also in State, had been the company's president.[8] Here were stakeholders planning to channel their wishes through a lawless agency that they happened to control in order to defend a private corporation's financial interests.

Planned from Florida and executed from within the territories of Guatemala's Central American neighbors, the 1954 coup concealed these private interests under the guise of anti-Communist intervention. While hostility and pressure mounted, Árbenz sought to stockpile weapons to protect his nation. Eight years prior to the nationalization of United Fruit's lands—after Guatemalans had ousted the repressive Ubico—the United States had cut off arms to Guatemala. As new pressure mounted in the wake of the land reform, the United States also blocked other would-be weapons suppliers from selling to Árbenz. There was no democratic rationale for the embargo: at the time, even Secretary Dulles admitted that it was "impossible to produce evidence clearly tying the Guatemalan government to Moscow."[9] Something would have to be fabricated. When US planes bombarded the nation with propaganda pamphlets, Árbenz ordered second-rate matériel from Czechoslovakia. When the ship carrying these Czech weapons, the *Alfhelm*, was intercepted, the United States depicted these purchases as sponsored by Moscow. But if they had been sponsored by Moscow, Árbenz would have gotten these weapons for free. He did not. Nevertheless, it became difficult for liberal Americans to continue to defend Árbenz, after the weapons were intercepted. Yet many did. *New York Times* reporter Sydney Gruson "wrote several articles after the *Alfhelm* incident suggesting that Guatemalans were rallying around their government and that they were caught up not in Communism but in 'fervent nationalism.'"

This was not what United Fruit and the Eisenhower Administration wished Americans to hear. Allen Dulles arranged a dinner with his friend Julius Adler, the business manager of the *Times*, and complained. Adler passed the complaint onto *Times* publisher Arthur Hays Sulzberger. A few days later, Gruson's boss pulled him out of Guatemala.[10]

The *Alfhelm* incident is a particularly potent example of US suspicions making themselves come true. The Eisenhower/Dulles clique created the crisis by plotting against Guatemala's elected government, and then ensuring through a weapons embargo that Árbenz protect himself via a means that affirmed American fears, the Czech weapons channel. As with the Soviets, whose overreaction to certain passages of *Doctor Zhivago* ensured the widespread dissemination of those same passages, the Americans also found that their actions made some of their worst fears come true: Árbenz was buying weapons from an Eastern bloc country. A tie to Moscow was found.

But Gruson at *The New York Times* wasn't the only figure who saw clearly that a distorted reading of events was about to congeal into policy. The CIA's Guatemala station chief, Birch O'Neill, was yanked from the country when he raised questions about the wisdom, or necessity, of the Agency's Operation SUCCESS. Indeed, as *New York Times* veteran Stephen Kinzer has written, Dulles was right about the poor evidence of a tie between Guatemala and Moscow. While Árbenz was certainly enthralled with Marxist ideas, "no evidence ever emerged to support" Dulles's conviction that the Soviets were behind Guatemala's nationalism during the Árbenz incumbency, "not in the vast archive of files the CIA captured after its coup, nor in any other document or testimony that has surfaced since. . ."[11]

Yet when media mogul Henry Luce's writers at *Time* magazine took a position "sympathetic to Árbenz," their articles "were rewritten at the magazine's editorial offices in New York to take a hard line against the Guatemalan government."[12]

Little magazines piled on. *The New Leader*'s Sol Levitas, an American Committee member who had changed his publication from newsprint to digest at the suggestion of the CIA,[13] dutifully ran stories urging invasion. He did so right after United Fruit ran expensive ads for charities like the Red Cross in *The New Leader*'s pages. The magazine's managing editor also wrote a book, *Red Design for the Americas*, which alleged that calls for land reform were a Soviet plot. United Fruit loved the book so much they bought it up and distributed it to the media. The CIA, planning the coup through the back door, also backed these efforts to win American and international support. John Day, the book's publisher, was one of those myriad CIA conduits who ran "black" printing operations for the CIA's propaganda needs. Another *New Leader* contributor during this time, Serafino Romualdi, was sent in the wake of the coup to "reorganize" Guatemala's labor unions. Flush with CIA money, here was another Agency man whose writing career, work with unions, and covert political vocations had blurred.[14]

Árbenz and the United States both had informants, yet even after public disavowals, specific hints were dropped about the coming coup by members of the American Committee.[15] As early as 1952, Arthur Schlesinger was consulted in preparation for the coup. Adlai Stevenson was running for president at the time. So the former US ambassador to Brazil, Adolf Berle, nudged Schlesinger, an advisor to Stevenson, to suggest that Stevenson's "advisors set up 'some sort of machinery'" to be put in place to liaise with the coup plotters in the event of Stevenson's election. He was not elected, so this became moot.[16]

Operation SUCCESS commenced at dawn on June 18, 1954, when a disgruntled military commander named Carlos Castillo Armas, hand-picked by the CIA to "lead" the coup, drove his handful of men six miles inside Guatemala, near its eastern border with Honduras.[17] They had embarked from a town owned by United Fruit.[18] CIA planes strafed targets throughout the country to give the impression of a large-scale revolt.[19] While the planes wrought terror throughout Guatemala's largely Amerindian population, the newly created "Voice of Liberation" radio (a CIA front, operated by David Atlee Phillips) helped foster the impression of a massive home-grown force. It used a hysterical repetition of disinformation about the rapid advances of huge numbers of rebel troops heroically en route to thwart Árbenz's Communist plot.[20] Again, it was a plot that did not exist. The United States' Catholic hierarchy was also in on the fiction. As the Vatican had helped distribute the CIA's Russian-language *Doctor Zhivago* at the 1958 World's Fair, Cardinal Spellman conspired with the Guatemalan clergy to smear Árbenz's government not only for being Communist but also "demonic."[21] Árbenz at last took to the radio in an attempt to counter the coup plotters. "Our crime is our patriotic wish to advance, to progress, to win an economic independence that would match our political independence. It is completely untrue that Communists are taking over the government. . ."[22]

This helped briefly. But as the strafing increased, civilians in Chiquimula, Gualán, and Zacapa ducked for cover. President Árbenz grew erratic. He took to drinking.[23] US Ambassador Puerifoy hinted to Guatemala's military that what was needed was a "clean sweep" of the administration. Even troops loyal to Árbenz could see that the Americans would stop at nothing to reel in their coup. Led by Colonel Carlos Enrique Díaz, Árbenz's commanders promised the president that if he resigned, they would allow him to address the country in order to prevent Castillo Armas from taking power.

In his radio farewell, President Árbenz argued solemnly that the nationalist reforms were important but were not worth the destruction of the country. A certain young Argentine doctor happened to be listening that day, and was infuriated. His name was Ernesto "Che" Guevara. Guevara was on a tour through Latin America, getting to know its people and checking its political pulse. He had landed in Guatemala just in time to witness these events firsthand, and he bristled at Árbenz's failure to arm the peasants or purge the nation of pro-US reactionaries when it had enacted its land reform. After Árbenz's overthrow, Guevara vowed revenge.[24]

Colonel Díaz took power. But in his own address to the nation he boldly promised to continue the program of resisting imperialism imposed from the outside. This got him in trouble. "Let me explain something to you," the CIA's Enno Hobbing told Díaz during a surprise visit to the barracks. "You made a big mistake when you took over government." After a short but meaningful pause, Hobbing explained, "Colonel, you're just not convenient for the requirements of American foreign policy."[25] The Guatemalan military personnel, who decided they could be as convenient to the requirements of American foreign policy as necessary, forced Díaz to resign at gunpoint. Castillo Armas took office in early July, while Árbenz began life in exile.

. . .

SUCCESS was a disastrous failure in every respect but its name. First, because the United States replaced a democratically elected leader with a dictator, it was the sort of behavior that incensed friendly democratic socialist moderates like Figueres worldwide. Castillo Armas immediately began a program of repression, which established a bloody precedent that lasted for more than forty years, continuing into the years after his assassination in 1957. The resulting decades of CIA juntas and military presidents culminated in 1982 with the regime of US School of the Americas graduate Efraín Ríos Montt, who perpetrated repression on a scale that a United Nations committee and a national court recently characterized as genocide.[26] Two-hundred thousand people, mostly civilians, died in the resulting civil war, often at the hand of right-wing death squads.

And in those years immediately after the operation, it was already clear what anti-Communist liberation meant for ordinary Guatemalans. Repressive officials from the days of Ubico returned to their posts. A National Committee banning Communism effectively outlawed most labor activities and empowered officials to name whomever they liked as subversive with no due process. By November, this committee had more than seventy thousand names on its list.[27]

Second, the invasion radicalized influential members of the Latin American nationalist and anti-imperialist movements, justifying the most anti-democratic readings of Marxist-Leninism as the "medicine" against such imperialism. Guevara's vow of revenge was enacted just five years later in the trials and executions of several hundred functionaries of the Fulgencio Batista regime.

In turn, those trials and executions surrounding what Cuba's leaders called Operation Truth made an impression on a young George Plimpton, who—along with Tennessee Williams and Kenneth Tynan—visited his idol Ernest Hemingway in early 1959, during a period when the United States had not yet made up its mind about Cuba. The trials also shaped the career and informed the journalistic impulses of young Gabriel García Márquez, who himself was inducted into politics through stories of a United Fruit massacre, which took place a short distance from where he grew up.

Thus, the third effect was on literary culture in Guatemala and throughout Latin America. After the CIA toppled Árbenz, Castillo Armas banned the illiterate from voting, disenfranchising three quarters of the population and prolonging their marginalization. His cronies also banned books, burning outright such masterpieces of world literature as Victor Hugo's *Les Misérables*, the works of Dostoyevsky, as well as books written by former president Juan José Arévalo. A sendup of United Fruit by Guatemala's future Nobel Prize winner Miguel Ángel Asturias was also expunged.[28] If the CIA helped nudge along the so-called Latin American boom in twentieth-century fiction, as some have argued, it was also responsible for the repression, torture, and execution of untold numbers of would-be writers who were killed by proxy under US foreign policy.

The fourth disastrous consequence of Operation SUCCESS was that the 1954 coup strengthened rampant anti-American feeling in the region, making its foreign policy aims harder to achieve. Rolling back anti-Americanism was among the major aims of the CCF, but now this was impossible. Julián Gorkin tested the waters to find them roiling. On the ground in Latin America just in time for the coup, the CCF had recently launched its flagship Spanish-language magazine, and Gorkin was *Cuadernos*'s first editor.[29] The ex-Communist had a colorful past. Having fallen out with the Soviets, he had fled to Mexico and survived an attempt on his life that left a hole in his skull.[30] Gorkin's central task was to present Latin American readers with a favorable representation of North American policy.[31] At a conference co-sponsored by the Latin American CCF affiliate, Gorkin read out a letter of greeting from none other than Carlos Castillo Armas to a cringing crowd.[32]

The faithful military dictator received a much warmer welcome when he was summoned to Washington and New York City. He was given a ticker tape parade and honorary degrees from Columbia University and Fordham University. In Washington, after a twenty-one-gun salute, Vice President Nixon raised a glass. "'We in the United States,' he said, 'have watched the people of Guatemala record an episode in their history deeply significant to all peoples.

> Led by the courageous soldier who is our guest this evening, the Guatemalan people revolted against Communist rule, which in collapsing, bore graphic witness to its inherent shallowness, falsity and corruption."[33]

By the end of 1954, both the State Department and the US Congress again justified the coup by obviating the Communist threat: "if [Árbenz] wasn't a Communist, he would do until a real one came along." Dissatisfied with these reports, Secretary of State Dulles phoned up C.D. Jackson, an expert on psychological warfare and defender of Radio Free Europe in the face of allegations it had incited the Hungarian bloodshed. Jackson was on vacation from his job at *Time* magazine. But Dulles had an unforgettable request for the veteran propagandist. "Dulles asked Jackson if the latter knew someone who might write a literary history of the Guatemalan affair." It would of course be fiction.

> He had in mind "a sort of historical novel" with an "Uncle Tom's Cabin or Ida Tarbell touch." The writer would have access to all the relevant documents except, of course, the CIA material, and the documentation would be published separately. Dulles did not specify whether the State Department's name would appear on the "opus in question," but he did mention that it would be translated into Spanish and circulated throughout Latin America as well as

the United States. Jackson considered the idea worth pursuing and promised Dulles he would get back to him . . .[34]

It's not clear how far the project got. But it again shows how for the Americans coups were activities of both the pen and the sword; history was to be made first through disinformation in support of military bullying, bombings, and bribes (what the agency called "executive actions"). Then it was to be given a literary makeover for posterity by the great writers whose pockets the CIA would stuff with cash.

In 2011, Guatemala's President Álvaro Colom issued a formal apology to Árbenz's son Juan Jacobo. "That day changed Guatemala and we have not recuperated from it yet," he said. "It was a crime to Guatemalan society and it was an act of aggression to a government starting its democratic spring."[35] As José Figueres Ferrer had put it to the Senate in 1958, US officials like Nixon would be spat upon because "you can't spit at a foreign policy."[36]

Boris Pasternak (second from right) at the First Congress of the Union of Soviet Writers in 1934. Two decades later, Pasternak would fall afoul of Party elite when his novel *Doctor Zhivago* included critiques of the Soviet Union and won the Nobel Prize. *The Paris Review* sent painter Olga Carlisle to Moscow to interview him in the aftermath of the controversy, known as the Pasternak Affair. Pasternak's only wish, he said, was for free time to finish his play, *Blind Beauty*. But he died in 1960, after only writing a portion of the three-part play.

Olga Ivinskaya, Pasternak's muse and the character Lara's prototype, suffered severely during the Pasternak Affair. As his de facto literary agent, Ivinskaya was browbeaten and tried after Pasternak's death for smuggling foreign currency—the profits from the novel—into the Soviet Union. She was sentenced to a remote labor camp, and wrote about the incident in her memoir, *A Captive of Time*. During her imprisonment, *The Paris Review* syndicated its Pasternak interview to the Congress for Cultural Freedom's magazines, and participated in a television panel about the suppressed novel.

Photograph: Wikimedia Commons.

Richard Wright in 1946, six years after the publication of his novel *Native Son*. An anti-communist who came to distrust the anti-communist movement, Wright complained, "My attitude to Communism has not altered but my position toward those . . . fighting Communism has. I lift my hand to fight Communism and I find that the hand of the Western world is sticking knives into my back. The Western world must make up its mind as to whether it hates colored people more than it hates Communists or . . . Communists more than . . . colored people."

Ernest Hemingway in 1953 at Finca Vigia (or Lookout Farm), his Cuban home, which he bought as a refuge from fame and surveillance. After the Cuban Revolution, George Plimpton visited the legendary author and witnessed war crime trials of functionaries of US-supported dictator Fulgencio Batista. In this period, the US petitioned for Hemingway to leave the island nation. His presence could hardly help in the propaganda war against Cuba and the Soviet Union. Convinced he was being spied on at home, Hemingway killed himself not long after he left Cuba.

Photograph: Hemingway Collection, John F. Kennedy Presidential Library and Museum.

Conservative pundit William F. Buckley with co-author L. Brent Bozell in 1954, holding their book *McCarthy and His Enemies*. Buckley had worked undercover with the CIA's E. Howard Hunt in Mexico in the 1950s. When he trained in Washington, D.C., he confirmed a fear that Peter Matthiessen confessed to Immy Humes: that other Yale classmates would recognize him and blow his cover. Buckley saw classmates but pretended to be in town for business involving his first book, *God and Man at Yale*. His cover was compromised in the 1970s during the Watergate scandal—President Nixon mentioning him as someone to feed an article to—and *The Paris Review* interviewed him on his spy novels in the 1990s.

Photograph: *Los Angeles Daily News Negatives*, Department of Special Collections, Charles E. Young Research Library, UCLA.

Harold "Doc" Humes in 1961, on the set of his silent film, "Don Peyote." The film culminates with a group of Greenwich Village Beatniks encircling a university professor who appears to have gotten too cozy with the system. To the original music of jazz great Ornette Coleman, the Beatniks shout, "Fink, fink, fink!"

Photograph courtesy of Immy Humes.

In August 1963, James Baldwin was left off the official roster of speakers at the March on Washington, but was invited to discuss civil rights on television. Here he appears in a photograph by the US Information Agency, the propaganda agency that sponsored the program, flanked by actors Charlton Heston and Marlon Brando (with Sidney Poitier and Harry Belafonte nearby). Baldwin's most critical comments about the FBI were censored.

Photograph courtesy of the National Archives (306-SSM-4D-87-8).

September 12, 1993   Jill Krementz

When Doc Humes asked George Plimpton (seated, front) and Peter
Matthiessen (standing, second from left) in 1966 to come clean about *The
Paris Review*'s CIA ties, he cited young writers like William Styron (seated
row, right) who had been "netted" by the magazine, and who could be
tarnished by any resulting scandal. Plimpton downplayed Humes's concerns. Indeed, so many media outlets were netted in the scandal in 1967
and 1977 when CIA media penetration was exposed that *The Paris Review*
was largely overshadowed. By the early 1980s, *Paris Review* founder John
Train (last row, second from right) would find his way into the "covert network" while working with media on anti-Soviet propaganda with a cover
in refugee relief. "I was a conduit," he told the author in 2015. Also pictured,
seated from left, are John Ashbery and E.L. Doctorow; with William Morris
(back left), Rose Styron (back center) and James Salter (back, right).

Immy Humes with Norman Mailer, while filming Humes's *Doc*, a documentary about her father. Family friend Peter Matthiessen spoke to Humes for the film, too, discussing his CIA service and how it may have affected Doc. Later he retracted much of what he said, including his CIA chain of command and details of his training. Segments of the interview languished on the cutting room floor for two decades while journalists tried to figure out the extent of his CIA work in the early 1950s.

Photograph courtesy of Immy Humes.

George Plimpton in 1993. Like her father, Immy Humes encouraged Plimpton to own up to *The Paris Review*'s ties to the CIA. But Plimpton demurred, she said. What obsessed Plimpton late in life, according to Robert Silvers, was the hope that, hidden in a little corner of the basement of the Ernest Hemingway museum outside Havana, was an undiscovered, unpublished Hemingway novel. Still "looking for Hemingway," Plimpton had tickets to fly to Cuba and was scheduled to arrive just days after his 2003 death.

Photograph by Nancy Wong, Wikimedia Commons.

Peter Matthiessen at the National Book Awards ceremony in 2008. Burnishing his late legend, Matthiessen's novel *Shadow Country* won the National Book Award that year. In interviews promoting the novel he confirmed much of what had already been known about his CIA service, but did not reveal any new details.

9

CUBA: A PORTRAIT BY FIGUERES, PLIMPTON, HEMINGWAY, GARCÍA MÁRQUEZ, PART 1

It is true that all mankind are delegates, that there is not a soul on the planet who is not a delegate, yet I am a member of the Congress in another way—I *know* I am; that is what makes me different from all my innumerable colleagues, present and future.

—Jorge Luis Borges, "The Congress"

Weeks after visiting the US Senate in 1958, Costa Rica's former President José Figueres Ferrer, aka "Don Pepe," and the American Committee's Norman Thomas launched *Combate*, the house magazine for Latin America's democratic, or non-Communist, left. The magazine was part of a greater scheme for creating a vade-mecum, a how-to manual, for social democracy in the hemisphere's Spanish-speaking countries. Figueres's Senate speech on spitting even appeared in the first issue.[1]

The link to the CIA was Sacha Volman,[2] a Romanian expat who had escaped arrest in his homeland in 1946. Having spent the war fighting both Nazi and Soviet occupation in Romania, Volman flew home from the war in a wooden box "in the belly of a British plane."[3] Given his experience, Volman was able to make himself indispensable to the growing anti-Communist labor movement in Europe. In France, he was hired as secretary for the International Center for Free Trade Unionists in Exile (ICFTUE), one of many in a vast payola network for labor ultimately funded by the CIA. These were unions staffed by anti-Communists and infused with money for ongoing operations, capital growth, and insurance against fiscal crises.[4] The graft was necessary to fight the unions thought to be penetrated by Communists. Volman met regularly with Agent Carmel Offie and corresponded with other CIA officers, some of whom were covert. In letters, he was good enough to abbreviate their names.[5] In 1952, Volman moved to New York to work directly for the Free Europe Committee, the CIA-sponsored group that ran Radio Free Europe and contained a book publishing wing. Volman remained there until 1955 and was described as a strange figure who "had his own rigid convictions and often thought that US propaganda outlets were making tactical mistakes."

> Although he was volatile and quick to anger, frequently clashing with colleagues, he spoke barely above a whisper. While talking his eyes shifted suspiciously about "like a spy in a silent film". . . . It was all so transparent that some assumed Volman couldn't possibly be a real spy . . .[6]

Volman met Norman Thomas at a socialist conference in June, 1953, and they became friends. Thomas was the perpetual US presidential candidate on the socialist ticket. He was an important member of the American Committee's left/socialist flank, but also able to call in favors from Allen Dulles when asked by his colleagues.[7] In addition to collaborating with Thomas, Volman fell in with men like Figueres and other high-profile leaders who were social democrats, anti-Communist, and militant interventionists. Over time, Volman's work with expatriates increasingly focused on Latin America, where he took up residence.

A rather heroic cabal of people plotting coups collaborated with these anti-Communist operatives in Latin America. Unlike the CIA, the cabal of social democrats had sought during and after World War II to topple right-wing dictators and death squad leaders, the very sort the United States was prone to installing. The interventionist nature of their militancy earned them a derisive nickname, "the Caribbean Legion."[8] Among those who made up the Caribbean Legion were Árbenz's predecessor in Guatemala, Juan José Arévalo, an elected president with social democratic leanings who admired Franklin Roosevelt; a future president of Cuba, Ramón Grau San Martín; Romulo Betancourt of Venezuela, sent into exile by dictator Marcos Pérez Jiménez, whose repression prompted the infamous spitting incident;[9] and the Dominican Republic's Juan Bosch, the white-haired, social-democratic short story writer and future president.

Beside *Combate* magazine, the most lasting achievement of the Caribbean Legion's interventions is commemorated by a little town in the mountains of Costa Rica called La Lucha, or the Struggle. In 1948 and 1949, Figueres sent empty planes to Arévalo in Guatemala, which returned with weapons and troops. Figueres then prevailed in a short civil war. The United States watched closely as his eighteen-month junta then gave women the vote, took measures to ban racism against black Costa Ricans,[10] nationalized certain industries, and kept foreign investments intact. Figueres's junta banned the Communist party and then (admirably, almost miraculously) he stepped down. He did so, however, after abolishing the military, which reinforced Costa Rica's reputation as the "Switzerland of the Americas"[11] and prevented the Americans from overthrowing him.

Some have suggested that had this "good" revolution happened later in the Cold War, the United States would have singled out the nationalization of industries as an excuse to intervene. According to journalist Stephen Kinzer, the CIA was too busy planning the Guatemala coup and managing its aftermath to commit to toppling Figueres. In fact, the abolition of the Costa Rican army meant the CIA had no play against Figueres; who could they pay off to eject him?[12]

Figueres's war of liberation made him a legend in his homeland. On the mountain road that leads into the village of La Lucha, a tawny-colored tank sits in a little valley of waterfalls surrounded by spikey cabuya plants and woodpecker-dotted cypresses. This village is where some of the bloodiest battles of the civil war took place. The tank commemorates this war to end wars in Costa Rica and is marked by a plaque whose inscription, covered in rust, translates: *To the fallen of both bands.*[13]

• • •

Figueres may have abolished his country's military, but *Combate* was his attempt to fight: to fight totalitarianism on the left and right, through articles, and through argument. Yet this new fight was to be carried out arm-in-arm with the CIA (those same agents and plotters who overthrew his friends in Guatemala). While the name of the magazine was a nod to Camus, the magazine's funding came from the same place as the rest of the CIA's publishing empire, specifically through an organization called the International Institute for Labor Research, or IILR. This was the FEC's side of the CIA, the same front used for propaganda support during the Pasternak affair. *Combate* magazine weighed in on US policy in Latin America, and it sprung up alongside a school for political training in Costa Rica, the Institute for Political Education.

The CIA money for *Combate* was first passed through the Kaplan Fund in New York. If *The Paris Review*'s first outside loan from the CIA came disguised through Fleischmann's yeast fortune and subsequent front foundation, the CIA monies for Norman Thomas and José Figueres's *Combate* came from Jacob M. Kaplan's grape and molasses fortune; this was the money behind Welch's Grape Juice.[14] After Kaplan's single donation of $35,000, the CIA funneled more than a million dollars to the IILR through the Kaplan Fund.[15]

Meanwhile, among the Bauhaus and Brutalist buildings, palm trees, and exhaust fumes from leaded-gas engines, the Institute for Political Education in Costa Rica's capital, San Jose, offered anti-Communist training classes on Latin American geography, history, politics, labor, and community organizing. Despite the anti-Communist aims of the IEP[16] campus, one American visitor was astonished that "His fellow students refused to condemn Fidel Castro . . . but were full of venom when it came to discussions of US occupations of their countries." This was the sort of reality that Latin Americans like Figueres tried to explain to the Americans time and again: blowback. Group study at the IEP could be so straightforward that it might simply mean reading aloud from two of the CIA's magazines in the region, *Combate* or *Cuadernos*. "While [the visiting American student] feared that these two magazines were overly critical of US foreign policy, he would not have known that neither . . . would have existed without a CIA subsidy, and he apparently couldn't see that they both consistently defended the United States within the framework of Cold War liberalism."[17]

Latin America faced the same problems as Europe with respect to top-down editorial control. In the minutes of an editorial planning meeting, Volman wrote that *Combate* was being "subjected to censorship of the smallest details by people other than board members."[18] "While we have succeeded in eliminating FEC censorship on all the texts to be printed," he added, "we have still not received the funds necessary to print *Combate*."[19] This was a banner year for CIA-sponsored censors. One month earlier Macdonald's "America! America!" was "vetoed" by *Encounter*. The delays in *Combate*'s launch that summer persisted, as a result of the CIA's wrangling for control. Motivating the bureaucracy, thought Figueres, was the very real Communist threat during that period. But "[t]he disadvantage was our lack of financial independence, or rather the strict policy veto imposed upon our activities."[20] Like *Encounter*, *Combate*'s editors were required to submit their texts for approval. Josselson's rationale during the 1958 Macdonald affair echoed the foot-dragging preventing *Combate's* launch. One recalls Nicolas Nabokov's exasperated reminder that anything controversial had to be run up the flagpole for approval. When *Combate*'s board asked to forgo FEC's formal oversight, the FEC at first agreed and then reneged.[21] (The censor- ship delayed *Combate*'s launch for a full year.)[22] When the United Fruit com- pany complained about *Combate*'s earliest editions,[23] with articles like the Figueres speech before the Senate in the first issue, the FEC even began suppressing supplies like paper and postage as well as operating funds.

When the Free Europe Committee wasn't screening *Combate*'s articles with an eye to censoring, it was "feeding the line," so to speak. In late 1959, Volman sent Thomas an article that had been accepted by the Free Europe Press for *Combate*'s next issue: "I have taken the liberty of drafting a letter [of acceptance] for your signature . . . and if you approve of it . . . I would forward it . . . to George Lieber, head of the Free Europe Press Department. . . . . Lieber is an old friend . . . and . . . a dedicated socialist . . ."[24] Since the Free Europe Press was a CIA-created and -funded front, this placed *Combate*'s output squarely in the propaganda camp, though in a channel separate from the CCF, with separate staff. The planning for *Combate* coincided with the Cuban Revolution, and the revolution's anticipated end may have made *Combate*'s launch feel urgent to its sponsors; this urgency may have greased the wheels toward a compromise on how much control the CIA could exert. But it is clear the CIA sought to control it through the FEC.

When Castro came to power on New Year's Day, 1959, Norman Thomas's associates were cautiously hopeful. Figueres had lent his support to the Cuban Revolution as it made its way from the swamps of the perim- eter through the Sierra Maestra and into the halls of Havana. Figueres's friend, Luis Alberto Monge, a thirty-three-year-old member of the Costa Rican legislature and a *Combate*/IILR board member, wrote Thomas in late

January, suggesting, "you and other North Americans [may be] slightly confused about what is happening in Cuba. It is really necessary to be there in order to interpret it. Not all that is happening there is desirable or perfect."[25] Indeed, Raul Castro is said to have presided over a mass execution of seventy of the ousted dictator Batista's soldiers with a machine gun and a bulldozer.[26] Even the official trials of the outgoing regime that were open to the public were highly contested in the US media. "But in my judgment," Monge continued, "we ought to realize that we are dealing with a movement that triumphed against an oppressive dictatorship; that the movement has decisive popular support in Cuba, and in Latin America, and finally that it offers a margin of hope for a return to the norm. Certain sectors of the [American] press have precipitated the very severe prejudice [against] Fidel Castro and his movement"[27] held by the North Americans.

In responding, Thomas cited uneasiness with the lack of due process in the trials against Batista's soldiers. "I think it is very important Castro should push social and economic reforms, whether or not certain sectors of the American press like it. I also, however, regret the way in which the present war trials have been carried on and this I have written privately to [Cuban President] Urrutia. More publicly, I have written and said that the American press was blameworthy for not informing our people on Batista's cruelties. However, I am too much a believer of the due process of trials, even of criminals, to applaud Castro's performance in this field. I do applaud his remarkable achievement in overcoming the Batista government, which had all too much support from the United States."[28]

In a vacuum, Thomas's and Monge's different emphases were compatible. They agree that "the norm"—Monge's phrase for democracy—was violated under the US-supported dictatorship preceding Castro's rise, that the US press had distorted recent events, and that Castro's current tribunals were "war trials." Given the confusions about the trials, and how bad a sign they may have been for Cuban democracy, Monge could only point ominously to the confusion engendered by American and European propaganda, which he didn't think was helping. ". . . Latin America is saturated with anti-Communist propaganda, and this abundance . . . may have developed a certain immunity against this propaganda."[29] Monge was merely being strategic, not purist. But he sought to use the propaganda in the service of the popular will, rather than to thwart it, writing, "I have recommended pamphlets which deal with the problems of our people. . . . We should speak of agrarian reform, of industrialization, and of economic integration. Within these major themes there is an ample margin within which to denounce the Communists. I am sure that

Compañero Thomas and other friends of the cause within the United States understand this viewpoint."[30]

The point, Monge argued, was that "To all these [propaganda] agencies are added the anti-Communist publications of the United States, English, and French embassies and those of the USIS [United States Information Service] . . . ."

> theoretically the publications of the Institute [for Political Education] were the best. [But] [m]any of the anti-Communist propaganda agencies have destroyed the authority of anti-Communism as an attitude.[31]

In other words, it was now difficult to get through to the Latin Americans torn between the politically correct view (anticommunism) and the discredited messenger of that view (US imperialists who overthrew Árbenz, backed Batista, Ubico, Trujillo, Somoza, etc., and who hid their role)—whose media were alarmist toward the revolution, to say the least.

Having stumbled before their CIA censors, the editors of *Combate* would now have to proceed with heightened sensitivity before the Latin Americans. The cabal that they both belonged to was self-avowedly engaged in propaganda. But Monge suggests that they would do best to advocate for the policies that Latin Americans, and in particular its intellectuals, actually favored and to prioritize this advocacy over advocacy for anticommunism. These were precisely the economic reforms that people like Árbenz had been pushing.

US foreign policy was incoherent. One minute the CIA was plotting to overthrow Pepe Figueres; the next it was funding his magazine. One minute it toppled democratic reformers and called them Communist to justify its criminality; the next its operatives must emphasize those same reforms in order to avoid pushing the new reformers toward Communism. If this was cultural freedom, it confused its own collaborators, such as the Costa Rican lawmaker Luis Alberto Monge.

· · ·

When *Combate* launched the summer before Castro's triumph in Havana, *The Paris Review*'s illustrious editor George Plimpton had just finished an interview with his idol, Ernest Hemingway.[32] The Hemingway, or "H. interview"—as the CCF called it—took even longer than the Pasternak one. Both interviews involved sending a correspondent abroad. Olga Carlisle traveled to Peredelkino, outside Moscow, for the peripatetic Pasternak conversation. Aware from the outset of Hemingway's interest in revolutions, even while he was chasing him to talk about fiction, Plimpton not only traveled to a Havana suburb to interview the illustrious Hemingway, he also returned for subsequent visits during the infamous post-revolutionary tribunals, which opened to the public in a program known as Operation Truth. All told, Plimpton chased Hemingway for most of the last decade of the elder writer's life. And nowhere was Hemingway's judgment more contested than in Cuba, where one was usually forced to take political sides in the battle between Cuba and the United States.

"Hemingway himself is an outrageous old man," Plimpton wrote William Styron in 1953, during *The Paris Review*'s launch when he first proposed to interview Hemingway to his co-editors. "I met him in the Ritz bar where he agreed to give us an interview. . . . His language is what you'd expect, and I should guess the most difficult problem of the interview would be to tone it down. . . . He is in Kenya at the moment, adding some Mau Mau filth to his vocabulary . . . and will be back here in November."[33] Plimpton came to idolize Hemingway. But if this progress report sounds less than adulatory it may have been tongue-in-cheek bravado. More likely, it pointed to the abuse that Hemingway doled out to the upstart editor, both verbal and physical abuse.

In his own first written response, Hemingway attributed his reluctance to be interviewed to injuries sustained after a pair of plane crashes in Uganda in early 1954. In a string of very bad luck, first his touring plane went down, then his rescue plane caught fire and crashed.

> My temper is a little bad from a slight surfeit of pain. I truly never mean to be rude ever but . . . I cannot talk like Forster, nor Graham Greene, nor [Irwin] Shaw and I might say fuck the Art of Fiction [though] what I would really mean was fuck talking about it. Let us practice it and shut up.
>
> My experience has been that when a writer talks about himself and his work except with his girl or other writers or to try to straighten kids out with whatever you know that can help them he is usually through, or a poseur or more or less a pompous ass.[34]

Undeterred, Plimpton later found his way to Spain and caught Hemingway during his annual visit to run with bulls. He wrote to his *Paris Review* colleagues: "I had a most splendid time in Pamplona . . . but I received the worst of it in the amateur [bull] fights, getting myself tossed and tromped on. I was carrying a furled umbrella at the time (someone had given it to me to hold) and the incident—while humiliating and painful to me—caused great merriment to 15,000 people and presumably one cow."[35]

. . .

Plimpton was a pioneer of a wing of New Journalism that some have taken to calling participatory journalism. He was also a serial exaggerator.[36] This combination of qualities charmed friends, fans, and readers alike, on the page, on television, and while entertaining guests at his legendary cocktail parties. As a writer, Plimpton admired the reporting of Paul Gallico, who believed that you could never write about sports until you enlisted to pitch against pro baseball's sluggers or stood in as quarterback for the Detroit Lions. Both of these Plimpton famously did. Plus he went on safari, played goalie for a professional hockey team, jumped from a plane, did standup comedy, played a bit part in a John Wayne Western, became a trapeze artist, and played triangle for a world-class New York City symphony orchestra. Throughout, short-form or long-, he wrote about it. Was it just a coincidence that this editor whose magazine had positive propaganda ties, secret though they were, was now writing pieces that celebrated American pastimes? Was it merely a matter of Plimpton listening to determine what was in harmony (and funded) and what was discordant with the music of the Cold War?

Whatever Gallico's influence, the letters between Plimpton and Hemingway make it clear, too, that Hemingway's heroism was also a major influence. Plimpton was using not just their interview to keep in touch with the novelist but also his own participatory writing. Plimpton's sports writing could at times be gimmicky, managing to be both self-flagellating and self-obsessed. He clearly had less at stake personally in some of these "stunts," as he called them, than other ones. Some of his more acclaimed literary friends viewed the participatory writing as downright silly and unserious. For example, the author James Salter said that Plimpton's participatory journalism was "a genre that really doesn't permit greatness."[37] But Plimpton used it in such a way—asking Hemingway for help finding a boxing coach, seeking his advice when his editor wouldn't let him print the athletes' curse words—so as to fold the novelist and man-of-action into the lore of *The Paris Review*, in its blue-chip canon of author interviews alongside the party hoppers and outsize personalities, and to enwrap the canonical writer into Plimpton's own legacy. He even got a great blurb out of it from Hemingway and he appeared to be having a great deal of fun. At the height of this bonding, they became friends and Hemingway often encouraged Plimpton more than Plimpton's own father, who dismissed the first issue of *The Paris Review* as "exhibitionist"[38] and could be a severe disciplinarian and scold.

While Hemingway was mercurial and cranky, he could be effusive with praise and occasionally earnest. In blurbing Plimpton's baseball book, *Out of My League*, he called Plimpton the "dark side of the moon of Walter Mitty." And it exercised him that Plimpton wouldn't be allowed to record the real color of conversations around the baseball diamond, when the publishers wouldn't allow him to print the players' colorful dialogue in full. Papa, as his admirers called him, could cuss—e.g. "fuck the art of fiction"—and the anger, frustration, and other emotions embedded in American dialogue were an indispensable component of his own literary technique. But whatever the elder writer's hang-ups, Plimpton won Hemingway over with charm and persistence. Courage was essential to the participatory journalist. As he fought championship boxers or played quarterback with professional football players, Plimpton found that success was both barred by the comic form of the amateur deliberately failing against the professionals and masters, and at the same time, given the low expectations, success was inevitable—so long as he survived. The bungling form of the amateur among the pros flattered both the amateurs that most readers feel we are, and it flattered the experts that Hemingway fancied himself and often was.

Plimpton's Hemingway interview—and their subsequent friendship—was itself part of this participatory experiment. One wrong move in an acolyte's attempt to immerse himself into the canon could be painful. On one of Plimpton's Cuba visits, Hemingway famously decked him over an impertinent question ("What is the significance of those white birds that sometimes turn up in your, ah, sex scenes?").[39] When Hemingway responded by scolding, then later punching, his young disciple in the head, he may have seen it as part of Plimpton's belated training. Plimpton shared Hemingway's interest in boxing and had fought the light middleweight champion, Archie Moore, in early 1959, as one of his writing stunts. Hemingway's friend, George Brown, served as Plimpton's trainer and Hemingway had tried to get Plimpton to enlist for preparatory fights. Hemingway's rage was couched in the common language between them, the language of sparring, and the reluctant Plimpton's prior evasions. Let's "see how good you are," Hemingway said as he hit Plimpton hard enough to make him cry, tears Plimpton described as a result of the condition he called "sympathetic response." Plimpton wrote that, while crying like this, "Suddenly I knew what to do.

> I dropped my hands and asked Papa a question. "How did you do that . . . how did you bring your hands up from that position?" turning him into an instructor, asking him in such wonder that he was enormously flattered. A smile appeared through those white whiskers.[40]

By seeking Hemingway's expertise, Plimpton had pacified him. But even after the interview ran, Plimpton's politely pestering letters make it clear he wanted more: namely, friendship. To lay oneself down before certain pain and survive was highly entertaining. To do so emotionally, on the other hand, was endearing. In one of their interview drafts, Hemingway had stated that he can only write when he's in love. In a reply, Plimpton wanted advice for his writerly heartbreak. "So I . . . watched all this from Versailles and Cannes, and then, Papa, when I got back here I found that my girl . . . had gone and got herself involved with an ex-Olympic ski champion. That hurt a lot, as much as anything I've ever known. I know what you mean when you say you can only write when you're in love. But what the hell do you do when it's unrequited?"[41] After apologizing and offering to rewrite his own interview questions—because they "were stiff and un-conversational in a few cases"—Plimpton added, "I know that you are doing this [interview] as a friend and I am more appreciative of that fact than I can put into words."[42]

To such prompts, a disarmed but cranky Hemingway replied, "I had the questions finished when I said I would. But they weren't right and I kept going over them to try to get them better." He finished,

> Mary [Welsh Hemingway, his fourth wife] says they are quite clear for you to have them copied for the printer. . . . It is never meant to be rude. I tried to make it sound like talk and we <u>are</u> friends.[43]

• • •

To finish his Art of Fiction interview with Hemingway, Plimpton traveled to the Havana suburb of San Francisco de Paula, where Hemingway now lived much of the time. But to earn this coveted visit—Plimpton had been rebuffed previously—he used Hemingway's favorite pastime, other than boxing, as a lure. Hemingway took seriously the macho quietude of fishing. He once mocked a friend with an invitation to come bonefishing, "if you want to bring your grandmother along."[44] In other words there was fishing for women and fishing for men. By inviting himself to fish for the womanly kind, Plimpton showed he learned to manage Hemingway's ego. As effective a self-deprecator in person as on the page, Plimpton steered away from Hemingway's competitive irritability and positioned himself as a fool before the master's throne. "If you want a talisman I'd have to admit I'm not the best to have around. Last time out on the Gulf Stream I had the smallest sailfish on the line ever seen in those parts."[45] Since childhood, Plimpton always had what Matthiessen described as a "social genius."[46] Using that genius, Plimpton signaled to Hemingway that he was no threat, that he needed the older writer's advice, his wisdom, and that in Plimpton he had a devoted disciple and friend.

It worked. Hemingway's third wife, the journalist and war correspondent Martha Gellhorn, had refused to stay in the hotel where Hemingway lived when they met. So she went house hunting in Cuba. The giant "ceiba" tree in front, with its pink late-winter blooms, endeared her to the farm that Plimpton would visit. Together she and Hemingway named it "Finca Vigia," or "Lookout Farm."[47] Hemingway wrote *For Whom the Bell Tolls* there; with his famous fishing boat, *Pilar*, he used the place as a base of operations to hunt for German subs during World War II. No subs were found, alas. But Hemingway used the ploy to up his gasoline rations. Today the house that the Hemingways cherished is a museum. When Plimpton visited it was late winter 1959, the ceiba would have been in bloom, and the day of fishing they shared had been sunny and fun.[48]

Plimpton's interview had finally run the spring before, and it remains much cited to this day, especially for its iceberg analogy: "I always try to write on the principle of the iceberg. There is seven-eighths of it underwater for every part that shows. Anything you know you can eliminate and it only strengthens your iceberg. It is the part that doesn't show. If a writer omits something because he does not know it then there is a hole in the story."[49]

Plimpton was proud of his ability to maneuver the older writer and his savvy had reeled in a difficult interview that he had pursued across Europe, New York, Cuba, and (by correspondence) Africa. Editorially, it was worth the trouble. That the propagandists wanted it must have made the little magazine feel that it was once again punching above its weight.

More than a year before it was out, the interview was sought by at least four of the CIA magazines for syndication. Melvin Lasky of the CCF wrote on *The Paris Review* letterhead, logo and address crossed out, to thank Paris editor Silvers for showing him a draft of the interview. Lasky asked to see the interview again when it was closer to done; but it was close enough to know he wanted it. For *Der Monat*, he wrote, "I should very much like to have first crack at the German rights. . ."

> But could you start the correspondence [for] an option on the Spanish, Italian, and possibly French translation rights. Our associated reviews in those languages might very well be interested too. In which case with a good lump sum most of the foreign rights would be disposed of.[50]

The Hemingway interview only touched on politics, specifically in discussing the Ezra Pound affair.[51] But as far as CCF magazines were concerned, the literary value of American and "pro-Western" authors was now a standard commodity used for positive cultural diplomacy. The five-year-old *Paris Review* was enabling a clutch of CCF magazines to offer a new snapshot of a popular American novelist who had won the 1954 Nobel Prize for Literature for his novel *The Old Man and the Sea*. In this short book, Hemingway had shown sensitivity to Cuban poverty by telling the story of the unlucky fisherman Santiago through the eyes of the young boy who takes care of him. The book examines obsession and fortune in a highly accessible, emotive, and at times allegorical language that in its way showed the plight of developing nations, populated by countless Santiagos who—without really great luck or the solidarity of a boy who gave up his berth on a more fortunate boat—might not eat a crumb for days at a time.

But cultural diplomacy was secondary to promoting *The Paris Review*. And for that, Hemingway's appeal was far-reaching. Aldrich wrote to the New York office, "Laski [sic] is coming to Paris any day now and I will give him the H. interview as per instructions." He continued, "If that doesn't work, I have already heard expressions of interest from magazines in the countries of our Axis allies: the Fisher-Verlag in Frankfurt and something or other in Japan. In short, I guess we shan't have much trouble selling Papa."[52]

Did Plimpton realize that he was making the defiantly leftist Hemingway into a US propaganda tool, even vaguely? Aldrich, for one, believed that Plimpton knew the CCF was a CIA front.[53] But did Hemingway know? Though many of the letters between Plimpton and Hemingway are archived, there is no hint in them that Hemingway was ever told his interview would be reprinted in covert state lit mags. Amidst all their friendly back and forth, in which recreational and editorial endeavors merged, not a word was dropped by Plimpton that the interview they had worked so hard on together, over which Hemingway toiled against his pain—rewriting it again and again despite health concerns and depression, fighting for time against his paying work in order to finish—could appear in the European and Asian magazines of the CCF. Was this because Plimpton assumed that Hemingway would demur?

·   ·   ·

Plimpton also tried to steer Hemingway's leftward politics back to the vital center. Months after visiting Hemingway in Cuba during a period when the Pasternak interview was also under way, Plimpton wrote Hemingway, "I hope to catch a glimpse of you on the way through [New York]. It's been a summer and fall of slow death, realizing what I missed; I just couldn't get away, try as I did.

> But there were good moments in the summer here. I wrote well. I did a few more stunts for the [participatory journalism] series . . . but you'll find me very much the listener come your arrival. I'm afraid it may have been worth shucking all responsibilities to see just a portion of what you saw this summer. I will always remember your initiation to it, and a steady smoldering rage at being unable to do anything about it.[54]

Note the change in tone. Among Plimpton's solicitous, jocular letters, this last sentence above stands out. It points to his disapproval for the tribunals of Batista's functionaries in Cuba, which Plimpton must have seen on that same trip when Hemingway punched him. According to two former *Paris Review* editors, Hemingway had taken Plimpton to watch those trials and executions, part of what the Cubans called Operation Truth. Plimpton could little have known how his own government had inspired those tribunals. Operation Truth began soon after Castro's revolutionaries came to power in Havana in early 1959. At stake were the hundreds of functionaries of the ousted dictatorship of Fulgencio Batista, the US ally who had fled into exile and left a long list of war crimes and criminals in his wake. Ernesto Guevara would now have his chance to put the lessons from Guatemala into action, lessons taught by the American overthrow there. For in Guatemala the mistake was allowing midlevel members of the old regime to stay, Guevara believed, and allowing those with mixed loyalties to hide in the new government and in particular in the armed forces. Even US ally José Figueres would have been overthrown by the Americans if he had left his military intact, as events later proved.

Knowing the Americans might attack Operation Truth in the media, the newly ascendant Castro had put out a call for writers to come in order to offset the propaganda they expected, by simply observing and listening at the tribunals. Younger writers, journalists, leftists, revolutionary idealists, anti-imperialist Latin Americans, and at least one future Nobel Prize winner—though a budding journalist then—were among those who attended.

Gabriel García Márquez's account is different enough from Plimpton's that the gap might simply point to the distortions-by-propaganda that Luis Alberto Monge described in his letter to Norman Thomas, in which he warned of the bad effect propaganda was having on the two regions' perspectives toward each other and suggesting that it helped to be on the ground to contextualize the confusion. Plimpton and García Márquez were both on the ground, of course. But only the latter spoke fluent Spanish, making Plimpton susceptible to the propaganda that was unleashed.

Operation Truth featured trials in which functionaries of Batista's regime were read their records, allowed a defense, and in many cases were executed. There were few pardons, though there was a formal means for them to petition for such. As with the attacks on Nixon's cavalcade in Venezuela the year before, the American media were loud and unanimous in their condemnation of what were treated as arbitrary executions. Historians describe the tribunals instead as a provisional justice to appease the people. "To demonstrate that these were war criminals and not simply followers of the ousted dictator,"[55] wrote scholars Ángel Esteban and Stéphanie Panichelli, Cuba opened the trials to the world. Castro hoped to show a contrast with his US-supported predecessor, the dictator Batista. García Márquez and his friend Plinio Apuleyo Mendoza were persuaded. They "had just arrived at the airport in Camaguey—they both must have looked exhausted—when Fidel appeared." Castro "looked at [García Márquez] and asked 'Have you eaten?,' showing an interest in making sure they were comfortable during their stay on the island.

Then they immediately attended the trial of Jésus Sosa Blanco, a colonel of Batista's army, accused of murdering various locals from a small rural area known as El Oro de Guisa who had supported the rebel army. He was sentenced to death. His wife and children asked many of the journalists to sign a document requesting a revised sentence.

García Márquez and Mendoza signed the appeal yet it was ultimately ineffective. But "both were confident that the trial and sentence had been just. . . . When they returned to Colombia a few days later, the two friends were already part of a group of intellectuals that were supportive of the Cuban Revolution."[56]

Plimpton's version of events was more lighthearted, though the smoldering rage that he recalled in his letter to Hemingway was voiced in Plimpton's literary treatment by New Yorker theater critic Kenneth Tynan. "That very evening there was going to be a lot of activity in the fortress," wrote Plimpton. The writers were drinking with an "American soldier of fortune," Captain Marks, who would "be delighted if we would consider joining him as his guests at what he referred to as 'the festivities.' . . . At this point there was a sudden eruption from Tynan. He had been sitting, rocking back and forth in his chair; he came out of it almost as if propelled." Plimpton continued in a sendup of the serious political convulsions that Cuba was experiencing:

> At first, I don't think Captain Marks was aware that these curious honked explosions of indignation from this gaunt arm-flapping man in a seersucker suit were directed at him, but then Tynan got his voice under control, and Captain Marks could see his opened eyes now, pale and furious, staring at him and the words became discernible—shouts that it was sickening to stay in the room with such a frightful specimen as an executioner of men ("l-l-l-loathsome!"), and as for the invitation, yes he was going to turn up all right, but in order to throw himself in front of the guns of the firing squad! He was going to stop the "festivities"—the word sprayed from him in rage—and with this he pulled his wife up out of her chair . . . and rushed to the exit.[57]

When Tynan's wife and biographer, Kathleen Tynan,[58] recapped the scene, it was clear that Plimpton was himself compelled to watch the executions. The allure of something so politically "loathsome" attracted him. Didn't the participatory style call for it? "Plimpton, to his own shame, wanted to attend that execution," she wrote, "and he went over to Hemingway's *finca* that afternoon to get some advice and tell him about Ken [Tynan], how Ken had stunned the man Marks and steamed with rage.

> Hemingway felt that it had been a mistake to ask Ken to an execution since his emotional makeup was just not suited to such things, that he would give the revolution a bad name. But he encouraged Plimpton to go.

Tynan continued, "Thus armed, Plimpton set off to meet [Tennessee] Williams for the event. Tennessee had discovered from Captain Marks that a German mercenary was scheduled to be shot that evening and he felt that if he had the chance to do so he would get close enough to give him a small encouraging smile."[59]

If not for Williams, Plimpton himself might have come off as the politically frivolous one. Between Tynan's righteous indignation and Williams's blasé flirtation, Plimpton positions himself (with an assist from Tynan's wife) as occupying a reasonable middle space—the vital center—from which he can make jokes and pass others' judgments without veering into the territory of Tynan's "hysterical" indignation or Williams's pure amusement. But the explosion of sensibilities was not to be. In the end, the event was canceled. "Frankly, I have no idea whether Tynan was actually responsible for the evening's 'festivities' being canceled," wrote Plimpton.

> I like to think that he was; that the officials got wind of his outraged reaction to Captain Marks in the Floridita [Café] . . . that he was going to throw himself in front of the guns. No, it was best to let things cool down; to let this weird fanatic clear off the island. At least they would not have to worry that just as everything was going along smoothly, the blindfolds nicely in place, not too tight, just right, Tynan's roar of rage would peal out of the darkness ("St-st-stop this in-in-infamous be-be-behaviour!"), and he would flap out at them across the courtyard, puffs of dirt issuing from his footfalls as he came at them like a berserk crane.[60]

Plimpton's version makes light of the varied responses, each of his friends' reactions almost satirically standing for different sensibilities of the political and cultural left. Hemingway, however, a veteran who had almost been killed in World War I, certainly wasn't attending the executions for entertainment. The debate did not end in the early 1960s. As late as 2009, *The*

Paris Review's former managing editor, James Scott Linville, reversed their positions in the neoconservative *Standpoint* magazine, showing Plimpton heroically drawing a line in the sand against injustice, like Tynan but without the silly stutter, while Hemingway drank and enjoyed the sunset executions.

In the mid-1990s, Linville was sent Guevara's *Motorcycle Diaries* in galleys. He asked to excerpt it in *The Paris Review*. The Cold War was over. The *Diaries* were more humanist than Marxist, he believed. So Linville was surprised when Plimpton, feet up on his desk, refused to publish an excerpt from that book or anything by Guevara. "It was right after the revolution," George told him, explaining his stance. Hemingway took him on an expedition.

> The nature of the expedition was a mystery; Hemingway made a shaker of drinks . . . . They got in the car . . . and drove . . . out of town. They got out, set up chairs . . . as if . . . to watch the sunset. Soon, a truck arrived. This, explained George, was what they'd been waiting for. It came, as Hemingway knew, the same time each day. It stopped and some men with guns got out. . . . In the back were a couple of dozen others who were tied up. Prisoners.
>
> The men with guns hustled the others out of the back of the truck, and lined them up. Then they shot them. They put the bodies back into the truck. I said to George something to the effect of "Oh my God."[61]

Linville described the executed men as "political prisoners," and compared these executions to those in Chile following the 1973 coup. "About Guevara's role in [their] execution," he finished, ". . . the world has taken less interest. For myself, after reading the accounts I was never able to feel the same way about some things ever again."[62] Here the famed editor of the apolitical *Paris Review* was being represented by a very political reading of history.

There have indeed been transgressions and worse over the years in Castro's Cuba. But propagandistic distortion had done nothing but cloud them. One prominent biographer has battled these distortions. "I have yet to find a single credible source pointing to a case where Che executed 'an innocent,'" *New Yorker* writer and Guevara biographer Jon Lee Anderson told a PBS forum in 1997. "Those persons executed by Guevara or on his orders were condemned for the usual crimes punishable by death at times of war or in its aftermath: desertion, treason, or crimes such as rape, torture, or murder."[63] A decade and a half after his biography appeared, Anderson doubled down on this sentiment in an email. Despite frequent challenges, he was certain that his reporting on the Operation Truth campaign held up:

> No one who has ever asked me about these outlandish claims has ever cited a piece of evidence . . . that might alter what I think I know—that around 340—or perhaps, as some say, a few more, maybe a total of 500—people accused of war crimes were executed after the revolutionary seizure of power in 1959 in the tribunals presided over by Che. As far as I know . . . these [more exaggerated] claims surfaced in the past seven or eight years courtesy of one Humberto Fontova of Miami, who runs an outfit dedicated to rewriting history . . .[64]

Linville didn't go as far as all this, but the insinuation seemed to. A regular guest on Fox News endorsed as "my American warrior blood brother" by Ted Nugent, Fontova has claimed that more than ten thousand were killed during Operation Truth. Distortions aimed at whitewashing the US atrocities in the region, multiple attempts to murder Castro, a terror campaign against the island called Operation Mongoose, and sanctions that punished Cuba's population lasted until Gabriel García Márquez's 2014 death when his friendship with Castro was held against him as a stain on his legacy. In a 2014 article in *The New York Times*, Cuba was slammed by eminent liberal critic Susan Sontag for having the world's highest prison rate. Never mind that when she had made this claim quoted by *The Times*—in the 1980s—as well as today, the US prison rate was higher than Cuba's. In other 2014 articles upon his death, García Márquez was condemned—also by Fontova, but picked up in the mainstream—for getting informants thrown into Castro's prisons and for getting American presidents (of the Democratic Party) to sing his praises despite his "rabid hatred" for the United States.[65]

After his death, Plimpton was praised for allegedly condemning Cuba; García Márquez was denounced for a laundry list of offenses by the propaganda stream of the American media. But despite Fontova's claims, García Márquez never hated the United States and Fontova was engaged in disinformation. The Nobel laureate may have hated the game the United States played, with intellectuals used as pawns in a black and white battle for hearts and minds. But he did not hate the players, even after he was tricked into their fold when the CIA claimed a publishing coup by excerpting two chapters from his masterpiece.

10

CUBA: A PORTRAIT BY PLIMPTON, HEMINGWAY, AND GARCÍA MÁRQUEZ, PART 2

Mr. Nixon could not see then what should have been obvious—and
. . . even more obvious when he made his ill-fated Latin American
trip in 1958—that unless the Cuban people, with our help, made
substantial economic progress, trouble was on its way. If this is the
kind of experience Mr. Nixon claims entitles him to be president,
then . . . the American people cannot afford many more such
experiences.

—John F. Kennedy[1]

The Bay of Pigs invasion was the disastrous covert operation handed off to
President Kennedy by the Eisenhower administration. During his campaign,
Kennedy had cited Cuba specifically to suggest that propping up dictators
who indulged in corruption was bound to backfire and that this exploitative
behavior on the part of the US fueled anti-imperialist and anti-American

rhetoric.[2] When Kennedy said this at a Democratic dinner in Cincinnati, the tribunals of Batista's functionaries and Operation Truth had already occurred and the American reaction was already under way. When he was voted in a month later, Kennedy inherited a CIA plan to neutralize the problem by force: a covert invasion was in the works. Faithful friends inside and outside the region insisted that an invasion would be counterproductive. First the American Committee's Arthur Schlesinger advised against the invasion,[3] then Costa Rica's Figueres did.[4] But the administration's hawks won the dispute.

On March 10, 1961, Sacha Volman, writing from San José, sent Norman Thomas in New York an urgent request. "Don Pepe is going to be in the US in about 10 days . . . . I know very much that he would like to have a meeting . . . with President Kennedy.

> In addition to this Don Romulo [Betancourt, Kennedy's close advisor and the president of Venezuela] also feels very strongly in favor of Don Pepe being able to greet the President. . . . Don Romulo has not only authorized me but also urged me to make clear his private views about this meeting.[5]

Volman urged Thomas to get in touch with Arthur Schlesinger, "making clear that . . . both he and Don Romulo (who can be quoted) are anxious about such a meeting."[6] Schlesinger was an advisor and "court historian" to the Kennedy administration. His critique of the American Committee had helped end that group in 1957. Schlesinger heard of the Bay of Pigs plan in February and claimed later that he opposed it in a memo, in which he wrote how "at one stroke you would dissipate all the extraordinary good will which has been rising toward the new Administration through the world. It would fix a malevolent image of the new Administration in the minds of millions." Schlesinger's warning was merely tactical. In the end, he advised an equally harebrained violent covert operation in its place.[7]

But as these letters corroborate, Schlesinger also tried to help Figueres make his case against invasion. Not only was Figueres a friend of the United States who collaborated secretly on a CIA-funded magazine and a social democratic training camp in San José. He had also appeared in Cuba in the early days of the revolution and was wrestled off a stage after criticizing Cuba's coziness toward the Soviet Union in a similar style to that which he used to criticize US policy before the US Senate—doing so in both cases as a concerned but blunt friend. Volman requested a cable be sent confirming that the meeting had been set up. On March 13, Thomas replied, "I just talked to Arthur Schlesinger by phone. He agreed that it was very important Don Pepe see President Kennedy." Arranged through Schlesinger, Figueres's visit with Kennedy was scheduled for just about three weeks before the Bay of Pigs. It was a race to stop a catastrophe.[8]

In January, *The New York Times* had reported that "the United States was training an exile army in Guatemala to invade Cuba."[9] Other rumors had leaked, too. Security in Florida, the command center, had been so bad that one of the coup plotters had his conversations about the attack overheard through the walls of his hotel room, schemes that were dutifully reported to the FBI. When the CIA's infamous plans to assassinate Castro (by poisoned food and exploding cigar) did not come to fruition, a new plan called for a covert invasion. In the period between John F. Kennedy's election and the days after his inauguration, murder was out: invasion was back in. The projected cost ballooned from four million to forty million. The required manpower had multiplied, too, from two hundred people to a full-scale secret war, which even included the Operation SUCCESS veteran who had ordered a bomb dropped onto a British ship, which sank it.[10]

Kennedy was skeptical enough that he forbade an outright escalation if anything went wrong and began pruning what he could. He changed the site of the landing to the swamps of Playa Girón and halted US air support plans to avoid an outright war.[11] The CIA assumed he would change his mind about hamstringing the invasion force.[12] So they never told the Cuban exiles who would execute the operation that it had been scaled back, which in turn led to their vitriolic hatred of Kennedy after the disastrous turn of events.

While the *Times* leaked the scheme and while certain partisans—such as Schlesinger, Thomas, Volman, and Figueres—acted to stop the invasion, Plimpton wrote to Hemingway in a subtle attempt to convince him to condemn the Cubans for moving into the Soviet camp. His plea came at the end of a long, arduous description of the night Norman Mailer, running for mayor of New York—with Harold "Doc" Humes as his campaign manager—stabbed his wife Adele. In a fit of pique, Mailer punctured her near her heart with a small knife. It was a brute response to an off-the-cuff, gay-baiting comment that she had made about his disheveled appearance[13] at a fund raising party filled with luminaries, celebrities, and down-and-out New Yorkers. Plimpton went on for six pages, some of them his best unpublished writing; Hemingway said so in his reply. They amounted to a long, confused meditation on the stifling atmosphere and confused allegiances of the early 1960s. At the end of this, Plimpton enclosed an open letter that Mailer would publish in the *Village Voice*,[14] after legal questions surrounding the stabbing were settled.

The letter begins with a litany of American sins, including the psychologically murderous behavior of US media and police. Finally, Mailer simply asks Castro to reconsider allying the proud Cubans—whose revolution Mailer described as heroic and pathway-lighting for soul-crushed North Americans—with the corrupted Soviets. It asks him to remain neutral, shy by yards of his alignment with the Soviets.[15] Was Plimpton trying to convince Hemingway to take a similar stance? If so, Plimpton's subtle pleading coincided with that of US officials who thought Hemingway's continued presence in Cuba was tantamount to treason, certainly unpatriotic.

While it's difficult to pin down Hemingway's precise politics in the period of the late 1950s and early 1960s, just before he died, one can say that he was somewhere between favorable to the Cuban Revolution and sometimes wary over how it would mature once in power.[16] He donated money to the Cuban Communist Party and famously went fishing with Castro and Guevara at the onset of their incumbency (in a fishing tournament in May 1960 that Castro won, and Hemingway judged). Clancy Sigal has written, "When the Batista regime fell, Hemingway wished Fidel 'all luck,' and later donated his Nobel Prize to Castro. Henceforth the new revolutionary government honored 'Ernesto' as an adopted son of Cuba."[17]

With Castro in power, Hemingway—returning from Spain—weighed in on the storm over Operation Truth by denouncing the US media for their Cuba-bashers, and he even kissed the Cuban flag. "I am happy to be here again, because I consider myself one more Cuban," he said. "My sympathies are with the Cuban Revolution and all our difficulties. I don't want to be considered a Yanqui."[18] The scholar Keneth Kinnamon recounts how Hemingway's doctor, Dr. José Luis Herrera Sotolongo, linked Hemingway to Fidel Castro. Hemingway had backed the overthrow of the dictator Gerardo Machado in the 1930s and had supported the Cuban Communist Party with donations amounting to $20,000 through the Cuban Revolutionary period.[19]

When Plimpton sent Hemingway Mailer's open letter in January 1961, the US ambassador to Cuba had just told Hemingway that his continued inhabitation of Cuba was regarded as unpatriotic by the United States. Valerie Hemingway, the writer's daughter-in-law, wrote that "Papa" bristled at the suggestion, "fiercely."[20]

Mailer's open letter made the case for reform, his main point being that non-alignment was better than Soviet alignment: an ideological and a moral plea. Practically, however, Hemingway knew that the Cubans would need to sell their sugar crop to somebody, and the United States wasn't buying. It wasn't just Fidel who chose the Soviets; it was the United States who forced Fidel's hand.

It was an art that Plimpton's magazine had taken part in now for almost a decade, appearing apolitical while making a political case. Without seeming to criticize Hemingway's vocal support for the revolution, Plimpton could make his point through Mailer. And there was no direct argument from Plimpton, no fingerprint from the apolitical *Paris Review*, just the enclosure from one writer to another sent as a personal matter between friends.

. . .

Meanwhile, Operation TRUTH had made Gabriel García Márquez so interested in the Cuban Revolution that he enlisted to work in Cuba's newly created media conglomerate. Prensa Latina was conceived when the Argentine writer Jorge Masetti criticized incessant US media attacks on post-Revolutionary Cuba and Guevara challenged Masetti to do something concrete; he offered the fellow Argentine resources to start Cuba's alternative media conglomerate. Named Prensa Latina, it was nicknamed Prela by those who regularly used it.[21]

A picture from his time at a Colombian newspaper in the late 1950s shows García Márquez with a thin mustache and prominent cheekbones. A tightly-rolled cigarette dangles from his thin lips. His hair is greased back and he wears a fine suit. This was the young man who joined as an enthusiastic recruit at Prela's Colombia desk. Though he was needed elsewhere, he would train in Havana. He wrote jokingly of how he did nothing there but work, that he could name only the small circle of restaurants around Prela's offices. The only other parts of Havana he memorized were his desk and the building's elevator. He and everyone there in those days worked so hard that, if anything would sink the revolution, he joked, it would be the light bill.[22] He worked with Masetti and Rodolfo Walsh, an author whom García Márquez admired and who was considered by some to be the continent's inventor of investigative journalism in Spanish. Walsh was also in charge of Prela's Special Services, an outgrowth of Prela's mediapolitics, as Deborah Davis has called the conflation of spying and journalism.[23]

Then something astonishing happened. One day in early 1961, Masetti "stumbled" across an encrypted telex from Washington, which he supposed could be important. Indeed, it was from the Americans, the CIA. He gave it to Walsh who, according to Walsh's wife, Poupée, spent several days in the dining room, blocks from the Prela office, until he successfully decoded it.[24] What it laid out were plans for the Bay of Pigs invasion. Masetti, García Márquez, and Walsh brought it to the Cuban government with a plan to surprise the Americans. But the three writers, who must have been stunned, were told that the Cubans already knew about the invasion and had their own plan. "In spite of that rebuff, it was an unforgettable event in the lives of the three journalists, which Gabo [García Márquez] would later immortalize in his 'Recuerdos de periodista,'"[25] in December 1981.

The story would be unbelievable, one of García Márquez's clique's own tall tales, if not for the fact of the widespread leaking, rumors, news reports, and security problems of the operation. And for speedy communication between CIA stations, the encrypted telex was the closest thing that could be found to an encrypted email or text message.

. . .

The Bay of Pigs was of course a failure. The scaled-back operations were blamed by many of the participants for the slaughter during which Fidel's men, warned of the attack in advance, gained the upper hand right away and beat back the invasion in short order.

On the morning of Saturday, April 15, Francis Taylor Pearsons Plimpton, George Plimpton's father and deputy ambassador to the United Nations, was just within the frame on the newsreel footage, when Ambassador Adlai Stevenson told the United Nations that Cuba's charges that the United States trained and sponsored the invading forces were "totally false and I deny them categorically."[26]

As it had in Guatemala, the United States had done covert air reconnaissance as an opening salvo in support of the Bay of Pigs ground invasion. Acting covertly on behalf of the United States, a pilot strafed strategic targets throughout Cuba—including the Cuban Air Force—and shifted the credit onto Cuban Air Force defectors. This was all a fabrication.[27] From the Cuban Air Force logo painted on the CIA plane's tail to the bullet holes shot into the fuselage, to the unidentified pilot (who initially hid his face on television as he disembarked in Florida after attacking his own nation), it was staged. Ambassador Pedersen described his boss as very "disturbed" to learn later that the CIA had tricked him into publicly lying and together the team wrote a letter of complaint to Washington. When asked long after by a CIA historian about this protest, Plimpton Senior indicated that he "'was in complete accord with everything' that Mr. Pedersen wrote about this episode."[28]

Two days later, the exile-mercenaries and the CIA team invaded the island. García Márquez felt he would have been safer there, on the beaches of the Bay of Pigs, than where he was. Since witnessing his colleagues decode the telex, he had been transferred to Prensa Latina's New York offices. In the city that never sleeps, his life and the life of his family were threatened, he later wrote. Going between the well-guarded Rockefeller Center office and Prela's office in the United Nations Secretariat Building, room 367,[29] he worked a stone's throw from where the world's governments negotiated, including Plimpton's father.

The threats Gabo faced came from those he described as "gusanos,"[30] reactionary or counterrevolutionary "worms" from the United States' unruly Cuban exile community. It sounds as if the aggressions that became Operation Mongoose were already roiling among the Cuban exile community. (A year later—for instance—in April 1962, Prensa Latina's New York offices were bombed. By then, García Márquez had already resigned. But the agency's international offices became regular targets of the broader US terror and surveillance campaign against Cuba that was code-named Operation Mongoose and also went by "Cuban Project.")[31]

Unlike in Guatemala, Castro's popular support and his abundant supplies during the Bay of Pigs invasion allowed him to do what Guevara had hoped Árbenz would have done seven years before: arm the citizens of the nation under attack and beat back the imperialist invasion. The exile-invaders, representing their bosses, funders, and planners in the north, had lost a major battle and those who weren't killed in the fighting were either imprisoned in Cuba or returned humiliated to their outposts in Miami or New York. The credibility of the United States and the Kennedy administration suffered. The United States had tried to use force, disguised through proxies, lied about it to the UN and before the world; the invasion had failed and the Americans were caught in their lie. On the Cold War scorecard, this was a full-scale loss for the United States.

Later, Stevenson himself compared it to the "U-2 disaster,"[32] whereby the Soviets insisted the United States was spying on them, the United States denied it, and then a U-2 surveillance plane crashed inside the Soviet Union with a pilot named Francis Gary Powers inside, who was kept in Soviet custody to make the point exceedingly clear about how bold the United States was with respect to public lying. Schlesinger and Figueres had warned them.

By some calculations, it might be argued that the Bay of Pigs was another lesson in the limits of coercive force: it undermined all that had been or could be won through cultural diplomacy. The refrain from the early 1950s, when the brutal refugee airdrops in Eastern Europe had failed, resounded over Cuba's Playa Girón as indeed it had over Guatemala: "We'd have been better off doing nothing."

Before the Bay of Pigs, the Latin American left could smell a US-funded magazine from a reasonable distance. Afterward this sniff test would be ever more acute. It was also becoming apparent that overt propaganda of the type that *Cuadernos* had tried, with no disguise—no diversity of opinion to point to—had failed to engage the readers they were meant to win over and refute. So instead of a moratorium on disastrous "executive actions," which would have been more effective than overt propaganda, the CIA would resurrect its plans to murder Fidel Castro while attempting to keep down the "noise" of such actions.[33] They would do this while at the same time launching a new CIA magazine for the region, and this magazine would adopt a line it called "Fidelismo sin Fidel"—Fidelism without Fidel—or revolution without dictatorship. This was a way of saying "subtler" anticommunism.

Meanwhile, Hemingway shot himself in his Ketchum, Idaho, home in July 1961, three months after the Bay of Pigs and exactly a year after he had been coerced into leaving the island he so loved after his presence there had grown contentious. Although no one believed him, he told everyone he could that he was being hounded endlessly by FBI agents, who followed his every move, standing at the corner of the bar in his hometown dive, the Casino Bar, staring at him outright. His FBI file released many years later revealed that, indeed, he was hounded as ruthlessly as he had said. One of the psychiatrists at Mayo Clinic in Rochester, Minnesota—where he received shock treatment—even "contacted the FBI to ask permission to tell his patient, who 'was concerned about an FBI investigation,' that 'the FBI is not concerned with his registering under an assumed name.'"[34] The irony is heartbreaking.

Whether the FBI ever worried that the constant surveillance might have had a calamitous effect on Hemingway's mental health is not clear.[35] Hemingway biographer and friend A.E. Hotchner wrote an op-ed fifty years after the author's suicide, admitting that he had minimized Hemingway's paranoia. "In the years since [his death], I have tried to reconcile Ernest's fear of the FBI, which I regretfully misjudged, with the reality of the FBI file. I now believe he truly sensed the surveillance, and that it substantially contributed to his anguish and his suicide."[36] But Hemingway wasn't just followed by the FBI and coerced into leaving Cuba, the island he so loved, by the State Department. As we have seen, has was subtly made in more Cold War propaganda by the CIA's magazines, funneled out to so many of them by *The Paris Review.*

If bullying, surveilling, and goading Americans—sometimes into suicide—was how the state sought to lure Europeans and the world's wavering Asians, Africans, and Latin Americans away from Communism and toward the American way, it might need a reboot.

11

TOOLS RUSH IN: PABLO NERUDA, MUNDO NUEVO, AND KEITH BOTSFORD

I do not want anybody to go around anymore being unwittingly a tool. —Keith Botsford

In the summer of 1962, the writer, editor, and CCF man Keith Botsford waited for Robert Lowell at the airport in Brazil. Lowell was coming on a CCF-sponsored campaign to overshadow the leftist Chilean poet Pablo Neruda. American officials were sending those they considered politically "responsible" to places like Latin America as "emissaries" to diminish the influence of those who scared them, like Neruda.

Lowell's first collection of poems had come out before his thirtieth birthday and had won him a Pulitzer Prize. Politically, he was fairly safe, of the left-liberal camp that the North Americans were trying to win over, and like Macdonald, he was aesthetically rather conservative. But as a Boston Brahmin, with blue blood coursing through his veins, Lowell might have been a better choice to send to London or Paris than post-Castro Latin America. Then again, Lowell's volcanic outbursts, produced by the manic phases of his bipolar disorder, made him in retrospect a liability anywhere. The trip ended with Lowell in a straitjacket.

Lowell had long wanted to visit his friend and fellow New England poet Elizabeth Bishop in Brazil, where she lived. In June 1962 he accepted the CCF's invitation to tour South America, and was ready to board his flight. "Who pays for the Congress for Cultural Freedom, anyway?" Bishop asked in a letter.[1] Lowell had just read Edmund Wilson's *Patriotic Gore*, a sharp critique of American empire, and he had also just been to Kennedy's White House. As a result, Lowell flew to the Caribbean and then on to Brazil with an imperial sense of his homeland. Keith Botsford met Lowell, his wife Elizabeth, and daughter Harriet, and escorted them south to Rio, where the Lowells were installed in the lavish Copacabana. Also at the airport was Bishop, and the CCF's Nicolas Nabokov. Lowell's biographer, Ian Hamilton, calls his duties "nebulous": "he was expected to give interviews and press conferences and to attend dinners."[2]

"[Lowell] was sort of vaguely there to be a famous literary man going through to pick up ideas," said Botsford, who served as Lowell's minder. "From the Congress's point of view he was an outstanding American to counteract, I suppose, Communist people like Neruda—our side's emissary."[3] Acclimatized to his new environment, Lowell was taken to his first stops—junkets and readings—on this US charm offensive. But then his wife and daughter returned to New England and in the beginning of September Lowell and Botsford were headed to Paraguay and Argentina. Bishop, familiar with Lowell's mental illness, noticed that he had begun to show signs of excitement. He was "overwrought," she thought, and had taken to getting sauced. When he began proclaiming his love for Bishop, as he had done during previous bouts of mania, she tried to dissuade him from going South.[4] Lowell, whose friends called him Cal, went anyway and Bishop stayed in Brazil. Botsford recalled what happened next. "When we got to Argentina, it was six double vodka martinis before lunch. And he made me drink with him. We went to lunch at the presidential palace, the Casa Rosada, and Cal promptly insulted the general, who was in fact about to be president . . . and started one of the many diplomatic rumpuses he caused on that trip." Botsford continued,

> Cal was sitting at this lunch in a very loud checked sports coat
> and open shirt, and all the generals were there, very uptight and

distinguished. And there was this wonderful opening scene when Cal was introduced to the cultural attaché ... The guy was an absolute idiot and asked stupid questions and obviously didn't know who Cal was. So Cal turned to him and said . . . "How can you be the cultural attaché? You're illiterate . . ." . . . and it went on from there. After his lunch Cal started his tour of the equestrian statues. He insisted on being taken to every statue in [Buenos Aires]—well, we didn't do every one, thank God. And he'd stop the car and start clambering up and sit next to the general on top of the statue.[5]

It was quite a performance. No one had yet seen Neruda do anything like *that*. Botsford thought Lowell simply needed rest and was drinking too much. He also thought that Lowell could use a primer on Latin American culture: "I considered it my task and my pleasure to inform him about a whole literature which I had discovered but which he knew nothing about."[6] Lowell himself, who had prepared an anthology of American poets for the Latin Americans, worried to friends that someone might draw out his ignorance on Latin American literature at one of his engagements. This wasn't the only thing he was worried about. He was falling apart, his mental health deteriorating rapidly. What began as a burst of energy morphed into a frenzy of lavish purchasing. "One of the striking aspects was the tremendous expenditure of physical energy. I'd never realized how strong Cal was." Botsford said,

> He was a very powerful swimmer—very strongly developed shoulders and chest and great long arms. And indefatigable. He couldn't sleep. He couldn't do anything for himself. I had to do everything, pay for everything . . . . And it got very expensive. I kept having to cable for more money. Cal felt the Congress was paying his expenses and that meant he had carte blanche. He insisted on buying everyone expensive presents, leather jackets. I couldn't control any of it.[7]

Along with this exuberant buying came a heady sense of entitlement that rankled Botsford. "And as he got higher and higher he began to treat me more and more as a flunky, a position which I resented. And all of a sudden for about a week he insisted I was homosexual. I think this was because he had a suitable component himself and was simply transferring it. But it was extremely burdensome to me and really rather painful. He kept on saying,

'You're saying that because you're queer.'" It became increasingly difficult to deal with Lowell.

> His whole conversation became very fragmentary and discon-
> nected. I used to think of it as a great knot which would twist
> and twist and twist and then a sentence would come out of it,
> pushed by a sort of strange breathy impulsion, and it was always
> in a totally unexpected direction. Eventually I was reduced to total
> flunkyism.[8]

Lowell took to quoting Wilson's *Patriotic Gore*, declaring that America was a new Roman Empire. He insisted that Botsford send Lowell's short letters to ex-President Eisenhower and the pope. Lowell was in perfect accord with *Patriotic Gore*'s sentiments: "The States have become a menace, seasquids as you say, and I guess they never were too good. . ." His ambivalence toward his nation's empire became an embrace. He hailed himself as the "Caesar of Argentina" and told Botsford: "I want you to travel with me always. You are my lieutenant."[9] He went on to extol the virtues of Hitler.[10]

But Botsford was done, and he returned to Rio. When Elizabeth Bishop got wind of his lieutenant leaving Lowell in Argentina, she was furious. "When I finally got Keith I asked him what the HELL he thought he was doing," she wrote Lowell's wife from Brazil, "didn't he know Cal's history? [He did.] WHY hadn't he called me before; what was he doing in Rio anyway, and WHY had he left Cal alone and sick in [Buenos Aires]?"[11]

At Bishop's prompting, Botsford returned to find Lowell even worse, albeit more tender, at the exiled left-wing Spanish poet Rafael Alberti's party. Lowell had thrown away his pills. Botsford petitioned guests for help returning him to the United States for treatment. But Alberti's guests instead called it a CIA plot to kidnap Lowell against his will. Look, wasn't he having a blast? The scene would have charmed Hemingway. The leftist Spanish poet was on the floor, arm-wrestling with Lowell, his CIA-funded, gringo counterpart. Finally, dangling a girl before him named Luisa, Botsford lured Lowell to a hotel where it took six men to wrestle him into a straitjacket. Lowell was dragged to the Clinica Bethlehem in Buenos Aires, where he was dosed with Thorazine. Was this what Bishop had meant by helping him? When Botsford visited, he found Lowell tied in leather straps, still violent despite the drugs, screaming for music.[12]

Botsford was born in Brussels to an aristocratic family,[13] which, after fleeing the Nazis, wound up in Balboa, California. He was badly burned as a child, a tragedy that inadvertently fostered his love of books. He claims he lay in bed reading for five years while his burns healed. Internet biographies boast of his being a descendant of Machiavelli, and he told one interviewer, "I know how to have servants, unlike the average American," and "I'm a man born to a certain class who expects things to be done in certain ways."[14] Multilingual, Botsford was raised around classical music, which would prove important to his duties as a CIA culture wrangler. After he finally institutionalized Lowell, his musical training came in especially handy. "I was brought up as a composer and all [Lowell] wanted me to do [at the hospital] was whistle. Sometimes it was 'Yankee Doodle Dandy' or 'The Battle Hymn of the Republic.' Or it was Brandenburg concertos, Mozart piano concertos, anything. It was the one thing he craved, the one thing that would calm him." These whistling sessions could last two or three hours.

> I'd be there . . . just whistling until I was dry in the mouth. I'd whistle all the parts in the Ninth Symphony or whatever, and he'd say, "Yeah, but do the tympani bit." He took great pleasure in this, and he was very tender and affectionate about it.[15]

Lowell didn't accomplish much in South America besides the junkets and the socializing. He later came out against the Vietnam War.

Much has been made of the power of Frank Wisner's corner of the CIA, often depicted through the image of a silent film or carnival organ, by which Wisner could control the media and the public like he was playing his own Wurlitzer. I like the image above better. Like Wisner, Lowell was bipolar; and the incident shows the aftermath of outburst, of bad behavior, and of "executive action." And this need to be whistled to tenderly—"familiar [Western] tunes of song"[16]—better captures the United States' anxieties, and its illness.

. . .

John Hunt was an old Iowa friend of Botsford's, a CIA man and National Book Award–winning novelist who became the CCF boss Josselson's own "lieutenant." Like Botsford, Hunt had ample experience in Latin America and one of their most infamous (and dubiously successful) missions was to deny Neruda the Nobel Prize.

It was yet another CCF errand that verged on censorship, though this time on the financial end. Denying money to left-wing writers was by now old hat for the CCF, implicit in many of its activities, explicit in others. And it worked as a means of training them to remain within certain rhetorical boundaries (think of that phrase of Botsford as Lowell's "leash" on the intellectuals). Between the carrot and the stick, the carrot was publication in the well-paying CIA magazines, or its junkets in New York, Europe, Latin America, or Asia, all expenses paid, or its networks of friends who could enable subsidies and enhance a writer's portfolio. To those writers who maintained their critical stance toward the American way came the stick. At minimum, this could mean marginalization, post-McCarthy blacklisting, publication bans, or other forms of censorship. In Neruda's Chile, the CCF's plotting also involved a smear campaign that, once blurred in their minds with the US coup, would traumatize those closest to Neruda for decades.

It was in early 1963 that Hunt was tipped off that Neruda was a candidate for the 1964 Nobel Prize. "This kind of inside information was extremely rare, as deliberations of the Nobel committee are supposed to be conducted in hermetic secrecy," wrote Frances Stonor Saunders. "Yet by December 1963, a whispering campaign against Neruda had been launched. Careful to obscure the Congress's role, when Irving Kristol asked Hunt if it was true the Congress was spreading rumors about Neruda, Hunt replied teasingly that it was inevitable that the poet's candidacy for the Nobel Prize would excite controversy."[17]

To damage Neruda's credibility, Hunt and the CCF wrote a white paper linking Neruda to Stalin. Among his crimes was accepting the cultural prize that Stalin had set up, originally named the Stalin Prize for Strengthening Peace Among Peoples, though Stalin had died by the time Neruda accepted it. Shortly after, it was renamed the Lenin Peace Prize; Nelson Mandela would be another winner, as was W.E.B. Du Bois and the Pakistani poet Faiz Ahmad Faiz. Hunt and Botsford's smear made no mention of what the situation was like in the period right after Stalin's death, when even Cold Warriors at the CIA saw signs that the Soviet Union was opening up. Some writers were openly critical; some were being pardoned. The Thaw was too short-lived, but the prize that Neruda received came at the very height of its optimism after Stalin's death. Going even further, however, the CCF also alleged that Neruda was involved in the 1940 attempt to murder Leon Trotsky in Mexico.

Curiously, fifty years later, Botsford maligned Neruda still, while denying it was even necessary. "Don Pablo was a caviar Communist," he wrote in an email from London in 2014. "He liked good living, expensive meals and the like. Everyone knew that, and in a country that had a [César] Vallejo or a [Nicanor] Parra, why would he need to be made ridiculous? Not everyone in Chile rated him that highly as a poet, and his 'Ode to Stalin' was odious."[18]

Soon the CIA went beyond merely discrediting him. They overthrew Neruda's friend, President Salvador Allende. Neruda himself died twelve days after the coup that installed General Augusto Pinochet. In fact, in 2011, Neruda's driver, Manuel Araya, wrote that he believed that Neruda was poisoned by the United States and by Pinochet's operatives in Santiago.[19] Neruda's cadaver was exhumed in 2013 for a belated autopsy in search of poison in his bones, though none was initially found.[20] The matter split members of Neruda's family, some of whom wanted to leave the past alone while others sought to pursue more conclusive tests.

In an acrobatic feat, the CIA's campaign to discredit Neruda did not preclude it from using his work to gain the trust and readership of Latin Americans. When the CIA and Botsford launched Latin America's *Mundo Nuevo*, its editor solicited Neruda's poetry from the beginning. The CIA was learning to make its public enemies into private cultural ambassadors to curtail blowback from its policies and, by doing so, to "leash" or rein them in when necessary.

Emir Rodríguez Monegal was tasked with editing *Mundo Nuevo*, the CIA's newest attempt to engage readers in Spanish.[21] Rodríguez Monegal was a Uruguayan critic, friends with many of the luminaries of Latin American letters. From the outset, Rodríguez Monegal's burden was to distance his new magazine from *Cuadernos*, the CIA's earlier effort, and from rumors of CIA ties. One sees this not only in his solicitation letters to Pablo Neruda, but also to Jorge Edwards (another Chilean writer) and Gabriel García Márquez. For its undisguised McCarthyite tone, *Cuadernos* was by many accounts a stark failure. It finally folded in early 1966,[22] and *Mundo Nuevo* was born out of its demise, taking over its Paris office and infrastructure, including writers, officers, and other collaborators.[23] And in at least one case the editor tried to camouflage the new magazine's CIA ties and appear independent by running a critique of the Vietnam War.[24]

During its brief life, *Mundo Nuevo* was marred by rumors over its funding. Yet it was undoubtedly one of the CCF's best magazines, reaching across the political divide, from anti-Castro Cuban exiles who deeply resented what was happening in Havana, to the revolutionary left who despised US foreign policy in Latin America and elsewhere. Additionally, subscribers were happy to be introduced to the work of Susan Sontag, Saul Bellow, and Robert Lowell, alongside rising and established Latin American icons.

The strategy was simple. By *Mundo Nuevo's* launch, the Congress finally recognized the need to engage the entire spectrum of political liberalism and leftism; it was a philosophy, again, that clever Josselson back in Paris dubbed "Fidelismo sin Fidel," or revolution without dictatorship.[25] Emphasizing these ideas would recognize a shared leftist and anti-imperialist commitment to social and economic justice, popular consensus issues from which to establish a foothold. The perspective might be described as *just too left enough.* It's reminiscent of a classic debate tactic to concede as much as you can as a means of persuading your opponent to adopt the must-have components of your position. But while people like Monge in Costa Rica appeared to be sincere with respect to the balance between reform-mindedness and anticommunism, this was not always true for the cultural CIA.

For two years, from July 1966 until Rodríguez Monegal resigned in 1968, the magazine left an impressive mark on Latin American letters, partly by scavenging other magazines such as *The Paris Review* for "content" it could translate and run as its own. With revelations of its sponsorship, the CIA and its defenders have cultivated the agency's reputation as a champion of the famous "Latin American Boom," the nickname for the movement that saw the rise of great writers such as Gabriel García Márquez, Julio Cortázar, Mario Vargas Llosa, and Carlos Fuentes, presiding over the use of magical realism—you might say—in the service of magical realpolitik. But the Boom was already well under way when the CCF discovered it (through Rodríguez Monegal) and used it secretly as a shield for its anticommunism and some of the movement's central figures would never forgive the organization for its sponsorship.

· · ·

Of the four titans—García Márquez, Cortázar, Fuentes, and Vargas Llosa—García Márquez was the least known when *Mundo Nuevo* launched.[26] By then the English term "boom" had made its way into usage in Latin America, crossing into Spanish via the language of economics. (One writer spelled it *búm.*) Early in the movement, literary forbear Jorge Luis Borges, Argentina's ironic mystic and winking lexicographer, shared the International Publishers' Prize with novelist and playwright Samuel Beckett, in 1961. A year later, Peruvian novelist Vargas Llosa became the first Latin American to win Spain's Premio Biblioteca Breve. And late in the Boom, which dwindled by the early 1970s, another forbear, Guatemala's Miguel Ángel Asturias, won the Nobel Prize in 1967.[27]

Before taking the helm at *Mundo Nuevo*, Rodríguez Monegal had written in *Encounter* that in the second half of the twentieth century, Latin American novelists would make their indelible mark on global letters.[28] This prediction boded well for his magazine. As the Chilean novelist José Donoso later wrote, "During the years it was directed with talent and [distinction] by Emir Rodríguez Monegal, this magazine exercised a decisive role in defining a generation. . . . *Mundo Nuevo* was the voice of the Latin American literature of its time. . . . I am convinced that the history of the Boom, at the moment in which it was most united, is written in the pages of *Mundo Nuevo* up to the moment Emir Rodríguez Monegal abandoned its directorship. . ."[29]

To bag the beloved leftist poet in a magazine widely suspected of US ties, Rodríguez Monegal described the new magazine to Neruda carefully in a February 1966 greeting. "Dear Pablo, I am preparing the launch of a magazine for Latin America that will be called *Mundo Nuevo* (New World), and whose direction is up! ('whose star is rising'?)[30] It's a project of great ambition, not just literary but also political."[31] Rodríguez Monegal detailed the ambition and inclusive political mission of the magazine. "I want for the first time to do justice to the greatness and creativity of *our* America, without McCarthyisms of either the right or the left; I have offered my magazine to the Cubans who are in a hostile mood."[32]

But Neruda didn't answer right away, though Rodríguez Monegal was his friend and the timing was good. Neruda finally replied three months later, signaling his approval of Rodríguez Monegal's gestures toward his Cuban counterparts. "You have the best intentions to correct errors, and moreover, time passes. Like us. I agree. With pleasure will I send you a poem or fragment as soon as it's typed out." The poet closed by asking Rodríguez Monegal if he was going to the International PEN meeting in New York.[33]

• • •

When the United States finally let Pablo Neruda into the country for a PEN conference in New York, he made his way eagerly to California, where he retraced the footsteps of Joaquin Murieta, sometimes known as the "Mexican Robin Hood." A Mexican gold speculator, Murieta's life ended badly in the 1850s at the hands of American race hatred. Neruda likely viewed him as a figure whose tragic trajectory reflected on his own times of vitriolic Cold War brinksmanship and violence. According to some accounts, Murieta, known variously as a bandit and an early campaigner for immigrants' rights, was killed by a posse. Reportedly his head wound up on display in a

San Francisco carnival stall. Neruda had known of the stall, having seen a photo of the displayed head in *National Geographic*, and wanted to write a play around Murieta's life in this perplexing land of opportunity and racism. Neruda's own head, after all, was on display during his visit in a more metaphorical carnival.[34]

But this was all a detour from the main event. If the FBI had followed this persona non grata, who until recently was banned from the United States—as it had followed James Baldwin, Ernest Hemingway, Richard Wright, and many others inside and outside the US border—the agency needn't have bothered. Neruda would be surrounded by spooks and friendly agents, some less witting than others. Having come under the auspices of the freedom of expression NGO, the PEN Club, for its June 1966 Congress of writers—with the theme of the writer as "independent spirit"—many of Neruda's hosts were anything but independent. The PEN organization bore new, secret ties to the intelligence community and could keep an eye on the maligned poet. This was because the CIA and the CCF had both campaigned to penetrate PEN that summer, and were largely successful.

International PEN, based in London, was the headquarter body for the freedom of expression organization, whose name stood for Poets/playwrights, Essayists and Novelists. It was widely seen as a champion for writers' rights and independence and was considered by UNESCO to be the organization most representative of global literary writers; it had seventy-five centers in fifty-five countries. Even though it had sworn off party politics within individual states, the CIA was keen to penetrate PEN.[35] In the months leading up to the New York PEN Congress, the American intelligence clique fought for control of the body's presidency, installing Arthur Miller as a liberal face to showcase American cultural freedom, and embedding the organization with friendly minds such as roving CCF correspondent Botsford and hard CIA agents with writing covers like Robie Macauley.

Thanks no doubt to his knowledge of Murieta's fate as much to his bad treatment by the Americans, Neruda came with trepidation. The thirty-fourth International PEN Congress in New York would be tricky for the famous poet, who had infamously taken the Stalin Prize. He was sure to be asked about Soviet writers Andrei Sinyavsky and Yuli Daniel, who had been sent to the gulag in 1965 for publishing in the West. To avoid persecution they had published under the pseudonyms Abram Tertz and Nikolai Arzhak.[36] This sentence showed yet again that the Soviets were at least as deaf to history as the Americans.

The PEN Congress, as many presciently called it, also promised Neruda a challenge simply for the fact of his having been labeled a subversive by the United States and banned from entering the country. But Neruda was one of the world's greats, he would be among his fellow writers from all over the world, and he wanted to come. Arthur Miller, himself once persona non grata with respect to cultural freedom, worked behind the scenes to help. As he told Neruda's biographer Adam Feinstein, the Johnson administration "became nervous that it would not be good to be seen banning such a famous figure and realized that it would be wise to relax the ban for Neruda."[37] Neruda loved New York, Washington, and California; he bought works by Shakespeare and Whitman in Manhattan, where he was fêted by his publisher Barney Rosset of Grove Press and gave a reading at the 92nd Street Y. Plimpton's former professor, Archibald MacLeish, introduced the Chilean poet as "all-American." Neruda did a reading at the Library of Congress in Washington, too. But he was unrelenting in his criticism of US policies in Vietnam. In pursuit of the truth of racial violence, Neruda spent his California trip researching his play on Murieta.[38] That image of his comrade's head displayed in a carnival stall must have traveled with him like a ghost.

Miller marveled that "a man of such all-embracing spirit could continue to countenance Stalinism."[39] But Neruda himself marveled that a democratic country built on generous, universal values could in that very moment behave so murderously toward the people of Southeast Asia. Indeed, as Nick Turse has documented, the US war in Vietnam (and its neighbors) killed an estimated two million Vietnamese before the decade-long incursion was over, and the majority were civilians targeted in a campaign to raise the body count and "kill anything that moved."[40] When an interviewer asked Neruda after the PEN Congress what one gift he would like to give the world, he was undoubtedly thinking of Vietnam when he replied, "The best gift would be the restoration of a true democracy in the United States. In other words, the elimination of regressive forces in that country who spill blood in faraway lands. A great country like the United States, divested of its political and economic arrogance, would be a grand gift for the world."[41]

The CCF's attempts to infiltrate PEN started as a result of American fears of Soviet cultural agents taking over its conferences. In the mid-1950s, the CCF worked with friends in PEN to stack conferences with partisans ready to respond to dirty tricks by the Soviets. But soon the CCF was staging full preemptive measures by stacking PEN events with experienced anti-Communist debaters such as Stephen Spender, Ignazio Silone, and Arthur Koestler. Debate in public was more than fair; it was part of the bargain. But CIA agent and novelist John Hunt decided to stack the headquarters in London as well. In 1964, Hunt believed that PEN's secretary, a large Brit named David Carver, friendly toward the CCF, needed "help" with his many duties. Botsford was sent to keep an eye on things. Botsford's staying on in Latin America after the Lowell visit had prepared him for the PEN action.

Since early 1962, he had made Brazil his base. After the Brazilian branch of the CCF had launched in 1958, it had been dominated by reactionaries and had thus failed to attract leftists. Botsford had been sent to reform the group.[42] But Brazil's reactionary atmosphere soon grew into a full-scale military coup. This coup took place in 1964, a decade after the Guatemala coup, and it used similar maneuvers. First President João Goulart of the Brazilian Labor Party was labeled a socialist. Then the Johnson administration backed a coup by members of the military to oust him. (President Kennedy first approved the coup in the summer of 1962. This was recorded for posterity in his first use of a new White House state-of-the-art recording system.)[43] After the Brazilian military coup saw academics targeted for firing and censorship and worse, Hunt asked the Brazilian wing of the CCF to condemn the crackdowns on academics, free speech, and other intellectuals. But the Brazilian CCF wasn't interested. They tended to smile upon these crackdowns and US officials did as well.[44] The military even suggested it would be a short period of military rule. The dictatorship instead lasted twenty-one years and even saw young women like Dilma Rouseff, later Brazil's president, tortured at the hands of the United States' allies.

The situation hopeless, Botsford then went to Mexico. In 1964, the CCF sent him to London to assist Carver with PEN. When the Americans proposed these and other staff changes, the French leveled charges of a cultural coup. The French wanted their own man in the PEN presidency, novelist Miguel Ángel Asturias.[45] But even Miller knew how shrewd a choice he himself was, though not until later did he fully understand how he was being used to disguise the United States' reactionary politics with a more liberal face. "The point now was that they had come to the end of the string. . . . [PEN had been] a victim of the Cold War," he said, "which had damaged if not destroyed its credit in smaller countries that were not entirely enlisted on the side of the West. The recent détente policy called for new attempts to tolerate East-West differences, which PEN had not yet gained the experience to do."[46]

Miller came to see how he and other left-wing or former left-wing cultural figures had become weaponized: "It passed through my mind—that the government might have wanted me to become president of PEN because they couldn't otherwise penetrate the Soviet Union, and they figured that traveling behind me could be their own people. They wouldn't expect me to do it, I don't think. One of the early people who approached me about PEN—I can't remember his name now—but people would later say about him, 'Why, that guy was an agent all the time.' . . . It was gossip."[47]

Meanwhile, if the CIA saw Asturias's candidacy as a threat, it was partly the CIA's own dirty dealings with him that had deepened the acrimony. Asturias was an example of the failure of CCF/CIA cultural diplomacy. Maybe it didn't care, with someone so clearly beyond the pale. Asturias was a writer whose anti-imperialism and whose opposition to American exploits in Latin America had been outspoken. While the CIA's military dictator-friends in Guatemala had burned Asturias's books after Operation SUCCESS had ended his job as ambassador to Paris, here the CIA's cultural wing was keeping him from getting a prestigious job at PEN. They wrote letters to French officials, risking creating a pathway from the government there back to PEN, which was inappropriate insofar as PEN's bylaws. Writing denunciations of Asturias to a number of stakeholders (Josselson calling the prospect of his presidency a "catastrophe"),[48] the Americans won the dispute and Miller became president of PEN. Miller had created the pained collaborator John Proctor in *The Crucible* and had broken off his friendship with Elia Kazan after the director had informed on his Communist friends before the House Un-American Activities Committee. Unaware until later of the degree of collaboration he was being ensnared into, Miller took the post in time for the New York PEN Congress of international writers. But having wrangled one leftist, they didn't want to take any chances. Political reliability was the currency. They sent Botsford to work the administrative side and doubled down by sending Robie Macauley to work from the margins. Macauley, a CIA case officer assigned to PEN, had advised Nelson Aldrich about writers like Olga Carlisle. Since his position was not public facing like Miller's, Macauley's more conservative politics weren't an issue. Macauley was sent to PEN not by someone in the CCF, incidentally, but by Cord Meyer, who originally recruited him (through the faithful P-Source) under the auspices of the CIA's International Organizations Divisions, or IOD.[49] This was the covert wing of the former Office of Policy Coordination, overseen during the 1950s by Frank Wisner. If the public story was that Miller had persuaded hawks to loosen the ban on leftists to let Neruda into the United States, then Miller's image as a liberal hero was burnished further by his *Paris Review* interview in the summer 1966 issue, which coincided with Miller's debut in the role of PEN president. The interviewers were Rose Styron and Olga Carlisle, veteran of the Art of Fiction series with her Pasternak interview.

The interview starts dramatically, with Miller suddenly picking up a rifle to shoot a woodchuck outside his spare upstairs office—as Hemingwayesque a moment as you could possibly dream up—and ends with him recounting his refusal to cooperate with the House Un-American Activities Committee during the 1950s.[50]

The Americans had also claimed to have accommodated Soviet anxieties in order to make space at the New York conference for an early episode of cultural détente. But Botsford himself was suspicious of this. At Bled, Yugoslavia in 1965, he had partaken in high-level negotiations with his Soviet counterparts, working out compromises by which the Soviets might send a delegation to the New York PEN Congress in 1966. In a letter to *Public Interest* editor and sociologist Daniel Bell, Botsford argued that Josselson and high-level US officials had betrayed these negotiations by deliberately dragging their feet to keep Soviet writers out of PEN conferences. "That the Russians did not come to NY," wrote Botsford, "could easily be blamed on their fear of the repercussions after Sinyavsky-Daniel—I do not doubt this played a part—but I am reasonably certain that the PEN's breach of faith was also responsible."[51]

The leftists who did come were welcomed. Neruda, for example, was embraced heartily by Miller, only to be cornered as a carnival attraction by others. In the style used at the Waldorf in 1949, Ignazio Silone treated the Chilean poet like a well-known spokesman for the Soviets, charging that Soviet writers "were mere instruments of the state, condemn[ing] the treatment of Boris Pasternak in the Soviet Union and enthusiastically cit[ing] the role played by Hungarian writers in the 1956 uprising." Neruda replied that Silone was rehashing Cold War dialogues that were tired and outdated.[52] But he didn't help his cause when he added that, like writers everywhere, some writers in socialist countries were happy and some unhappy. "But I must add," he concluded, "the happiest writers I have found [are] in the socialist countries."[53]

On his way home, in Mexico, Neruda missed another chance to condemn the Soviet gulags when author José Revueltas asked him about his position on this repression.[54] Neruda didn't bite. It's a shame the solidarity he felt with Latin Americans from an earlier time, such as Murieta, wasn't the same solidarity he felt with gulag prisoners. Despite such silence, Neruda's appearance in New York nevertheless infuriated those on the revolutionary left in Latin America. In July, a group of one hundred Cuban intellectuals, who had opted not to come at the last minute, denounced Neruda's new dealings with the United States and its repressive allies. This hurt Neruda,[55] and it must have been in his mind as he weighed which of his work to send his friend Emir Rodríguez Monegal for inclusion in the CIA's *Mundo Nuevo* magazine. Neruda offered Rodríguez Monegal poetry for the magazine's fourth issue, which ultimately ran three short sections excerpted from his collection *La Barcarola*.[56] The second part was an elegy to Paris, titled "Paris Serenade."

. . .

Another writer who was banned from the United States but was solicited for *Mundo Nuevo*'s pages was Gabriel García Márquez. Two months after introducing Neruda to *Mundo Nuevo*, Rodríguez Monegal bagged one of the great novelists of twentieth century Spanish letters, whose own "star was rising." As he had yet to publish his masterpiece (*One Hundred Years of Solitude*, which would go on to sell more copies than any book in Spanish except the Bible),[57] today we'd call the García Márquez of 1966 an emerging voice. García Márquez was an important constituent for *Mundo Nuevo*, one of the leftists sought out by the magazine's brain trust.[58]

Not engaging writers like García Márquez or Neruda was precisely where *Cuadernos* had failed. It had modeled itself partly on Victoria Ocampo's *Sur*, with which Jorge Luis Borges was associated in Buenos Aires. While *Sur* was cosmopolitan, anti-provincial, urbane, pro-American, and, thanks partly to the editorial sensibility of Waldo Frank, pan-Americanist, it had slightly different aims than a Cold War magazine for the anti-Communist cause. But there was much overlap. In fact, *Sur* had introduced many Spanish readers to northern writers translated by Borges, and served the Congress's purposes so well that it was the de facto magazine for the Argentine branch of the Congress for Cultural Freedom.[59] Though it started with an antifascist bent,[60] it signaled in various ways that it was "above" politics, though what this meant in practice was that it disdained certain strains of leftism, namely the pro-Cuban strain. Like *The Paris Review*, it camouflaged its agenda behind an urbane, nineteenth century, art-for-art's sake air, often called belles lettres. Through *Sur*'s association with the CCF, *The Paris Review* syndicated its author interviews to the Argentine magazine; Carlisle's Pasternak interview was one candidate for reprint there.[61]

But after rising resentment over the United States' foreign policy in the region came to discordant climax in the early to mid-1960s, *Sur*'s anti-revolutionary stance would become hard to maintain. Ocampo criticized one of her editors for participating in a Cuban literary conference, which prompted his resignation.[62] Rodríguez Monegal had undoubtedly known much of this. Number-crunching, recollecting *Cuadernos*'s failure, and other ways of projecting impact suggested that *Mundo Nuevo* should embrace both the *Sur* belletristic anti-Communists as well as the growing scrolls of revolutionary leftists. Only then would it drain off some of the energy from Casa de las Americas, Cuba's publishing house, which Castro had set up as part of his cultural mission.

Engaging writers like García Márquez would perfectly fulfill this embrace. After reading the draft of his new novel, Rodríguez Monegal wrote to García Márquez ecstatically in February, months before launch, hoping *Mundo Nuevo* might participate somehow in the novel's release. "It's magnificent! . . . I read it dazzled and with great happiness,"[63] gushed Rodríguez Monegal, who promised to write a long essay on it. The following month, García Márquez calmly offered to give him any of the chapters he liked to excerpt in his new magazine. "Gabo," as Rodríguez Monegal and other friends called him, suggested the second chapter might be the best for excerpting, the "most rounded."

"The title of this novel (that I hope to turn in in July)," Gabo added, "is *One Hundred Years of Solitude*."[64] A year later, he would regret offering it to *Mundo Nuevo*.

• • •

García Márquez's masterful novel owes itself to a childhood listening to his grandmother's stories. But it also owed much to a youth dedicated to reading writers like William Faulkner, whom he first read in translation, possibly in *Sur*. During his secondary school and university days, García Márquez read poetry and Karl Marx, and soon—like Narayan after going to the United States—he considered himself socialist.[65] While he came of age politically during law school in Bogotá in the late 1940s, several incidents reveal his heart was more invested in literary pursuits than political ones.

In April 1948, Eliécer Gaitán, the liberal candidate favored to win the next presidential election in Colombia, was gunned down by an assassin in Bogotá. The resulting riots, which led to years of violence, are known as the Bogotazo.[66] On the day of the assassination, the riots erupted in an initial ten hours of mayhem, during which supporters of Gaitán destroyed much of the city. The word on the streets and over the radio was that conservatives were culpable for the killing. The young lawyer Fidel Castro was in town that day and had met with Gaitán two days earlier at his office on Seventh Street. They had liked each other and Gaitán had promised to help Castro stage an anti-imperialism rally. One block over, in low-income student housing on Eighth Street, the young law student who dabbled in short fiction, García Márquez, was preparing to eat lunch. When he and his roommates heard the commotion on the day of the murder, they knew exactly what must have happened and ran to Seventh Street. But their candidate had already been rushed to the hospital, where he was declared dead on arrival. Emotions were high: the killer was torn to shreds and the city was ablaze; García Márquez ran home to find his house was also on fire. A friend was stunned when he found García Márquez crying.

"I didn't realize you were such a devoted disciple of Gaitán," said the friend.

"No, what are you talking about," he said. "It's that my stories burned."

García Márquez ran to the pawn shop that held his typewriter as collateral for a small loan. Thankfully, the place was intact. Castro, meanwhile, raided the nearby police station, liberating its guns. Soon enough, however, Castro realized that this was not revolution in the streets, just rioting. Some writers have suggested that this incident caused him to prefer rural guerrilla action over revolutionary organizing in cities. Castro claims to have told the story of the day of the assassination in front of García Márquez, describing the destruction of windows and storefronts, the looting of everything from pianos to armoires. "The most vocal unleashed their frustration by shouting from the street corners, garden terraces, and smoky buildings," Castro began. He continued,

> One man vented his fury by attacking his typewriter, beating it, and then to save himself the laborious effort, he threw it up into the air, and it smashed to bits when it hit the pavement.
>
> As I spoke, Gabo listened, probably confirming to himself the certainty that in Latin America and the Caribbean, writers don't have to make very much up, because reality is more interesting than anything you could imagine, and maybe the challenge is to make that incredible reality believable. As I was finishing telling my story, I knew that Gabo had been there too, and the coincidence was very telling, maybe we had run through the same streets and witnessed the same harrowing events, which had made me just one more character in that suddenly roiling mob. I asked the question with my usual dispassionate curiosity:

"And what were you doing during the Bogotazo?"

And he, calmly, entrenched within his vibrant, provocative, exceptional imagination, answered simply, smiling, ingenious with his natural use of metaphor:

"Fidel, I was that man with the typewriter."[67]

. . .

Evidence of CIA involvement in the Gaitán murder is sparse. But García Márquez himself was curious about it. In 2000, a writer recalled that García Márquez had tipped him off about a Cuban documentary that featured a former CIA agent who confessed to agency involvement in the Gaitán murder.[68] The coup that upended Colombia five years later certainly bore the marks of American support, and this one had even more direct impact on García Márquez's life and career.

On June 13, 1953, partisans for the liberal and conservative oligarchies eagerly cheered on the coup of General Gustavo Rojas Pinilla, who went on to preside over a period of roughly four years of restrictions on civil liberties across the country. García Márquez and his friends did not cheer the coup or the man behind it, though General Rojas Pinilla received the Legion of Merit Award from the United States. García Márquez wanted "the world to be Socialist and I believe that sooner or later it will happen."[69] But to the chagrin of some of his friends, his first novel, *The Leaf Storm*, had no obvious political message in it, although the book appeared not long into Pinilla's dictatorship. Some felt that while his work showcased clear leftist sympathies, at the same time it was "less a tool for transformation than a source of enjoyment." This was tantamount to calling García Márquez bourgeois. The slander prodded García Márquez to declare that he opposed "committed literature." "Far from accelerating any process of raising consciousness," he argued, such literature "actually slows it down. Latin Americans expect more from a novel than an exposé of the oppression and injustice they know all too well. Many of my militant friends who so often feel the need to dictate to writers what they should or should not write are, unconsciously perhaps, taking a reactionary stance inasmuch as they are imposing restrictions on creative freedom. I believe a novel about love is as valid as any other. When it comes right down to it, a writer's duty—his revolutionary duty, if you like—is to write well."[70]

Here was a socialist who didn't defend the Soviet Union's definition of literature (who in fact didn't defend the Soviet Union), a writer of the non-Communist Left over whom the Cold War propagandists would eventually fight. A survey of García Márquez's career before the Cuban Revolution, and of what he absorbed in order to write *One Hundred Years of Solitude*, reveals an ability to pair the journalist's and novelist's sensibilities in interpreting historical events. An aesthetic hedonist, he held robust, anti-imperialist views toward the United States but believed in embracing characters with a generous, bird's-eye humor. His love of American writers, including Hemingway, Faulkner, and John Dos Passos, make any claims of anti-Americanism against him too narrow. At the same time, efforts to damn him by his association with Fidel Castro, as were made upon his death in 2014, have failed to mar his brilliant legacy.

During the early years of the Rojas Pinilla reign, García Márquez moved between Bogotá and the coastal towns where he'd grown up. In Cartagena, he found work writing for newspapers. Aracataca, the inspiration for Macondo, the fictional town at the center of *One Hundred Years of Solitude*'s gyrating universe, lies due east of Cartagena, southeast of Barranquilla, and southwest of Riohacha. He was happy to be back on the Caribbean while he worked on freelance pieces and as a bookseller.

Searching for stability, he took a staff position at *El Espectador* in Bogotá, where he wrote a column about the city as well as criticism, including film reviews. He also wrote daily news pieces. But like Plimpton, he was most interested as a nonfiction writer in leveraging the skills he took from the novelists and great literary writers he loved into a new kind of journalism, what today might be called "longform" or "reportage."

One day he was handed a story that would change his life. In late February 1955, after repairs in Mobile, Alabama, the Colombian Naval destroyer, *Caldas*, lost eight crew members sailing for Cartagena. For four days, the US Panama Canal Authority searched for the men, who had been tossed overboard, but then it gave up. Ten days after the incident, a man named Luis Alejandro Velasco washed ashore in northern Colombia. Velasco had been one of the crew and had survived those ten days on a simple raft. The media was ravenous for one-off stories about his survival and resilience. But what actually happened to him was obscured by the fact of his having been lionized as a national hero—one who was soon promoting watches, shoes, and other goods in various advertising campaigns.

But as the attention waned and as his credibility strained under all the self-promotion, Velasco turned up at *El Espectador*'s editorial offices and wanted to tell the full, detailed version of his story for the first time. Told over a series of twenty sessions, each six hours at a time, the true tale of

Velasco's survival had many of the elements of great storytelling. García Márquez later said the twenty-year-old shipwreck survivor had "an exceptional instinct for the art of narrative, an astonishing memory and ability to synthesize, and enough uncultivated dignity to be able to laugh at his own story."[71]

The resemblance to Hemingway's *Old Man and the Sea* was not lost on García Márquez. Not long after receiving the Nobel Prize, Hemingway was approached by Cuba's *Bohemia* magazine, who offered to pay him $5,000 to run the full novel in their magazine. (*Life* had paid $30,000.) Hemingway said he would do it for no fee whatsoever, provided the magazine would donate $1,000 to a leper colony. *Bohemia*'s full excerpt—and the book's first Spanish translation—was published in 1953, just two years before the *Caldas* incident made Velasco famous.[72]

So Velasco's intact memories of his attempt at survival felt like literature to many Latin American readers who were familiar with Hemingway's popular novel. Here was a real-life Santiago. García Márquez serialized the story over fourteen issues of the paper. It represented the widest readership he had ever seen for his work, even if he ultimately gave Velasco the byline.

The dictator Rojas Pinilla had been following the story with admiration but the ending took him by surprise. According to Velasco, the great weight of the cargo had hindered the ship's maneuvering, and it was this that led to the ship's foundering and the crew being thrown overboard. And what was that cargo? The ship was carrying illegal black market goods from the United States: refrigerators, washing machines, and TVs. The series amounted to a life-or-death visual for the heavy, sluggish weight of corruption on the Colombian economy. And so, in the end, García Márquez was chased from Colombia by General Rojas Pinilla for telling the story of Velasco's shipwreck and the general's corruption.[73]

. . .

Afterward, García Márquez went to France as *El Espectador*'s Europe correspondent to cover NATO and economic summits. The stuffy conferences bored him so he lit out to explore the Soviet Union and its satellites. In 1955, and again in 1957, he volunteered for assignments to survey countries behind the Iron Curtain. Even without any rhetorical help from the United States, he was somehow able to gauge the deficiencies of the Soviet system as he found it in the Eastern bloc. In Poland, he wrote, "A dense, disheveled, depressed crowd wandered around disoriented through narrow streets. . ."

There were large groups of people who spent hours staring at shopping windows of state-owned department stores where new items were being displayed. The items looked old. At any rate, no one was able to afford them.[74] In 1957, he wrote of East Germany as "a system imposed from the outside by the Soviet Union through dogmatic, unimaginative local Communist parties whose sole thought was to enforce the Soviet model in a society where it did not fit."[75] As Octavio Paz came to see it, he was convinced that Soviet Communism was not true socialism but a perversion of it.

When he returned to France, where he planned to settle, García Márquez found he was out of a job. While he was in the east, the press freedom crisis in Colombia concomitant with the coup had climaxed. As the Soviet leaders did during that same period to the Polish magazine *Opinie* (for running selections from *Doctor Zhivago*), our man in Bogotá simply shut García Márquez's newspaper down.[76]

García Márquez drifted, briefly enjoying the freedom of joblessness in Paris. It gave him time to write fiction. But his extreme destitution forced him to earn meals by returning bottles. He wasn't yet married though he was in love. How could he support a family like this? After scrambling to pay the bills in Paris through freelance work commissioned through friends— work too inconsistent to live on—he finally returned to the Caribbean coast, if not exactly to his homeland. A friend offered him a job in Venezuela and he arrived just in time for another regime change.

. . .

Like General Pinilla Rojas of Colombia, Marcos Pérez Jiménez, who ruled Venezuela when García Márquez arrived, had also received the Legion of Merit award from the United States, though he and his security czar, Pedro Estrada, were international villains. After a long career of torture and the political murders of their enemies, Pérez Jiménez and Estrada were chased from Venezuela in January of 1958 by a massive grassroots student movement. This was a year before Fulgencio Batista would be chased out of Cuba. Both Batista and Pérez Jiménez would seek shelter in the United States: Pérez Jiménez was granted safe passage en route to Europe while Batista was not.

It must have been a heady moment for Latin Americans. First, Rojas Pinilla had fallen in Colombia. Batista would soon fall in Cuba. (García Márquez's Paris friends had apprised him of the progress of the "bearded ones'"—as Castro's ungroomed forces were known—who fought their way seemingly inevitably from the Sierra Maestra toward Havana.) And now Venezuela was liberated from the monstrous Pérez Jiménez. On top of this, García Márquez had a job, working at *Momento* with his new friend Plinio Apuleyo Mendoza.

In March, García Márquez made an important trip to Barranquilla, where he married Mercedes Barcha Pardo, who had faithfully waited out his exile and poverty in Europe. He had an ambitious novel in mind, *La Casa*. After their marriage he promised Mercedes (a Sophia Loren looka-like, some felt) that, although he needed to support their family now by working—and although he hadn't quite worked out the voice, pacing, or structure of his book—nevertheless, by the time he was forty, he would pub-lish his masterpiece.

But on May 13, 1958, when Vice President Nixon's cavalcade rolled through Caracas, García Márquez's fate again would change. Plinio Mendoza's boss at *Momento* told him to run "an editorial note that the civil unrest didn't represent the feelings of most Caracas dwellers and that Venezuela and the United States were nations that were eager to explore their natural connections." In the wake of the US-backed dictatorship, this was too much for Mendoza. He refused to run it and was subsequently fired.[77] Loyal to his friend, García Márquez walked out in solidarity. Thanks to a Latin American dictator's favor by the United States, a contentious visit by the American vice president, and García Márquez's own left-wing reflexes, the young writer was out of a job—again.

12

THE VITAL CENTER CANNOT HOLD

Today I realize that the reticence was not so much theirs as mine, for I never could overcome the bitterness with which my grandparents had evoked their frustrated wars and the atrocious slaughters of the banana companies.

—Gabriel García Márquez, *Living to Tell the Tale*

Around 1965, García Márquez and his wife Mercedes were driving to the sea for a long-planned beach vacation in Acapulco, a four-hour drive due south from Mexico City through Cuernavaca and Chilpancingo. Suddenly, Gabo understood how to write *La Casa*, the working title for the book that would become *One Hundred Years of Solitude*. They pulled the car over and he told her they had to go back to the capital.[1]

Why? Because now he knew how to make the novel sing. He would follow the style that his grandmother used to tell stories. "What was most important was the expression she had on her face. She did not change her expression at all when telling her stories, and everyone was surprised. In previous attempts to write *One Hundred Years of Solitude*, I tried to tell the story without believing in it. I discovered that what I had to do was believe in them myself and write them with the same expression with which my grandmother told them: with a brick face."[2]

García Márquez and Mercedes by now had two sons, Rodrigo and Gonzalo. His children represented real responsibilities. Nevertheless, when he discovered how to write the novel, he secluded himself in his "Mafia Cave," as he called his smoke-filled writing space at Calle Lomas #19 in Mexico City. Once ensconced, he left the work of getting by to Mercedes. As Ilan Stavans writes, "During those eighteen months, the García Márquezes were overwhelmed with debt. He tapped into savings from his journalism and screenplays."

> Mercedes was in charge of the family finances and used the scant resources to buy food and clothes for the boys.... García Márquez would recall that he didn't even have enough to photocopy and post the manuscript. They were $10,000 in debt (roughly 120,000 Mexican pesos) when he finished it.... Mercedes, always a source of strength for her husband, persuaded their landlord to let them fall behind with the rent for seven months.[3]

On one of the rare occasions when he saw friends during this intense bout of writing, he told them, "Either I'm going to succeed big time or fall miserably on my face."[4] With a final manuscript at 1,300 pages, no wonder he fretted. He wrote in eight-hour shifts, Stavans notes, with few days off. As he worked his way toward the end, he knew he'd "found" the book he meant to write, just as he'd promised his wife after returning from Paris and asking for her hand. A selfish act of artistic excess, it was also a love letter to Latin American history, told through the Buendía family, that would change his and his family's lives. And he needed it to be good enough to justify his wife's sacrifices. In one of the book's many iconic scenes he recorded something he may have remembered from watching the execution of Jésus Sosa Blanco in Cuba, a colonel in Batista's army:

> For the rest of his life he would remember the livid flash of the six simultaneous shots and the echo of the discharge as it broke against the hills and the sad smile and perplexed eyes of the man being shot, who stood erect while his shirt became soaked with blood, and who was still smiling even when they untied him from

the post and put him in a box filled with quicklime. "He's alive,"
he thought.[5]

In a scene involving executions ordered to protect the local arm of
the US fruit conglomerate, one of the family scions, José Arcadio Segundo,
wakes up among the dead. A political killing is again described as an act of
being buried alive, as if on a train among corpses piled like fruit:

> . . . Trying to flee from the nightmare, José Arcadio Segundo dragged
> himself from one car to another in the direction in which the train
> was heading, and . . . he saw man corpses, woman corpses, child
> corpses who would be thrown into the sea like rejected bananas. . .[6]

Recorded for posterity was the aftermath of the United Fruit Company breaking
a strike, when the US military ordered its Colombian counterpart to open fire
on its own population. It was a real example and it took place in his native
country. García Márquez had heard the story many times while growing up
a short distance from the massacre site. Now he'd transformed it into a vivid
memento mori for the history of conflict and commerce between these two
lands, folding it into the experiences of the Buendías, the "Good-days," and
commemorating the atrocity to millions of readers around the world.

García Márquez and Mercedes allegedly didn't have money for postage
to send one of the initial four copies of the novel to a publisher. He had to
send the first half, pawn some kitchen appliances, then send the second half.
Eventually he had sent it off to several. Editorial Losada rejected it. Another,
Carlos Barral, who had launched Carlos Fuentes and Guillermo Cabrera
Infante, was on vacation when the manuscript arrived and his assistant
rejected it, a fact that dismayed Barral for the rest of his life. By the time he
got to his friend's masterful book, Editorial Sudamerica had won the rights
and was already printing it.[7] The CIA's *Mundo Nuevo* was too—as well as
the magazines *Amaru* in Lima, and *Eco* in Bogotá. The book's prospects
seemed foreordained. "If everything is like this fragment," said future Nobel
laureate Mario Vargas Llosa, "the novel must be a marvel."[8]

But did García Márquez want the novel he'd promised to his wife
excerpted in a US propaganda front? Rodríguez Monegal would have an
answer soon.

• • •

As a result of the global reach of the CIA's family of associated magazines, including *The Paris Review*, people around the world could—theoretically—have experienced the phenomenon of this masterpiece simultaneously in multiple translations. But it's not clear if other CCF magazines ran it. It appears that only Emir Rodríguez Monegal, editor of one of the last of these perfect-bound miniature showrooms for American culture, had the knowledge and good taste to champion this book and he did so just as the secret program was being exposed.

In *Mundo Nuevo*'s last days, just before the scheme would blow up in the CCF's faces, more writers reading this new work by Neruda and García Márquez would trust their own work to the magazine, thereby increasing the size of the boom. By the time of its exposure, *Mundo Nuevo* boasted fiction by Clarice Lispector, writing by Jorge Luis Borges on (what else?) labyrinths, Sartre on myth and reality in theater, and the Mexican poet and future Nobel laureate Octavio Paz—on his idol, André Breton. While Paz grew increasingly anti-Communist throughout his career, he reportedly disliked the CCF, sensing its official provenance,[9] and was only wrangled into its pages through the charisma and intelligence of Rodríguez Monegal.

Magazines in Latin America had a unique cultural importance absent elsewhere. Given the limited book publishing infrastructure, *they* were the public square and the commons. The infrastructure of democracy was formed in magazines in this region. "For *Mundo Nuevo* . . . part of [its] context was the venerable tradition in Latin America of literary production through magazines or cultural supplements to newspapers."[10]

But it wasn't just Rodríguez Monegal's connections from his days at the Uruguayan publication *Marcha* that enabled this literary public square. Botsford was himself well connected, having done hard time as the CCF's man in Latin America. He was friends with American masters like Saul Bellow, Mary McCarthy, and Susan Sontag, who also soon found their way into *Mundo Nuevo*'s pages. Sontag's contribution to *Mundo Nuevo*, a beloved essay titled "Against Interpretation," argued against Freudian or Marxist readings of literary or artistic texts—an argument with an interesting subtext in this magazine created by the CIA. And while American writers like Erskine Caldwell had been appropriated by the Soviets for stories demonstrating viscerally America's historical exploitation and callous disregard for the poor, *Mundo Nuevo* answered by excerpting Oscar Lewis's "The Culture of Poverty" from *Scientific American*. The "culture of poverty" was Lewis's term for a group of hyper-alienated poor he had seen in Mexico, Puerto Rico, and New York. The essay ran in *Scientific American* in October

1966 and in *Mundo Nuevo* the following month, showing the speed with which the latter magazine could get work translated and printed. Lewis's essay ends,

> By creating basic structural changes in society, by redistributing wealth, by organizing the poor and giving them a sense of belonging, of power and of leadership, revolutions frequently succeed in abolishing some of the basic characteristics of the culture of poverty even when they do not succeed in curing poverty itself.[11]

Was this a subtle argument against revolution? This new scientism would emerge as a full-flung system called modernization theory. It was essentially anticommunism remade as "science." Few were willing to claim it as their brainchild, but its leading proponent was probably Walt Rostow, who went on to join President Johnson's cabinet. Rostow began his career in the OSS during World War II, where he chose the targets upon which to drop Allied bombs. He landed at MIT, where he worked with CIA-linked academics and recommended that the United States vastly increase its foreign economic aid. When Eisenhower took up Rostow's cause, Congress was facing economic recession and it saw aid to nonaligned and other poor nations as wasteful.

In response, Eisenhower weaponized the aid for members of Congress who had no interest in helping the foreign poor, by suggesting it would prevent the Soviets from winning them over. And he took his case to the public: "We must use our skills and knowledge and, at times, our substance, to help others rise from misery, however far the scene of suffering may be from our shores. For wherever in the world a people knows desperate want, there must appear at least the spark of hope, the hope of progress, or there will surely rise at last the flames of conflict."[12] As a synopsis of modernization theory, Rostow's 1960 book—*The Stages of Economic Growth: A Non-Communist Manifesto*—best laid out the five stages of economic growth: "the traditional society, the preconditions for take-off, the take-off, the drive to maturity, and the age of high mass-consumption."

James Baldwin got a whiff of modernization theory from his old friend Richard Wright, who told audiences at the Congress of Black Writers and Artists in Paris in the mid-1950s that exposure to advanced countries was good for under-developed ones. If you were to ask Jayaprakash Narayan during the British occupation of India, might he not point to the school fees he had to pay, the biases embedded in the curricula at the British-supported institutions of higher learning, and the censorship of the India Congress Party's publications, not to mention the slaughter of protesters? Baldwin himself may have been ambivalent about the developing world in the mid-1950s when he heard Wright espouse the theory. But the theory was little more than a rationalization for Western interventionist power.

· · ·

By the mid-1960s, Irving Kristol had left *Encounter* and, with Dan Bell, had founded *The Public Interest* with a $10,000 grant from the CCF/CIA.[13] Bell had been tasked with interviewing *The Paris Review*'s candidate for "joint emploi," in Aldrich's phrase. And he eventually left *The Public Interest* as Kristol's politics veered rightward. Kristol came to embrace the derogatory term "neoconservative," which he defined as "a liberal who's been mugged by reality."

The Public Interest quietly joined the "Grande Famille," as Mike Josselson called his magazines, actively sharing content with *Mundo Nuevo*. *The Paris Review* reprints started to appear in the pages of *Mundo Nuevo*, too. An interview with Harold Pinter appeared in *Mundo Nuevo*'s issue 13. Conducted by *The Paris Review*'s Paris editor Larry Bensky, it originally ran in the *Review*'s Fall 1966 issue, number 39. Bensky himself even took some government money to attend a junket, where he subverted his funders, he recalled later, by using the trip to denounce the Vietnam War.[14]

The exchange between *The Paris Review* and others in the Grande Famille was mutually beneficial to the magazines—a readymade bouquet of "content" at their disposal. In February 1967, Rodríguez Monegal wrote to *The Paris Review*'s Maxine Groffsky to request permission not just for the Pinter interview, but also William Flanagan's interview with Edward Albee. In May, Rodríguez Monegal asked for *The Paris Review*'s Borges interview and in December for its Nabokov interview. Rodríguez Monegal arranged content-syndication deals with other CCF magazines, as well. He wrote Melvin Lasky, now editor at *Encounter*, to request the rights to such pieces as Sidney Hook's pamphlet on Marxism, articles by Theodor Adorno on Spengler, Edmund Wilson on Freud, Martin Turnell on Roland Barthes, and Ernst Gombrich on Claude Lévi-Strauss. Hearing nothing back, he wrote again to request the same arrangement he had with *Preuves*. "When I ask them and they are free to give them to me, they do not reply. No answer means a positive answer. . . . If I do not hear from you, can I assume the same?"[15]

In cultural and political propaganda for the West, silence was understood as consent. But if consent was unspoken between editors, how could it be gotten from the author? In some public spaces, the work was getting less and less overt. It was melting into the backdrops. For many confused readers, it was getting harder to separate literature from propaganda—a disservice to the former though a boon to the latter. As when Rodríguez Monegal ran a decoy story criticizing the Vietnam War to hide his ties to US intelligence, tightly controlled and limited dissent was recast as proof of cultural freedom—as quiet, subtle propaganda for the Western way. All "content"—whether of the left, right, or center—was viable as propaganda, proof (again) for the Americans' vision of their own freedom. Sometimes the work said little more than this: we are here. Sometimes the left-wing or critical argument was used to cover the trail of the hawkish or reactionary one. The Americans could not be denied their voice. Their way would prevail. They had the intellectuals. More importantly, they had money and their money was backed up by guns. And they had had the foresight to keep their propaganda secret. Thus would it be more effective.

Finally, Rodríguez Monegal sent nothing more than simple lists. The rumors were closing in on him. The CIA ties were being whispered about. But as long as he could, he kept working, writing to the other CCF editors, reminding them of previous requests, adding new titles to those he sought to reprint as he found and read them. According to the CCF scholar for Latin America, Russell Cobb, these editorial sharing arrangements did not involve an exchange of money; *Mundo Nuevo* was syndicating (and being syndicated) for free. Whatever infrastructure was being created to further Latin American letters, globally writers were getting the shaft each time their pieces went into another language for yet another CCF magazine. Their work was being multiplied; but their pay rate shrank.

Yet as we saw with Pasternak and *The Paris Review*, even those magazines that were paid made no efforts to seek permission for these reprints from the interview *subjects*. In journalism, the interviewer is considered the writer, the creator who controls rights to the interview. And while it would have been hard for *The Paris Review* or Olga Carlisle to get Pasternak's permission to run reprints of their interview anyway, had he lived, one nevertheless imagines that leftist writers like Hemingway or Harold Pinter, and others like Faulkner, would have been annoyed to find that having agreed to an interview with, say, *The* ("apolitical") *Paris Review*, they somehow wound up in the magazines of a CIA front.

The system reeked of coercion. The apolitical posture was a trick. Freedom means, to paraphrase Octavio Paz, the right to say yes or no. Hemingway, Pasternak, Faulkner, García Márquez, Clarice Lispector, and most of the magazines' authors and interview subjects whose words were foisted into the literary propaganda mags of the CIA were denied—thanks to the secrecy—their right to refuse, even as Stalin, Khrushchev, the CIA, and the FBI denied these authors' rights to free speech and privacy.

. . .

On March 10, 1966, Plimpton responded to Doc Humes's challenge to come clean or take him off the masthead. Doc was unwell. Living in London, his wife had left him on Christmas and had taken the children back to the United States, where she ended up marrying Nelson Aldrich in 1967. She had met him at a *Paris Review* party. Some stories described Doc doing too much LSD and never coming down from his trip. Others have him constantly looking over his shoulder at the surveillance. Nevertheless, his letters sound lucid.

Doc had prodded his co-founders to come clean about Matthiessen's ties to the CIA. Rumors had come and gone in the 1950s about *Encounter*, *The Paris Review*, and other magazines' funding. Matthiessen may have been influenced by the chatter and was ready to tell the truth. In Immy Humes's documentary "Doc," Matthiessen and Plimpton argue indirectly in a series of intercut interviews over the appropriateness and timing of Matthiessen's revelations to Doc.

Matthiessen says he thought it was a good time to come clean and adds defensively that he didn't think his revelations made Doc's condition any worse. *I didn't think you did*, Immy Humes says in the footage. It's not clear Matthiessen even knew about *The Paris Review*'s ties to the CCF. These were George's ties. The exchanges suggest that Matthiessen only told Doc about his early days in the CIA. In his letter to Plimpton, Doc was sympathetic to Peter and had suggested to Plimpton that the CIA makes victims of its instruments. But he underlined, too, that the magazine's disclosure to readers now and for future generations was important.

In March, George replied, "Peter is back, and he's talked to me about your meetings . . . [Peter] says that if you resign, he's going to resign."

All of this puts a great deal of pressure and dismay on an innocent third party—namely humble old GAP [Plimpton's initials]. I under-stand about the principles involved, of course, and your feelings and Peter's, but I would hasten to point out that whatever overt acts you do—such as resignations, or press conferences, or a long "confession" by Peter in the SatEvePost (your suggestion)—can only harm, even destroy the magazine. What a paradox it would be if the magazine which stood up through that most tenuous CIA relationship in those early days was now destroyed when there is no relationship whatsoever![16]

In fact, the ties between the Congress and *The Paris Review* in early 1966 remained intact. The staff ties appeared to end when Nelson Aldrich moved from *The Paris Review* and the Congress's Paris headquarters, to working specifically on propaganda for Africa and then returned to the United States to work for the likes of *Harper's*. But when Humes and Plimpton exchanged these letters, engaging in a transatlantic argument about journalistic disclosure, the ties remained in content and ad sharing, none of which could quite match the glory of being used as a cover. The ties continued even after this ultimatum from Humes with Larry Bensky's fall interview with Harold Pinter running in *Mundo Nuevo* number 13.

Plimpton continued, "All of this may be quite academic, Doc. As you know, I have never accepted a resignation."

Listen, I wish you'd come home. That's really why I'm writing. You have too many friends here to stay away from them for so long. I don't pretend to know what your personal problems are. That doesn't make any difference. You are always welcome to stay here at 541 [East 72nd Street] until you get things straightened out. (I'll amend that to a one year limit) and such resources, and cash, and all the rest of it would be forthcoming from any number of friends. Things aren't so bad here. All sorts of projects. The little publishing house is going OK, I think, and what should I be involved with but films![17] Stumbling, but learning. Come back in time for the second annual Paris Review Revel, which is on April 28, a Thursday. That would make it a celebration indeed![18]

Plimpton's generosity in this letter has been noted, among others, by Doc's daughter Immy. Nevertheless, Humes himself may have felt that he was being treated again as a hysteric, gaslighted and so just as he had threatened to do, he resolutely resigned.

On March 12, Plimpton's patience was exhausted. He responded, "I have your letter of resignation at hand. I'm somewhat puzzled as to what it is you expect me to do—that is 'to take urgent counsel with the best and wisest heads you can find.'" Referring to these wise heads, Plimpton continued,

> What can these Solomons suggest? I'm not even sure I could present the facts to them with a straight face. Peter's clandestine occupations in the early fifties have nothing to do with the *Review* or its policies. When he described his connection with the CIA to me, he spoke of the *Review* as being a "convenient" front, not that it was "set up" by him as a front. Besides, Doc, I'd always assumed <u>you</u> had founded the magazine. For God's sake, don't let your anti-CIA sympathies deny you <u>that</u> important statistic![19]

We've seen how it annoyed Matthiessen when Plimpton was described as *The Paris Review*'s founder. Now Plimpton was appealing to Humes's vanity, calling him the founder to keep him quiet, trapping Humes with his own earlier claims.

Writer Bryant Urstadt unearthed a letter in an unprocessed folder of *The Paris Review*'s archives at the Morgan Library in midtown Manhattan, in which Doc Humes makes a strange argument. On February 25, 1953, Humes argued "that the *Review* was his idea from the start, challenging Plimpton to check with James Baldwin, with whom he discussed it in the summer of 1950 at the Metro Café on the Rue de Four, a year before Matthiessen would arrive."

Urstadt continues, "Humes not only claims that the magazine was his idea alone, but that he caused Matthiessen to suggest [it] to him. . . . [Humes] describes some management techniques he had learned while working for William Sheppard on the Marshall Plan in Paris."

> Among "Sheppard's Rules" were instructions on how to convince colleagues to advance your own ideas as theirs. Humes claims he worked on Matthiessen in this regard for some time, writing, "Do you think it is an easy thing to build up steam for the idea of the Paris-American Review in Peter Matthiessen's cold, New England boilers?"[20]

Reflecting this back to Humes, Plimpton tries to placate and convince his former colleague that neither Humes's nor Plimpton's nor Matthiessen's coming clean about the CIA ties would be good for the magazine. He must have feared Doc's knack for publicity, the press conferences for the writers' union with screenwriters, the New York City Police campaign. Despite Doc's talents for raising a public stink, Plimpton was adamant that no good could come of revelations about Matthiessen, *The Paris Review*, and the CIA. What had the CIA even done for the magazine, really? "May I remind you that *Encounter*'s Congress for Cultural Freedom backing is actually, or was until its present private sponsorship, from CIA funds," wrote Plimpton.

> Dwight Macdonald discovered this not long ago, and began a long article of indignation and suspension. He dropped it almost immediately—for a number of reasons, but chief among that that the editors' integrity remained their own, and that there was apparently no interference.[21]

Plimpton hoped that by contrasting his magazine with *Encounter*, he might dodge the reckoning Doc was requesting. But then Plimpton baited Humes, asking how he never figured out Matthiessen's ties sooner, and he even halfheartedly accused Humes himself of spying. "You must admit that the CIA-*Encounter* bond is a far more tenable one than the CIA-*Paris Review* connection—this latter indeed non-existent," he wrote.

> I suppose every CIA agent must have a job of sorts. Otherwise his presence in a foreign city looks suspicious. I'm not outraged by the thought of a CIA man selecting Tea at Le Gord for the mag. If you want to know, I always thought <u>you</u> were in the CIA, truly. You knew more about underground currents (how was it that you never smelled out Peter M. before this?) than anyone. And then you grew that beard and read *Huck Finn* day after day in the cafés, and I always assumed you were waiting for someone to slip a note to. . .
>
> Don't resign, Doc, at least not on this score. I don't know why more editors aren't . . . resigning because of the poetry lately, which seems very bad to me, and a much better reason for throwing in the sponge.[22]

It was as masterful as Plimpton's trapeze act for one of his writing "stunts." He contrasted *The Paris Review*'s nebulous ties with *Encounter*'s very real ones, hoping to downplay the former. And to cover any anticipated pushback from Humes, he underlined the myth of *Encounter*'s editorial freedom. Why did it matter to Humes anyway? It was old news.

. . .

A month and a half later, *The New York Times* ran the third in a series of articles about the extended reach of the CIA. The article began with details about new satellite surveillance technologies: "American Samos and Soviet Cosmos satellites gather more data in one 90-minute-orbit than an army of earthbound spies."[23]

But satellite surveillance wasn't the only new technology the CIA was using to extend its reach. "The agency is now developing a highly sensitive device that will pick up from afar indoor conversations, by recording the window vibrations caused by the speakers' voices. . . . This is only one of the many nefarious gadgets that have made the word 'privacy' an anachronism."

As the scandal deepened, it was backlit for Humes by Plimpton's comparison. *The New York Times* tied *Encounter* to the CIA through the CCF. "[T]he CIA has supported groups of exiles from Cuba and refugees from Communism in Europe, or anti-Communist but liberal organizations of intellectuals such as the Congress for Cultural Freedom, and some of their newspapers and magazines." Hadn't Plimpton privately outed *Encounter* before the story was even in print, dismissing the ties as having ended? Even if this was partly true (the Ford Foundation had been added as an extra layer of buffer between the CIA and *Encounter*), how did Plimpton even know this?

The *Times* named *Encounter* as a beneficiary of funds and went on to call the CIA a "Frankenstein's monster" that "no one can fully control." However Plimpton had downplayed the story, it must have read like a vast conspiracy to Humes, affirming his worst fears. The "revelations" continued to seep out for more than a year, a vast American conspiracy was being documented after almost two decades in the darkness, and the paranoid—like Doc Humes—must have been terrified and enthralled.

The response to these allegations was at first muted in Latin America, since revelations were coming primarily in English. Yet colleagues wrote one another to check the mood. Rodríguez Monegal wrote to Dan Bell at *The Public Interest* to request an article by conservative sociologist Robert A. Nisbet. They chatted about the revelations in the exchange. The Nisbet article, meanwhile, defended another conspiracy just dragged out into the light. This was the US Army's secret plan, recently uncovered, to use Chile as a testing ground for the scientific study of the prevention of revolution, and examining precisely what happens when a society collapses. Chilean institutions of higher learning had been penetrated by American sociologists who were actually working for the US military, undercover. When the plan, Project Camelot, was made public, Chileans were outraged. This was just two years before the CIA would go into the early but decisive stages of plotting a coup in Chile, what it later called Track 1, first controlling the elections and later blocking President Salvador Allende from taking office. The agency may have already funded the Christian Democratic party headed by Eduardo Frei. (As in Italy, the strategy was to pry the socialists, social democrats, and other liberals away from the Communists, a strategy that resulted in propping up the center-left party with bribes.) The CIA spent three million on the 1964 Chilean elections. As Evan Thomas reported, this meant that the United States spent a dollar per vote to buy that election for its favored party.[24] The CIA doubled down by propping up Chile's high-circulation conservative newspaper *El Mercurio*. The propaganda that this newspaper put out would help instill a climate of fear against the popularly elected President Allende, making way for the strongman, General Augusto Pinochet, on September 11, 1973.

The *Mundo Nuevo* translation of Nisbet's *Public Interest* article defending Project Camelot ran in the same issue as the second excerpt of García Márquez's *One Hundred Years of Solitude*. Had Nisbet known about the purchase of Chilean elections he might not have been as dismissive of the Chileans as he was when he wrote, "One of the ways [to treat Project Camelot with overblown importance] was to turn the whole thing over to a left-wing newspaper which, after months of the usual dreary leftist copy, had, for a change, something of Stop Press significance." Nisbet continued,

> It is not difficult to imagine the theme: American diplomacy, after a century of working through banana royalists had now turned to behavioral science royalists, that is, from industrial to academic tycoons, etc. etc. In any event, the news of Camelot was out—in Chile at least.[25]

Nisbet wiggled acrobatically away from the event itself, offering, if not a defense of the plan, then a defense of the military's use of social sciences, which could only make the generals and colonels better informed deciders. Wasn't this an appeal to modernization theory? Indeed, while the CIA funded a right-wing newspaper conspiring to overthrow the government, Robert Nisbet, *The Public Interest*, and *Mundo Nuevo* bashed a left-wing newspaper for exposing what everyone was really doing. Institutions in the developing world needed this kind of contact with American ones, as per modernization theory, the way an ulcer needs chili powder.

. . .

The same month that the *Times* outed the CCF, the liberal Catholic magazine *Ramparts* ran a story that exposed a secret CIA partnership with Michigan State University. The Michigan State story was a kind of Project Camelot for Vietnam. The article was written by *Ramparts* staffers Warren Hinckle and Robert Scheer—with whistleblower Stanley Sheinbaum writing an introduction. It told the story of United States university professors taking huge pay increases to militarize and weaponize their expertise on behalf of Vietnam's strongman, and in tandem with the interests behind the Vietnam War in the United States.

Ramparts started as a liberal Catholic quarterly based on the West Coast under its founder and longtime funder, Edward Keating. But the magazine quickly developed a voice unlike any magazine of its time. It grew increasingly playful and taunting in its acts of dissent toward American power. It was not shy about engaging with racial politics and the travesty of US foreign policy, especially in Vietnam. Events of the day pushed Keating and *Ramparts* ever leftward, while also attracting truly independent journalists like Hinckle and Scheer, and increasingly, brave and disgusted whistleblowers—like the academic Stanley Sheinbaum.

Sheinbaum had been on faculty in the economics department at Michigan State University starting in 1955. Two years into his stint he became a coordinator at the university's Vietnam Project, a $25 million contract job to advise South Vietnamese president Ngo Dinh Diem. Diem was roughly the equivalent of Batista, a corrupt killer propped up by US money. The United States was in the process of securing his "mandate" through the creation of a police state in his native land and by stuffing ballot boxes. MSU faculty who signed on to the Vietnam Project doubled their salaries and improved their likelihood for tenure. Additionally, Sheinbaum and others discovered that a whole wing of a university building they had attempted to visit was off-limits to faculty and staff and said to be filled with undercover CIA agents. Sheinbaum had wanted to mark his career by helping developing economies to grow but the project he was ensnared into was something else entirely. It used real academic social scientists as cover for paramilitary activities and as camouflage for agents.[26]

The professors were paid to retrofit their expertise in other fields in order to help arm and train the Vietnamese Bureau of Investigation, or VBI. This was Diem's secret police. The professors were also expected to keep silent in the face of "investigations" that led to the removal of dissidents, in at least one case to a known "concentration camp."[27] Sheinbaum himself knew that the MSU Vietnam Project was presiding over and enabling torture in Diem's Vietnam. Here—again—was the sponsorship of culture, plus expertise, as a cover for atrocities at its most crass. This was modernization.

Sheinbaum wrote of being visited in the United States by four high-level Vietnamese officials. One of them was Diem's nephew, who told Sheinbaum that he planned to kill another member of the visiting quartet. The plan was thwarted when Sheinbaum sent the target to hospital for fake TB-like symptoms. This had been too much for Sheinbaum and he finally quit. The connection between MSU faculty and the CIA was about as close as possible, according to *Ramparts*.

"The professors not only trained Diem's security forces," wrote Sheinbaum's co-authors, "but, in the early years of the Project, actually supplied them with guns and ammunition.

> In doing so, the East Lansing contingent helped to secure Diem's dictatorship and to provide the base and the arms for the "secret police" which were to make [Diem's sister-in-law] Madame Nhu and her brother infamous at a later date.[28]

The *Ramparts* writers wrote in a brisk, sarcastic style that blended sweeping reporting—names, titles, quotes, dates; original as well as previously published material—with shrewd analysis and acerbic observations that taunted the targets of their scoop. Challenging US foreign policy, *Ramparts* even slammed another CIA-tied magazine, *The New Leader*, for publishing a hagiography of Diem by the most corrupt of the MSU professors, who had the closest relationship to Diem and the nicest villa of all the professors. The *Ramparts* article implied that the university broke international laws and ended with appropriate bravado. "To question the assumption that the academician of tomorrow must be an operator is to ask but part of the essential question about MSU's 'Vietnam Adventure,'" argued the muckrakers.

> And to ask whether the University officials are liars, or whether the MSU Project broke the spirit of the Geneva Accords, is also neglecting the primary question.

The essential query, which must be asked before the discussion of Michigan State's behavior can be put into any rational perspective, is this: what the hell is a university doing buying guns, anyway?[29]

·   ·   ·

By naming undercover spies, *Ramparts* got the agency's attention. In mid-April, Director of Central Intelligence William Raborn asked for a "rundown" on *Ramparts* on "a high-priority basis." Legally such an investigation was questionable; it violated the ban on domestic operations that established the agency in 1947 and would therefore require a cover-up. But the CIA's director of security, Howard Osborn, was unafraid of such cover and made the orders explicit. "The Director [Raborn] is particularly interested in the authors of the article, namely, Stanley Sheinbaum and Robert Scheer," began one memo. "He is also interested in any other individuals who worked for the magazine."[30]

Within two days, the agents had collected dossiers on twenty-two of *Ramparts'* fifty-five staffers. Osborn reported on *Ramparts'* start as a lay Catholic journal and its turn under Hinckle and Scheer to muckraking and whistleblowing. In addition to its San Francisco headquarters, it had offices in New York, Paris, and Munich. It had two former-Communist staff members, but its most outspoken critic of US policy—a former Green beret named Donald Duncan—was arguing from a pragmatic position, invoking national security: "We will continue to be in danger as long as the CIA is deciding policy and manipulating nations."[31]

The intelligence agents reported that *Ramparts* planned follow-up stories and that there would be further revelations about the agency. Two of *Ramparts'* editors were even planning to run for Congress on an antiwar platform. This information ultimately went to President Johnson via his aide, Bill Moyers, and on to Walt Rostow, the man later replaced by Henry Kissinger as national security advisor. "Within days [of launching its rundown on the magazine]," the author Angus Mackenzie wrote indelibly, "the CIA had progressed from investigating a news publication to sending domestic political intelligence to the White House, just as a few members of Congress had feared 19 years earlier [when they tried to block the establishment of the CIA]."[32]

The public outcry over the *Ramparts* revelations—violation of academic freedom being the common refrain—was so loud that Johnson set up a task force made up of the attorney general, the secretaries of health, education, and welfare and the CIA's Richard Helms. Helms also set up a task force within the CIA to vet agency relationships with academia—"but that review, from all appearances, was designed only to ensure that these operations remained secret."[33]

The CIA investigated the magazine's funding and it requested that the FBI treat *Ramparts* as a subversive organization, even without evidence of wrongdoing. But the real point, wrote Mackenzie, "was to place *Ramparts* reporters under such close surveillance that any CIA officials involved in domestic operations would have time to rehearse cover stories before the reporters arrived to question them."[34] *Ramparts* was now the stuff of legend but it was far from the only prominent intellectual journal of the 1960s to be suppressed. Another was *The New York Review of Books*. In a passing reference to another "rundown" of a magazine, the CIA's Lee Williams, the agent who likely sent Macdonald's "America! America!" to CIA HQ in Washington, told an interviewer, "We had a big problem with the yin and the yang of *The New York Review* crowd, especially when it got so anti-Vietnam and so left-wing."[35] The CIA had come a long way from funding culture for the aim of beating Soviet soft power influence.

. . .

But even the constant surveillance on *Ramparts* couldn't stop their next story about academia and the CIA. In January 1967, Hinckle met Michael Wood, a former employee of the National Student Association (NSA), which had also contracted with the CIA.

Twenty-four years old, a dropout of Pomona College, Wood had done fund-raising for the National Student Association. The National Student Association represented three million American college students. Fund-raisers like Wood attended a number of international meetings on behalf of the members. In the course of his work, Wood, like Sheinbaum at Michigan State, had learned that the organization was largely funded through the CIA. The money came from the agency's Covert Action Division Number 5, funneled through a series of nonprofit foundations. The CIA invested money into the NSA to battle the international student organizations it presumed were penetrated by Communists. Hinckle and Wood met in New York, in the Algonquin Hotel's dining room, where Dorothy Parker had once hosted her famous Round Table discussions. The two men chatted while sharing a slice of chocolate cake.

When Wood turned over the National Student Association's financial records at the end of their discussion, having recounted his discovery of the CIA's penetration, Hinckle was dubious. The last thing he needed was to give the CIA reason to question his credibility by printing something that wasn't properly vetted. Was he being set up? At first he wondered. "Wood's story was not one to instill faith in the skeptic," he wrote in his memoir.[36] But he enlisted his reporting and research staff, who found a remarkable means of corroborating Wood's story. Texas Congressman Wright Patman had three years earlier investigated nonprofits that served as front organizations, or conduits, for channeling CIA money to cultural institutions. These philanthropic organizations had been dubbed "the Patman Eight." These were the same foundations that were funding the National Student Association, as recorded in the documents turned over by Wood. Hinckle wasn't just surprised that the nervous dropout was telling the truth. He was dumbfounded that, even after their philanthropic conduits had been outed by a Congressional investigation, the CIA continued to use them.[37]

It was shoddy "spycraft." But while the records helped, the cone of silence ordered by the CIA made the investigation difficult. "The CIA knew we were onto their game before we had time to discover what it really was," Hinckle wrote. "Doors slammed in the faces of our inquiring reporters. . . . The blank walls were impressive."[38] Nevertheless *Ramparts* was able to report the story, even without some of the witnesses the CIA had warned off.

The United States National Student Association (NSA) rose up as a counter to the presumably Communist-penetrated International Union of Students (IUS) and little by little the organizations' roles reversed. As Sol Stern described it in his *Ramparts* article, "Most student unions, originally attracted to the organization out of resentment against the strictures imposed by the [Communist-influenced] IUS, became alienated from it when, partly under NSA's prodding, the ISC [International Student Conference] began to set forth its own tight Cold War positions."[39] In other words, the CIA's NSA was becoming more doctrinaire and high-handed than the Communist-penetrated student union had been. Stern outed an organization that was apparently democratic in its makeup at home (with members voting on decisions), but elitist and hermetic in its makeup abroad. It was a charade, a schizophrenic doubling where the American arm's visible democratic decision making was a cover for the international arm, controlled by the CIA, where the real decision making powers lay. Stern wrote, "In the '50s, NSA took even more liberal stands than the prevailing apathy among students might have suggested. And in the '60s, NSA responded to the new militant protest mood on the campuses. It supported students against the draft, opposed the war in Vietnam, and participated in civil rights struggles. It played a crucial role in the formation of the Student Nonviolent Coordinating Committee and was one of its staunchest supporters, a position which cost it the affiliation of many schools in 1961."[40]

But as laudable as all this may have been, it appeared to be a cover for the NSA abroad, which was a different animal altogether. "Despite its liberal rhetoric, NSA-ers abroad seemed more like professional diplomats than students; there was something tough and secretive about them that was out of keeping with their openness and spontaneity back home."[41] Stern continued, "the operations of NSA's international staff were debated by a select few who could usually move the rest of the Congress on the basis of their esoteric expertise. Overseas representatives of NSA and delegates to the ISC were never elected by the NSA Congress."[42] They were an elite; that is, they were witting collaborators with the CIA.

Stern could have been talking about the CCF or any number of CIA fronts, from *Imprint* magazine in India to *Combate* and the Institute for Political Education in Costa Rica. The New York–based Kaplan Fund filtered CIA money to both *Combate* and to *Mundo Nuevo*, commingling that money, laundering it after a fashion, with a Ford Foundation filter—and through many smaller foundations expressly set up to channel "philanthropic" Cold War money. In other words, the money that came to the NSA or *Mundo Nuevo* passed through Kaplan Fund accounts to disguise its CIA origin. This was, of course, illegal, and masked the money so those outside the witting leadership might never know. Stern wrote:

> It turned out that a number of other foundations had contributed to the Kaplan Fund during the crucial years of 1961–63 when the Fund had been serving the CIA. Five of these foundations were not even on the Internal Revenue Service's list of tax-exempt foundations. . . . The implication was clear that some or all of these were the channel through which the CIA money passed into the Kaplan foundation coffers.[43]

Stern reported, too, that students and other anti-Communist delegates had received funding to attend festivals across Europe, from Vienna to Helsinki. They went through a front called the Independent Research Service, which actively recruited a delegation of hundreds of young Americans to attend the festivals in order to actively oppose the Communists. The travel expenses of all the delegates were fully paid for and the bill was footed as well for a jazz group, an exhibition of famous American painters and a daily newspaper printed in five languages, all of which accompanied the delegates.[44]

After it failed to prevent this whistleblower, the CIA scrambled to deny *Ramparts* its scoop. Administration had shifted over at Langley. Raborn was out as director of Central Intelligence and Richard Helms was in. Helms moved the *Ramparts* operation under the Directorate of Plans (later of Operations; later National Clandestine Services). This meant that until his death in July of that year, the man responsible for the operations against *Ramparts* was Frank Wisner's protégé, Desmond Fitzgerald.[45] However, when the CIA realized they had no mechanisms in place to directly suppress the magazine since it wasn't one they had started, the CIA quickly planned a preemptive press conference where National Student Association officers would admit to the CIA tie. As part of the charade, they insisted that the relationship had ended. If revelations into the secret workings of government were the fuel of journalistic prestige, the CIA would preempt such revelations where it could.

But Hinckle and *Ramparts* had their own informants inside the NSA and they heard of the preemption. "I was damned if I was going to let the CIA scoop me," Hinckle wrote in his memoir. "I bought a full-page advertisement in *The New York Times* and *The Washington Post* to scoop myself, which seemed the preferable alternative."[46] The ads provided a bullet point recounting of what Stern's reporting had revealed. The CIA was outmaneuvered, but it wasn't ready to give up. As author Evan Thomas has reported,

"I had all sorts of dirty tricks to hurt their circulation and financing," said [Agent Edgar] Applewhite. "The people running *Ramparts* were vulnerable to blackmail. We had awful things in mind, some of which we carried off. . . . We were not the least inhibited by the fact that the CIA had no internal security role in the United States." When Applewhite returned to brief Fitzgerald on his dirty tricks (which he declined to describe twenty-five years later), the clandestine chief was bemused. "Eddie," he said, "you have a spot of blood on your pinafore."[47]

This records a rare glimpse of a CIA agent gloating over an operation to kill off a media institution as retribution for its truthful reporting. With the slipshod creation of the CIA as a secret, extralegal institution, the American and world press had drifted into rapids that were pounding against its erstwhile liberties. In such a system of secrecy, the public debate regarding relevant policy questions was relegated always to the period after key decisions had already been made.

· · ·

The *Ramparts* article on the NSA was attacked by the former head of United States Information Service, Carl Rowan, in his new capacity as syndicated columnist.[48] This diligent defender of the American Way printed a much-cited piece alleging as fact, first, that Scheer and others at *Ramparts* were Communists who had come from meetings in Prague before publishing the NSA story and, second, that their revelation of the CIA role in student life was actually a Communist-planted story. This, of course, was disinformation. To make the story *feel* true, a trip to Cuba Scheer had taken years before was alleged to have taken place after it was illegal to go there, rather than when he actually went.

Scheer was then invited onto William F. Buckley's new television debate show, *Firing Line*, after the magazine Buckley had founded, *The National Review*, repeated Rowan's false claims. *The National Review* was launched by several CIA veterans in the mid-1950s,[49] and like that magazine, *Firing Line* was a media institution with a hidden agenda. When Scheer came on to discuss *Ramparts*, Buckley attacked. None of the facts about the National Student Association or Michigan State articles were discussed. Instead, in classic ad hominem style, Buckley tried to label Scheer—and the magazine he worked for—as "anti-American." But calling the phrase a rhetorical one used to silence critics, Scheer slammed Buckley for refusing to define the term.

The two then debated the US preference for right-wing and not left-wing killers. Buckley threatened, "The trouble with resisting Ho Chi Minh [the Vietnamese revolutionary fighting the Americans] is that you get shot if you do, and that a lot of people aren't prepared to do. Maybe you wouldn't even publish *Ramparts* if you got shot for doing so."[50] This was right-wing irony, intended to whitewash Diem's own crimes, which his American collaborators knew meant exactly this type of extrajudicial murder of dissidents. Scheer said he would take Castro over Batista and Ho Chi Minh over the murderous Diem.

Buckley might have been barred from telling his audience the truth of his CIA ties, but there were certainly hints if you were paying attention. After serving as Tom Guinzburg's editor-in-chief at the *Yale Daily News*, Buckley had joined the agency in the 1950s and worked under his friend E. Howard Hunt in Mexico; he knew of the CIA's covert propaganda funding of various fronts like the CCF[51] when he was a deep cover agent. The year he trained in DC, he confirmed Matthiessen's fears of being spotted by friends—and outed as CIA. When he ran into a college friend in the capital, this friend of Buckley's had admitted he was training for the Agency but Buckley held his tongue. Using a book as a cover, he pretended he was researching a follow-up to his bestselling *God and Man at Yale*. Others associated with the CIA signed on when Buckley's new magazine launched,[52] one of many conservative magazines that make up the CIA's legacy. A few years later, Buckley even had Hunt himself on *Firing Line* to counter the allegations that Hunt was blackmailing the president during the Watergate sentencing period.[53]

When Watergate broke, Buckley's work in the CIA was outed. As an undercover agent, he did propaganda—getting useful books published—and spied on friends. Subsequently, he admitted to some of this. Hunt's own "retirement" from the Agency has been questioned by journalists and researchers, one who wrote, "CIA history is littered with instances where CIA officers have tendered their 'resignation' as a means of creating deniability while continuing to work closely with the agency." The example cited was none other than Buckley's old boss Hunt, writing that Hunt's "resignation" in 1970 "left him in a position to find work in the Nixon White House—where he promptly began a 'liaison' relationship with his old bosses."[54] Evidence for Buckley's ongoing relationship with the Agency arose on the Watergate tapes. Buckley biographer John Judis recalls, "When the Watergate tapes were released, there was one embarrassing reference to Buckley and Hunt in them. On January 8, 1973, Nixon had said to Charles Colson in regard to Hunt's bid for clemency: 'Hunt's is a simple case. We'll build that son of a bitch up like nobody's business. We'll have Buckley write a column and say, you know, that he, that he should have clemency, if you've given eighteen years of service.'"[55]

The above suggests that attacking Scheer was not just a matter of politics for Buckley. It was his job. Not only did Buckley republish propagandist Rowan's column calling the *Ramparts* editors "Communists" in *The National Review*, but even after *The National Review* promised to correct the misinformation, Buckley repeated it on television. He also pretended Scheer had never sent Buckley a detailed letter correcting the mistake. Calling Scheer anti-American was not just an insult. It was code for denying patronage and credibility.

But despite the attacks from Buckley and other operators, *Ramparts* bore up well—at least for a little bit longer. Against the stream of persecution, it kept its adversarial role toward American power and worked against the rampant corruption of that power. It ran, in this period, a stream of exposés and countercultural coups in its pages that were perhaps best typified by a translation of Sartre's call for genocide charges against the United States in Vietnam. For roughly eight more years, *Ramparts* ran articles that proved that despite the sabotage, attacks, and whisper campaigns to chill its advertisers and staff, its independence was intact. Without that independence, even an erudite journal was just not doing journalism so much as publicity, no matter how urbane its tone. And in maintaining its antagonistic posture, *Ramparts* wasn't alone. Though they may have felt outnumbered by publications with ties, they were beginning to inspire others.

At the outset of the 1966 PEN Congress in New York (the one attended by Neruda), the author and public intellectual Conor Cruise O'Brien challenged the conference's theme: "writer as independent spirit." O'Brien suggested in a pointed speech at NYU that intellectuals were serving American power, flattering it as propagandists, rather than questioning the assumptions and crimes within that power. He called the operators around *Encounter* particularly to task for "the inculcation of uniformly favorable attitudes in Britain towards American policies and practices."[56]

Naturally, *Encounter* (under editor Melvin Lasky) attacked his credibility. This prompted a libel lawsuit. O'Brien not only sued but by taking his claim into Irish jurisdiction, he won. The Irish had a healthy skepticism toward Anglo empires. While *Encounter* attacked O'Brien for questioning the intellectuals' independence, the CIA's sub rosa persecution of *Ramparts* sought pretexts to close them down on the basis of a foreign funding tie, which was the Cold War euphemism for the infamous tie to Moscow. They never found one, but the search itself was especially ironic.

. . .

In July of 1966, *The New York Times* reported that the CCF's "Arab Review," *Hiwar*, based in Beirut, Lebanon, had been banned in Egypt as a result of its "foreign ties" to the CIA.[57] In the article announcing the ban, *The Times* cited its own April 27, 1966 article and quoted the single phrase it reported on the CCF as the likely trigger for the ban on *Hiwar*: "the CIA has supported groups of exiles from Cuba and refugees from Communism in Europe, or anti-Communist but liberal organizations of intellectuals such as the Congress for Cultural Freedom, and some of their newspapers and magazines."[58] This was enough for the Cairene leftists to presume that *Hiwar* was imperialist propaganda.

The July article quoted Dr. Louis Awad, a left-leaning literary critic at the Egyptian newspaper *Al Ahram*, who pointed to *The New York Times* revelations as justification for banning *Hiwar* and *Encounter* both. Awad may have known that other magazines like *The Paris Review* had its interviews regularly syndicated in *Hiwar* from the Arab magazine's first issue. The pressure from Humes probably distracted Plimpton from this latest revelation amounting to a mere footnote in the history of *The Paris Review*. Nevertheless, Plimpton's staff had been in touch repeatedly with *Hiwar*'s editor Tawfiq Sayigh.

Paris editor Patrick Bowles wrote Sayigh in July 1964 and enclosed proofs of an interview with Jean Cocteau for reprint in *Hiwar*, as Sayigh had requested. Bowles requested payment for reprints of several past interviews in *Hiwar*.[59] The fall before, in middle October, Bowles had written Sayigh to note that "I have of course received your copies of HIWAR containing the Henry Miller and Lawrence Durrell interviews, and although I cannot, unfortunately, read a single word of Arabic, I am able to appreciate the presentation of your magazine. . ."[60] Even someone who couldn't read Arabic could see that the CCF magazine in Arabic shared a certain belletristic, small-digest elegance that defined official and unofficial CCF magazines from *The New Leader* and *Partisan Review* to *Encounter*, *Preuves*, *Mundo Nuevo*, and *The Paris Review*. Of its first thirteen issues, *Hiwar* printed a *Paris Review* interview in at least six.[61]

And through syndication these magazines could casually be linked; it even happened that work that appeared in *Hiwar* later appeared on at least one occasion in the Muslim Brotherhood of Syria's journal *Hadarat al-Islam*.[62] (But this was in the days when the CIA had only dabbled in weaponizing Islamism. More would come on that front.) *The New York Times* notes that while Dr. Awad had published poetry in *Hiwar*, he called upon Sayigh to resign, "because carrying on would infringe upon any writer's patriotism." Likewise, the leftists of Cairo had convinced another writer, Yusuf Idris, to refuse the nearly $3,000 literary prize he won from *Hiwar*.

As Michael Vazquez has written, *Hiwar*'s foreign ties turned out to be detrimental; the magazine's demise followed the revelations of ties to the

CCF. "Sayigh was a Palestinian Christian and a modernist poet who translated T.S. Eliot into Arabic."

> He'd founded *Hiwar* in Beirut in 1964 [sic], and the journal was wildly successful, if only for publishing the first short stories of Tayeb Salih, which in turn convinced Salih to return to the abandoned manuscript that would become *Season of Migration to the North*. *Hiwar* was also wildly controversial; even without the CIA connection, the CCF and its Anglo-American milieu rankled both the Nasserites and the Francophiles. When the story broke, Sayigh made a full-throated defense of CCF, and when it was confirmed, he was left holding the bag. The magazine folded and he went into exile—another exile—in California, where he died a few years later, much too young.[63]

Sayigh's death indeed sounds lonely. He returned home from a dinner at a friend's house in Berkeley, where he taught at the University of California (where the professor of psychology, Edward Tolman, had once mounted opposition to the McCarthy-era campaign to make professors sign a loyalty oath and had been fired) and upon taking the elevator to his floor Sayigh died quietly of a heart attack, slumping over between floors. Two girls who lived in the building were said to have found him. He died, it was said, with a beatific smile.[64]

13

BLOWBACK

... our knowledge and plans for the future of our Country cannot
be built on twisted and distorted history.
                    —Blanche Ames Ames (Plimpton's grandmother)[1]

Following the wave of revelations and CIA outings, the intellectuals began to attack one another and their funders. While American Committee members like Arthur Schlesinger, Irving Kristol, and Stephen Spender defended the secret patronage from the CIA along those outlines Plimpton had set down for Humes, others took a different stance. García Márquez and Dwight Macdonald depicted the patronage as an unwarranted betrayal of the adversarial media and of US democratic principles, along the lines of Doc Humes's own arguments. García Márquez wrote to his friend and editor Rodríguez Monegal to complain further that in light of the CIA patronage he felt like a cuckold.[2] India's Jayaprakash Narayan wrote, "It was not enough to assess that the Congress had always functioned with independence . . . . The Agency was only doing what it must have considered useful for itself." His colleague, K.K. Sinha, wrote to announce that he was quitting, adding, "Had I any idea . . . that there was a time bomb concealed in the Paris headquarters, I would not have touched the Congress."[3]

Though he opted not to comment publicly, Keith Botsford, the poet Robert Lowell's leash and lieutenant, called *Cuadernos* a "fink magazine"— its readers the "paralytic wing of the liberal reaction" and its editor himself a "fink." Claiming he hadn't known of the CIA patronage of the CCF, he alleged to Dan Bell that constant pressure from Josselson at Paris headquarters amounted to a severe censorship throughout Botsford's three-year stint in Latin America. In a remarkable seven-page letter, Botsford sets out to prove methodically, point by point, that Bell's defense of the CIA's "no strings attached" reputation was untenable. He compares them all to legitimate scientists who have been working for the advancement of science, but then find out that secretly their work was financed by the Department of Defense, and now the "possibility has been introduced" that there were other purposes for their work "of which [the scientist] has no cognizance, over which he has no control, and of which he may not approve."[4]

While intellectuals argued over who knew what when, the CIA targeted the antiwar newspapers and celebrated its assassination of Che Guevara. In July 1967, Desmond Fitzgerald died of a heart attack and Thomas Karamessines was made director of plans. Counterintelligence chief James Jesus Angleton, reporting to Karamessines, was in charge of a new Special Operations Group. This group would be called Operation MHCHAOS.

The purpose of MHCHAOS, or simply Chaos, was to make war on journalism itself. The collective antiwar press, with a cumulative circulation of seven million,[5] assailed American policymakers on a daily basis for the United States' crimes in Vietnam. Teamed up with the formidable student press, these often penniless papers punched above their weight in shaping the minds of the young who were ashamed of the brutalities of American policy. Angleton and Agent Richard Ober, the large redhead about whom little was known, were tasked with crushing this editorial cohort.

The Directorate of Plans under Karamessines prioritized Chaos as high as operations against the Soviets and the Chinese. The plan got under way in late summer 1967. Intellectuals debated all spring and summer over who knew that *Encounter* and the other CCF magazines were CIA-funded and whether they ever censored content. But they missed the more important story. The CCF had been created to fund magazines that were largely responsible for disseminating pro-American cultural creations and polemics and the fact of editorial interference, however common, was an exception, restricted largely to controversial articles that rode on the back, as it were, of masses of uncontroversial cultural pieces. But Chaos was a scheme to spy on and destroy a large, independent strain of the American free press, bluntly quashing all homespun editorial opposition and preemptively striking against embarrassing stories. The exception, in other words, became the rule. As the CIA turned twenty, it "had moved from forswearing internal security functions to assigning domestic political espionage the highest level of priority."[6] The battle over control of magazines and independent newspapers was the vehicle that got the CIA here.

Agent Ober described to the Rockefeller Commission his reaction to the illegality of Operation Chaos: "I can still vividly remember saying to myself at that moment, as I walked back to my office, that I had a bear by the tail. I was convinced then that the project would leak with explosive results."[7] He believed that there was a structural problem with Chaos. It was such a high-priority operation that there were multiple agents across multiple departments, and he was certain there would be leaks. He made sure everyone involved had signed a secrecy contract and created a telephone number for agents to call if someone asked them about the program: by calling the number they could find out if the person discussing Chaos also had clearance to do so. Ober also brought the administration of Chaos into the building's basement, wrangled the use of computers with unprecedented strength, and used the subterranean room's shields against electronic surveillance to keep its anti–First Amendment sabotage and snooping totally secret.

The CIA also leveraged partnerships with the Army, FBI, and local police, transforming these agencies into surveillance and political outposts. When one officer at Army Intelligence complained that the operation was in violation of the National Security Act, his position as CIA liaison was terminated.[8]

One victim of Operation Chaos was *Quicksilver Times*, an antiwar newspaper that was feminist, and pro–racial equality and LGBT rights. Sympathetic to Black Power, it was founded in the aftermath of Malcolm X's killing. Terrence Becker was an antiwar activist who had learned his trade while working at his college newspaper. But while Becker prepared to launch *Quicksilver*, a mysterious figure named Sal Ferrera finagled an introduction to the editor. The mutual friend who introduced Ferrerra to Becker says he didn't know until much later that Ferrera wasn't who he said he was.[9] Ferrera posed as a hipster with an interest in antiwar publishing. In fact, he was a secret agent for the CIA hired by Ober to penetrate newspapers like *Quicksilver* in order to sow dissension among the staff. Ferrera had been recruited for the agency as an undergrad at Loyola University in Chicago. There he did his thesis on Marxism and paid special attention to Fidel Castro, Che Guevara, and a French leftist-philosopher, Régis Debray. Debray had written an analysis of Guevara's guerrilla warfare strategy, *Revolution Within the Revolution?*, which Barney Rosset's Grove Press published in the United States. Debray then followed Guevara to Bolivia to study the progress of Guevara's revolution in real time. Bolivia was suffering under a right-wing military junta which had decimated workers and unions. Only a small Communist faction remained, and it hoped to convert the vast populace of rural Indians who lived in abject poverty into a base of support. In April of 1967, Debray was arrested as a subversive and in November he was convicted and sentenced to thirty years for being part of Guevara's revolution. But his book and his ideas remained influential.

After studying the work of Debray, Ferrera went to graduate school and continued to master the factional fissures of the left for maximal cover. He donned a hipster look and lingo, and applied his expertise to the task of wedging apart New Left groups in the antiwar publishing sphere. He spied on an antiwar paper, *Repress*, which was interested in rising police surveillance. Thanks to Ferrera's efforts, *Repress* never managed to launch because of these illegal incursions against press freedom by the CIA and Ferrera. Ferrera also spied on the lawyers for the Chicago Nine, the activists who had disrupted the Democratic convention. He posed as a journalist to take notes on the case for his boss at the CIA.[10]

For the *Quicksilver* sabotage mission, Ferrera, slight of build with dark hair and a "Beatles-style haircut,"[11] was given at least nine FBI informants who posed as new volunteers in the paper's editorial and marketing ranks. They flooded staff meetings and "sowed opposition to the paper's founders, which led to a shutdown of the newspaper at a critical moment. Several of the super-militant newcomers took control of the *Quicksilver* office and literally hurled Becker [the editor]'s allies out the front door and down the stairs. A white female supporter of Becker was called a white racist by the black leader among the newcomers, who threw her to the floor and hit her in the face. Becker's allies did manage to get some of their production equipment out of the building, but publication had to be suspended" just as the United States announced the Cambodia invasion,[12] an important time for it to weigh in.

When *Quicksilver* reconstituted itself in its new space, Becker knew that, thanks to this penetration by government informants, the only way to survive was to be less democratic and far more paranoid. Becker grew suspicious of newcomers. Even Sal Ferrera was gently pushed out, though his true aim was not revealed until much later. "We collectivized at that point," Becker said. "If you worked on the paper, you had to live in the house. No outside income. If you had outside income, you pooled it. The paper paid everybody's bills. We were criticized for being too closed, but it was the only way to avoid a repetition of what had happened."[13]

Collectivization was Becker's response to penetration; Occupy Wall Street's response decades later would be horizontalization. No single leader meant no one could be overthrown, marginalized, or ganged up on. But that also meant anyone could filibuster, as the movement found when it was infiltrated by undercover FBI informants and saboteurs.[14] Despite Becker's collectivization, the *Quicksilver Times* was killed off just three years after its launch, because it was penetrated by a covert CIA agent who fostered an atmosphere of such distrust that the paper's decision making was hindered.

Through its intellectual magazines like *Encounter* and through its friends like the *Partisan* and *The Paris Review*, the CIA was already able to make these newspapers aesthetically marginal, visually outside the consensus. The CIA magazines had money to pay staff, and money for materials. These magazines could signal their officialdom and reasonableness through their ability to stay solvent. But the antiwar press didn't have anywhere close to the same resources and one could see this in their broadsheet format. Even if their principled arguments in favor of pacifism, equality, and freedom of the press were universal and would hold up, the paper these arguments were printed on was utterly disposable and ephemeral. Instead of pay, some of these independent newspapers might give out four hundred copies to staff to sell for a quarter apiece. By rigging the market on this already marginal enterprise, the CIA made their difficult and noble slog harder, adding pressure, sleepless nights, fears, censorship, surveillance, the inability to trust one's friends—psychic bullets, Norman Mailer called them in the letter Plimpton sent Hemingway—along with all-too-real handcuffs.

Yet despite their poverty and persecution, the antiwar press remained formidable. For example, *Dispatch News* ran Seymour Hersh's expose of the United States' massacre at My Lai in Vietnam, when soldiers opened fire on women and children, killing roughly five hundred. The massacre happened in 1968, but the story broke only in 1969, resulting in significant mainstream coverage. Several mainstream outlets had had the opportunity to break the landmark story before *Dispatch News*, but they'd been too timorous. Some must have regretted a missed change when Hersh's reporting won the Pulitzer Prize in 1970. Until the CIA is ordered to release its records on this operation, as a result of being hammered with relentless FOIA requests on the topic, Americans will never know how many of our antiwar newspapers, university presses, and other independent media were penetrated and subverted under Operation Chaos.

. . .

It's not clear, either, if the left-wing factionalism that helped destabilize *Quicksilver Times* played a part in Che Guevara's capture and death. When Guevara landed in Bolivia in late 1966, still disguised as a balding businessman, he met with the urban-based Communist Party operatives. Already the factionalism was severe. Guevara made the case for leading his guerrilla faction united with Bolivians in the villages dotting the Andes. But the official party leadership chose instead to isolate the Cuban and his freelance guerrillas.

In early 1967, Guevara's Bolivian faction went into training and then gained a small victory or two, taking soldiers' positions and some weapons; they hoped these victories would yield recruits. But Guevara's Bolivian troops were not well trained for counterinsurgency warfare. It seems clear that if the Bolivian Communists had supported the foreigners, and if the Americans had stayed out, things may have turned out better for Guevara. As it happened, Guevara's platoon split up and never regrouped. Guevara's guerrillas were cornered in a ravine in late September. He was barefoot and suffering from chronic asthma. In early October, he was shot in the leg during an ambush.

The Bolivian military leaked stories that Guevara was taken prisoner and that his battle wounds were grave enough that he died in captivity. But nobody really knew what had happened. When journalist Michèle Ray heard that New York publishers, some with official ties to the United States' intractable propaganda protocol, were hot on the trail of Guevara's guerrilla war diary, she headed straight for Bolivia's capital, La Paz. A friend told Ray, a French reporter who goes by Ray-Gavras today, that a representative of Magnum, "the US-dominated news consortium," was signing a contract for the publishing rights to Guevara's diary the next day. Ray-Gavras found it "bizarre and unjust that the diary of this man who had dedicated his life and death to the fight against American imperialism should be exploited, expurgated, perhaps falsified, to the profit of the very political line he abhorred." Ray-Gavras was armed with book publisher Jean-Jacques Pauvert's permission to negotiate for the rights to the diary and little more. Fueled by her progressive political convictions, she proceeded with uncanny skill. As she recounted in *Ramparts* in March 1968, "Rushing to Bolivia with one thought uppermost in my mind—keep the Americans from getting hold of the diary—I had no idea that weeks later I would leave having reconstructed the last day of Che's life and assured myself that the CIA was responsible for his death."[15]

Ray-Gavras's *Ramparts* exposé is a startling first-person report in two parts. In the first, she describes her efforts to sabotage the negotiations between Andrew St. George, a reporter negotiating for Magnum with alleged ties to American intelligence and the Bolivian military establishment, while she was also being spied on by the latter. Ray-Gavras shows how even with the generals reading her cables to Pauvert, her intervention was successful because, knowing this, she was able to bluff about how much she would pay, causing the Bolivian generals to drive up the price for the diary. Once she got the price prohibitively high enough to slow things down, she leaked the story to the media so as to alert Guevara's widow, who signaled the likelihood of a war over who controlled the rights to Che's story: the generals who had killed Che, or his family. With that, Magnum pulled out.

In the second part of her narrative, the story deepens. Ray-Gavras gets a tip from a Bolivian journalist who wants help getting to France. He mentions the multiple times the soldiers shot Che in captivity. Check for holes in the schoolroom wall where they held him, he tells her. The town where the killing took place was blockaded by the military leadership. But she still confirms the Bolivian journalist's story through a Swiss priest who had shown up an hour after the execution. Between the local journalist's account, the priest's, and the fearful soldier's (afraid Che's disciples will come for revenge), she pieces together how the CIA, in violation of the Geneva Conventions, was responsible for Che's execution without a trial. Two CIA agents, Félix Ramos and Eduardo Gonzales, had commanded the hunt for Che himself and at least one has overseen his execution. Ray-Gavras initially determined that it was Gonzales who supervised Che's execution.[16] Later it emerged that it was probably Ramos, whose real name was Félix Rodriguez, a Cuban exile who had partaken in the Bay of Pigs as part of the pre-invasion infiltration force and who had volunteered to assassinate Fidel Castro.

But now there was a new bidder for the rights to Che's story: Sol Stein. Stein was the president and founder, with his wife, of the publishing house Stein & Day. He was also the former executive director of the American Committee for Cultural Freedom who had published James Baldwin's essays and had promised that the government would buy their next book together in quantity. He was an across-the-board propagandist who had published anti-Communist authors as a book editor, and who had longed for the blood-and-thunder early days of the Cold War. He'd done radio, film, and even theater, attempting to turn Whittaker Chambers's tell-all memoir of finking out friends in the McCarthy days into a play.

Stein quickly became the leading bidder for the diary as far as the Bolivian dictatorship was concerned. But he had only a questionable legal claim on Guevara's work. Four months after Ray-Gavras's *Ramparts* piece, on July 1, *The New York Times* announced a deal between Castro and *Ramparts*; Castro would publish the book in Havana and *Ramparts* would serialize it in the United States. When this was announced, physical publication was already under way, since both sides were also trying to thwart each other. Stein & Day and McGraw-Hill were worried that the Guevara estate and the Cubans would block them. (Aleida March de Guevara, Che's widow, had signed over rights to the Cuban state publishers.) Meanwhile, McGraw-Hill was being blocked by the Bolivians because they had a preexisting publishing contract with *Ramparts*. The Bolivian generals despised that magazine thanks to Michèle Ray-Gavras's exposé of the generals' murder of Che.[17]

Two days later, on July 3, the *Times* reported that "In addition to the publication yesterday in *Ramparts* magazine of an English translation of the Cuban copy of the diary, *Evergreen Review* is coming out Friday with a collection of Guevara documents its editors obtained in Bolivia."[18] Barney Rosset was the owner of the high-end rebel publishing house Grove Press and founder of *Evergreen*, from which *The Paris Review* excerpted its first pieces by Samuel Beckett. Rosset was a legendary maverick who used his own inheritance to fight the US ban on such books as D.H. Lawrence's *Lady Chatterley's Lover* and Henry Miller's *Tropic of Cancer*. Rosset had already published work about (and written by) both Che Guevara and Fidel Castro and he was keen to get into the diary action. He sent a CBS reporter friend named Joe Liss to negotiate for a section of the diary and another book. Rosset knew enough to cable and speak to his agent in a kind of code, this no doubt from having read Ray-Gavras's *Ramparts* story. But even the radical publisher could be accused of collaboration with the CIA in such a climate.

In an early draft of his forthcoming memoir, Rosset writes, "Having somehow learned of Liss's meeting with the generals, a radical priest, favorable to Grove, who had been brought to meet him by the Bolivian writers, accused Liss of being with the CIA, and nothing Joe said could sway the good father."

The deal was on the verge of foundering. But this priest had been in New York and had heard of Grove. Joe said, "I told him about all the officers of Grove Press and pretty soon with my knowledge of Grove I think he became convinced that I was not a CIA agent, but a representative of Grove Press."[19]

After publishing the six pages of the diary, Rosset's office was bombed. "On July 26, 1968, while the issue of *Evergreen Review*, No. 57 (August 1968), featuring the pages we had obtained from Che's Bolivian diary, was on the newsstands," Rosset wrote, "Cuban exiles bombed Grove's offices on University Place with a grenade launcher. After the bomb exploded, a man with a Spanish accent called the Associated Press to say we had been bombed in retaliation for our publication of Che's diary and our perceived support of Communism."[20]

This wasn't the first time that those angry at Guevara had expressed themselves with military weaponry in New York City. When Guevara had spoken at the United Nations in late 1964, someone, presumably a Cuban exile, fired a bazooka across the East River. It landed in the water just shy of the UN building, which shook from the blast; according to *The New York Times*, Guevara didn't even pause during his speech.[21]

On July 4, Stein warned *Evergreen*, *Ramparts*, and now the book publisher Bantam to back off: he had secured "exclusive rights" from the Bolivian dictatorship.[22] For others to publish the diary now, Stein said, would be "in violation of our rights." The Bolivian Army claimed "ownership of the documents on the basis of a decree signed last December by President Rene Barrientos Ortuno," and the Army had cabled Stein to award him those rights. Stein's competitors shrugged, telling *The New York Times* they would go forward with publication. While Stein was apparently unconcerned that he was legitimizing a right-wing dictatorship, he couldn't help but accuse his fellow publishers of doing publicity work for the enemy.

"Bantam knows what it is publishing is incomplete," he said. "They agreed with the Cuban government to publish every word without editorial explanations. This is a great coup for Castro, in that he has compelled innocent publishers to help his propaganda."[23] But *were* there any innocent publishers left? Years later, when the lawyer had passed away who helped him to violate Guevara's widow's copyright, Stein wrote in tribute, again boasting about his "editorial explanations":

When Stein & Day acquired the publishing rights to Che Guevara's diaries in 1968, and planned to publish them with detailed explanatory material by Daniel James (who was to become Guevara's biographer), we knew the news-making importance of the revelations in that volume and also that Fidel Castro would do everything he could to undermine its publication. . . . In brief, the work required [the lawyer] to have a massive amount of material translated from the Spanish within a day—and by unbiased translators. It was done, the advice rendered, and *The Complete Bolivian Diaries of Che Guevara* was rushed to publication, but not before Castro released expurgated versions of two of the five diaries in an attempt to abort or hurt our publication. However . . . the news in our unexpurgated book drew 36 reporters and four television crews to a press conference.[24]

In this scramble for control of history, the Berne Convention (which regulates copyright) had collided with the Geneva Conventions (which regulates the treatment of prisoners). The CIA and its proxies had acted in violation of both. The agency had commanded Bolivian forces on the hunt for Guevara. Having secured his capture, the agency lied about who killed him and the lies had leaked out through the media. The liaison between the Johnson administration and the CIA's covert team, incidentally, was modernization guru Walt Rostow.[25] Modernization theorists were not interested in following international standards over treatment of prisoners or due process, this incident suggests. Now the CIA was acting as executor of Guevara's literary estate. Killing Guevara was one thing, but they doubled down on his ideas; they must have control of the publication of his combat diary. In the CIA's definition of cultural freedom, ideas were too important to be left free to circulate. Disagreeing with Guevara's views wasn't enough. Those views would have to be falsified, or at least severely annotated by a man who had worked for the same agency, so to speak, that had helped kill the author with no trial.

To fully grasp all this, one would have to pick through the record carefully. And what was at first an open secret later came out in boasts. For instance, Agent Rodriguez repeated a joke that he uses to justify his role in killing Guevara. It's a light way of reminding audiences what kind of a man he had helped the Bolivians kill. While Guevara was his prisoner in a little Bolivian schoolroom, Rodriguez asked him how he became Fidel Castro's chief economist. Guevara told him that he had raised his hand at a cabinet meeting when Fidel asked if anyone was a trained economist. But he realized later that he had misheard Castro. Guevara raised his hand because he "thought Fidel asked if anyone was a trained Communist."[26] With that one little rhyming misunderstanding, Guevara's entitlement to Geneva protections disappeared. Guevara was nothing more than a Communist. But Guevara asked explicitly to be remembered as a man and, grateful that Guevara hadn't resorted to sniveling or tears, Rodriguez had indicated he would be treated as such, that he would relay a message to Guevara's wife. When his assassin came in shivering and with a nervous look in his eye, Guevara told him that there was nothing to be afraid of because the soldier was "only killing a man."[27] Did the CIA not believe that men and women of the left deserved to be tried before a jury? If they did not, what was the telling difference between us and them? We both killed, their side and ours, with no trial.

There was considerable fear in Washington that, once captured, Guevara might still get away alive. To prove that he was dead, the guerrilla fighter's hands were cut off and shipped north and Félix Rodriguez kept the prisoner's watch (although he had promised Guevara he would send it to his widow). Guevara's body had an interesting afterlife. Initially, Guevara's killers proposed to send his severed head to Washington. Alas, another head (like that of Joaquin Murieta) would be on display in the halls of American amusement and power. But this was too brutal. Rodriguez proposed to send Washington one of Guevara's fingers. Sending both his severed hands was the compromise they struck.[28]

After Washington got his hands, Rodriguez got his watch, the Bolivian assassin got Guevara's pipe, and the Bolivian generals kept Guevara's diaries. The military dictatorship tried to monetize their bequest through the likes of that old friend of the Congress, Sol Stein. CIA money, which is to say US taxpayer money, could be spotted at every station of the cross on this passion play of the Argentine doctor, Ernesto Che Guevara. The CIA and US military's sponsorship of the operations to capture and kill Guevara is well known. Agent Rodriguez admits routinely that he was an agent with the CIA, boasting of it in the title of a memoir.[29] Stein himself had been on the CIA's payroll at least twice, while working for the American Committee and for Voice of America radio. The CIA's largesse inspired loyalty in some of its former operatives. How widely that largesse spread is still unknown; the agency's budget remains secret and unaccountable. One glimpse into the size of that largesse came via Thomas Braden, one of the CIA's former officers who told a television journalist, "If the director of CIA wanted to extend a present, say, to someone in Europe—a labor leader—suppose he just thought, *This man can use fifty thousand dollars, he's working well and doing a good job*—he could hand it to him and never have to account to any-body . . . There was simply no limit to the money it could spend and no limit to the people it could hire . . . to conduct the war—the secret war. . ."[30]

When the Republican and Democratic members of Congress refused to grant Eisenhower the amount of foreign aid he had asked for in 1958, he took them aside and made the case one on one, and then he hammered them in the media. One of his biggest opponents was concerned that the money was unaccountable and that this had already been reflected in inci-dents involving corruption of those receiving the money. It seems that one solution was that the CIA became the workaround; and of some of those funds laundered through CIA conduits, the media was the vehicle.

. . .

Meanwhile, Doc Humes never convinced his co-founders at *The Paris Review* to clarify publicly the magazine's ties to the CIA. One story leaked while Humes was alive. But if his wish had been for Matthiessen and Plimpton to offer full disclosure to friends and readers, then Humes died frustrated in that wish. It would fall to his daughter, the filmmaker Immy Humes, to serve as midwife to this disclosure. When Humes was finally able to obtain her father's FBI file, it was a revelation. It turned out that her dad—who, like Hemingway, had been called paranoid—was right about a lot more than he had been given credit for.

An Oscar-nominated documentarian, Humes had wanted to make a film about her father since 1992, when she found those letters between her father and George Plimpton. In dismissing Doc's rationale for clarifying the magazine's CIA ties, Plimpton had kept his word. The only inkling of the clarification Humes had requested had appeared despite Matthiessen's best efforts to keep his past a secret.

When Immy Humes arrived to interview Matthiessen at his idyllic house in Sagaponack, New York—one of her favorite places—Humes in a way was following up on her father's wish. But things took a turn for the strange. The visit started in the kitchen, with just the two of them. "I went out there with love and admiration for him. Even though my mother hated him, I knew my father loved him."[31] It had been roughly twenty years since John Crewdson reported on Matthiessen's service in *The New York Times*, Humes knew. This alarming December 1977 article had also claimed that the CIA had an agent or a contract agent at a newspaper in every capital on earth, who could make stories run when favorable to the agency's aims, or cut them when unfavorable.[32] But with respect to Matthiessen, she "had never heard anything from him. I knew that he had told the *Times*, 'Yes it's true,' but that he hadn't elaborated."

He served her a tuna sandwich. "I want to talk to you about Doc and I want to talk to you about everything," she said after taking a bite, "including your experience in the CIA and what you told Doc [about that]." Humes had brought the letters between her father and Plimpton, in which they discussed Matthiessen's CIA service, with her to Sagaponack.

"I don't want to talk about *that*," said Matthiessen.

"We *have* to talk about that. Everyone *else* has talked about that. Why do you think I came out here if you don't want to talk about that?"

Who was talking about it? he asked.

"Everybody knows, Peter, and talks about it all the time."

Humes didn't understand Matthiessen's caginess. "It was this incredible example of an open secret. [And] it was also an important part of Doc's story, not because it changed Doc's life but because thematically it was so important and historically it was so important and it was important to Doc." The impetus for the film Humes planned to make had been her frustrated attempts to account for her father's life and mind. She didn't know much about him after his breakdown in London, and his absconding to Italy in the late 1960s. Before she could fill in the gaps of his mysterious life, he had died. Matthiessen listened. Perhaps to stall, he invited Humes for a walk.

Strolling under the trees, she asked why he'd never discussed his CIA service. "Talking about it will make you a hero," she argued. They passed the Zendo Matthiessen had had built on the property; he was now a Zen priest. "You have this very large audience of young people who love you for your Buddhism, your environmentalism, and they would really love if you could stand up and tell this story of your experience of having worked for the CIA. And if you could come clean and tell them this story, it would make you even more of a great man to your particular audience." Humes was improvising. She tried to play down the finality of an interview. "We'll record the interview, and you can be completely free to say whatever you want to say. And then when the interview is over, I'll give you the videotapes. And then you can decide later whether you want to give me the tapes back."

She told him what would become his most frequent defense: that joining the CIA was seen as a patriotic thing to do back in the early 1950s, adding a caveat that "the only thing that's a shame [was] not to come clean."

One of the reasons Matthiessen resisted talking about it was because he wanted to write a memoir, he said. But Matthiessen was already pushing seventy. Humes told him, "Well, you better hurry up. . . . Peter, you better get *on* that." She even framed the interview as a way to start the memoir.

When he finally agreed, Matthiessen took Humes to his writing space. There, after she set up her camera, he enthralled her with the details of his life as a spy: his refusal to go to DC, his training in a New York safe house, his monitoring the French left, his being asked to spy on his own friends. Could one of these friends have been her father? She had wondered this previously, and had applied for Freedom of Information Act access to government surveillance files on her father, but her request had not yet been resolved and would not be resolved until after her interview with Matthiessen. When the pages and pages of spy notes and reports finally came, she was appalled to see that her father was correct—but she was also gratified. The documents showed that her father's first appearance in the FBI's surveillance files was in 1948, the year he arrived in Paris. "But in 1951, there was somebody reporting to the FBI that Doc was a Communist or a fellow traveler, which was a real joke because Doc was so anti-Communist. But somebody was finking him out . . . and I can't help worrying that it was Peter. Because—who knows who it was? But it feels like it could have been Peter."

There were hints of this in Doc's novel, *Underground City*. The novel traced the story of the French Resistance during World War II, the layers of detail which perplexed not just Plimpton, who wondered how Doc knew so much about underground currents, but Immy, too, who had different questions. "There were all these things that I figured out after the interview that point to Peter and [his wife] Patsy. Now, Patsy was Doc's favorite person in the world. In Doc's novel, there's this amazing scene when the hero, Stone— basically a Doc stand-in, this all-American in Paris—is in what, to me, is Matthiessen's apartment. And there are these Smith girls, who are Patsy, it seems like. And he's showing off to the Smith girls, bragging—you know, being a cool guy and saying provocative things—and saying, 'There is no God,' and running down religion. And being a groovy, hipster atheist. And the next day or the day after, he's hauled in at work because somebody has reported him for this conversation where he's an atheistic Commie. And [his fictional stand-in] says to himself, 'Well, even Smith girls have to make a living.' To me, it's very generous."

If she had gotten her FOIA documents or put any of this together while interviewing Matthiessen, she would have pressed him. But then again, so many people besides her father's dear friend Peter were spying on their friends then that it could have been anyone. "That was the fact of life in

Paris, and also in the United States: everybody was informing on everybody else, and everybody was aware that everybody was informing on everybody else and that that was McCarthyism. So my immediate question—was it Matthiessen who informed on Doc?—may be naïve. It could have been one of a million people; everybody was in the business. But I would have asked Matthiessen if I'd known of it."

Humes showed Matthiessen the letters between Doc and Plimpton. Doc's line of thinking in those letters was clear. But when they were written, Matthiessen knew, Doc was losing his grip on reality. He had grown obsessed with the surveillance state, the assassination of JFK, the Vietnam War, friends spying on friends, hidden microphones in the bedposts. All of these were the atmospheric triggers for Doc's unraveling. *The Paris Review*'s ties to the CIA couldn't have helped him.

"Doc at the time of the letters was in and out of London mental institutions," she said. "And he was staying part of the time with [theater critic Kenneth] Tynan, and Tynan was trying to get him into treatment with R. D. Laing." Influenced by existentialist philosophy and by New Left politics, Laing had written that there was almost nothing wrong with schizophrenics, that they were actually better at seeing a deeper pattern into which reality was starting to fit than most of us. "If the human race survives," Laing wrote in *The Politics of Experience*, "future men will, I suspect, look back on our enlightened epoch as a veritable age of Darkness. They will presumably be able to savor the irony of the situation with more amusement than we can extract from it. The laugh's on us. They will see that what we call 'schizophrenia' was one of the forms in which, often through quite ordinary people, the light began to break through the cracks in our all-too-closed minds."[33] This romantic view of schizophrenia may not even have applied to Doc Humes. The closest he had come to a diagnosis was "manic depression with paranoid overtones," Immy Humes said. But even if her father's mindset was the result of an illness, Doc's letters confirmed there was deep wisdom embedded in his fears.

·   ·   ·

When the interview was over, Humes was as good as her word. To her relief, Matthiessen said she could keep the interview tapes. But she forgot to ask him for a signed release before the interview. When she remembered this after the interview, she hesitated to make him sign anything. After all, she had pushed him for answers all day. Even though she had a bombshell of an interview on her hands, the centerpiece of her film, she left without the signed release. Letting her keep the tapes was gracious, she thought. "To me, that was like him saying, 'I wanted to say this. I'm gonna say it. You keep them.' But on the other hand, it wasn't as specific as a signed release."

Many years later, Humes had edited her rough cut. She has trouble determining how long the film took, since she worked on it between other projects and interviewed people on camera sporadically over the better part of a decade. But she hadn't forgotten how hard it was to convince Matthiessen to discuss his CIA service and she was anxious whether he was still "feeling good" about their interview. When she sent him a release form, she enclosed a cover letter asking him to sign, and he returned the signed release right away with a note of good luck. "I was delighted, and thought he was down with it."

Humes invited Matthiessen to see a rough cut. After all, he was like an uncle to her, and she thought his blessing would help the film's fund raising and word-of-mouth buzz. She wanted Matthiessen to be able to correct any second thoughts or misstated facts. "I arranged to show it at Sarah Plimpton's house." Plimpton himself had died in September 2003, of a heart attack at the age of seventy-six. Matthiessen, Immy, and a friend of Immy's watched the rough cut with George's widow, Sarah. Humes was excited and nervous.

When the film began, Humes strained to read Matthiessen's responses. In one scene, Plimpton criticized Peter for choosing that spring of 1966 as the moment to drop his bombshell on Doc, in the aftermath of the Kennedy assassination and during the beginning of the incessant revelations of CIA spying and overreach, and after Doc's wife had left him. Doc had been in a state of near-total psychological breakdown when Peter's confession had come. Plimpton said that it "backfired, that it was the *worst* conceivable therapy." That scene, crosscut with Peter's rationalization ("It was before the ugly stuff. . .") may have been the trigger for what happened next.

When it was over, Matthiessen was upset. He said to Immy, "I can't believe you used that." Despite having signed a release, Matthiessen complained that his service with the agency was irrelevant to Doc's story. He prodded her, "Why don't you take that out, take the whole CIA [segment] out!"

Immy repeated what she had told him in Sagaponack, that it *was* central to Doc's story. "I think it's important as the cultural, political, and historical context of Doc's paranoia," she told me. In front of the others, Humes tried to mollify Matthiessen. He argued that he hadn't been allowed to elaborate on the context for *why* he joined. In fact, he says in the version of the film that they argued over that "[t]here were so many guys signing up for the CIA, it was kind of the thing to do. . . . I had a lot friends who did it. So did George. And we still do." But then Matthiessen did something curious. If adding more historical context to explain his joining would take up too much film time, he said, Immy could cut some of her mother's interview. It was boring. According to Immy, her mother, Anna Lou Humes Aldrich, had never gotten along with Matthiessen, but never let him know. The suggestion made Immy wonder if Matthiessen had sensed that her mother disliked him. But the other way Immy made sense of it was that in front of Sarah Plimpton, Matthiessen was perhaps also suggesting he would protest the film less if it included more context for why he joined CIA. First he wanted the discussion of his CIA service cut; then he paired an insult to Immy's mother with a disingenuous plea for more screen time and attention to his CIA service; namely, to the question of why he joined.

But Matthiessen wasn't done. He began to call Immy late at night. "I think he was in his cups," said Humes, "which I never thought of as a Peter thing. And he would harangue me. He would be very angry, and get stuck on wanting me to take [those scenes] out." The more she did to mollify him, the worse it got. "I wanted Uncle Peter to be pleased. And at the same time, I wanted to do what I wanted to do." She stuck to her position but the episode depressed her. It especially stung when he suggested she'd betrayed his trust. "You sandbagged me. You've been a bad journalist," he said. He even threatened her with the treatment that evidently most terrified Peter himself: to "expose" her.

. . .

When the film was done in 2008, sixteen years after Humes had begun it, *The Paris Review* had been scheduled to host a screening. At the last moment, Humes got a note from one of its editors saying that a board member had complained and that *The Paris Review* had changed its mind and wouldn't present the film.

She was disappointed. The right way for the magazine to deal with such a legacy, she said, was to own it. "Just come out with it. Own it. Explain it. . . . The only answer for *The Paris Review*—and I said this to George before he died—is to do an interview . . . dealing with *The Paris Review*'s CIA stuff. And we'll put Doc's great letter in. And it'll be a history lesson, a retrospective corrective, an opportunity for meditation. There are no real disputes about the facts. And so *The Paris Review* is perfectly suited to tell the story, which is what Doc said in 1966. He said, 'You know, God forbid, [you should clear the air] in the pages of *The Paris Review* itself.' George was horrified at this idea," she said.

One of the ways Matthiessen got journalists off the topic of his covert life was to mention his work with Native Americans. "He said it to me and every time a journalist brought it up," said Humes. Matthiessen had a deep voice and Humes lowered hers in imitation: "'You don't want to put that in because I'm on the side of the Native Americans, and I'm very liberal, and I've done a lot of good stuff. And the Native Americans,' he always said, 'are very paranoid.'" Lowering her voice, she sounded somewhat like him. "'And it would be really devastating [for them] to find out I used to work for the CIA.' It was this horrific thing where he was saying, 'If you publish this, you will be betraying the Native American cause,'" she laughed, "never realizing that the Native Americans also use Google." In my own case, Matthiessen promised an interview one or two months into the future and canceled the day of. He did this five or six times between 2011 and 2012, once doing so the moment I was getting on the train to Sagaponack.

What was the real reason Matthiessen wouldn't talk? Many have asked Humes, she said, "What if Peter never left the CIA? What if he was doing good work? What if he was working with Free Tibet? What if he was on the side of the angels?" More likely, said Humes, there was deep shame. But if the ties went further than any one of the magazine's former editors, they would be betraying one another by clearing the air. Maybe that was too much. Their silence was a passive consensus. And what if another *Paris Review* veteran had ties that lasted until the present day?

John Crewdson's *New York Times* article pointed to something called "Mockingbird," a deep media penetration plan by the CIA. Fronts like the National Student Association and the CCF would become Chaos (since the CIA created Chaos to protect these programs' secrecy). And Chaos, it seems, became Mockingbird, an operation outed by Carl Bernstein in *Rolling Stone* in 1977. Mockingbird saw the American media share editors, reporters, producers, and other key staff with the CIA. Name a mainstream television station, newspaper, or magazine: it likely had an agent. These weren't always low-level staff members. As Bernstein wrote, sometimes the executives at these media outlets were themselves involved:

A few executives—Arthur Hays Sulzberger of the *New York Times* among them—signed secrecy agreements. But such formal understandings [with the CIA] were rare: relationships between Agency officials and media executives were usually social—"The P and Q Street axis in Georgetown,"[34] said one source. "You don't tell [CBS CEO] William Paley to sign a piece of paper saying he won't fink."[35]

From subtle editorial curation to outright intimidation to making sure that every influential media body was penetrated with its own personal CIA agent ready to plant or kill stories . . . What next? Had the CIA perfected the use of the media for state power? And if it had done so by the mid to late 1970s, what would it look like in the age of terror? To answer this, we can turn again to *The Paris Review*, whose body of founders had one last, fuzzy tie to this propaganda and spying apparatus, its most astonishing tie yet. Through the magazine's founding managing editor, John Train—who collaborated with George on a number of projects—Plimpton's blurred social and professional ties now linked him to the disastrous policies that led up to the terrorist attacks of September 11, 2001.

CODA

AFGHANISTAN

The people we're fighting today we were supporting in the fight against the Soviets.

—Hillary Clinton

In November 1982, thirty years after the launch of *The Paris Review*, John Train, the founding managing editor of the magazine, wrote to the president of Freedom House, a democracy watchdog organization. Train wanted to found a new nonprofit group whose "activity will be collecting money . . . to be used within the general area of the media, to encourage the dissemination of pro-freedom and pro-democratic ideas [in Afghanistan]." Train would synchronize his efforts with those of the CIA-supported mujahideen to battle against the Soviet presence there. The mujahideen, of course, are those fighters who engage in jihad. Made up of local and foreign fighters, this was the ilk out of which Osama bin Laden and Al-Qaeda emerged. In the same letter, Train volunteered his NGO, the Afghanistan Relief Committee, to finance a "film on Afghanistan." The film "will be shown first on public television and thereafter on the Christian Broadcasting Network in Norfolk, Virginia." Train named colleges as one of the films' key target audiences. He was doing Cold War propaganda on broadcast television.

Train had come a long way from the Pasternak campaign. In addition to putting up money for *The Paris Review*'s launch and having given it its name, Train also sponsored the magazine with a subsidy provided through an indefinitely recurring ad for his finance company. Train also helped streamline *The Paris Review*'s Paris operation, trying to convince its associates there—including the future creators of *Charlie Hebdo* magazine—to help sponsor *The Paris Review* either by erasing its rent or another scheme. Acting at apparent cross-purposes, he worked out the logistics for the Pasternak interview after having pushed the magazine away from publishing criticism and remaining apolitical, forsaking those "axe-grinders" and "drum-beaters."[1] Here, though, he appeared to be taking a different tack. The cousin of US senator Claiborne Pell, a whiz in finance and a master of launching profitable companies, Train is known today for his books about finance and global capitalism (he claims to have burnished Warren Buffett's early reputation). But his main job is as an investment advisor. Working out of the same office today from which he hosted Doc Humes's campaign against the New York City police and its racist performers' laws, Train remains the chairman of Montrose Group, and was tapped to serve Presidents Reagan through Clinton as consultant. But he appears never to have spoken of his work as a propagandist against the Soviets during the Afghanistan invasion of the early 1980s. When I visited him at his office on Park Avenue, he told me bluntly, "I was a conduit."[2]

As early as the 1950s, Train allegedly had direct ties to the covert state through a shell company with a CIA code name.[3] And his archive from the early to mid-1980s document the use of a shell nonprofit to foster schemes to penetrate Afghanistan with foundation money and with journalists on intelligence and propaganda missions. While Train's Afghanistan Relief Committee (ARC), founded in 1980, billed itself as "the first American organization to start sending aid to relieve the suffering of victims inside Afghanistan itself,"[4] a look at its spending shows it focused primarily on the media.[5] In one proposal, Islamist commander Gulbuddin Hekmatyar was floated as a fixer between Train and his propagandists on the ground: today, Hekmatyar is designated by the US government as a terrorist who openly supports ISIS, the Islamic State terrorist group. Here—in one *Paris Review* founder—we find all the previous CIA anti-Communist schemes—penetration of NGOs, universities, secret money pass-throughs, covert media campaigns, corrupting alliances with militants—all done sub rosa in the name of cultural freedom.

. . .

To understand John Train's turning up in Afghanistan, you need to understand the country's convulsions during the second half of the twentieth century. In the 1950s and 1960s, women participated in significant numbers in educational and civic life in Afghanistan's cities. The country was a station on the hippy trail in the early to mid-1970s, along which pilgrims made their way to India. But while the cities were relatively urbane, the countryside was conservative, owing in particular to a lack of infrastructure linking village to city. Rural Afghanistan was governed by tribal clans and elders through patronage networks. Traditional hierarchies reigned peaceably in villages, while in the cities tension was rising between Communists and nationalists—who admired the likes of Che Guevara—and Islamists who hoped to usher in a conservative, militant brand of political Islam. Leftist and Communist protesters, angry that a conservative dictatorship killed a prominent member of the left, rallied in Afghanistan's first large-scale protests in the late 1970s. These protests grew until the movement morphed into a coup, which the Americans and Soviets both watched. The leftists took power, followed by immediate infighting and factionalism. There was a counter-coup of sorts. Then the Soviets invaded. And only *then* did the Americans enter. So it ran in the US media.

The United States has copped to a certain amount of blame for the rise of radical Islam in the service of anticommunism in Afghanistan, but the record has suggested that this sponsorship of radical Islam as part of a wider intervention took place only after the Soviet invasion. This turned out not to be true. Afghanistan actually represents another version of rollback, the failed policies of the early 1950s, or as we call it today regime change. If Islamists could overthrow a Western-backed Shah in Iran, as they had in 1979, national security hawks in the United States foresaw Islamists' power in Central Asia and in the Soviet Union's Muslim borderlands. National Security Advisor Zbigniew Brzezinski called this thinking the "arc of Islam." The doctrine actually married George Kennan's containment and Frank Wisner and Allen W. Dulles's old, failed policy of rollback—where masses of Eastern Europeans were killed after being sent over the border in the early 1950s.

The Asia Foundation, that old CIA front that had helped the Vietnam lobby start the Vietnam War, had been operating at Kabul University since the late 1950s. The Eisenhower administration had wanted a study of Afghanistan's strategic importance in the region. The Foundation had two or three full-time staff members and as many as two dozen US advisors and consultants.[6]

While Afghanistan remained low priority in the 1960s, Cold War hawks had announced a mandate to cultivate Third World hearts and minds. The idea was to frame the debate before the Che Guevaras of the world could get there. In the name of this preemptive political and cultural penetration, the CIA increased its covert influence beyond the academic subsidies. A secretive group called "the professors" rose up in Kabul University, linking anticommunism to militant Islam. By the early to mid-1970s, the CIA's university penetration through the Asia Foundation gave way to conservative Muslim death squads that liquidated leftists of all stripes.[7] Foreign partisans from the ranks of the Muslim Brotherhood, Arab Islamists, and Iranians (working as advisors and spies) all followed the trickle and then flood of Saudi and American money, which came into the nation as early as 1973.[8]

It is important to note that before the US-backed foreign fighters arrived, Afghanistan's version of Islam was devout yet relatively apolitical. But the mélange of outside forces—from Pakistan and Egypt, with funds from Saudi Arabia—would indeed roll back Afghanistan's milder practice of Islam and the institutions around it.

Brzezinski, later United States secretary of state, has admitted that the official date of US entry into the conflict has been fudged: "According to the official version of history, CIA aid to the mujahideen began during 1980, that is to say, after the Soviet army invaded Afghanistan, 24 Dec 1979. But the reality, secretly guarded until now, is completely otherwise: Indeed, it was July 3, 1979 that President Carter signed the first directive for secret aid to the opponents of the pro-Soviet regime in Kabul. And that very day, I wrote a note to the president in which I explained to him that in my opinion this aid was going to induce a Soviet military intervention."[9] Read that again. Despite what histories had said until then, the Soviets came into Afghanistan *after* the United States lured them there.

After the CIA, Gulbuddin Hekmatyar and other local Afghani and foreign Islamist fighters succeeded in driving out the Soviets, the focus of the CIA-backed rebels veered toward control of the country, and the weapons and money were turned on each other in a breakdown along ethnic lines. Sound familiar? In the aftermath these foreign fighters created a "university of jihad," and exported the jihad to "Algeria, Azerbaijan, Bangladesh, Bosnia, Burma, China, Egypt, India, Morocco, Pakistan, Sudan, Tadzhikistan,

Tunisia, Uzbekistan, Yemen—and the United States," wrote Tim Weiner in *The New York Times.* Weiner and others called Hekmatyar the "dean of the University of Jihad."[10] Hekmatyar spent years shelling civilians in the capital, killing more than ten thousand people. He fought the many Islamist factions for control of government and swore he would build the caliphate, which would burn and shell and tear down borders.

. . .

No detail was too small and no heart or mind too young for indoctrination when fighting the Soviets. The textbooks that were designed to teach Afghanistan's refugees to read were filled with propaganda for the armed struggle against the infidels: J for Jihad, K for Kalashnikov, and so on. These infamous textbooks were a CIA-funded scheme conceived, designed, and printed through the University of Nebraska's Center for Afghanistan Studies. The man tasked to carry it out was Thomas Gouttierre, a former Peace Corps volunteer who brought basketball to Afghan villages and coached the national team.[11] Gouttierre and Hekmatyar were both collaborators with *The Paris Review*'s co-founder, John Train. Hekmatyar was a fixer for Train's TV propaganda against the Soviets in the mid-1980s, according to letters, and Gouttierre was on the Afghanistan Relief Committee's masthead as an advisor.

One memo from Train outlines the "Seitz idea," conceived by Train, the Freedom House, and Russell Seitz.[12] Freedom House is the democracy and freedom watchdog founded in 1941. Seitz, a Harvard physicist and Cold War interventionist alumnus, is known today for a plan to fight global warming using tiny synthetic bubbles. But his name graces the pages of a document that most explicitly links ARC and John Train to the Cold War brinksmanship that gave us Al-Qaeda, and arguably also ISIS. Found among Train's papers, the document has all proper names but two blacked out and begins with the following goal: "To impose on the Soviet Union in Afghanistan the sort of television coverage that proved fatal to the American presence in Vietnam." By 1980, the Cold Warriors were adamant that they were going to serve the Soviets their Waterloo—that is, their Vietnam—in Afghanistan. Train's cohort patriotically took up the media side of that Waterloo. Train wrote to Seitz in 1983 to praise a successful media penetration in Afghanistan by Italian national television, and cited Pakistani intelligence for helping the network. The Seitz idea sought to emulate this penetration as a kind of intelligence operation. The outline lists two principal players, described as "1" and "2." Principal 1 "is well acquainted with and has secured the cooperation of the Jamiat-i-Islam and the Hezb-i-Islam of Gulb-ud-din [sic] Hekmatyar." Hekmatyar was cited as an asset with ties to Principal 1 and he could be enlisted to help create a "Vietnam for the Soviets."[13]

The memo lists under its "assumptions" that the project "will be treated by the Department of State with, at least, benign neglect." It also promises that "Network TV and USIA/Administration interest in the area will increase during the course of the next 12 to 18 months. . ." It includes under "Uncertainties" the question of the "Response of Pakistan if informed in detail." The memo's "Best Case" section envisioned a brutal Russian response and the Afghan dismay at such a response. "Russians: Coverage live of air assault and destruction of a rural village and mosque. Reprisal killings, use of CBW." (In military jargon this typically translates as "chemical or biological weapons.") "Scorched earth policy in action, conscription and deportation into USSR."[14] Such a reprisal could certainly be used to show the true nature of Soviet Communism to Afghanis and the world. If the United States could precipitate such Soviet violence, then the violence could be used as propaganda to discredit them. This seemed to take propaganda to a whole new level that completely dehumanized the victims of the violence in the service of some apocalyptic bet between angels and demons.

The best case scenario listed more pluses: the "Afghans: Recapture of an urban area, even if temporary. Use of improved/captured weapons to inter-dict Soviet aircraft and armor, capture or surrender of Soviet troops and their confrontation with residents of the area they formerly occupied." The filming scenarios that Train's co-plotters optimistically dreamed of were "[m]oving accounts of surviving Afghan victims of Soviet atrocities—injured women and children telling how they were injured."[15] American hawks, with *The Paris Review*'s John Train as one of their collaborators and funders, were in a cynical race to the bottom, a race cloaked in patriotic robes and the language of human rights.

But with American and European media crews penetrating Afghanistan to engage knowingly in secret propaganda, it's helpful to turn again to Carl Bernstein's 25,000-word cover story for *Rolling Stone*, which exposed the depth of the domestic side of the undemocratic marriage of US media and spying. "Legitimate, accredited staff members of news organizations—usually reporters" were one form of Operation Mockingbird media penetration, wrote Bernstein in 1977. This partnership of convenience would of course apply to willing war reporters working overseas in America's mission-critical conflicts. "Some were paid; some worked for the Agency on a purely voluntary basis.

> This group includes many of the best-known journalists who carried out tasks for the CIA. The files show that the salaries paid to reporters by newspaper and broadcast networks were sometimes supplemented by nominal payments from the CIA, either in the form of retainers, travel expenses or outlays for specific services performed. Almost all the payments were made in cash. The accredited category also includes photographers, administrative personnel of foreign news bureaus and members of broadcast technical crews.[16]

Compare the above with the Seitz memo, which concluded by brandishing the journalists' "legitimate" credentials. "Both principals and cameramen/technicians are bona fide journalists. Neither principal objects to [two lines blacked out]. While any and all footage will be available to all Federal agencies in real time the canon of journalistic ethics and the project's credibility both demand that all participating agencies must agree to refrain from deletion and unnecessary delay of footage en route to commercial broadcasters." In the event of Soviet escalation, the memo called for "withdrawal to areas of complete mujahideen control": in other words, a retreat to safety among friends.

In a September 26 letter to Seitz himself, Train lauded the Italian national television "operation," conducted "with the cooperation of Pakistani authorities, who broadcast a half-hour show live from Afghanistan." Train signaled that the program could recreate action-packed, preferably bloody propaganda for the mujahideen, writing that "The mujahideen obligingly attacked a Soviet post for [these camera crews'] benefit, which was shown in full." This was of course a real battle. Beyond its being watched and recorded by journalists, it was apparently one where journalists inspired the fighters to battle. Since this was actionable information in support of his group's memo, Train then listed the makeup of the crew, including technical positions and equipment, plus "a very competent Major Rafid from Pakistani intelligence, the C.I.D. who was able to arrange relationships with the local tribes.... The signal was relayed back to Peshawar."[17] In the propagandists' yearning for battle footage, one recalls Sol Stein's nostalgia for the action-packed days of the Korean War. Never mind that men and women were dying or that the moral quandary with Stalin had begun supposedly with the loss of innocent life in his gulags. Here Cold Warriors like John

Train had come full circle. In wishing for war crimes to capture on camera after their government had goaded the Soviets to invade, they were confessing something perverse: that they were eager to countenance—and even instigate—the loss of innocent (Asian) life in order to capture their enemies committing atrocities on camera.

．　．　．

All of this took place under the auspices of the Northcote Parkinson Fund, created for Afghanistan propaganda and named for Professor C. Northcote Parkinson, the peripatetic British professor and writer who was best known for his humorous take on bureaucratic time wasting. For the board of the new media outfit, Train nominated Virginia Armat of *Reader's Digest*. Train had worked with *Reader's Digest*'s John Dimitri Panitza on a number of magazine-related projects and had a friendly relationship with this conservative magazine. For example, Train brainstormed with Panitza over whether billionaire Sir James Goldsmith (whose son, as of this writing, has just lost a virulently anti-Muslim campaign for mayor of London) might buy two of those magazines famous in the days of the "clearinghouse" of little magazines: *Encounter* and *Survey*. Train and his associates in refugee advocacy also "placed" friends' articles in *Foreign Affairs* and *Reader's Digest*.[18]

The propaganda value of the actual work with refugees—as opposed to its use as a cover—was not lost on Train, who wrote to Freedom House collaborator Rosanne Klass: "It is almost impossible to subvert the Afghan refugee effort. The thing speaks for itself too clearly. It has, indeed, occasioned massive defections from the extreme left in Europe, like the Hitler-Stalin pact in its day.

> I therefore do not think that we should be too concerned with Europeans who want to join in the effort [who may] have, e.g. Socialist backgrounds, particularly if the embassy has no objection to them. In other areas of political struggle, it has often turned out that the disillusioned member of the far left becomes the most affected member of the other side, simply because he can recognize what is really going on. That has been true in a number of most effective labor union people, e.g., Jay Lovestone.[19]

Lovestone's network of nonprofit fronts, of course, were the original conduits for laundering CIA money.

In another letter to Klass, Train suggested that a mutual contact use the UN's High Commission on Refugees as a "conduit" to pass funds.[20] This too was interesting; his Harvard classmate and *Paris Review* colleague Sadruddin Aga Khan held that position later at the UN. The ties between the US's most prominent refugee relief organization, the International Rescue Committee, and the CIA went back to the early days of CIA airdrops inside the Iron Curtain, where the early refugee organizations recruited from students and union leaders in the refugee camps themselves. Train was the sort of operator who wrote to colleagues at Doctors Without Borders, whose operatives disbursed ARC's funds to refugees: "I get the impression that it would be better for a team of physicians to go openly to Afghanistan, rather than a single individual in a semi-clandestine way. There would be some embarrassment if a single individual were apprehended . . . a bona fide medical team would be harder to paint as an intelligence operation. . . . One would want to check with friends on the inside in Washington to see what was really thought here . . ."[21]

Train was wise enough to be circumspect when asked in writing about his organizational work. When a daughter of one of Train's friends wrote to inquire about the possibility of Train funding one of her organizations, Train was reluctant. He described the sizeable financial commitment that ARC already represented, and then named the Northcote Parkinson Fund and an unnamed media nonprofit as additional financial obligations. He wrote her: "Please come to New York and I'll describe the last two activities."[22] Train was operating with discretion in order to keep details of the propaganda schemes he worked on out of the written record.

Other familiar names supported Train's work. CIA alumnus William F. Buckley was ready to skewer the craven, supposedly liberal media for not championing Train's hard-hitting exposé on the KGB in the United States. The title of Buckley's column said it all: "Why Won't TV Show This Documentary?" Describing the Train group's KGB film as "the most powerful two-hour documentary on the subject of underground Soviet activity ever put together," Buckley went on to complain to readers across America that "the producers can't get it shown in the United States."[23] That it didn't show on TV here was proof that we don't have real freedom of speech, he wrote. It finally did show, and made a lot of money, as Train boasted to friends. The stink Buckley raised even got it shown at the White House to all staff.[24]

Train worked in Afghanistan "relief" long enough to witness the blowback of US involvement. The great world powers he helped pit against one another in covert, adrenaline-addled and warlord-enabled propaganda schemes had turned Afghanistan into a failed state. In 1995, he visited

Afghanistan as a representative of ARC to help with infrastructure projects there. Reporting back to the ARC executive committee, he wrote of his convoy's having been attacked by "brigands." "We could never be quite sure," he wrote, "whether these were uncontrolled Hekmatyar followers, or just volunteers profiting from an unstable situation."[25]

Train's work propagandizing these groups' efforts to beat the Soviets may have been well-intentioned. Funding conservative, anti-Communist operatives and Islamist fighters was the thing to do at the time, the culmination of an ill-conceived brinksmanship that led to the rise of Al Qaeda and Osama bin Laden, and many figures associated with the CIA's anti-Communist elite would be linked to these Islamists. From Guatemala to Afghanistan, the American record on Cold War invasion and intervention had been a long string of failures that had to be rewritten by the propagandists. The little magazines, the television crews instrumentalized for warfare and other secret propaganda instruments played an important role in erasing—and collectively forgetting—these mistakes. Forgetting, of course, starts with secrecy, and secrecy was written into their contracts and winking bonds of friendship so that they could avoid accountability. And avoiding accountability, incidentally, was corruption. This was the setup that Doc Humes, Train's old friend and colleague, had foreseen before any of his friends were willing to listen, in 1966.

Across the border in Pakistan, when General Zia-ul-Haq came to power in a Reagan-supported military coup, his advisor, a lawyer named A.K. Brohi, was "brought in to rationalize Zia's martial law," wrote historian Stephen Cohen.[26] Brohi came into his own as a leader in Pakistan's Committee for Cultural Freedom and his thinking developed into a meditation on sacrifice of the individual: "The individual if necessary has to be sacrificed in order that the life of the organism be saved. Collectivity has a special sanctity attached to it in Islam."[27] Brohi also wrote to justify jihad through a "just war" theory, which would have put his efforts during the Cold War into concert with those of the West. The CCF was comfortable with intervention; indeed, it at times appeared to treat intervention as its religion, though articulated through a seemingly apolitical theory of development called modernization. It had many other names as well: militant liberty, cultural freedom, and a number of sub-articulations on the cultural side that downplayed the politics of art, from abstract expressionism to New Criticism. But if you looked at the details with some skepticism and could keep straight what the paper trail truly looked like across the constellation of archives and cover stories, modernization theory was jihad. Even if it was American jihad.

The Paris Review's ties may seem inconsequential from some angles. After all, how long had it been since Train was on their staff? And was the CCF even an entity this late in the Cold War? But the magazine's apolitical stance allowed it to roll with the times, and absorb a subtle second role that its public disavowal of politics suggested was a mere disguise. The champion of the novelist Aleksandr Solzhenitsyn who tried to place a non-interview Art of Fiction interview with the novelist in his erstwhile magazine, Train proved to be just the latest founder with ties to the covert state. The magazine that he helped launch and name was part of a social and editorial nexus of organizations interested in the success of the covert state in a way that was undeniably political, and that bound these instruments together with militant, often violent and illegal operations.

The role these organs played put them at odds with the traditional adversarial role of media, a role that at least theoretically checked government power and guarded against overreach and corruption. It had gone nearly absent for the prior three decades, if it had existed with any solidity before that. Indeed, these operators, despite their patriotism, put the United States at odds with its own founding vision, the insistence upon freedom of expression that the nation advocates for its international friends and adversaries. In the name of cultural and political freedom, these media, labor, student, charity, academic, and legal organizations linked here through John Train and elsewhere through the magazine clearinghouse and the Congress for Cultural Freedom—and IILR, and FEC and so on—behaved slavishly toward a perverse mission of state. The most involved among them feared they might go to jail if they violated their secrecy oaths. It's not anathema to our purposes of exposing this history to have sympathy for the young men and women who signed under duress, pressure, or surprise, with little experience, and in some cases under illness. Many of them did not know what they were getting into.[28] The less central members, who may not have feared arrest, no doubt still feared they would be blacklisted. This has resulted in outlets like The Paris Review's reluctance to discuss its own past. And this has translated into a diminishment of our own freedom to know the truth.

When readers and fans—and even editors of the magazine—hail The Paris Review's accomplishments, I readily acknowledge that the accomplishments are real and deserve recognition. Many people I admire enormously are still linked to the magazine and are no doubt left in an awkward position by the truth of the history. As a result, what gets left out of the legacy is the terrible and corrupting effect of something so prevalent during the Cold War: open secrets. The founders who stayed on the board and pulled the plug on a screening of Immy Humes's documentary, her truthful attempt to clear the air in the name of her father's legacy and our muddled history—and in the name of moral clarity and our founding principles— those founders were part of a vast network of Americans and others who may indeed have meant well, but who left us, in our practice of cultural and press freedom, seriously weakened.

All of these problems conjure up the CIA's hasty creation and its ill-conceived efforts to deal with the atmospheric Cold War fears and obsessions. In 1947, in debates preceding the passing of the National Security Act, Republican Congressman Clarence J. Brown of Ohio grilled Secretary of the Navy James Forrestal (later secretary of defense) about the potential for abuse embedded in the new security laws and their sloppy wording.

"I am not interested in setting up here, in the United States, any particular central policy agency under any president," said Brown, "and I do not care what his name may be, and just allowing him to have a Gestapo of his own if he wants it."

Forrestal shot back that the CIA's power would be "limited definitely to purposes outside this country."

"Is that stated in the law?"

"It is not; no sir," Forrestal admitted.[29]

Forrestal's underhanded dealings with President Truman's opponent in the 1948 election, Thomas Dewey, were outed by a journalist and cost him his job as secretary of defense. The stress of being overworked and in command of such a paranoid post and then being asked to resign caused Forrestal to seek psychiatric help. In a letter to Ernest Hemingway, which is worth repeating, the writer Malcolm Cowley described the paranoia that was bestowed on the country by men like Forrestal.

"What we had really been living through was paranoia that had passed from mind to mind like measles running through a school. Not so long afterwards," Cowley recalled of Forrestal's sad end, "he had been carried off to the loony bin shouting, 'The Russians are after me.' This great nation has been adopting its policies on the advice of a paranoiac secretary of defense. Maybe this is the age of paranoia, of international delusions of persecution and grandeur. Maybe persons like Forrestal . . . are the chosen representatives and suffering Christs of an era."[30]

ACKNOWLEDGMENTS

A book—like a child—takes a village to raise. Friends and colleagues who read the manuscript during the beginning, middle, and end of my research and drafting bear my deepest gratitude. In the very beginning . . . were my friend Genevieve Walker, my brother Jake Whitney, my friend and ex-neighbor Grace Bonner, my colleague and friend Tana Wojczuk, my neighbor and friend John O'Connor, and my friend Stephen Raleigh Byler. Among those who read it later are friend and colleague Lisa Lucas, the historian of modern India Ramachandra Guha, the environmental writer (and my current neighbor) Andrew Blackwell, *Salon* founder and friend David Talbot, author Peter Richardson, and my colleague and friend Suzanne Menghraj. I owe thanks to Kerry Lauer and Dave Daley, *Salon*'s former and current editor-in-chief for publishing the long 2012 article, "*The Paris Review*, the Cold War, and the CIA," out of which this book morphed.

I am indebted to those many former stakeholders and bearers of five- and six-decade-old memories who let me interview them, short format or long. They added context to very old archives and accounts, or otherwise helped me reenvision the partially erased past. Nelson Aldrich spoke to me many times, Sarah Plimpton spoke to me for a magazine piece on Plimpton and Hemingway that got folded into this narrative instead; Bob Silvers talked to me several times by phone and email and read a draft of that same magazine piece and offered suggestions and comments—for which I'm very grateful. Former *Paris Review* Paris editor Larry Bensky, author John Berger, author William Blum, author Henrietta Boggs, author and CCF graduate Keith Botsford, author Olga Carlisle, author and scholar Russell Cobb, author Peter Finn, author Philip Knightley, poet Frederick Seidel, author Sol Stein, and author and scholar Hugh Wilford gave short interviews or answered a quick question or two (or three) or otherwise pointed me forward—or backward—and I'm grateful to them, as well. I'm grateful to Lorin Stein and Jonathan Galassi for help contacting one or two on the list above, and Lorin for pointing me to an academic paper relating to those questions in this book. The author and scholar Patrick Iber has been exceedingly supportive and informative on questions about the Congress for Cultural Freedom in Latin America. Critic George Scialabba answered my nitpicky questions about Dwight Macdonald.

Frances Stonor Saunders was especially helpful not just for her inspiring book, *Who Paid the Piper?* as it was called in the UK (*The Cultural Cold War* as I read it in the New Press's edition in the United States); I'm grateful for the several instances during which she answered questions and partook in a long transatlantic telephone interview about her own research break-throughs, techniques, and difficulties getting her book published in the United States, where she was told by her editor (before the New Press saved the day) to insert a disclaimer stating that the CIA were "on the side of the angels." I'm grateful for all the cussing she did over the phone in response to that memory. My own Chapter 5 on CCF censorship is the one that owes the most to her important research and I'm glad, in short, she withstood the same casual censorship we take for granted here in the United States.

Thanks to archivists at the Morgan Library (especially Maria Molestina-Kurlat) and at Princeton, Seton Hall (Alan Delozier and Amanda); Columbia Rare Books and Manuscript Library's archivists (Thai Jones in particular)—and to *The Baffler's* John Summers for the tip here—and NYU's Tamiment Library (especially Sarah Moazeni), plus NYPL and BPL.

I'm grateful to OR Books' founders Colin Robinson and John Oakes for the great company they've built and to my editor John Oakes in particular for many graces, deadline indulgences, good advice, laughs, and guidance. I thank him, too, for the story about his former boss Barney Rosset which led to the search that this book grew into; and for his patience after the very scope of the book expanded to include all these places and names and people which resulted in late deadline after late deadline for two and a half years. I'm grateful to Justin Humphries for fine work right-sizing the book and to Natascha Ullman in the publicity department. I'm grateful to my fact checker and Bennington Field Work Term research assistant for the winter of 2014–2015, Layne Eckensberger. And I'm grateful to my colleagues at *Guernica: A Magazine of Art and Politics* for keeping the site going with distinction while I took a short leave to finish a few freelance pieces under a tight deadline (which corroded into a luxuriously long book leave). The brilliant filmmaker and my friend, Immy Humes, is very close to the heart of this book and I thank her for those first letters she showed me, for making a great documentary film about her father, Doc, and for caring about this topic before me, for sharing her post-production experiences and for being a great guide.

And thanks especially to my newly indispensable first reader, who calls me B though there isn't a B anywhere in my name. And thanks to my family—my three brothers and one sister—for unquestioning moral support, and to my parents Peter and Victoria for more than I can name: from unbending principles in pursuit of justice (on the lofty side) to putting me up, loaning of laptops, feeding me when this project was an incoherent freelance summer of what may have appeared to be—and was—temporary joblessness (on the less lofty).

SOURCES

ARCHIVES

Letters and other primary source information about *The Paris Review*, Doc Humes, John Train, the American Committee for Cultural Freedom, *Mundo Nuevo*, Emir Rodríguez Monegal, Keith Botsford, and Hemingway come from the following archives:

Columbia University – Rare Book & Manuscript Library Collections (RBML), *The New Leader* Papers

Columbia University – Rare Book and Manuscript Library Collections (RBML), Sol Stein Papers

The J.P. Morgan Library and Museum – *The Paris Review* Papers and editorial letters

The J.P. Morgan Library and Museum – The Harold L. "Doc" Humes Papers

New York University (NYU) – Tamiment Library within Bobst Library, the American Committee for Cultural Freedom Papers

New York Public Library (NYPL) – Norman Thomas Papers

Princeton University – Emir Rodríguez Monegal Papers in Rare Books Firestone Library

Seton Hall – The John Train Papers (1960–2003), The Msgr William Noé Field Archives & Special Collections Center, Seton Hall University Library

Stanford University – Hoover–Karpeles Manuscript Library

ONLINE ARCHIVES

CIA –The CIA's online FOIA Library is also helpful for memos and documents released to other journalists and citizens via Freedom of Information Act requests, accessible at www.foia.cia.gov.

Encounter – The online archive at UNZ.org can be used to search all of *Encounter* here: http://www.unz.org/Pub/Encounter.

Freedom First – India's CCF-sponsored journal *Freedom First* can be found here, along with documents for the Swatantra Party – http://www.freedomfirst.in/archives/archives.aspx.

Jet – *Jet* magazine's online archives regarding Emmett Till are here: http://www.jetmag.com/?s=emmett+till.

Mundo Nuevo – The entire issue archive for the CCF's Latin American magazine *Mundo Nuevo* can be found online at the site Publicaciones Pediodicas de Uruguay, available at http://www.periodicas.edu.uy/v2/minisites/mundo-nuevo/indice-de-numeros.htm.

Paris Review interviews – The quarterly generously shares all its interviews with online readers here: http://www.theparisreview.org/interviews/.

Public Interest – Issues of the now-defunct *Public Interest* can be found here: http://www.nationalaffairs.com/archive/public_interest/.

Quest – CCF's India magazine, *Quest*, can be found archived here: http://www.freedomfirst.in/quest/quest-archives.aspx.

Ramparts – The online archive at UNZ.org can be used to search all of *Ramparts* here: http://www.unz.org/Pub/ramparts.

Saginaw Valley State University Library Archives

Tempo Presente – Issues of the Congress for Cultural Freedom's Italian magazine, *Tempo Presente*, can be found here: http://www.bibliotecaginobianco.it/?e=flip&id=1.

UNZ.org can be used to search many of the intellectual magazines of the Cold War era.

SELECTED INTERVIEWS (e = email; v = voice)

Nelson Aldrich – May 2012, July 2013 (v)

Jon Lee Anderson -- May 8, 2013 (e)

Larry Bensky – July 2012, June 2015 (v)

John Berger – August 31, 2015 (v)

William Blum – March 30, 2015 (e)

Henrietta Boggs – January 3, 2013 (e, v)

Keith Botsford – June 24, 2014 (e)

Olga Carlisle – March 26, 2016 (v)

Russell Cobb – March 30, 2015 (e)

Peter Finn – August 6, 2014 (e)

Ram Guha – August 26, 2014 (e) and March 18, 2016 (e)

Immy Humes – March 2015 (v)

Philip Knightley – November 10, 2014 (v, e)

Sarah Plimpton – July 2013 (v)

Félix Rodriguez – July 30, 2015 (v)

Astrid Meyers Rosset – February 2012 (v)

Frances Stonor Saunders – February 14, 2016 (v)

Frederick Seidel – May 2012 (v)

Bob Silvers – May 2012 (v)

Sol Stein – June 8, 2015 (v)

Hugh Wilford – July 13, 2013 (e)

SELECTED BOOKS AND ARTICLES

Achebe, Chinua. "An Image of Africa," in *Hopes and Impediments*. New York: Knopf Doubleday Publishing Group, 2012.

Adams, Jad and Philip Whitehead. *Dynasty: The Nehru-Gandhi Story*. Darby, PA: Diane Pub Co., 1997.

Adler, Jack. Soulmates from the Pages of History: From Mythical to Contemporary, 75 Examples of the Power of Friendship. New York: Algora Publishing, 2013.

Akenson, Donald Harman. *Conor: A Biography of Conor Cruise O'Brien*. Ithaca: Cornell University Press, 1994.

Alape, Arturo. "La Confesion del Agente Espirito." *El Tiempo*, October 15, 2000: http://www.eltiempo.com/archivo/documento/MAM-1294995.

Aldrich, Nelson. *George, Being George*. New York: Random House, 2008.

Alexander, Robert Jackson. *Rómulo Betancourt and the Transformation of Venezuela*. Dulles, VA: Transaction Publishers, 1982.

Ali, Tariq. The Clash of Fundamentalisms: Crusades, Jihads and Modernity. London: Verso, 2003.

Ali, Tariq. The Duel: On the Flight Path of American Power. New York: Scribner, 2009.

Alinder, Mary Street. *Ansel Adams: A Biography*. New York: Bloomsbury, 2014.

Anderson, Jon Lee. *Che Guevara: A Revolutionary Life*. New York: Grove Press, 1997.

"Arab Magazine Banned in Cairo: Leftists Charge Periodical Received C.I.A. Subsidies." *New York Times*, July 24, 1966.

Baker, Russ. Family of Secrets: The Bush Dynasty, America's Secret Government, and the Hidden History of the Last Fifty Years. New York: Bloomsbury, 2009.

Baldwin, James. "Princes and Powers," *Encounter* (January 1957): 52–3 (see *Encounter* archives listing above for all *Encounter* articles).

Bardach, Anna Louise. "Scavenger Hunt." *Slate*, October 6, 2004: http://www.slate.com/articles/news_and_politics/interrogation/2004/10/scavenger_hunt.single.html.

Barnes, Christopher. *Boris Pasternak, A Literary Biography*. New York: Cambridge University Press, 2004.

Bass, Gary. The Blood Telegram: Nixon, Kissinger, and a Forgotten Genocide. New York: Vintage, 2014.

Bellow, Saul and Keith Botsford. *Editors: The Best from Five Decades*. London & Connecticut: The Toby Press, 2001.

Bennett, Eric. Workshops of Empire: Stegner, Engle, and American Creative Writing During the Cold War. Iowa City: University of Iowa Press, 2015.

Berger, John. *A Painter of Our Time*. London: Writers and Readers Publishing Cooperative, 1976.

Berman, Marshall. *All That Is Solid Melts into Air*. New York: Penguin Books, 1988.

Bernstein, Barton. *Towards a New Past: Dissenting Essays in American History*. New York & Toronto: Random House, 1968.

Bernstein, Fred A. "In Costa Rica, Built for Books and Breezes." *New York Times*, October 4, 2007, F5: http://www.nytimes.com/2007/10/04/garden/04costarica.html?_r=0.

Biesecker, Michael. "Ex-Blackwater Employees' Felony Charges Dropped." *Huffington Post*, February 22, 2013.

Bigart, Homer. "Bazooka Fired at UN as Cuban Speaks." *New York Times*, December 12, 1964, A1: http://www.nytimes.com/1964/12/12/bazooka-fired-at-un-as-cuban-speaks.html.

"Birmingham and Beyond: The Negro's Push for Equality." *Time*, May 17, 1963, cover image here: http://content.time.com/time/covers/0,16641,19630517,00.html.

Blauner, Bob. Resisting McCarthyism: To Sign or Not to Sign California's Loyalty Oath. Redwood City: Stanford University Press, 2009.

Boyd, Herb. Baldwin's Harlem: A Biography of James Baldwin. New York: Atria Books, 2008.

Boggs, Henrietta. *Married to a Legend*. Lulu Press, 2011.

Boston, Andrew. "Radical Islam's Goal Is Global Conquest." *FrontPage*, July 2, 2007: http://archive.frontpagemag.com/readArticle.aspx?ARTID=27244.

Boullata, Issa J. "The Beleaguered Unicorn." *Journal of Arabic Literature*, Col. 4 (1973): 69–93.

Brogan, D.W. "America South." *Encounter* (July 1958): 88–89.

Brown, Judith M. *Gandhi: Prisoner of Hope*. New Haven: Yale University Press, 1991.

Braden, Thomas. "I'm Glad the C.I.A. is 'Immoral.'" *Saturday Evening Post,* May 20, 1967: http://www.cambridgeclarion.org/press_cuttings/braden_20may1967.html.

Buckley, William F. "Why Won't TV Show This Documentary?" *Milwaukee Sentinel*, October 22, 1981: http://www.newspapers.com/newspage/143409729/.

Bush, George. "President Bush's Statement on Execution of Saddam Hussein." The White House Web Archives of President George Bush, December 29, 2006: http://georgewbush-whitehouse.archives.gov/news/releases/2006/12/20061229-15.html.

Campbell, James. Exiled in Paris: Richard Wright, James Baldwin, Samuel Beckett, and Others on the Left Bank. Berkeley: University of California Press, 2003.

Campbell, James. *Talking at the Gates: A Life of James Baldwin*. Berkeley: University of California Press, January 2002.

Carlisle, Olga. "The Art of Fiction, No. 25: Boris Pasternak." *Paris Review* Summer-Fall (1960).

Carlisle, Olga. *Under A New Sky: A Reunion with Russia*. New York: Ticknor & Fields, 1993.

Chazanoff, William. *Welch's Grape Juice: From Corporation to Co-Operative*. Syracuse, NY: Syracuse University Press, 1977.

Chomsky, Noam. *The Essential Chomsky*. New York: The New Press, 2009.

Cobb, Russell. "Our Men in Paris? *Mundo Nuevo*, the Cuban revolution, and the Politics of Cultural Freedom." Texas: Texas Scholar Works, University of Texas Libraries (2007): https://repositories.lib.utexas.edu/bitstream/handle/2152/3179/cobbd58005.pdf?seq.

Cobb, Russell. "The Politics of Literary Prestige: Promoting the Latin American Boom in the Pages of *Mundo Nuevo*." *A Contra Corriente: A Journal on Social History and Literature in Latin America* (Spring 2008): 75–94.

Cohen, Karl. "The Cartoon That Came in from the Cold." *The Guardian*, March 7, 2003.

Cohen, Stephen. *The Idea of Pakistan*. Washington, DC: Brookings Institution Press, 2006.

Coleman, Peter. The Liberal Conspiracy: The Congress for Cultural Freedom and the Struggle for the Mind of Postwar Europe. New York: The Free Press/Macmillan, 1989.

Conquest, Robert. *The Pasternak Affair: The Courage of Genius*. New York: Octagon Books, 1961.

Cooperman, Alan. "A Father's Madness, a Daughter's Perseverance." *Washington Post*, October 17, 2008: http://voices.washingtonpost.com/shortstack/2008/10/a_fathers_madness_a_daughters.html

Corn, David. *Blond Ghost: Ted Shackley and the CIA's Crusades*. New York: Simon & Schuster, 1994.

Malcolm Cowley. *The Long Voyage: Selected Letters of Malcolm Cowley, 1915–1987.* (Letter from Malcolm Cowley to Ernest Hemingway, May 3, 1949.) Cambridge: Harvard University Press, 2014.

Crewdson, John. "Worldwide Propaganda Network Built by the CIA." *The New York Times,* December 26, 1977: http://query.nytimes.com/gst/abstract .html?res=9B04E1D9143AE334BC4E51DFB467838C669EDE.

Cummings, Richard. "The Fiction of the State: *The Paris Review* and the Invisible World of American Letters." *Smoke Signals*: http://smokesignalsmag .com/3/parisreview.html.

Davis, Deborah. *Katharine the Great: Katharine Graham and the Washington Post.* New York and London: Harcourt Brace Jovanovich, 1979.

Duberman, Martin Bauml. *Paul Robeson.* New York: The New Press, 1995.

Dreyfuss, Robert. Devil's Game: How the United States Helped Unleash Fundamentalist Islam. New York: Metropolitan Books, 2005.

Earley, Pete. "White House Screening Boosts 'KGB Connection.'" *Washington Post,* March 10, 1982: http://www.washingtonpost.com/archive/ politics/1982/03/10/white-house-screening-boosts-kgb-connection/ 29d3f189-9331-44ba-b4e3-a4074879c871/.

Ensor, Josie. "Gabriel García Márquez dies aged 87." *Telegraph,* April 17, 2014: http://www.telegraph.co.uk/culture/books/booknews/10774255/Gabriel-Garcia-Marquez-dies-aged-87.html.

Esteban, Angel and Stephanie Panichelli. Fidel & Gabo: A Portrait of the Legendary Friendship between Fidel Castro & Gabriel García Márquez. New York: Pegasus, 2009.

Fabre, Michel. *The World of Richard Wright.* Jackson: University Press of Mississippi, 1985.

Feinstein, Adam. *Pablo Neruda: A Passion for Life.* New York & London: Bloomsbury, 2004.

Feinstein, Adam. "Why the Pablo Neruda 'Poisoning' Saga Rolls On." *The Guardian,* December 30, 2013: http://www.theguardian.com/books/2013/ dec/30/pablo-neruda-chile-pinochet.

Feltrinelli, Carlo. "Comrade Millionaire." *The Guardian,* November 3, 2001: http://www.theguardian.com/theguardian/2001/nov/03/weekend7.weekend8.

Figueres Ferrer, José. "No se puede escupir a una politica exterior." *Combate* I, no. 1 (1958): 64–69.

Figueres Ferrer, José. *El Espíritu del 48*. San Jose: Editorial Costa Rica, 1987.

Finn, Peter, and Petra Couvée. The Zhivago Affair: The Kremlin, the CIA, and the Battle Over a Forbidden Book. New York: Pantheon, 2014.

Fleishman, Lazar. *Boris Pasternak: The Poet and his Politics*. Cambridge: Harvard University Press, 1990.

Fontova, Humberto. "Gabriel García Márquez: Castro's Propagandist and Snitch." Frontpagemag.com, April 28, 2014: http://www.frontpagemag.com/fpm/224013/gabriel-garcia-marquez-castros-propagandist-snitch-humberto-fontova.

Frye, Dean. "Dwight Macdonald's *Against the American Grain*." *Ramparts* (September 1963): 94–96.

Futehally, Laeeq and Arshia Sattar. *The Best of Quest*. Chennai: Tranquebar Press, 2011.

García Lorca, Federico. "Theory and Play of the Duende." Translated by A.S. Kline: http://www.poetryintranslation.com/PITBR/Spanish/LorcaDuende.htm.

García Márquez, Gabriel. *Living to Tell the Tale*. New York: Knopf/Borzoi, 2003.

García Márquez, Gabriel. *One Hundred Years of Solitude*. 1967.

Gates, Robert. From the Shadows: The Ultimate Insider's Story of Five Presidents and How They Won the Cold War,. New York: Simon & Schuster, 2007.

Gelb, Arthur. "Inquiry on Police Weighed by State." *New York Times*, November 16, 1960.

Gellhorn, Martha. "Cuba Revisited." *Granta*, Number 20 (Winter 1986): http://granta.com/cuba-revisited/.

Glass, Loren. Counterculture Colophon: Grove Press, the Evergreen Review, and the Incorporation of the Avant-Garde. Redwood City: Stanford University Press, 2013.

Gold, Hannah K. "Why Did the FBI Spy on James Baldwin?" *The Intercept*, August 15, 2015: https://theintercept.com/2015/08/15/fbi-spy-james-baldwin/.

Gottfried, Martin. *Arthur Miller; His Life and Work*. Cambridge: Da Capo Press/Perseus, 2003.

Granville, Johanna. "'Caught with Jam on Our Fingers': Radio Free Europe and the Hungarian Revolt of 1956." *Diplomatic History*, vol. 29, no. 5 (2005): 811–839.

Greenberg, David. "The Hidden History of the Espionage Act." *Slate*, December 27, 2010: http://www.slate.com/articles/news_and_politics/history_lesson/2010/12/the_hidden_history_of_the_espionage_act.html.

Gross, Neil. *Richard Rorty: The Making of an American Philosopher.* Chicago: University of Chicago Press, 2008.

Guha, Ramachandra. *The Makers of Modern India.* Cambridge: Belknap Press, 2011.

Guha, Ramachandra. India After Gandhi: The History of the World's Largest Democracy. New York: Ecco, 2007.

Hamilton, Ian. *Robert Lowell: A Biography.* London: Faber and Faber, 2011.

Hayward, Max. "Pasternak's 'Doctor Zhivago.'" *Encounter* (May 1958): 38–48.

"Hemingway in Bohemia." *Juventud Rebelde Magazine* (April 6, 2008): http://www.juventudrebelde.cu/columnas/lectura/2008-04-06/hemingway-en-bohemia-/; see also Karpeles Manuscript Library, which has a folio of the manuscript with the agreement.

Hemingway, Ernest. *A Moveable Feast.* New York: Scribner, 1964.

Hemingway, Ernest. *Old Man and the Sea.* New York, Scribner, 1952.

Hemingway, Ernest. *Selected Letters.* New York: Scribner, 2003.

Hemingway, Valerie. "Hemingway's Cuba, Cuba's Hemingway." *Smithsonian* (August 2007): http://www.smithsonianmag.com/people-places/hemingways-cuba-cubas-hemingway-159858952/?no-ist.

Hemming, A.D. "How Jimmy Carter and I Started the Mujahideen." *Counterpunch* (January 15, 1998): http://www.counterpunch.org/1998/01/15/how-jimmy-carter-and-i-started-the-mujahideen/.

Hendrickson, Paul. Hemingway's Boat: Everything He Loved in Life, and Lost: 1934–1961. New York: Vintage, 2012.

Hinckle, Warren, et al. "MSU: The University on the Make." *Ramparts* (April 1966): 11–22.

Hinckle, Warren. *If You Have a Lemon, Make Lemonade.* New York: W. W. Norton & Company, 1990.

Hofstadter, Richard. "The Paranoid Style in American Politics." *Harper's*, November 1964: http://harpers.org/archive/1964/11/the-paranoid-style-in-american-politics/.

Holzman, Michael. *James Jesus Angleton, the CIA, and the Craft of Counterintelligence.* Amherst: University of Massachusetts Press, 2008.

Horne, Gerald. *Communist Front? The Civil Rights Congress, 1946–1956.* Madison, NJ: Fairleigh Dickinson University Press, 1988.

Horvath, Robert. *Legacy of Soviet Dissent*. New York: Routledge, 2012.

Hotchner, A.E. "Hemingway, Hounded by the Feds." *The New York Times*, July 1, 2011: http://www.nytimes.com/2011/07/02/opinion/02hotchner.html.

Hunt, E. Howard. An American Spy: My Secret History in the CIA, Watergate & Beyond. New York: Wiley, 2007.

Iber, Patrick J. Neither Peace Nor Freedom: The Cultural Cold War in Latin America. Cambridge: Harvard University Press, 2015.

Iber, Patrick J. "'Who Will Impose Democracy?': Sacha Volman and the Contradictions of CIA Support for the Anticommunist Left in Latin America." *Diplomatic History*, Vol. 37, No. 5 (2013).

Ignotus, Paul. "Fiddler of Our Time." *Encounter* (February 1959): 76–78.

Immerman, Richard. *The CIA in Guatemala: The Foreign Policy of Intervention*. Austin: University of Texas Press, 1982.

Institute for Policy Studies, Report on Afghanistan Relief Committee: http://rightweb.irc-online.org/articles/display/Afghanistan_Relief_Committee.

Ivinskaya, Olga. *A Captive of Time: My Years with Pasternak*. New York: Doubleday, 1978.

Jay, Mike. "The Reality Show," *Aeon*, August 23, 2013: https://aeon.co/essays/a-culture-of-hyper-reality-made-paranoid-delusions-true.

Johnson, Scott. *The Wolf and the Watchman: A CIA Childhood*. New York: W. W. Norton & Company, 2013.

Jones, Derek (ed.). *Censorship: A World Encyclopedia*. New York: Routledge, 2015.

Joseph, Peniel. *Stokely: A Life*. New York: Basic Civitas Books, 2014.

Judis, John B. William F. Buckley: Patron Saint of the Conservatives. New York: Simon & Schuster, 2001.

Kachka, Boris. Hothouse: The Art of Survival and the Survival Art at America's Most Celebrated Publishing House, Farrar, Straus and Giroux. New York: Simon & Schuster, 2014.

Kempton, Murray. "The Shadow Saint." *New York Review of Books*, July 11, 1996: http://www.nybooks.com/articles/1996/07/11/the-shadow-saint/.

Kennan, George. "The Long Telegram." http://nsarchive.gwu.edu/coldwar/documents/episode-1/kennan.htm.

Kennedy, John F. "Speech of Senator John F. Kennedy," Cincinnati, Ohio, Democratic Dinner, October 6, 1960, The American Presidency Project at UCSD, http://www.presidency.ucsb.edu/ws/index.php?pid=25660.

Kinnamon, Keneth. "Hemingway's Politics," in Scott Donaldson, *The Cambridge Companion to Hemingway*. New York: Cambridge University Press, 1996.

Kinzer, Stephen. The Brothers: John Foster Dulles, Allen Dulles, and Their Secret World War. New York: Times Books, 2013.

Kinzer, Stephen. Overthrow: America's Century of Regime Change, From Hawaii to Iraq. New York: Times Books, 2007.

Kinzer, Stephen, and Stephen Schlesinger. *Bitter Fruit: The Story of the American Coup in Guatemala*. Cambridge: David Rockefeller Center for Latin American Studies, 2005.

Kolhatkar, Sonali and James Ingalls. *Bleeding Afghanistan: Washington, Warlords, and the Propaganda of Silence*. New York: Seven Stories Press, 2011.

Knightley, Phillip. *A Hack's Progress*, London: Vintage UK. 1998.

Krauze, Enrique. *Redeemers: Ideas and Power in Latin America*. New York: Harper Perennial, 2012.

Kristol, Irving. Reflections of a Neoconservative: Looking Back, Looking Ahead. New York: Basic Books, 1983.

Kristol, Irving. *The Neoconservative Persuasion: Selected Essays* (1942–2009). New York: Basic Books, 2011.

Laing, R.D. *The Politics of Experience*. New York: Pantheon, 1983.

Lasch, Christopher. "The Cultural Cold War," in *Towards a New Past: Dissenting Essays in American History*, edited by Barton Bernstein. New York & Toronto: Random House, 1968.

"The Legacy of Ernesto Che Guevara." PBS, November 20, 1997: http://www.pbs.org/newshour/updates/latin_america-july-dec97-guevara_11-20/.

Lewis, Oscar. "The Culture of Poverty." *Scientific American* (October 1966): http://www.scientificamerican.com/article/the-culture-of-poverty/.

Lewis, Paul. "Harry Rositzke, 91, Linguist and American Spymaster." *New York Times*, November 8, 2002: http://www.nytimes.com/2002/11/08/us/harry-rositzke-91-linguist-and-american-spymaster.html.

Linville, James Scott. "Shooting Script." *Standpoint*, January 2009: http://www.standpointmag.co.uk/node/764/full.

Longley, Kyle. Sparrow and the Hawk: Costa Rica and the United States During the Rise of Jose Figueres. Tuscaloosa: University Alabama Press, 1997.

"Lord Buckley's Police Station Interview, October 1960." http://www.lordbuckley.com/Speak_The_Jive/PoliceInterview.html.

Macdonald, Dwight. "America! America!" *Dissent*, Fall 1958.

Macdonald, Dwight. "No Miracle in Milan." *Encounter* (December 1955): 68–74.

Mackenzie, Angus. *Secrets: The C.I.A.'s War at Home*. Berkeley: University of California Press, 1997.

Mailer, Norman. "An Open Letter to Castro and Kennedy." *Village Voice*, April 27, 1961: https://news.google.com/newspapers?id=RmoQAAAAIBAJ&sjid=3osDAAAAIBAJ&pg=5119,2073910&hl=.

Malkin, Elisabeth. "An Apology for a Guatemalan Coup, 57 Years Later." *The New York Times*, October 20, 2011: http://www.nytimes.com/2011/10/21/world/americas/an-apology-for-a-guatemalan-coup-57-years-later.html?_r=1.

Mancosu, Paolo. *Inside the Zhivago Storm: The Editorial Adventures of Pasternak's Masterpiece*. Milan: Feltrinelli Editore, section 1.1, via Google Books, snippet preview.

Marin, Francisco and Mario Casasus. *El Doble Asesinato de Neruda: Con el Testimonio de Manuel Araya*. Santiago: OchoLibros, 2013.

Matthiessen, Peter. *Snow Leopard*. New York: Penguin, 1978.

Maxwell, William J. FB Eyes: How J. Edgar Hoover's Ghostreaders Framed African American Literature. Princeton: Princeton University Press, 2015.

McGilligan, Patrick. *Alfred Hitchcock: A Life in Darkness and Light*. New York: Harper Collins, 2004.

McSmith, Andy. Fear and the Muse: The Russian Masters—From Akhmatova and Pasternak to Shostakovich and Eisenstein—Under Stalin. New York: New Press, 2015.

"Miles Davis Seized." *New York Times*, August 26, 1959.

Miller, Arthur. *Timebends: A Life*. New York: Grove Press, 2013.

Narayan, Jayaprakash. "Nehru and Hungary's Revolt." *The New Leader*, Vol 39, Issue 51 (November 17, 1956).

Nisbet, Robert. "Project Camelot: An Autopsy." *Public Interest*, Number 5 (Fall 1966).

Orwell, George. *Animal Farm & 1984*. New York: Houghton Mifflin Harcourt, June 1, 2003.

Pace, Eric. "Jose Figueres Ferrer Is Dead at 83." *The New York Times*, June 9, 1990: http://www.nytimes.com/1990/06/09/obituaries/jose-figueres-ferrer-is-dead-at-83-led-costa-ricans-to-democracy.html.

Paget, Karen. Patriotic Betrayal: The Inside Story of the CIA's Secret Campaign to Enroll American Students in the Crusade Against Communism. New Haven: Yale University Press, 2015.

Pasternak, Boris. *Doctor Zhivago*. New York: Pantheon, 1957.

Pfeiffer, Jack. "Adlai Stevenson and the Bay of Pigs." *Studies in Intelligence*, Volume 27, (Fall 1983): 37–38.

Phillips, David Atlee. *The Night Watch*. New York: Ballantine Books, 1982.

Plimpton, George. "The Art of Fiction, Number 21, An Interview with Ernest Hemingway." *Paris Review*, Number 18, Spring 1958 (see interviews archive link above).

Plimpton, George. *The Best of Plimpton*. New York: Atlantic Monthly Press, 1994.

Plimpton, George. "Kennedy and Hemingway: Two Tricky Men to Eat With." *Sydney Morning Herald*, Dec. 27, 1980, https://news.google.com/newspapers?nid=1301&dat=19801227&id=0p5WAAAAIBAJ&sjid=L-cDAAAAIBAJ&pg=6154,7860647&hl=en.

Plimpton, George. "My Last Cobra: Stalking the Wild Prevarication." *Harper's*, September, 1994: http://harpers.org/archive/1994/09/my-last-cobra/.

Plimpton, George. *Shadow Box: An Amateur in the Ring*. New York: Lyons Press, 2010.

Pugliese, Stanislao. *Bitter Spring: A Life of Ignazio Silone*. New York: Macmillan, 2009.

Al Rahim, Muddathir Abd. "Reminiscences of Al Faruki," in Imtiyaf Yusuf, *Islam and Knowledge: Al Faruqi's Concept of Religion in Islamic Thought*. London: I.B. Tauris, 2012.

Ratner, Michael and Michael Steven Smith. *Who Killed Che? How the CIA Got Away with Murder*. New York: OR Books, 2011.

Ray, Michèle. "In Cold Blood." *Ramparts* (March 1968): 23–37.

Raymont, Henry. "Guevara Papers Published Here." *The New York Times*, July 3, 1968: http://query.nytimes.com/gst/abstract.html?res=9D07E6D81638 E134BC4B53DFB1668383679EDE.

Raymont, Henry. "Publisher Warns Rivals Over Diary." *The New York Times*, July 4, 1968: http://query.nytimes.com/gst/abstract.html?res=9C06EFD61230 E034BC4C53DFB1668383679EDE.

Raymont, Henry. "Ramparts to Publish Manuscript Said to be Guevara's Diary." *The New York Times*, July 1, 1968: http://query.nytimes.com/gst/abstract.html?res=9B02E7DD1131E034BC4953DFB1668383679EDE.

"Report of the Attorney General to the Congress of the United States on the Administration of the Foreign Agents Registration Act of 1938, As Amended for the Calendar Year 1962," October 1963.

Richardson, Peter. A Bomb in Every Issue: How the Short, Unruly Life of Ramparts Magazine Changed America. New York: The New Press, 2010.

Robins, Natalie. *Alien Ink: The FBI's War on Freedom of Expression*. New Brunswick: Rutgers University Press, 1993.

Rodriguez, Félix and John Weisman. *Shadow Warrior: The CIA Hero of a Hundred Unknown Battles*. New York: Simon & Schuster, 1989.

Rodríguez Monegal, Emir. "In Praise of Quimaraes Rosa." *Commentary* (January 1966): 65–66.

Roiphe, Anne. Art and Madness: A Memoir of Lust Without Reason. New York: Anchor, 2012.

Rosenfeld, Seth. Subversives: The FBI's War on Student Radicals and Reagan's Rise to Power. New York: Farrar, Straus and Giroux, 2012.

Rosset, Barney. "Evergreen Review and Che Guevara's Diary," unpublished manuscript chapter, courtesy Astrid Myers Rosset. In Rosset, Barney. *Rosset: My Life in Publishing and How I Fought Censorship*. New York: OR Books, May 2016.

Rostow, W.W. *The Stages of Economic Growth: A Non-Communist Manifesto*. New York: Cambridge University Press, 1991.

De Rougemont, Denis. "Looking for India." *Encounter* (October 1953): 36–42.

Ruge, Gerd. "Letter from Moscow: A Visit to Pasternak." *Encounter* (March 1958): 22–25.

Ruiz Galvete, Marta. "Cuadernos del Congreso por la Libertad de la Cultura: Anticomunismo y guerra fria en America Latina." *El Argonauta Español 3* (2006): https://argonauta.revues.org/1095.

Sabin, Margery. "The Politics of Cultural Freedom: India in the Nineteen Fifties." *Raritan*, Vol. 14, No. 4 (March 1, 1995): 45–65.

Said, Edward. *Culture and Imperialism*. New York: Vintage, 1994.

Said, Edward. *Orientalism*. New York: Vintage, 1979.

Schmidt, Michael S. and Colin Moynihan. "FBI Counterterrorism Agents Monitored Occupy Movements, Records Show." *New York Times*, December 24, 2012: http://www.nytimes.com/2012/12/25/nyregion/occupy-movement-was-investigated-by-fbi-counterterrorism-agents-records-show.html.

Saunders, Frances Stonor. The Cultural Cold War: The CIA and the World of Arts and Letters. New York: The New Press, 2001.

Saunders, Frances Stonor. "The Writer and the Valet." *London Review of Books*, September 25, 2014: http://www.lrb.co.uk/v36/n18/frances-stonorsaunders/the-writer-and-the-valet.

Scammell, Michael. Koestler: The Literary and Political Odyssey of a Twentieth-Century Skeptic. New York: Random House, 2009.

Scarfe, Allan and Wendy Scarfe. *J.P., His Biography*. Hyderabad: Orient Blackswan, 1998.

Schlesinger, Arthur. *The Letters of Arthur Schlesinger*, edited by Andrew Schlesinger and Stephen Schlesinger. Random House, 2013.

Seidel, Frederick. *Nice Weather: Poems*. New York: Farrar, Straus and Giroux, 2012.

Sen, Amartya. "Foreword," in Rabindranath Tagore, *Boyhood Days*. London: Hesperus Press, 2011. Excerpted as "Childhood Reasons" in *Guernica: A Magazine of Art and Politics*, April 15, 2011: http://www.guernicamag.com/features/sen_tagore_4_15_11/.

Sherman, Scott. "In His League: Being George Plimpton." *The Nation*, February 2, 2009: http://www.thenation.com/article/his-league-being-george-plimpton/.

Sigal, Clancy,. Hemingway Lives: Why Reading Ernest Hemingway Matters Today. New York: OR Books, 2013.

Solzhenitsyn, Aleksandr. *The Gulag Archipelago*. New York: Harper & Row, 1974.

Stavans, Ilan. *Gabriel García Márquez: The Early Years*. New York: Palgrave/Macmillan, 2010.

Stein, Sol, and James Baldwin. *Native Sons*. New York: One World/Ballantine, 2005.

Steinfels, Peter. The Neoconservatives: The Men Who Are Changing America's Politics. New York: Touchstone, 1980.

Stern, Sol. "NSA and the CIA" *Ramparts* (March 1967): 29–39.

Stone, Peter H. "Art of Fiction number 69: Gabriel García Márquez." *Paris Review*, No. 82 (Winter 1981).

Tagore, Rabindranath. *The Essential Tagore*. Cambridge: Belknap Press, 2011.

Talese, Gay. "Looking for Hemingway." *Esquire*, 1963, republished in Longform .com: http://longform.org/stories/looking-for-hemingway-gay-talese.

Teitelboim, Volodia. *Neruda: An Intimate Biography*. Austin: University of Texas Press, 1991.

Tennyson, Hallam. "A Dynasty of Saints." *Encounter* (December 1954): 3–7.

Thomas, Evan. The Very Best Men: Four Who Dared: The Early Years of the CIA. New York: Simon & Schuster, 1996.

Thompson, Catherine. "UNCENSORED: FBI Pushed MLK to Kill Himself Over Threatened Sex Stories." Talking Points Memo, November 21, 2014: http://talkingpointsmemo.com/livewire/read-fbi-letter-threatening-mlk.

Toor, Saadia. The State of Islam: Culture and Cold War Politics in Pakistan. New York: Oxford University Press, 2014.

Turkel, Stanley. *Heroes of the American Reconstruction*. Jefferson, NC: Macfarland, 2005.

Turse, Nick. Kill Anything That Moves: The Real American War in Vietnam. New York: Metropolitan Books, 2013.

Tynan, Kathleen. *The Life of Kenneth Tynan*. New York: William Morrow & Co, 1987.

Urstadt, Bryant. "Paris, Paranoia, the CIA, Humes." 3QuarksDaily, December 29, 2008: http://www.3quarksdaily.com/3quarksdaily/2008/12/paris.html.

Ernest van den Haag. "Social Science Testimony in the Desegregation Cases—A Reply to Professor Kenneth Clark." *Villanova Law Review* 69, Vol. 6, No. 1 (1960): http://digitalcommons.law.villanova.edu/cgi/viewcontent .cgi?article=1502&context=vlr.

Vazquez, Michael. "The Bequest of Quest." *Bidoun*, Issue 26: Soft Power: http://bidoun.org/articles/the-bequest-of-quest.

Volkov, Solomon. The Magical Chorus: A History of Russian Culture from Tolstoy to Solzhenitsyn. New York: Vintage, 2009.

Warner, William Eaton. "Products of a Reading of an English Translation of Doctor Zhivago's Italian Publisher." *AGNI* Online, October 2004: http://www.bu.edu/agni/essays/online/2004/warner2.html.

Webster, Paul. "Flying into a Literary Storm." *The Guardian*, June 23, 2000: http://www.theguardian.com/books/2000/jun/24/biography.books.

Weiner, Tim. "Blowback From the Afghan Battlefield." *New York Times*, March 13, 1994: http://www.nytimes.com/1994/03/13/magazine/blowback-from-the-afghan-battlefield.html?pagewanted=all.

Weiner, Tim. The Legacy of Ashes: The History of the CIA. New York: Anchor, 2008.

Wicker, Tom, et al. "Electronic Prying Grows." *New York Times*, April 27, 1966: http://query.nytimes.com/gst/abstract.html?res=9401E6DB1F39EF34BC4F51DFB266838D679EDE.

Wilford, Hugh. America's Great Game: The CIA's Secret Arabists and the Shaping of the Modern Middle East. New York: Basic Books, 2013.

Wilford, Hugh. *The Mighty Wurlitzer: How the CIA Played America*. Cambridge: Harvard University Press, 2009.

Wiskari, Werner. "Author Tells Swedes He Cannot Accept Nobel Literature Award." *New York Times*, October 30, 1958: http://www.nytimes.com/packages/html/books/nobel-Pasternak2.pdf.

Raymond Wolters. *Race and Education, 1954–2007*. Columbia: University of Missouri Press, 2008.

Wreszin, Michael. Rebel in Defense of Tradition: The Life and Politics of Dwight Macdonald. New York: Basic Books, 1994.

Yusuf, Imtiyaz. Islam and Knowledge: Al Faruqi's Concept of Religion in Islamic Thought. London: I.B.Tauris, 2012.

FILMS AND VIDEOS

Animal Farm, directed by Joy Batchelor and John Halas, 1954.

"Bay of Pigs Invasion Newsreel," CSPAN, April 1, 1961, http://www.c-span.org/video/?101118-1/bay-pigs-invasion-newsreel.

Plimpton!: Starring George Plimpton as Himself, directed by Tom Bean, 2012.

Civil Rights Roundtable (USIS), August 28, 1963, http://www.youtube.com/watch?v=ZjZBZxPk4Pc.

"Doc," an episode of the documentary series *Independent Lens*, directed by Immy Humes (2008).

The KGB Connections, directed by Martyn Burke, 1982.

Eric Lichtblau interview with Amy Goodman and Juan Gonzalez on *Democracy Now*, October 31, 2014.

The Paris Review: Early Chapters, directed by by Paula Heredia, 2001.

"May 1958: Nixon Ordeal – Venezuela Mob, and Hero's Welcome Home," May 13, 1958. https://www.youtube.com/watch?v=nvigX1doz2U.

ENDNOTES

INTRODUCTION

1. Harold "Doc" Humes to George Plimpton, March 4, 1966, Harold Humes Archives at the J.P. Morgan Library and Museum.
2. Ibid.
3. Nelson Aldrich, *George, Being George*, New York: Random House (2008), 134.
4. Ibid., blurbs page.
5. Ibid., 110.
6. This was originally said by Humes himself, who was being self-deprecating, said his daughter Immy Humes, who saw many copies and believed it was a high-quality little magazine. *The Paris Review* Founders biographical page credits the full description to John Ciardi as, "the best fourth-rate imitation of *The New Yorker* I have ever seen."
7. Humes to Plimpton, March 1966, Harold Humes Archives at the J.P. Morgan Library and Museum.
8. It was Keith Botsford's use of this word, "finks," that gave the book its name; other characters in the book use it too.
9. Humes to Plimpton, March 1966, Harold Humes Archives at the J.P. Morgan Library and Museum.
10. John M. Crewdson, "Worldwide Propaganda Network Built by the CIA," *New York Times*, December 26, 1977.

CHAPTER 1

1. Michael Holzman, *James Jesus Angleton* (Amherst: University of Massachusetts Press, 2008), 18.
2. Michael Holzman, "The Ideological Origins of American Studies at Yale," http://journals.ku.edu/index.php/amerstud/article/viewFile/2679/2638.
3. Ibid.
4. Interview with Immy Humes, transcribed from her film outtakes, 2012; video originals are in the Harold Humes Archives at the J.P. Morgan Library and Museum.
5. Ibid.

6. Peter Matthiessen, *The Snow Leopard*, 43–44.
7. Interview with Immy Humes.
8. Ibid.
9. Evan Thomas, *The Very Best Men*, 15–16.
10. Interview with Immy Humes.
11. Appropriated for the CIA by author David Martin, among others.
12. Interview with Immy Humes.
13. Interview with Immy Humes.
14. Aldrich, *George, Being George*, 90.
15. *Plimpton! Starring George Plimpton as Himself*, Tom Bean, director (2012).
16. Aldrich, *George, Being George*, 61, 64.
17. Ibid., 57.
18. Ibid., 12.
19. *Plimpton!*, Bean (dir.).
20. Doc Humes to Gay Talese, cited in Aldrich, *George, Being George*.
21. Letter from Matthiessen to Plimpton, undated, *Paris Review* Archives, Morgan Library.
22. The conspiracist will be tempted to think Michael Josselson, of the Congress for Cultural Freedom.
23. Aldrich, *George, Being George*, 112.
24. Ibid., 90.
25. Interview with Immy Humes.
26. James Campbell, *Exiled in Paris: Richard Wright, James Baldwin, Samuel Beckett, and Others on the Left Bank*, 88.
27. Ibid., 68.
28. Ibid., 69.
29. Campbell, *Exiled in Paris*, 69.
30. Crewdson, "Worldwide Propaganda Network Built by the CIA."
31. Interview with Immy Humes.
32. Frances Stonor Saunders, *The Cultural Cold War*, 86.
33. Campbell, *Exiled in Paris*, 99.
34. Michel Fabre, *The World of Richard Wright*, 185.
35. Interview with Immy Humes.
36. Interview with Immy Humes.
37. Ibid
38. "Doc," an episode of the documentary series *Independent Lens*, directed by Immy Humes (2008).
39. Interview with Immy Humes.
40. Campbell, *Exiled in Paris*, 65.
41. Anne Roiphe, *Art and Madness*, New York: Nan A. Talese (2011), 67.
42. Holzman, *James Jesus Angleton*, 15.
43. Ibid., 8–10.
44. Ibid., 18.
45. Ibid., 18–24.
46. Ibid., 87.
47. Thomas, *The Very Best Men*, 38–40, 68.
48. Interview with Immy Humes.
49. Ibid.

CHAPTER 2

1. George Kennan, "The Long Telegram," http://nsarchive.gwu.edu/coldwar/documents/episode-1/kennan.htm.
2. Psychological warfare was an American mistranslation of the Nazi-era German notion of Worldview Warfare, writes Johanna Granville in "'Caught with Jam on Our Fingers': Radio Free Europe and the Hungarian Revolution of 1956," *Diplomatic History* 29, no. 5 (November 2005): 811–839, http://www.scribd.com/doc/13866301/RFE-and-the-Hungarian-Revolt-of-1956-by-Johanna-Granville.
3. Saunders, *The Cultural Cold War*, 1.
4. Ibid., 127.
5. One of those accounts was *The Paris Review*'s Nelson Aldrich. Aldrich had been the Paris editor for the magazine and while transitioning to the CCF in the late 1950s; he talks about knowing it was a CIA front in his book about George Plimpton, *George, Being George*. See page 151.
6. Formally called the Molotov–Ribbentrop Pact.
7. Michael Wreszin, *A Rebel in Defense of Tradition: The Life and Politics of Dwight Macdonald*, 213–214.
8. See: Sol Stein to Sidney Hook, February 3, 1955, ACCF Papers, Tamiment Library at NYU Bobst Library.
9. Russell Cobb, "Our Men in Paris? *Mundo Nuevo*, the Cuban Revolution, and the Politics of Cultural Freedom," PhD dissertation, University of Texas at Austin (2007), 103.
10. Richard Hofstadter, "The Paranoid Style in American Politics," *Harper's*, November 1964.
11. Saunders, *The Cultural Cold War*, 41–42.
12. Ibid., 42.
13. Wreszin, *A Rebel in Defense of Tradition*, 218.
14. Ibid., 217.
15. Ibid., 220.
16. Ibid., 221.
17. Ibid., 222.
18. Ibid., 223.
19. Malcolm Cowley to Ernest Hemingway, May 3, 1949, from Malcolm Cowley, *The Long Voyage, Selected Letters of Malcolm Cowley, 1915–1987*, (Cambridge: Harvard University Press 2014), 404.
20. See under, Dashiell Hammett.
21. Dan Bell to Jack White, June 9, 1953, ACCF Papers, Tamiment Library, NYU Bobst Library.
22. Irving Kristol to Dr. Lewis A. Wilson, October 6, 1952, ACCF Papers, Tamiment Library, NYU Bobst Library.
23. Bob Blauner, *Resisting McCarthyism: To Sign or Not to Sign California's Loyalty Oath*, 206; see also George R. Stewart, *The Year of the Oath: The Fight for Academic Freedom at the University of California*.
24. The phrase is cited back to John Kenneth Galbraith by ACCF's Sol Stein as the proper attitude for dealing with public issues; Sol Stein to J.K. Galbraith, March 29, 1955, ACCF Papers, Tamiment Library, NYU Bobst Library.

25. American Committee proposal to Ford Foundation, "Request for a grant to prepare a major study of Communist influence on large non-Communist sections of the American population," February 1956, ACCF Papers, Tamiment Library, NYU Bobst Library.

26. Ibid.

27. Arnold Beichman to Dr. Harry J. Carman, October 25, 1954, ACCF Papers, Tamiment Library, NYU Bobst Library.

28. See *Jet* Magazine's online archives here: http://www.jetmag.com/?s=emmett+till.

29. Gerald Horne, *Communist Front? The Civil Rights Congress, 1946–1956*, 13–17. They were ahead of their time, in many ways, in Horne's version. "Decades before the issue became a live one in the civil rights movement," Horne writes, "CRC and their allies were arguing before the US Supreme Court that an employer had to hire Afro-Americans, as Euro-Americans quit or transferred, until the proportion of Black clerks to white clerks approximated the proportion of Black customers to white customers (about 50%)" at a given store. Summarizing the blunt notion of a front as it applied to radicals, Horne writes, "Although Americans for Democratic Action would not be tagged a 'Democratic Party front' or the *Wall Street Journal* or *New York Herald Tribune* would not be tagged as 'GOP fronts,' seemingly only organizations that were influenced" by the Communist party could earn such a reductive epithet.

30. Martin Bauml Duberman, *Paul Robeson*, 328–330.

31. Horne, *Communist Front?*, 13–18.

32. "Request for a grant for a conference of magazine editors," ACCF Papers.

33. Ibid.

34. Ibid.

35. Saunders, *The Cultural Cold War*, 25.

36. Ibid., 26.

37. "Request for a grant for a conference of magazine editors," ACCF Papers.

38. Ibid.

39. Across many letters: for instance, Henry Schwarzschild to Francis Brown, August 20, 1954, ACCF Papers, Tamiment Library, NYU Bobst Library.

40. David Greenberg, "The Hidden History of the Espionage Act," *Slate*, December 27, 2010.

41. Peter Viereck to Irving Kristol, undated cable, ACCF Papers, Tamiment Library, NYU Bobst Library.

42. Sol Stein to Peter Viereck, December 17, 1953, ACCF Papers, Tamiment Library, NYU Bobst Library.

43. "Proposal for a grant for a conference for editors," ACCF Papers, Tamiment Library, NYU Bobst Library.

44. The ACCF would later rally to raise funds for *The New Leader* within the dark budgets of CIA.

45. "Request for a grant for a conference of magazine editors," ACCF Papers, Tamiment Library, NYU Bobst Library.

46. Saunders, *The Cultural Cold War*, 141.

47. Ibid., 146.

48. Ibid., 10–11.

49. Ibid., 12.

50. Hugh Wilford, *America's Great Game: The CIA's Secret Arabists and the Shaping of the Modern Middle East*, 163.

51. Peter Matthiessen to Julius Fleischmann, undated letter, Matthiessen folder, *Paris Review* Archives, PR1, J.P. Morgan Library and Museum.

52. Aldrich, *George, Being George*, 97.

53. Campbell, *Exiled in Paris*, 67.

54. William Styron, "Feature," *The Paris Review*, number 1, Spring 1953.

55. Campbell, *Exiled in Paris*, 66.

56. Matthiessen to Plimpton, undated, *Paris Review* Archives, PR1, J.P. Morgan Library and Museum.

57. Tom Guinzburg to George Plimpton, dated 1953, *Paris Review* Archives, PR1, Guinzburg Folder, J.P. Morgan Library and Museum.

58. Ibid.

59. Matthiessen to Plimpton, 1954, *Paris Review* Archives, PR1, J.P. Morgan Library and Museum.

60. See the Train biography on *The Paris Review* masthead online.

61. Aldrich, *George, Being George*, 110.

62. Ibid., 109–110.

63. Matthiessen to Plimpton, undated letter, *Paris Review* Morgan Archive, PR1, Matthiessen Folder.

64. Spender to Kristol, letters spanning from February to May 1953, ACCF Papers, Spender Folder, Tamiment Library, NYU Bobst Library.

65. Ibid.

66. Hugh Wilford, *The Mighty Wurlitzer: How the CIA Played America*, 105.

67. See Columbia University – Rare Book and Manuscript Library Collections (RBML) *The New Leader* Papers, in particular the Lovestone and Offie folders.

68. Irving Kristol to Stephen Spender, letters spanning from February to May 1953, ACCF Papers, Spender Folder, Tamiment Library, NYU Bobst Library.

69. Ibid.

70. Saunders, *The Cultural Cold War*, 138.

71. Aldrich, *George, Being George*, 110.

72. Ibid., 97–98.

73. George Plimpton to Tom Guinzburg, 1954, *Paris Review* Archives, PR1, Plimpton Folder, J.P. Morgan Library and Museum.

74. Scott Sherman, "In his League: Being George Plimpton," *The Nation*, February 2, 2009.

75. Aldrich, *George, Being George*, 114.

76. Gay Talese, "Looking for Hemingway," Esquire, July 1963, republished in Longform, http://longform.org/stories/looking-for-hemingway-gay-talese.

CHAPTER 3

1. Thomas, *The Very Best Men*, 150.

2. Ibid., 38.

3. Ibid.

4. Ibid.

5. For instance: "Consider that in 1800 Western powers claimed 55 percent but actually held approximately 35 percent of the earth's surface, and that by 1874 the proportion was 67 percent, a rate of increase of 83,000 square miles per year. By 1914, the annual

rate had risen to an astonishing 240,000 square miles, and Europe held a grand total of roughly 85 percent of the earth as colonies, protectorates, dependencies, dominions, and commonwealths." Edward Said, *Culture and Imperialism*, 8.

6. Thomas, *The Very Best Men*, 68.
7. The agent was Frank Lindsay; Thomas, *The Very Best Men*, 71.
8. Thomas, *The Very Best Men*, 40.
9. Holzman, *James Jesus Angleton*, 155–156.
10. Hugh Wilford, *The Mighty Wurlitzer*, 7.
11. Holzman, *James Jesus Angleton*, 158.
12. Ibid., 155–157.
13. Ibid., 155–156.
14. Thomas, *The Very Best Men*, 144–145.
15. Indian Committee for Cultural Freedom newsletter, Fall 1956, ACCF Papers, Tamiment Library, NYU Bobst Library.
16. Thomas, *The Very Best Men*, 147.
17. Ibid.
18. Ibid., 146.
19. Ibid., 162.
20. Holzman, *James Jesus Angleton*, 161.
21. Ibid., 125.
22. Thomas, *The Very Best Men*, 148; the friend was Clare Boothe Luce.
23. The letter appears in translation in the ACCF Papers (S Folder), ACCF Papers, Tamiment Library, NYU Bobst Library.
24. John Pauker to Sol Stein, October 20, 1955, ACCF Papers, Tamiment Library, NYU Bobst Library.
25. Sol Stein to Eric Bentley, January 4, 1955, ACCF Papers, Tamiment Library, NYU Bobst Library.
26. Pauker to Stein, October 20, 1955, ACCF Papers, Tamiment Library, NYU Bobst Library.
27. ACCF to William D. Kennedy, date not visible, ACCF Papers, Tamiment Library, NYU Bobst Library.
28. The full quote to Hook was: "Things were easier [for anti-Communists] when the conflict was more dramatic as at the time of the outbreak of the Korean War when the Congress for Cultural Freedom was founded." Stein to Sidney Hook, June 3, 1955, ACCF Papers, Tamiment Library, NYU Bobst Library.
29. Werner Wiskari, "Author Tells Swedes He Cannot Accept Nobel Literature Award," *New York Times*, October 30, 1958.
30. George Plimpton to Nelson Aldrich, October 30, 1958, Plimpton Folder, *Paris Review* Archives, PR1, J.P. Morgan Library and Museum.
31. Peter Finn and Petra Couvée, *The Zhivago Affair: The Kremlin, the CIA, and the Battle over a Forbidden Book*, (New York: Pantheon 2014), 4.
32. Ibid., 5.
33. Ibid.
34. "He remembered approaching the city's cathedral (in Milan), seeing it from various angles as he came closer . . . 'When at last a narrow platform placed me at its foot and I craned my head, it slid into me with the whole choral murmur of its pillars and turrets, like a plug of snow down the jointed column of a drainpipe.'" Cited in Peter Finn and Petra Couvée, *The Zhivago Affair*, 6.

35. Finn and Couvée, *The Zhivago Affair*, 6.
36. Ibid., 8.
37. Ibid., 9.
38. Ibid., 12.
39. Olga Ivinskaya, *A Captive of Time: My Years with Pasternak*, (New York: Doubleday 1978) 199; also in Lazar Fleishman, *Boris Pasternak: The Poet and His Politics*, (Cambridge: Harvard University Press 1990), 275 (I combine two translations).
40. Ivinskaya, *A Captive of Time*, 199; also in Fleishman, *Boris Pasternak*, 201–202.
41. Ibid.
42. Boris Pasternak, *Doctor Zhivago*, tr. Richard Pevear and Larissa Volokhonsky. New York: Pantheon Books (2010), 128-129.
43. Ibid., 128.
44. Ibid., 173.
45. Ibid., 304.
46. Finn and Couvée, *The Zhivago Affair*, 32.
47. Andy McSmith, *Fear and the Muse: The Russian Masters—From Akhmatova and Pasternak to Shostakovich and Eisenstein—Under Stalin*, New Press, page 134.
48. Christopher Barnes, *Boris Pasternak, A Literary Biography*, 75.
49. Marshall Berman, *All That is Solid Melts Into Air*, Penguin Books, 282.
50. Ivinskaya, *A Captive of Time*, 61; also in Jack Adler, *Soulmates from the Pages of History*, 317.
51. Fleishman, *Boris Pasternak*, 180.
52. Ivinskaya, *A Captive of Time*, 62; Ivinskaya cites Anna Akhmatova and Nadezhda Mandelstam, whose versions differ slightly. It was the Finn/Couvée account where the author first saw the dialogue written out as in a play or screenplay.
53. Ibid., 63; Finn and Couvée, 40–41.
54. Finn and Couvée, *The Zhivago Affair*, 41.
55. Ibid.
56. Ivinskaya, *A Captive of Time*, 59.
57. Ibid., 58.
58. Finn and Couvée, *The Zhivago Affair*, 43.
59. Solomon Volkov, *The Magical Chorus*, 201.
60. Finn and Couvée, *The Zhivago Affair*, 97.
61. Ibid., 66.
62. Ibid., 67.
63. Ivinskaya, *A Captive of Time*, see 98–103
64. Finn and Couvée, *The Zhivago Affair*, 68.
65. Ibid., 71.
66. Ibid., 72.
67. Ibid., 73.
68. Ivinskaya, *A Captive of Time*, 410; in footnote 57, translator Max Hayward, a Russia scholar and expert, writes that "by 1960 most people sentenced unjustly before 1953 had been released. . ."
69. Fleishman, *Boris Pasternak*, 270.
70. Ibid., 271.
71. Ibid.
72. Ivinskaya, *A Captive of Time*, 197; Finn and Couvée, *The Zhivago Affair*, 90.
73. Carlo Feltrinelli, "Comrade Millionaire," *The Guardian*, November 2, 2001.

74. Finn and Couvée, *The Zhivago Affair*, 95–96.

75. Fleishman, *Boris Pasternak*, 278.

76. Whitney is being dramatic. After false starts, a sort of thaw would be back under way by the early 1960s.

77. Fleishman, *Boris Pasternak*, 283.

78. Ibid., 282.

79. Finn and Couvée, *The Zhivago Affair*, 111.

80. Ibid.

81. Ibid., 112.

82. For instance, see Fleishman, *Boris Pasternak*, 284.

83. William Eaton Warner, "Products of a Reading of an English Translation of *Doctor Zhivago*'s Italian Publisher," *AGNI*, October 2004.

84. Fleishman, *Boris Pasternak*, 284 dates this to November 22 but Finn and Couvée to November 15.

85. Fleishman, *Boris Pasternak*, 287.

86. Ibid., 282.

87. Ibid., 286.

88. Finn and Couvée, *The Zhivago Affair*, 115.

89. Ibid., 115.

90. Memo from Western Europe Chief to Unknown, January 2, 1958, CIA FOIA Library, http://www.foia.cia.gov/sites/default/files/document_conversions/1822135/DOC_0005795616.pdf.

91. Ibid.

92. Ibid.

93. Finn and Couvée, *The Zhivago Affair*, 132–133.

94. Ibid., 134.

95. Letter to Henry Poor, Esq., November 12, 1958, the CIA Online FOIA Library, http://www.foia.cia.gov/sites/default/files/document_conversions/1822135/DOC_0002389319.pdf.

96. Memo from General Cable, October 29, 1958, the CIA Online FOIA Library, http://www.foia.cia.gov/sites/default/files/document_conversions/5829/CIA-RDP80B01676R002700050011-8.pdf.

97. Allen Dulles to Victor Bator, January 22, 1959, the CIA Online FOIA Library, http://www.foia.cia.gov/sites/default/files/document_conversions/5829/CIA-RDP80R01731R000400580002-7.pdf.

98. Commercial Staff to General Counsel, February 5, 1959, the CIA Online FOIA Library, http://www.foia.cia.gov/sites/default/files/document_conversions/1822135/DOC_0002389298.pdf.

99. Letter to Henry Poor, Esq, November 12, 1958, The CIA Online FOIA Library, http://www.foia.cia.gov/sites/default/files/document_conversions/1822135/DOC_0002389319.pdf.

100. See page 3 of this memo, item 9c: http://www.foia.cia.gov/sites/default/files/document_conversions/1822135/DOC_0005796343.pdf.

101. Memo for the Record, July 28, 1958, the CIA FOIA library, http://www.foia.cia.gov/sites/default/files/document_conversions/1822135/DOC_0005795653.pdf.

102. Memo for Soviet/Russia Chief, July 14, 1958, the CIA FOIA library, http://www.foia.cia.gov/sites/default/files/document_conversions/1822135/DOC_0005795648.pdf. This opinion was provided to the CIA before publication. Another post-mortem legal

analysis told them that what they did was probably illegal: http://www.foia.cia.gov/sites/default/files/document_conversions/1822135/DOC_0002387886.pdf.

103. Finn and Couvée, *The Zhivago Affair*, 144.

104. Ibid., 131–132.

105. Robert Horvath, *Legacy of Soviet Dissent*, 52.

106. The hand-scrawled note at the bottom of this memo shows the CIA coordinating over and tracking deadlines for magazines planning to profile Pasternak and review the book, and when the review would appear: http://www.foia.cia.gov/sites/default/files/document_conversions/1822135/DOC_0005795618.pdf. And this June 1958 memo shows the CIA tracking reviews by Alberto Moravia, and Max Hayward, the latter probably referring to one of the CIA's own translators for the book: http://www.foia.cia.gov/sites/default/files/document_conversions/1822135/DOC_0005795618.pdf.

107. "Editions of Dr. Zhivago," March 23, 1959, The CIA Online FOIA Library, retrieved October 19, 2014 http://www.foia.cia.gov/sites/default/files/document_conversions/1822135/DOC_0005796367.pdf.

108. See this September 1959 memo, called AEDINOSAUR Renewal: http://www.foia.cia.gov/sites/default/files/document_conversions/1822135/DOC_0005796413.pdf.

109. Finn and Couvée, *The Zhivago Affair*, 143.

110. Memo for Director of Central Intelligence, undated, the CIA FOIA Library, http://www.foia.cia.gov/sites/default/files/document_conversions/1822135/DOC_0005796341.pdf.

CHAPTER 4

1. Frederick Seidel, "A Toast to Lorin Stein," *Nice Weather*, 62–3.

2. George Plimpton to Nelson Aldrich, October 30, 1958, PR1 Series, *Paris Review* Archives, J.P. Morgan Library and Museum.

3. Ibid.

4. Ibid.

5. Ibid.

6. Issue is here: http://www.bibliotecaginobianco.it/flip/TEP/03/1100/

7. Ibid.

8. See chapter 2.

9. Gerd Ruge, "Letter from Moscow: A Visit to Pasternak,"*Encounter*, March 1958, 22–25.

10. Max Hayward, "Pasternak's 'Doctor Zhivago,'" *Encounter*, May 1958, 38–48.

11. The best information about her is in her memoir *A Captive of Time: My Years with Pasternak*.

12. Ivinskaya, *A Captive of Time*, 216.

13. Ibid., 217.

14. Ibid.

15. Ibid., 217.

16. Puzikov and Kotov were the others; see Ivinskaya, *A Captive of Time*, 205.

17. Ivinskaya, *A Captive of Time*, 217–218.

18. Ibid., 224–225.

19. Ibid., 225.

20. Ibid., 227–228.

21. Ibid., 228.

22. Ibid.
23. Ibid., 233.
24. Ibid.
25. Ibid., 234.
26. Ibid., 235.
27. Ibid., 236–237.
28. Ibid., 276.
29. Ibid.
30. Ibid., 238.
31. Ibid., 278–280.
32. Ibid., 293.
33. Ibid., 286.
34. Ibid., 294.
35. Ibid.
36. Ibid., 298–9.
37. Ibid., 299.
38. Ibid.
39. Olga Carlisle, *Under A New Sky: A Reunion with Russia*, 12.
40. Ibid.
41. Nelson Aldrich to George Plimpton, undated (November or December), 1958, PR1 Series, *Paris Review* Archives, J.P. Morgan Library and Museum.
42. http://www.people.com/people/archive/article/0,,20100033,00.html.
43. Ivinskaya, *A Captive of Time*, 301.
44. Olga Carlisle, *Voices in the Snow: Encounters with Russian Writers*, (New York City: Random House 1962).
45. Nelson Aldrich to George Plimpton, June 28, 1960, Aldrich Folder, *Paris Review* Archives, PR1, J.P. Morgan Library and Museum.
46. Its name changes appear to have been designed to avoid mastery and accountability: Office of Policy Coordination, before the CIA was born, then the Directorate of Plans, then the Directorate of Operations, and finally, as of 2005, the National Clandestine Services.
47. George Plimpton to Nelson Aldrich, July 5, 1960, Plimpton Folder, *Paris Review* Archives, PR1, J.P. Morgan Library and Museum.
48. Olga Carlisle, "The Art of Fiction, No. 25: Boris Pasternak," *Paris Review*, Summer–Fall 1960.
49. Ivinskaya, *A Captive of Time*, 312–313.
50. Olga Carlisle, *Under A New Sky*, 14.
51. Olga Carlisle, interview with author, May 1, 2016.
52. Nelson Aldrich to George Plimpton, undated, Aldrich Folder, *Paris Review* Archives, PR1, J.P. Morgan Library and Museum.
53. Aldrich, *George, Being George*, 151.
54. Robert Silvers to Plimpton, Aldrich, et al., undated, S Folder, *Paris Review* Archives, PR1, J.P. Morgan Library and Museum.
55. Robert Silvers interview, May 24, 2012.
56. Robert Silvers, email to the author, May 24, 2012.
57. George Plimpton to Patrick Bowles, August 6, 1962, *Paris Review* Archives, PR1, J.P. Morgan Library and Museum.

58. Ivinskaya, *A Captive of Time*, 313.

59. Finn and Couvée, *The Zhivago Affair*, 143.

60. Ivinskaya, *A Captive of Time*, 350.

61. Finn and Couvée, *The Zhivago Affair*, 144.

62. Ivinskaya, *A Captive of Time*, 350.

63. Ibid.

64. Ibid., 331–332.

65. Ibid., 332–333.

66. Ibid., 333.

67. Ibid., 339.

68. Ibid., 343.

69. George Plimpton to Nelson Aldrich, January 4, 1961, Plimpton Folder, *Paris Review* Archives, PR1, J.P. Morgan Library and Museum.

70. George Plimpton to Nelson Aldrich, January 28, 1961, Plimpton Folder, *Paris Review* Archives, PR1, J.P. Morgan Library and Museum.

71. Joel Whitney, "The Paris Review, the Cold War, and the CIA," *Salon*, May 27, 2012.

72. Nelson Aldrich interview, July 2013.

73. George Plimpton to Nelson Aldrich and Blair Fuller, March 5, 1961, Plimpton Folder, *Paris Review* Archives, PR1, J.P. Morgan Library and Museum.

74. Olga Carlisle, interview with author, May 1, 2016.

75. Nelson Aldrich to George Plimpton and Bob Silvers, undated, Aldrich Folder, *Paris Review* Archives, PR1, J.P. Morgan Library and Museum.

76. Nelson Aldrich to Plimpton, undated, Aldrich Folder, *Paris Review* Archives, PR1, J.P. Morgan Library and Museum.

77. Aldrich to Plimpton, undated, Aldrich Folder, *Paris Review* Archives, PR1, J.P. Morgan Library and Museum.

78. Plimpton to Aldrich, July 5, 1960, Plimpton Folder, *Paris Review* Archives, PR1, J.P. Morgan Library and Museum.

79. Plimpton to Aldrich and Fuller, February 20, 1961, Aldrich Folder, *Paris Review* Archives, PR1, J.P. Morgan Library and Museum.

80. Aldrich to Silvers, March 3, 1961, Aldrich Folder, *Paris Review* Archives, PR1, J.P. Morgan Library and Museum.

81. Plimpton to Aldrich, June 1, 1961, PR1, Aldrich Folder, *Paris Review* Archives, PR1, J.P. Morgan Library and Museum.

82. Blair Fuller to Ivan Kats, June 23, 1961, CCF Folder, *Paris Review* Archives, PR1, J.P. Morgan Library and Museum.

83. Ivan Kats to Joan Moseley, June 26, 1961, CCF Folder, *Paris Review* Archives, PR1, J.P. Morgan Library and Museum.

84. $200 at the time.

85. Frederick Seidel to Hoki Ishihara, July 5, 1961, CCF Folder, *Paris Review* Archives, PR1, J.P. Morgan Library and Museum.

86. This was first pointed out to me in a discussion with the filmmaker Immy Humes, Harold "Doc" Humes's daughter and archivist.

87. Carlisle, *Under A New Sky*, 11.

CHAPTER 5

1.   Dwight Macdonald, "America! America!" *Dissent*, Fall 1958.
2.   Ibid.
3.   Ibid.
4.   Saunders, *The Cultural Cold War*, 266.
5.   Ibid.
6.   Ibid., 267.
7.   Ibid., 270.
8.   Ibid., 267.
9.   In this example it was Pan-Africanist and socialist George Padmore's *Pan-Africanism or Communism?* The book was Padmore's defense of African independence movements from the charge that they were invariably Communist-inspired.
10. Saunders, *The Cultural Cold War*, 272.
11. Ibid.
12. Ibid.
13. Ibid., 269.
14. Ibid., 266.
15. Ibid., 272.
16. Ibid., 273.
17. Ibid.
18. Ibid.
19. Ibid.
20. Ibid., 274.
21. Warren Manshel to Henry Schwarzschild, ACCF Papers, Tamiment Library, NYU Bobst Library.
22. Saunders, *The Cultural Cold War*, 274.
23. Ibid., 269.
24. Ibid.
25. Ibid., 388, footnote 17.
26. Wreszin, *A Rebel in Defense of Tradition*, 303–305.
27. Peter Steinfels, *The Neoconservatives: The Men Who Are Changing America's Politics*, 85.
28. Keith Botsford to Dan Bell, May 27, 1967, Princeton's Emir Rodríguez Monegal Papers.
29. Dwight Macdonald, "America! America!."
30. Ibid.
31. John Berger, *A Painter of Our Time*, 191.
32. Derek Jones (ed.), *Censorship: A World Encyclopedia*, (Routledge, 2015); Paul Ignotus was the son of a Hungarian poet. Ignotus, meaning "unknown," was the pen name of the father adopted by the son. Paul Ignotus's *Encounter* attack on Berger was mild compared to Spender's.
33. "The greatest violinist," Ignotus quotes Berger, "cannot be justified in playing his violin on the bank of a river in which a drowning man is shouting for help."
34. John Berger, interview with the author, August 31, 2015.
35. Ibid.
36. John Berger, *A Painter of Our Time*, 191.

37. Wilford, *The Mighty Wurlitzer*, 118.
38. Saunders, *The Cultural Cold War*, 239–240.
39. Ibid., 240.
40. Ibid.
41. Ibid.
42. Ibid., 243.
43. George Orwell, *Animal Farm & 1984*, 84.
44. E. Howard Hunt, *An American Spy*, 50.
45. Karl Cohen, "The cartoon that came in from the cold," *The Guardian*, March 7, 2003.
46. Hunt, *An American Spy*, 50.
47. Ibid.
48. Wilford, *The Mighty Wurlitzer*, 119.
49. Ibid., 121.
50. Patrick McGilligan, *Alfred Hitchcock: A Life in Darkness and Light*, 376.
51. Saunders, *The Cultural Cold War*, 246.
52. Ibid.
53. Ibid., 244.
54. Ibid.
55. Ibid., 246.
56. Hugh Wilford, *The Mighty Wurlitzer*, 120.
57. Seth Rosenfeld, *Subversives: The FBI's War on Student Radicals and Reagan's Rise to Power*, 147.
58. Schlesinger to Sol Stein, February 15, 1954, Schlesinger Folder, ACCF Papers, Tamiment Library, NYU Bobst Library.
59. Roger Baldwin to Sol Stein, July 16, 1954, B Folder, ACCF Papers, Tamiment Library, NYU Bobst Library.
60. R.M. MacIver to Irving Kristol, November 3, 1952, M Folder, ACCF Papers, Tamiment Library, NYU Bobst Library.
61. Henry Schwarzschild to Ernest van den Haag, January 25, 1954, V Folder, ACCF Papers, Tamiment Library, NYU Bobst Library.
62. Ernest van den Haag, "Social Science Testimony in the Desegregation Cases - A Reply to Professor Kenneth Clark," *Villanova Law Review* 69, 1960. http://digitalcommons.law.villanova.edu/cgi/viewcontent.cgi?article=1502&context=vlr. See also Raymond Wolters, *Race and Education, 1954–2007*, 36–38.
63. James T. Farrell to Robert M. Hutchins, March 6, 1956, F Folder, ACCF Papers, Tamiment Library, NYU Bobst Library.
64. Norman Jacobs to members of the board of directors of the American Committee for Cultural Freedom, January 14, 1957, ACCF Papers, Tamiment Library, NYU Bobst Library.
65. Ibid.
66. Irving Kristol to W.L. White, March 24, 1953, ACCF Papers, Tamiment Library, NYU Bobst Library.

CHAPTER 6

1. James Campbell, *Talking at the Gates: A Life of James Baldwin*, 178.
2. Ibid., 172.
3. Ibid., 62–63.
4. In its final issue of 1956, it included Gore Vidal, Paul Bowles, Wallace Stevens. Campbell, *Talking at the Gates*, 62–36.
5. Campbell, *Talking at the Gates*, 64.
6. Ibid., 63.
7. James Baldwin & Sol Stein, *Native Sons*, 24.
8. I have friends who write for Beacon today, and admire much of what survives there. But given these ties—ubiquitous and nebulous ones, admittedly—I especially admire their in-house slogan, "Hearts and Minds."
9. Jacket copy for James Baldwin's *Notes of a Native Son*, from James Baldwin & Sol Stein, *Native Sons*, 51.
10. James Baldwin, "Princes and Powers," *Encounter*, January 1957, 52–53.
11. Ibid.
12. Ibid.
13. Sol Stein, "Working for the CIA and Not Knowing it," Columbia University—Rare Book and Manuscript Library Collections (RBML), Sol Stein Papers.
14. Baldwin and Stein, *Native Sons*, 93.
15. Baldwin and Stein, *Native Sons*, 93–94.
16. Ibid., 82–83.
17. Ibid., 73.
18. Sol Stein to Anthony Micocci, Chief, Evaluation Division, USIA, April 2, 1954, ACCF Papers, Tamiment Library at NYU's Bobst Library.
19. Campbell, *Talking at the Gates*, 136.
20. Ibid., 113.
21. Ibid., 146–147.
22. Harold Humes to James Baldwin, undated (1963), Pierpont Morgan Library and Museum, Humes Archives.
23. "Birmingham and Beyond: The Negro's Push for Equality," runs the corner banner on that same cover; *Time*, May 17, 1963.
24. Campbell, *Talking at the Gates*, 119.
25. Ibid., 75.
26. Aldrich, *George, Being George*, 92–93.
27. Campbell, *Talking at the Gates*, 81.
28. Ibid., 90–91.
29. Ibid., 125.
30. Ibid., 123.
31. Ibid., 98–99.
32. Ibid., 178.
33. William Faulkner, The Art of Fiction No. 12, *The Paris Review*, Spring 1956.
34. Campbell, *Talking at the Gates*, 98–99.
35. Aldrich, *George, Being George*, 92–93.

36. Harold Humes to James Baldwin, undated, Harold Humes Archive, J.P. Morgan Library and Museum (it may not have been sent).
37. Ibid.
38. Wilford, *The Mighty Wurlitzer*, 209.
39. Campbell, *Talking at the Gates*, 178.
40. Ibid., 180.
41. Peniel E. Joseph, *Stokely: A Life*, 50–51.
42. Ibid., 54.
43. Ibid.
44. Ibid., 55.
45. Campbell, *Talking at the Gates*, 163–171.
46. Rebecca Onion, "Video: When Heston, Poitier, Brando, Baldwin, and Belafonte Sat Down to talk Civil Rights," Slate, May 28, 2013: http://www.slate.com/blogs/the_vault/2013/05/28/video_charlton_heston_sidney_poitier_marlon_brando_harry_belafonte_james.html.
47. "Hollywood Roundtable," September 21, 2012, Unwritten Record Blog, National Archives, http://unwritten-record.blogs.archives.gov/2012/09/21/hollywood-roundtable/.
48. Ibid.
49. D.W. Brogan, "America South," *Encounter*, July 1958, 88–89.

CHAPTER 7

1. Murray Kempton, "The Shadow Saint," *New York Review of Books*, July 11, 1996, http://www.nybooks.com/articles/1996/07/11/the-shadow-saint/.
2. Tishani Doshi interviews George Saunders, "Writing Fiction is a Moral Act," *The Hindu*, February 13, 2016.
3. Edward Said, *Culture and Imperialism*, First Vintage Books Edition, 8; the historian Ramachandra Guha disputes this point, writing, "It is true that large parts of the world were under the political control of the European colonists, but the land itself was cultivated by peasants, under the direct control of native landlords who (in places like India and China) had oppressed them from far before the white man arrived. And direct corporate control over land per se could never even have been as high as 10%."
4. Allan and Wendy Scarfe, *J.P.: His Biography*, 24.
5. Ibid., 25.
6. Ibid., 33.
7. Ibid.
8. Ibid.
9. Ibid., 36.
10. Ibid.
11. Ibid., 39.
12. Ibid., 42.
13. Ibid., 44.
14. Ibid., 45.
15. Ramachandra Guha, *The Makers of Modern India*, 370.
16. Ibid.

17. Scarfe, *J.P.: His Biography*, 5–6.
18. Ibid.
19. Stephen Kinzer, *The Brothers: John Foster Dulles, Allen Dulles and Their Secret World*, 128.
20. Ibid., 206.
21. Ibid., 203.
22. Jayaprakash Narayan, "Nehru and Hungary's Revolt," *The New Leader*, November 17, 1956.
23. Scarfe, *J.P., his Biography*, 174; India's great historian Ramachandra Guha reminds us that "Nehru spoke late in criticizing the Soviet action in 1956, but he did speak against it—he was not silent." Guha, Ramachandra to the author, March 18, 2016, email.
24. Margery Sabin, "The Politics of Cultural Freedom: India in the Nineteen Fifties," *Raritan*, March 1, 1995, 45–65.
25. John Train to George Plimpton, October 14, 1958; see the John Train Folder at The Pierpont Morgan Library, New York, The *Paris Review* Archives.
26. Sabin, "The Politics of Cultural Freedom."
27. Saunders, *The Cultural Cold War*, 181.
28. Ibid.
29. Sabin, "The Politics of Cultural Freedom."
30. James Farrell to Robert Blum, September 21, 1955, ACCF Papers, NYU Bobst Library.
31. Dilip Chitre to the *Paris Review*, April 17, 1961, Morgan Library, *Paris Review* Papers.
32. Saunders, *The Cultural Cold War*, 181.
33. Irving Kristol to James Wechsler, September 16, 1952, ACCF Papers, Tamiment Library, NYU Bobst Library.
34. Sabin, "The Politics of Cultural Freedom."
35. Ibid.
36. Ibid.
37. Laeeq Futehally, "Someone like Nissim," in Laeeq Futehally, *The Best of Quest*, xix.
38. Molly Daniels, "Memories of Nissim," in Laeeq Futehally, *The Best of Quest*, page xxvi.
39. Michael Scammell, *Koestler, The Literary and Political Odyssey of a Twentieth Century Skeptic*, (New York: Random House 2009), 384–385.
40. Sabin, "The Politics of Cultural Freedom."
41. Ibid.
42. Ibid.
43. See Edward Said, *Orientalism*, Pantheon Books (1978).
44. Sabin, "The Politics of Cultural Freedom."
45. If his financial and political fortunes had not been tied explicitly to the translatlantic friendship, would he have seen that anti-Americanism as the natural outgrowth of British geographical-cultural occupation?.
46. Sabin, "The Politics of Cultural Freedom."
47. Ibid.
48. Ibid.
49. Ibid.
50. Dwight Macdonald, "No Miracle in Milan," *Encounter*, December 1955, 68–74.
51. Ibid.
52. Ibid.
53. See the *Quest* archives on the site with their partner *Freedom First*'s archives (see Sources for URL).

54. Laeeq Futehally et al, *Best of the Quest*, (Chennai: Tranquebar Press 2011), 59.
55. Phillip Knightley, *A Hack's Progress*, 83.
56. Ibid., 84.
57. Ibid., 85.
58. Ibid., 88.
59. Ibid.
60. Ibid., 89.
61. Ibid., 89–90.
62. Paul Webster, "Flying into a Literary Story," *The Guardian*, June 23, 2000.
63. Denis de Rougemont, "Looking for India," *Encounter*, October 1953, 36–42.
64. Chinua Achebe, "An Image of Africa (chapter 1)," *Hopes and Impediments*, 1 - 19.
65. Knightley, *A Hack's Progress*, 87.
66. Ibid., 90.
67. Ibid.
68. Ibid.
69. Ibid.
70. Paul Lewis, "Harry Rositzke, 91, Linguist and American Spymaster," *New York Times*, November 8, 2002.
71. Knightley, *A Hack's Progress*, 91.
72. Ibid., 91–92.
73. David Corn, *Blond Ghost: Ted Shackley and the CIA's Crusades*, 44.
74. Ibid., 45.
75. Eric Lichtblau interview with Amy Goodman and Juan Gonzalez on *Democracy Now*, October 31, 2014.
76. David Corn, *Blond Ghost*, 44.

CHAPTER 8

1. Dwight Macdonald wrote about the episode in "America! America!" Footage of the protests here: http://www.youtube.com/watch?v=EHRldBTJrRA; the quote upon his return is here: http://www.youtube.com/watch?v=nvigX1doz2U.
2. Eric Pace, "José Figueres Ferrer is dead at 83," *The New York Times*, June 9, 1990.
3. After calls for his arrest, Estrada fled and was granted asylum in the US, where he was safely installed (as was the dictator himself). There he sat, in Miami, effectively protected from arrest or extradition, when Nixon's caravan rolled through Caracas.
4. Robert Jackson Alexander, *Rómulo Betancourt and the Transformation of Venezuela*, 360.
5. Richard Immerman, *The CIA in Guatemala: The Foreign Policy of Intervention*, 129.
6. The first was Juan José Arévalo.
7. See Stephen Kinzer, *Overthrow: America's Century of Regime Change, From Hawaii to Iraq*.
8. Kinzer, *Overthrow*, 129–130.
9. Ibid., 136.
10. Ibid., 140.
11. Ibid. 136.
12. Thomas, *The Very Best Men*, 117.

13. See the Carmel Offie and Irving Brown Folders, Columbia University—Rare Book and Manuscript Library Collections (RBML), *The New Leader* Papers. It was paid back through thousands of subscriptions underwritten by the CIA in the UK, India, and elsewhere.

14. Stephen Schlesinger and Stephen Kinzer, *Bitter Fruit: The Story of the American Coup in Guatemala*, 89.

15. Thomas, *The Very Best Men*, 116.

16. Immerman, *The CIA in Guatemala*, 129.

17. Kinzer, *Overthrow*, 141.

18. Schlesinger and Kinzer, *Bitter Fruit*, 170.

19. Kinzer, *Overthrow*, 141.

20. Ibid., 142.

21. Ibid., 138.

22. Ibid., 142–143.

23. Schlesinger and Kinzer, *Bitter Fruit*, 183.

24. Jon Lee Anderson makes this explicit throughout his Che biography. On page 389, he adds: "He never tired of telling his Cuban comrades that in Guatemala Arbenz had fallen because he had not purged his armed forces of disloyal elements, a mistake that permitted the CIA to penetrate and overthrow his regime."

25. Kinzer, *Overthrow*, 146.

26. Elizabeth Malkin, "Former Leader of Guatemala is Guilty of Genocide Against Mayan Group," *The New York Times*, May 10, 2013.

27. Schlesinger and Kinzer, *Bitter Fruit*, 221.

28. Ibid., 221–222.

29. Though Francois Bondy spent a time as its director, and as Gorkin's boss, and Germán Arciniegas helped, and later became editor.

30. Saunders, *The Cultural Cold War*, 347–348.

31. Peter Coleman, *The Liberal Conspiracy*, cited in Marta Ruiz Galvete, *Cuadernos del Congreso por la Libertad de la Cultura: Anticomunismo y guerra fria en America Latina*.

32. Patrick Iber, *Neither Peace Nor Freedom*, 100.

33. Immerman, *The CIA in Guatemala*, 180.

34. Ibid., 181.

35. Elizabeth Malkin, "An Apology for a Guatemalan Coup, 57 Years Later," *New York Times*, October 20, 2011.

36. José Figueres, "No se puede escupir a una politica exterior," *Combate* I, no. 1 (1958), 64–69; cited also in Patrick J. Iber, "'Who Will Impose Democracy?': Sacha Volman and the Contradictions of CIA Support for the Anti-Communist Left in Latin America," *Diplomatic History*, Vol. 37, No. 5 (2013).

CHAPTER 9

1. José Figueres, "No se puede escupir a una politica exterior," *Combate* I, no. 1 (1958), 64–69; cited also in Patrick J. Iber, "'Who Will Impose Democracy?': Sacha Volman and the Contradictions of CIA Support for the Anti-Communist Left in Latin America," *Diplomatic History*, Vol. 37, No. 5 (2013).
2. Iber, "'Who Will Impose Democracy?': Sacha Volman and the Contradictions of CIA Support for the Anti-Communist Left in Latin America," 6.
3. Ibid., 4.
4. Ibid., 5.
5. Ibid., 6–7.
6. Ibid., 7.
7. See two letters: Norman Thomas to Sol Stein, April 28, 1955, and Norman Thomas to Sol Stein, May 10, 1955, both in Tamiment Library, NYU Bobst Library.
8. The name was meant to make the group "seem a more substantial threat to regional order than the bungled invasions of dozens of men really warranted," writes Iber. But recall that the *Granma* itself landed in Cuba with "dozens of men" and Fidel and his guerrillas bungled their way out of the swamps and into government.
9. Pedro Estrada's boss.
10. Kyle Longley, *The Sparrow and The Hawk*, 88 and 104.
11. Despite which, Figueres is said to have returned the favor afforded him by Arévalo; in 1958 he sent a plane-load of weapons to the Cuban guerrillas trying to oust the US-supported dictatorship of Fulgencio Batista.
12. Stephen Kinzer, *The Brothers*, 158–159; Kyle Longley hints that the CIA may have played a role in the Nicaragua/Somoza-backed coup attempt in January 1955 against Figueres, but halfheartedly and cowed by international outrage. See Kyle Longley, *The Sparrow and the Hawk*, 144–146.
13. "A los caidos de ambos bandos."
14. Kaplan sold the company in 1956, according to Patrick Iber, citing William Chazanoff's *Welch's Grape Juice: From Corporation to Co-Operative* (Syracuse, NY: Syracuse University Press, 1977).
15. Iber, "'Who Will Impose Democracy?'," 12.
16. IEP in Spanish for Instituto de Educacion Politica.
17. Iber, "'Who Will Impose Democracy?'," page 14.
18. Minutes from IILR Board Meeting, May 22, 1958, 3, Norman Thomas Papers NYPL.
19. Sacha Volman to Members of the IILR Board, June 10, 1958, Norman Thomas Papers NYPL.
20. Sacha Volman to Norman Thomas, July 12, 1958 Norman Thomas Papers, NYPL.
21. Sacha Volman to Edward McHale, August 5, 1958, Norman Thomas Papers, NYPL.
22. Sacha Volman to Norman Thomas, July 12, 1958 Norman Thomas Papers, NYPL.
23. Memo: United Fruit Company's Criticisms of the Institute of International Labor Research and ORIT, August 20, 1958, Norman Thomas Papers, NYPL.
24. Sacha Volman to Norman Thomas, September 24, 1959, Norman Thomas Papers, NYPL.
25. Luis Alberto Monge to Norman Thomas, January 27, 1959, Norman Thomas Papers, NYPL.

26. Jon Lee Anderson, *Che Guevara: A Revolutionary Life*, 388.
27. Monge to Thomas, January 27, 1959, Norman Thomas Papers, NYPL.
28. Thomas to Monge, January 30, 1959, Norman Thomas Papers, NYPL.
29. Luis Alberto Monge to Neal Buhler, February 7, 1959, Norman Thomas Papers, NYPL.
30. Ibid.
31. Ibid.
32. *Combate*'s predecessor in the region, *Cuadernos*, launched almost concurrently with *The Paris Review*.
33. Plimpton to William Styron, September 22, 1953, The Pierpont Morgan Library, New York, *Paris Review* Archives.
34. Hemingway to Plimpton, reprinted in a letter from Plimpton to Matthiessen, May 7, 1954, The Pierpont Morgan Library, New York, *Paris Review* Archives.
35. Plimpton to Guinzburg et al., undated, The Pierpont Morgan Library, New York, The *Paris Review* Archives.
36. The most amusing confession of this, the essay, "My Last Cobra: Stalking the Wild Prevarication," ran in *Harper's* in September 1994.
37. *Plimpton! Starring George Plimpton as Himself*, Tom Bean (dir.).
38. Aldrich, *George, Being George*, 117,
39. George Plimpton, *Shadow Box*; the section was excerpted in the *Sydney Morning Herald*, "Kennedy and Hemingway: Two Tricky Men to Eat With," December 27, 1980,.
40. Ibid.
41. Plimpton to Hemingway, July 3, 1957, The Pierpont Morgan Library, New York, *Paris Review* Archives.
42. Ibid.
43. Hemingway to Plimpton, undated 1957, The Pierpont Morgan Library, New York, *Paris Review* Archives.
44. Paul Hendrickson, *Hemingway's Boat: Everything He Loved in Life, and Lost: 1934–1961*, 292.
45. Plimpton to Hemingway, undated 1958, Plimpton Folder, Morgan Archive.
46. *Plimpton!*, by Tom Bean (dir.).
47. Martha Gellhorn, "Cuba Revisited," *Granta*, Number 20, Winter 1986.
48. Plimpton, "Kennedy and Hemingway."
49. George Plimpton, "The Art of Fiction, Number 21, An Interview with Ernest Hemingway," *Paris Review*, Number 18, Spring 1958.
50. Melvin Lasky to Robert Silvers, undated 1958, The Pierpont Morgan Library, New York, *Paris Review* Archives.
51. Pound had been institutionalized for treason over his pro-fascist and anti-Semitic radio rants during World War II, and Hemingway and others were trying to get him freed.
52. Aldrich to Plimpton, undated, The Pierpont Morgan Library, New York, The *Paris Review* Archives.
53. Aldrich interview, May 2012.
54. Plimpton to Hemingway, October 22, 1959, The Pierpont Morgan Library, New York, *Paris Review* Archives.
55. Ángel Esteban and Stéphanie Panichelli, *Fidel & Gabo: A Portrait of the Legendary Friendship between Fidel Castro and Gabriel García Márquez*, 20.
56. Ibid.
57. Plimpton, *Shadow Box*, 142–147; cited in Kathleen Tynan, *The Life of Kenneth Tynan*, 215.
58. Not the same wife he traveled to Cuba with.

59. Tynan, *The Life of Kenneth Tynan*, 215–216.
60. Plimpton, *Shadow Box*, 142–147; cited in Tynan, *The Life of Kenneth Tynan*, 216.
61. James Scott Linville, "Shooting Script," *Standpoint*, January 2009.
62. Ibid.
63. "The Legacy of Che Guevara," November 20, 1997, PBS, http://www.pbs.org/newshour/updates/latin_america-july-dec97-guevara_11-20/.
64. Jon Lee Anderson, Interview, May 8, 2013.
65. Humberto Fontova, "Gabriel García Márquez: Castro's Propagandist and Snitch," Frontpagemag.com, April 28, 2014; The online site's motto screams moderately beneath its logo: "Inside Every Liberal is a Totalitarian Screaming to Get Out."

CHAPTER 10

1. John F. Kennedy, "Speech of Senator John F. Kennedy," Cincinnati, Ohio, Democratic Dinner October 6, 1960.
2. Ibid.
3. Thomas, *The Very Best Men*, 251.
4. Eric Pace, "José Figueres Ferrer Is Dead at 83."
5. Sacha Volman to Norman Thomas, March 10, 1961, Norman Thomas Papers NYPL.
6. Thomas to Volman, March 13, 1961, Norman Thomas Papers NYPL.
7. Kinzer, *The Brothers*, 298.
8. Thomas to Volman, March 13, 1961, Norman Thomas Papers NYPL.
9. Thomas, *The Very Best Men*, 243.
10. Ibid., 242–243.
11. Tim Weiner, *Legacy of Ashes*, 200–201.
12. Thomas, *The Very Best Men*, 247.
13. Plimpton described the comment as Adele saying to Mailer, "Jesus, you look like a fairy who's been rolled by a couple of sailors." See Plimpton to Hemingway, December 10, 1960, *Paris Review* Archives, PR1, J.P. Morgan Library and Museum.
14. Norman Mailer, "An Open Letter to Castro and Kennedy," *Village Voice*, April 27, 1961.
15. Ibid.
16. Keneth Kinnamon, "Hemingway and Politics," in *The Cambridge Companion to Hemingway*, 149–169.
17. Clancy Sigal, *Hemingway Lives: Why Reading Ernest Hemingway Matters Today*, 136.
18. Aside from his distaste for Batista, his revolutionary fervor as a much younger man had been summed up in *Esquire*: "For instance the world was much closer to revolution in the years after the war than it is now. In those days we who believed in it, looked for it at any time, expected it, hoped for it—for it was the logical thing. But everywhere it came it was aborted. For a long time I could not understand it but finally I figured it out. If you study history you will see that there can never be a Communist revolution without, first, a complete military debacle."
19. Kinnamon, "Hemingway and Politics," in *The Cambridge Companion to Hemingway*, 166–167.
20. Valerie Hemingway, "Hemingway's Cuba, Cuba's Hemingway," *Smithsonian*, August 2007.
21. Esteban and Panichelli, *Fidel & Gabo*, 39–41.

22. Ibid., 24.

23. Deborah Davis, *Katherine the Great: Katherine Graham and the Washington Post*, 119; Davis defines it as "reporting of politics with an eye toward government interests."

24. According to author Enrique Arrosagaray, Walsh's wife thought he knew how to decipher encrypted messages from reading code-breaking books and pamphlets like one in French called *Je Sais Tout*.

25. Esteban and Panichelli, *Fidel & Gabo*, 24.

26. "Bay of Pigs Invasion Newsreel," CSPAN website.

27. Tim Weiner's account in *Legacy of Ashes* starts on page 201.

28. Jack Pfeiffer, "Adlai Stevenson and the Bay of Pigs," 46 (endnote).

29. "Report of the Attorney General to the Congress of the United States on the Administration of the Foreign Agents Registration Act of 1938, As Amended for the Calendar Year 1962," October 1963.

30. Esteban and Panichelli, *Fidel & Gabo*, 42.

31. See this July 25, 1961 memo summarizing Phase 1, typified by invasion preparations: http://nsarchive.gwu.edu/nsa/cuba_mis_cri/620725%20Review%20of%20Op.%20 Mongoose.pdf, and this October 4, 1962 memo for some understanding of what Phase 2 was like: http://nsarchive.gwu.edu/nsa/cuba_mis_cri/621004%20Minutes%20 of%20Meeting%20of%20Special.pdf.

32. Pfeiffer, "Adlai Stevenson and the Bay of Pigs," 43.

33. Again, see the memos above.

34. Natalie Robins, *Alien Ink: The FBI's War on Freedom of Expression*, 213.

35. Even if these were unintended consequences, the FBI would deliberately goad another famous American into suicide—though it didn't work. FBI boss J. Edgar Hoover tried to nudge Martin Luther King into suicide in a deceptive letter, finally released in its uncensored version in the fall of 2014. Written with help from William C. Sullivan, head of the FBI's domestic intelligence unit, Hoover alluded to King's alleged extramarital affairs and added that the names of King's sexual liaisons would be released if King didn't act. "King, there is only one thing left for you to do," they wrote. "You know what it is." See Catherine Thompson, "FBI Pushed MLK to Kill Himself Over Threatened Sex Stories," Talking Points Memo, November 21, 2014; see also William J. Maxwell, *FB Eyes: How J. Edgar Hoover's Ghostreaders Framed African American Literature*; moreover, some have cited the deliberate misspellings and slang to suggest that the agents were trying to sound like a black former admirer of King's.

36. A.E. Hotchner, "Hemingway, Hounded by the Feds," *The New York Times*, July 1, 2011.

CHAPTER 11

1. Poet Bishop was famous for writing of the broadest form of unwitting collaboration (in the human race), "you are an *I*, you are an *Elizabeth*, you are one of *them*. Why should you be one, too?."

2. Ian Hamilton, *Robert Lowell: A Biography*, 300.

3. Ibid.

4. Ibid.

5. Ibid., p 300–301.

6. Ibid., 301.

7. Ibid.
8. Ibid.
9. Ibid., 302.
10. Saunders, The Cultural Cold War, 292.
11. Hamilton, *Robert Lowell*, 302.
12. Ibid., 302–303.
13. His mother has six names: Carolina Elena Rangoni-Machiavelli-Publicola-Santacroce.
14. Fred A. Bernstein, "In Costa Rica, Built for Books and Breezes," *New York Times*, October 4, 2007.
15. Hamilton, *Robert Lowell*, 303.
16. "Familiar English tunes of song" was what the settlers (who lost family members at Roanoke's Lost Colony) sang into the woods as their rescue boat was being diverted back to England in the middle 1580s.
17. Saunders, *The Cultural Cold War*, 293–294.
18. Keith Botsford, interview with author, June 24, 2014.
19. Francisco Marín and Mario Casasús, *El Doble Asesinato de Neruda: Con el Testimonio de Manuel Araya*.
20. Adam Feinstein, "Why the Pablo Neruda 'Poisoning' Saga Rolls On," *Guardian*, December 30, 2013. Though when former Chilean president and CIA funding beneficiary Eduardo Frei was exhumed in 2006, his autopsy indeed found he had been poisoned with mustard gas and thallium during the US-supported Pinochet regime, although his death had previously been attributed to septic shock during an operation.
21. *Mundo Nuevo* was the Congress's third magazine in the region, after *Cuadernos* and *Combate*; fourth, if you count the Spanish version of *Encounter*. Fifth, if you count *Aportes*; sixth if you count *Cadernos Brasileiros*, in Portuguese. Seventh, if you count *Examen*. Eighth, if you count the one on China. And so on.
22. Russell Cobb, *Our Men in Paris?*, 10.
23. Ibid.
24. Iber, *Neither Peace Nor Freedom*, 207.
25. Cobb, *Our Men in Paris?*, 26.
26. Russell Cobb, "The Politics of Literary Prestige: Promoting the Latin American Boom in the Pages of *Mundo Nuevo*," *A Contra Corriente: A Journal on Social History and Literature in Latin America*, Spring 2008, 75–94.
27. Ibid.
28. Ibid.
29. Ibid., 80.
30. Rodríguez Monegal to Neruda, February 24, 1966, Princeton's Emir Rodríguez Monegal Papers. This is my translation of "cuya direccion es arriba."
31. Rodríguez Monegal to Neruda, February 24, 1966, Princeton's Emir Rodríguez Monegal Papers.
32. Ibid.
33. Pablo Neruda to Emir Rodríguez Monegal, May 13, 1966, Princeton's Emir Rodríguez Monegal Papers.
34. Volodia Teitelboim, *Neruda: An Intimate Biography*, 405.
35. Saunders, *The Cultural Cold War*, 304–305.
36. Adam Feinstein, *Pablo Neruda*, 343.
37. Ibid.

38. Teitelboim, *Neruda*, 405.

39. Feinstein, *Pablo Neruda*, 343.

40. See Nick Turse, *Kill Anything That Moves*.

41. Teitelboim, *Neruda*, 413; Teitelboim refers to an interview in *Enfoque Internacional*, no. 31, July 1969.

42. Iber, *Neither Peace nor Freedom*, 179–183.

43. Weiner, *Legacy of Ashes*, 218.

44. Iber, *Neither Peace Nor Freedom*, 184.

45. Saunders, *The Cultural Cold War*, 305–306.

46. Arthur Miller, *Timebends: A Life*, 566.

47. Saunders, *The Cultural Cold War*, 307; Saunders cites Robin, *Alien Ink*.

48. Ibid., 307.

49. Saunders, *The Cultural Cold War*, 307.

50. Arthur Miller, "The Art of Theater No. 2," *The Paris Review*, Summer 1966.

51. Botsford to Dan Bell, May 26, 1967, Princeton's Emir Rodríguez Monegal Papers, Firestone Library.

52. Feinstein, *Pablo Neruda*, 345–346.

53. Stanislao Pugliese, *Bitter Spring: A Life of Ignazio Silone*, 220–221.

54. Feinstein, *Pablo Neruda*, 346.

55. Ibid.

56. See this index online of all the issues of *Mundo Nuevo*; see issue 4: http://www.periodicas.edu.uy/v2/minisites/mundo-nuevo/indice-de-numeros.htm.

57. Josie Ensor, "Gabriel García Márquez dies aged 87," *Telegraph*, April 17, 2014.

58. Botsford to Bell, May 1967, Emir Rodríguez Monegal Papers, Firestone Library, Princeton University.

59. Iber, *Neither Peace Nor Freedom*, 179.

60. Ibid., 65.

61. See Congress for Cultural Freedom Folder in the *Paris Review* Archives in the J.P. Morgan Library & Museum.

62. Cobb, *Our Men in Paris?*, 62.

63. Rodríguez Monegal to García Márquez, January 19, 1967, Emir Rodríguez Monegal Papers, Firestone Library, Princeton University.

64. García Márquez to Rodriguez Monegal, March 30, 1966, Emir Rodriguez Monegal Papers, Firestone Library, Princeton University.

65. Esteban and Panichelli, *Fidel & Gabo*, 16.

66. For a very detailed synopsis of the Bogotazo, see Esteban and Panichelli, *Fidel & Gabo*, 11–14.

67. Fidel Castro, "La novela y sus recuerdos," 1–2; cited in Esteban and Panichelli, *Fidel & Gabo*, 13–14 (Esteban and Panichelli assume that García Márquez's line ending the vignette was a joke). Stavans, *García Márquez*, 63–64.

68. Arturo Alape, "La Confesion del Agente Espirito," *El Tiempo*, October 15, 2000.

69. Stavans, *García Márquez*, 63.

70. Stavans, *García Márquez*, 63–64.

71. The above information on Velasco and García Márquez comes from Stavans, *Gabriel García Márquez*, 73–78.

72. "Hemingway in Bohemia," *Juventud Rebelde*, April 6, 2008. See also Karpeles Manuscript Library, which has a folio of the manuscript with the agreement. That

issue of *Bohemia* reportedly had a print run of 260,000 and its publishers estimated that each copy of the issue was read by eight readers who shared it.

73. Stavans, *Gabriel García Márquez*, 73–78.
74. Ibid., 83.
75. Stavans, *Gabriel García Márquez*, 85.
76. Ibid.
77. Ibid., 87–88.

CHAPTER 12

1. One version of this story can be found in Stavans, *Gabriel García Márquez*, 4.
2. "Art of Fiction number 69: Gabriel García Márquez," *Paris Review*, No. 82, Winter 1981; Stavans, *Gabriel García Márquez*, 29.
3. Stavans, *Gabriel García Márquez*, 144.
4. Ibid., 145.
5. Gabriel García Márquez, *One Hundred Years of Solitude*, Harper Perennial, 201.
6. Ibid., 329–330.
7. Stavans, *Gabriel García Márquez*, 145.
8. Ibid.
9. Peter Coleman, *The Liberal Conspiracy: The Congress for Cultural Freedom and the Struggle for the Mind of Postward Europe*, 207.
10. Cobb, *Our Men in Paris?*, 34.
11. Oscar Lewis, "La cultura de la pobreza," *Mundo Nuevo*, Issue 5, November 1966, 42.
12. See "Primary Sources: Second Inaugural Address, 1957," January 21, 1957, PBS TV: http://www.pbs.org/wgbh/americanexperience/features/primary-resources/eisenhower-inaugural57/.
13. Saunders, *The Cultural Cold War*, 338.
14. Larry Bensky interview, July 2012
15. Emir Rodríguez Monegal to Melvin Lasky, February 1967, Emir Rodríguez Monegal Papers, Princeton's Firestone Library.
16. Plimpton to Humes, March 12, 1966, J.P. Morgan Library and Museum, Harold Humes Archive.
17. Alan Alda starred in a screen adaptation of Plimpton's *Paper Lion*, released in 1968.
18. Plimpton to Humes, March 10, 1966, J.P. Morgan Library and Museum, Harold Humes Archive.
19. Ibid..
20. Bryant Urstadt, "Paris, Paranoia and the CIA," 3QuarksDaily, December 29, 2008.
21. Plimpton to Humes, March 10, 1966, J.P. Morgan Library and Museum, Harold Humes Archive.
22. Ibid.
23. Tom Wicker et al., "Electronic Prying Grows," *New York Times*, April 27, 1966.
24. Thomas, *The Very Best Men*, 324.
25. Robert A. Nisbet, "Project Camelot: An Autopsy," *Public Interest*, Number 5, Fall 1966, http://www.nationalaffairs.com/doclib/20080516_06projectcamelotanautopsyrobertanisbet.pdf.
26. Warren Hinckle et al., "MSU: University on the Make," *Ramparts*, April 1966, 11–22.

27. Ibid.
28. Ibid. The article can be read, as can all of *Ramparts* and all of *Encounter*, on UNZ.org.
29. Ibid.
30. Angus Mackenzie, *Secrets: The CIA's War at Home*, 17.
31. Ibid.
32. Ibid.
33. Ibid., 18.
34. Ibid., 19.
35. Saunders, *The Cultural Cold War*, 304.
36. Warren Hinckle, *If You Have a Lemon, Make Lemonade*, 190; Mackenzie, *Secrets*, 19–20.
37. Ibid., 19.
38. Hinckle, *If You Have a Lemon, Make Lemonade*, 185; Mackenzie, *Secrets*, 20.
39. Sol Stern, "NSA and the CIA," *Ramparts*, March 1967, 29–39.
40. Ibid.
41. Ibid.
42. Ibid.
43. Ibid.
44. Ibid.
45. Like Nelson Aldrich, Fitzgerald's daughter Frances had gone from an internship at *The Paris Review* to the Congress for Cultural Freedom, making it a repeat pathway. She went on to write a scorching book about the Vietnam War, *Fire in the Lake*.
46. Hinckle, *If You Have a Lemon, Make Lemonade*, 179; cited in Peter Richardson, *A Bomb in Every Issue: How the Short, Unruly Life of* Ramparts *Magazine Changed America*, 77.
47. Thomas, *The Very Best Men*, 330.
48. Richardson, *A Bomb in Every Issue*, 78.
49. John B. Judis, *William F. Buckley: Patron Saint of the Conservatives*, 359.
50. Transcript of the full show at Stanford's Hoover Institution's Library and Archives, Stanford University.
51. Michael Wreszin, *Rebel in Defense of Tradition*, 424.
52. Judis, *William F. Buckley*, 358.
53. During this period, Hunt was alleged to have threatened to reveal the illicit business he did as one of Nixon's "plumbers" if a certain amount of money, more than a hundred thousand dollars, weren't paid him by the US's spy patronage networks. In that episode of *Firing Line*, which bears on Buckley's covert role, Buckley went into detail on how an incarcerated covert agent is expected to get back pay and how the money Hunt demanded was actually a request for salary in arrears. Buckley admitted up front that Hunt was a close friend, though not, of course, his one-time employer; this would be buried by the focus mostly on Nixon. Though later, despite its promise to showcase "the non-drum beaters and non-axe grinders," *The Paris Review* even ran an interview with Buckley, who was not exactly known for his belletristic high literary style.
54. Russ Baker, *Family of Secrets: The Bush Dynasty, America's Secret Government, and the Hidden History of the Last Fifty Years*, 13.
55. Judis, *William F. Buckley*, 358.
56. Saunders, *The Cultural Cold War*, 309.
57. "Arab Magazine Banned in Cairo: Leftists Charge Periodical Received CIA Subsidies," *New York Times*, July 24, 1966.
58. Wicker, "Electronic Prying Grows."

59. Patrick Bowles to Tawfiq Sayigh, July 16, 1964, Patrick Bowles folder, *Paris Review* Archives, J.P. Morgan Library and Museum.
60. Ibid.
61. See Congress for Cultural Freedom folder, *Paris Review* Archives, PR1, J.P. Morgan Library & Museum.
62. See Muddathir Abd al Rahim, "Reminiscences of Al Faruki," (footnote 30) in Imtiyaf Yusuf, *Islam and Knowledge.*
63. Michael Vazquez, "The Bequest of Quest," *Bidoun*, Issue 26: Soft Power; Vazquez gets one key fact wrong; Sayigh actually founded *Hiwar* in 1962.
64. Issa J. Boullata, "The Beleaguered Unicorn," *Journal of Arabic Literature*, Col. 4 (1973), 69–93.

CHAPTER 13

1. Stanley Turkel, *Heroes of the American Reconstruction*, 19.
2. García Márquez to Rodríguez Monegal, May 24, 1967, Princeton's Emir Rodríguez Monegal Papers.
3. Saunders, *The Cultural Cold War*, 343.
4. Keith Botsford to Dan Bell, May 27, 1967, Princeton's Emir Rodríguez Monegal Papers.
5. Mackenzie, *Secrets*, 27.
6. Ibid.
7. Ibid.
8. Ralph Stein; see Mackenzie, *Secrets*, 30.
9. William Blum, email interview, March 30, 2015.
10. Mackenzie, *Secrets*, 37.
11. Ibid., 32.
12. Ibid., 33.
13. Ibid., 34.
14. Michael S. Schmidt, "FBI Counterterrorism Agents Monitored Occupy Movements, Records Show," *New York Times*, December 24, 2012.
15. Michèle Ray, "In Cold Blood," *Ramparts*, March 1968, 23–37.
16. Ibid.
17. Henry Raymont, "Ramparts to Publish Manuscript Said to be Guevara's Diary," *The New York Times*, July 1, 1968.
18. Henry Raymont, "Guevara Papers Published Here," *The New York Times*, July 3, 1968.
19. Barney Rosset, "Evergreen Review and Che Guevara's Diary," unpublished manuscript chapter, courtesy Astrid Myers Rosset, 5.
20. Ibid., 6.
21. Homer Bigart, "Bazooka Fired at UN as Cuban Speaks," *The New York Times*, December 12, 1964.
22. Henry Raymont, "Publisher Warns Rivals Over Diary," *The New York Times*, July 4, 1968.
23. Ibid.
24. Sol Stein, "Che, Castro and the Heroic Lawyer," letter to the editor *New York Times*, January 19, 1992.
25. See Ratner and Smith, *Who Killed Che?*.

26. Rodriguez told this story many times, including in a phone interview with me on January 30, 2015.

27. Anderson, *Che Guevara*, 709–712.

28. Ibid., 709–712; on the decision to cut off Che's hands in particular, see 713.

29. Félix I. Rodriguez and John Weisman, *Shadow Warrior: The CIA Hero of a Hundred Unknown Battles*.

30. Thomas Braden, interview for the Granada Television program *World in Action: The Rise and Fall of the CIA*, 1975.

31. All the quotes from Immy Humes in this chapter come from an interview on March 28, 2015 and a follow-up interview on February 18, 2016.

32. Crewdson, "Worldwide Propaganda Network Built by the CIA."

33. R.D. Laing, *The Politics of Experience*, 107.

34. "Q Street in Georgetown became synonymous with the CIA," wrote C. David Heymann in *The Georgetown Ladies' Social Club: Power, Passion, and Politics in the Nation's Capital* (Simon & Schuster, 2004). "By happenstance, many of the journalists of the day had homes on P Street. The proximity of the two, and the social connections that then linked the CIA to the world of Washington journalists gave rise to a code name: the P & Q Street Axis" (p. 53).

35. Carl Bernstein, "The CIA and the Media," *Rolling Stone*, October 20, 1977.

CODA

1. See *The Paris Review*'s online masthead, the Founders biographical page: www.theparisreview.org/about/founding-editors#john-train.

2. Interviews by phone (November 5, 2015) and in person (November 19, 2015).

3. Russ Baker, *Family of Secrets: The Bush Dynasty, America's Secret Government, and the Hidden History of the Last Fifty Years*, 14.

4. Afghanistan Relief Committee memo, undated, Saginaw Valley State University Library Archives, www.svsu.edu/library/archives/public/Follett/documents/44_50/KFP046_37d.pdf.

5. The group admitted that until 1982, it indeed focused on media to increase US government spending on refugee relief inside Afghanistan. But it claimed that a shift in strategy and circumstances allowed it to focus on direct relief, disbursed via on-the-ground organizations like Doctors Without Borders, after 1982. The progressive Institute for Policy Studies, however, looked at its budgets from the time. The vast majority of its spending fell into two buckets: more than half for media and 45 percent for administration and fund raising. That left less than 5 percent of its 1986 budget for the suffering of victims "inside Afghanistan itself." http://rightweb.irc-online.org/articles/display/Afghanistan_Relief_Committee.

6. Robert Dreyfuss, *Devil's Game: How the United States Helped Unleash Fundamentalist Islam*, 258.

7. The American Committee even worked with two groups in Indonesia in the mid-1950s: Darul Islam and Moslem State.

8. See Robert Dreyfuss's *Devil's Game* for a detailed recounting of this history.

9. Sonali Kolhatkar and James Ingalls, *Bleeding Afghanistan: Washington, Warlords and the Propaganda of Silence*; see also the widely syndicated interview with Zbigniew

Brzezinski by A.D. Hemming, "How Jimmy Carter and I Started the Mujahideen," *Counterpunch*, January 15, 1998: http://www.counterpunch.org/1998/01/15/how-jimmy-carter-and-i-started-the-mujahideen/.

10. Tim Weiner, "Blowback from the Afghan Battlefield," *The New York Times*, March 13, 1994.
11. Dreyfuss, *Devil's Game*, 328–329.
12. The Seitz memo, found by the author in the John Train Papers, Seton Hall University Library, was probably from 1983, as another letter on similar topics from Train to Russell Seitz was listed for September 1983.
13. Ibid.
14. Ibid.
15. Ibid.
16. Carl Bernstein, "The CIA and the Media," *Rolling Stone*, October 20, 1977.
17. John Train to Russell Seitz, September 26, 1983, John Train Papers, Seton Hall University Library.
18. John Train to Dimitri Panitza, November 1981, John Train Papers, Seton Hall University Library.
19. John Train to Rosanne Klass, April 4, 1983, John Train Papers, Seton Hall University Library.
20. Train to Klass, December 10, 1983, John Train Papers, Seton Hall University Library.
21. Train to Terese Jarchow, July 22, 1983, John Train Papers, Seton Hall University Library.
22. Train to Elizabeth Paddock, December 21, 1983, John Train Papers, Seton Hall University Library.
23. William F. Buckley, "Why Won't TV Show This Documentary?" *Milwaukee Sentinel*, October 22, 1981.
24. Pete Earley, "White House Screening Boosts 'KGB Connection,'" *Washington Post*, March 10, 1982.
25. John Train to Executive Committee, Board of Directors, Afghanistan Relief Committee, June 28, 1995, John Train Papers, Seton Hall University Library.
26. Stephen Cohen, *The Idea of Pakistan*, 85.
27. Andrew Boston, "Radical Islam's Goal Is Global Conquest," *FrontPage Magazine*, July 2, 2007.
28. Karen Paget, *Patriotic Betrayal: The Inside Story of the CIA's Secret Campaign to Enroll American Students in the Crusade Against Communism.*
29. Mackenzie, *Secrets*, 10.
30. Cowley to Hemingway, May 3, 1949, from Cowley, *The Long Voyage, Selected Letters of Malcolm Cowley, 1915–1987*, 404.

INDEX

Cypherpunks
Freedom and the Future of the Internet
JULIAN ASSANGE with
JACOB APPELBAUM, ANDY MÜLLER-MAGUHN, AND
JÉRÉMIE ZIMMERMANN

When Google Met Wikileaks
JULIAN ASSANGE

Kingdom of the Unjust
Behind the U.S.–Saudi Connection
MEDEA BENJAMIN

A Narco History
How the US and Mexico Jointly Created
the "Mexican Drug War"
CARMEN BOULLOSA AND
MIKE WALLACE

Beautiful Trouble
A Toolbox for Revolution
ASSEMBLED BY ANDREW BOYD
WITH DAVE OSWALD MITCHELL

Bowie
SIMON CRITCHLEY

Extinction
A Radical History
ASHLEY DAWSON

Black Ops Advertising
Native Ads, Content Marketing, and the
Covert World of the Digital Sell
MARA EINSTEIN

Beautiful Solutions
A Toolbox for Liberation
EDITED BY ELI FEGHALI, RACHEL
PLATTUS, AND ELANDRIA WILLIAMS

Remembering Akbar
Inside the Iranian Revolution
BEHROOZ GHAMARI

The Optician of Lampedusa
Based on a True Story
EMMA JANE KIRBY

Folding the Red into the Black
or Developing a Viable *Un*topia for
Human Survival in the 21st Century
WALTER MOSLEY

Inferno
(A Poet's Novel)
EILEEN MYLES

Trump Unveiled
Exposing the Bigoted Billionaire
JOHN K. WILSON